Landmarks in the History
of the German Language

Britische und Irische Studien
zur deutschen Sprache und Literatur

British and Irish Studies
in German Language and Literature

Etudes britanniques et irlandaises
sur la langue et la littérature allemandes

Edited by H.S. Reiss and W.E. Yates

Band 52

PETER LANG
Oxford · Bern · Berlin · Bruxelles · Frankfurt/M. · New York · Wien

Landmarks in the History
of the German Language

Geraldine Horan, Nils Langer
and Sheila Watts (eds)

PETER LANG
Oxford · Bern · Berlin · Bruxelles · Frankfurt/M. · New York · Wien

Bibliographic information published by Die Deutsche Bibliothek
Die Deutsche Bibliothek lists this publication in the Deutsche
Nationalbibliografie; detailed bibliographic data is available on the
Internet at ‹http://dnb.ddb.de›.

A catalogue record for this book is available from The British Library.

Library of Congress Cataloging-in-Publication Data:

Landmarks in the history of the German language / Geraldine Horan, Nils
Langer and Sheila Watts [editors].
    p. cm. -- (British and Irish studies in German language and
literature ; 52)
  Some essays were originally delivered as lectures at the University of
Cambridge.
  ISBN 978-3-03911-890-8 (alk. paper)
  1. German language--History. 2. German language--Social aspects. 3.
Sociolinguistics--Germany. I. Horan, Geraldine. II. Langer, Nils, 1969-
III. Watts, Sheila.
  PF3075.L36 2009
  430.9--dc22
                                    2009023956

ISSN 0171-6662
ISBN 978-3-03911-890-8

© Peter Lang AG, International Academic Publishers, Bern 2009
Hochfeldstrasse 32, CH-3012 Bern, Switzerland
info@peterlang.com, www.peterlang.com, www.peterlang.net

Printed in Germany

Contents

Acknowledgements

In preparing this volume we have been grateful for the support of our institutions: the Department of German, University College London (Horan), the School of Modern Languages at the University of Bristol (Langer) and the Department of German and Dutch at the University of Cambridge, and Newnham College, Cambridge (Watts). Each has supported this volume financially and through grants of research leave. Particular thanks are due to Dr Chris Young (Cambridge), who, with Sheila Watts, organized the original lecture series in which many of the papers published here were given, and to Pembroke College, Cambridge, which was a generous host to speakers. We are very grateful also to Caroline Smith (Cambridge) who helped immeasurably in checking the bibliographies and preparing them for publication. Thanks also to Rox Thomson (Bristol) for her help with indexing. Graham Speake of Peter Lang has been extraordinarily patient, and we thank him for helping us finally bring this project to fruition.

Our families, man and beast, have supported us throughout, and deserve our thanks.

GERALDINE HORAN, NILS LANGER, SHEILA WATTS

Introduction

The history of the German language has been the subject of intense academic study for at least two hundred years, and of scholarly interest for perhaps another two hundred before that. This research has had several different strands, from the cultural nationalism of earlier periods to the central role of German and the Germanic language family in the development of comparative and historical linguistics as academic disciplines. While historical linguistics looks at language change as a universal phenomenon and considers individual languages as exemplars of general trends, the task of language history is to take a single language in order 'das Werden [dieser] Sprache zu verfolgen und die Korrelation zwischen Menschengeschichte und Sprachentwicklung zu beleuchten' (Scardigli 1994: 82). This definition reflects the understanding that every language embeds social and geographic variation, and that a language is the sum of linguistic knowledge and attitudes of the communities that speak it.[1] Language history is thus both linguistic and historical,[2] and aims to create a narrative which should describe how the language has been used, when, and by whom, what linguistic forms meant to different speakers at different times, and how their beliefs about and attitudes towards their language have influenced its development. In this sense language history is, as Hermann Paul defined it, a *Kulturwissenschaft*, rather than a *Gesetzeswissenschaft* (1886; as quoted in Gardt et al. 1995: 1), or what Romaine labels an 'aesthetic rather than a scientific pursuit' (1982: 274). Linguistics in its

---

1   This view, the 'sociolinguistic turn' in language studies, began to have importance for historical linguistics after the seminal article on the subject by Weinreich, Labov and Herzog (1968).
2   Lass has argued that language users, 'their properties and actions belong to another subject-area, not historical (or perhaps any) linguistics proper' (1997: xvii–i). It is not our intention to argue over whether language history in the sense in which it is used here does or does not belong to linguistics: it is essentially an interdisciplinary pursuit.

historical dimension today covers a spectrum from the purely theoretical – in which German material continues to be of central importance, and is widely cited in general introductions to historical linguistics and language change[3] – and the socio-historical, studies which look at the broader context of languages, their speakers, and their historical development of the people as a speech community. This volume aims to complement existing English-language works on German language history by illuminating recent research at this socio-historical end of the spectrum.

For a language historian, German is a rewarding study, as it has a number of features which make it distinctive even amongst its European neighbours. Firstly, the corpus of German historical texts is comparatively rich, both with regard to the age of the oldest texts, which date from the eighth century AD, and to the diversity of text types that have survived since the Middle Ages. Secondly, due to the large geographical area in which German has been spoken, the surviving texts display a wide range of regional differences, which continue to survive in dialectal variation today. At the boundaries of this large territory, due to the number of neighbouring languages and instances of multilingualism in German speakers, language contact phenomena can be studied for many historical periods. There is also a considerable range of texts, especially from the late Middle High German (MHG) period onwards, which can be differentiated in terms of register or sociolect thanks to the complex stratification of German-speaking society. Thirdly, the German language underwent a comparatively late and complex standardisation process with no clear or unique geographical or socio-cultural foundation: unlike English or French, the German standard language is *not* the dialect of a particular town or area. Lastly, German has been the native language of important figures nationally and internationally throughout its history, from figures of general historical significance such as Charlemagne, Gutenberg and Luther, to academics such as Leibniz or the brothers Grimm who have put their own language and culture at the centre of international scholarly discourse.

---

3   German is extensively used for exemplification in general introductions and textbooks such as Bynon (1977), Trask (1996), Lass (1997), Campbell (1998), Schendl (2001) and even in Crowley (1973), which emphasises its focus on Pacific languages and away from traditional Indo-European data.

It has become conventional to divide the history of a language into two parts: its internal history, which describes linguistic forms and their changes over time, and its external history, which considers the reciprocal relationship between political, social and cultural events on the one hand, and language users and usage on the other. Studying the internal history of a language involves identifying and labelling chronological stages in its development, describing each stage in terms of its phonology, morphology, syntax and lexis, and looking at how these linguistic systems change and develop. Although language history is modelled as a succession of periods which are described as synchronic states, in reality no language is ever in stasis, and changes occur at all times and in all linguistic domains. Thus we no longer pronounce <so> as /so/, but as /zo/,[4] a change from late Old High German (OHG); we no longer use a zero ending on any predicative adjectives, so we cannot say *ein gut Mensch*, a change from Early New High German (ENHG); and for us, the word *englisch* no longer primarily means 'angelic' but 'English' (a change from Middle New High German).[5] These are just a few examples from a host of changes from across the attested history of German, including many which are still in process, for instance in

> **phonology**: monophthongization; diphthongization; lenition; (af)frication
>
> **morphology and syntax**: loss of overt case distinction on nouns, so that articles are required more often; fewer distinctive number endings on verbs, so that subject pronouns tend to become obligatory
>
> **lexis and semantics**: changes in the meaning of words; expansion of the lexicon by various types of lexical borrowing

These phenomena show a common dynamic of language change: changes in pronunciation, caused partly by the natural speed and rhythm of speech, lead to loss of distinctiveness in endings, so that grammatical information has to be supplied by the use of extra words such as pronouns and auxiliaries. Over

---

4   In Northern and Central varieties of German.

5   The period of Middle New High German has recently been suggest by Elspaß (2008) and covers the period of 1650–1950.

the whole development of the language from earliest times one can speak of a change from synthesis, where grammatical meaning is expressed morphologically, to analysis, where it is expressed syntactically, a large-scale change which appears to be common to all (formerly) inflected languages. At the same time, if we look at words rather than rules we see lexical change caused by fashion, technological advance and contact with other cultures. Changes like these can be described, but they can be explained only to a limited extent, and theories of language change lack predictive power beyond some general trends.[6] This is intrinsic to the nature of language as a social phenomenon, subject to the same unpredictable forces that affect its users.

The internal history of German is, on the whole, well studied and understood, thanks largely to the involvement of native German speakers in the development of historical linguistics as an academic discipline, and to the support which these scholars received because of the importance of the language in the historiography of the German nation (cf. e.g. Leyhausen 2005). New findings in the study of the internal history of German are essentially of two different types. On the one hand, new theoretical models are applied to the known data, usually contextualizing German material within a broad typological understanding of how languages in general work: such studies tend to belong to the domain of historical linguistics rather than of language history in the sense which has been outlined above. On the other hand, it is also possible to draw on different data, whether it is texts which have been re-discovered after loss – such as fragments of medieval manuscripts –, or data, even whole text types, that were known about in principle but never investigated because they were not considered valuable for academic, specifically linguistic study, for instance, private letters from nineteenth-century German emigrants to America (Elspaß 2005). Such texts lend themselves particularly well to an inclusive, broad language history in our sense, and with their inclusion in our scholarly interest, we constantly add to the body of material that constitutes the history of German.

6   There is a very considerable literature on the nature of explanation in linguistics, which is bound up in the debate about whether or not linguistics is a science and what its empirical base is. See, for example, Davis and Iverson (1992), Romaine (1982) and Lass (1997).

The description of the history of a language as a set of chronologically-sequenced autonomous entities is arguably a taxonomic pre-requisite for a description which integrates the study of the same changing linguistic forms with an analysis of their importance for their speakers and the society and culture in which they live. When we refer to language users as speakers, we immediately confront one of the most difficult problems for the language historian, namely that, although spoken language has been recognised as the primary object of linguistic study since Saussure, the historical record is a written one, and we are dependent on chance to have determined what has survived fires, wars, general decay and the risk of being discarded as uninteresting and irrelevant.[7] The written word has to be interpreted: at the level of the sound system, there is no absolute one-to-one relationship between letters and sounds across time and space, while grammatical forms and lexical choices also typically show writers making different choices from speakers. The community of writers in the past was much smaller than the community of speakers, being limited in the main to an educated elite, mostly of men: the voices of women, children and the poor are not generally reflected in writing until the early modern period. Furthermore, the genres or text types which have survived from earlier periods are often from very formal registers even within writing, such as courtly poetry, legal contracts or exegetical religious texts, while more 'speech-like' genres such as letters or diaries, dependent on cheaply available writing materials and leisure time for their composition, typically survive only from relatively modern times.

One of the qualities which has been distinctive in more recent research into the history of German has been a desire to look at 'low' culture as well as 'high', and to consider groups and communities who have been less well-studied than the dominant literate elite. This has inevitably led to a focus on more recent material than the traditional early medieval texts on which much language history has been based, because it is only since about 1500 that there has been sufficient, and sufficiently varied, data to have empirical validity for

---

7   The high cost of producing vellum means that many early medieval texts, in particular, were either written in margins or were erased so that other texts could be written over them (palimpsests). Personal documents of precisely the kind that of key interest in socio-historical linguistics are also more likely to be thrown away than formal, official documents.

sociolinguistic assessment. Linguistic interest now includes, and in many ways prefers, non-printed and informal texts, as they appear to present a more unfiltered impression of how people spoke in the past. As an important further development, a recent drive towards a *Language History from Below* (cf. Elspaß et al. 2007) consciously focuses not only on informal language sources such as diaries and letters from writers and politicians, but also on voices from below and outside, such as peasants, workers, and, often across social strata, women. This change of direction allows for a much fuller treatment of the German language in the past and makes space for new insights particularly into the nature and processes of standardisation, challenging the textbook idea that German was fully standardised by about 1750. The social focus of this way of considering language history allows us to compare standard languages directly with natural speech, and to consider planned and deliberate changes alongside those which occur spontaneously. When a language is standardized, change is slower: although speakers continue to innovate, 'gatekeepers' such as language academies, grammarians and educators deny these new forms access to the standard. A social consensus operates, most powerfully amongst educated, middle-class speakers, which is conservative and tends to assume that established, older forms, are better than the innovations which are appearing in the speech community, and that change represents decline and decay. A history of the language needs to appreciate the effects that its speakers' attitudes will have on its development, and on the divergence of standard from non-standard, the delineation of what is regional or dialectal from what is merely colloquial, and the shifts in these categories over time.

While earlier cultural nationalists took it for granted that 'great men' had played an important role in determining the course of German language history, this view has long been out of fashion. The first two contributions to this volume give it a new twist, by re-examining two key figures, Charlemagne and Luther, both variously credited with creating the foundations of the German language. McKitterick looks at the claim, already made in contemporary sources, that Charlemagne was a patron of writing in German who strove to promote an interest in his native culture, an idea which inspired Alfred the Great in his considerably more successful efforts to promote English. She finds in Charlemagne instead a European figure, whose interests were in the Roman form of Christianity and in the unity of his empire – both of which required him to do far more to promote Latin than he could do for German.

As with Charlemagne and Alfred, Luther and Tyndale are another German-English pairing who yield interesting comparisons, which Flood draws out in an article which shows that both left a lasting mark on their respective languages in terms of style and vocabulary, and that in their interaction with one another, Luther can be seen as an 'uncle' of English as much as a 'father' of German.

The history of a language is not mainly created by individual members of the community, but is more typically a collective effort. Three essays consider how the ideas of particularly influential groups have worked on the developing German standard: grammatographers (McLelland), lexicographers (Jones) and purists (Pfalzgraf). McLelland addresses the important period of the seventeenth century, the age of cultural patriotism when Germans used their language's history and form as arguments to boost its status, felt to be lagging behind that of competitors French or Italian. Grammarians of this era felt that by defining and describing the forms of German, and by breaking away from purely Latin-inspired categories, they could give it a respectability which would be a source of national pride, and they began a long tradition of admiration for the intricate grammatical forms which make German special. Grammars, like dictionaries, are ideological creations, and it is this aspect which Jones addresses in his essay on the development of German lexicography. Collecting words began even earlier than the description of grammatical forms, and lent itself in equal measure to national self-aggrandisement, making a claim for linguistic prestige by virtue of the copiousness, antiquity and special qualities of German words. Jones traces the path of dictionary-makers from the mysticism of the national idea in the seventeenth century to the practical work of the eighteenth and nineteenth centuries, through more of the giants of the German language, Adelung and the Grimms.

Grammars and dictionaries are just two of many types of text which are found in earlier periods of German and whose analysis is fruitful for a study of language history. In her essay on text linguistics, Lange introduces the reader to the formal study of text types which has been a very fruitful approach to honing the interpretation and appreciation of different registers and styles in the past. A style which has often been difficult to interpret is purist discourse, which is the subject of Pfalzgraf's contribution. Pfalzgraf considers how defining German in order to build its prestige has involved excluding elements which are considered to be not-German: foreign words as emblems of cultural dependence or inferiority. As a discourse it requires careful interpretation: nationalism and patriotism have been both negatively and positively valued in the history of German, and linguistic purism has been used for a range of ideological and political purposes. Periods of intense puristic activity are often a symptom of the speech community feeling under stress, and Pfalzgraf discusses the impact right up to the contemporary (over-)reaction to the influence of English.

The notion of self-definition is also at the heart of Durrell's contribution, which considers the history of words for 'German' and the ideologies which have informed them. Germans are known to their European neighbours under a great diversity of terms, and have held a long scholarly discussion about their identity, with the popular idea that it resides in the language being set against the legal notion that it resides in the blood, the *ius sanguinis*. Durrell traces the complex interrelationhsip of *deutsch* and *Teuton* and their role in the national story.

Nationalism is a key element of the nineteenth century, and Davies' contribution deals specifically with this period. Traditionally, textbook histories of German have tended to assume that their work was done soon after 1750, with few further developments to report, but Davies develops a much more nuanced view of how the prejudices and ideas about the standard were developed as a way for the *Bildungsbürgertum* to mark themselves out as the prestige social grouping with access to the prestige linguistic variety, which they were able to define and develop in their own image. The notion that there is one correct form of the German language emerges, of course, from the suppression of otherness, and Langer's contribution is to describe one of the chief other German languages, the Low German language – dialect of the North. Langer traces the fall of Low German from its high status in the Middle Ages as a contrast to the rise of High German, such that the dominant perception of the prestige of High German has led to even Low German's own speakers deserting it, a process now only beginning to be reversed as part of the Europe-wide trend of support for minority languages.

The final two essays in this volume are devoted to the twentieth century, and specifically to its middle years: both contribute to the study of language history from 'below' or 'without'. While the Nazi period and its aftermath are probably the most-studied areas of German history, they have received very little attention from language historians, and these articles aim to redress that balance. Horan pays attention to the discourse of National Socialist times by looking at the writing of women involved with the movement, and considers how linguistic analytical processes can help to interpret what is being said, how and why, and to place these texts in the historical continuum which is the story of German. That continuum is generally considered to have broken by the caesura of Germany's catastrophic defeat in the Second World War, and Wells concludes our volume by considering the late 1940s as a time of both continuities and new beginnings for the German language. Wells pulls away the simplifications of previous work on this area to reveal a complex social network of public and private spaces in which language was used, far from the expected totalitarian monolith.

Over the course of its history the status and idea of what German is has changed in the minds of both its own speakers and the outside world. The seventeenth-century struggle for recognition for German as a *Haubtsprache* gave way to the nineteenth-century idea of German as a *Kultursprache*, a defining element in the *Kultur- und Sprachnation*,[8] building an identity on the high culture of literature and thought, of the *Land der Dichter und Denker*. For Germans, living in a country (if, indeed, we can call it a country) with much more fluid geographical boundaries than, for instance, France or England, and with changing capital cities, the German language, and important people who have used it, have been key reference points creating a sense of belonging as part of the German nation. To give some sense of the complexity and diversity of the interplay between the German language and its speakers is the goal of these landmarks in the history of German.

References

Bynon, T. (1977), *Historical Linguistics*, Cambridge: Cambridge University Press.
Campbell, L. (1998), *Historical Linguistics. An Introduction*, Edinburgh: Edinburgh University Press.
Crowley, T. (1973), *An Introduction to Historical Linguistics*, Oxford: Oxford University Press.

8   For a comprehensive history of these terms, see Gardt (2000).

Davis, G.W. and G.K. Iverson (eds) (1992), *Explanation in Historical Linguistics*, Amsterdam, Philadelphia: Benjamins.

Elspaß, S. (2008), 'Vom Mittelneuhochdeutschen (bis ca. 1950) zum Gegenwartsdeutsch.' In: *ZDL 75*: 1–20.

Elspaß, S., N. Langer, J. Scharloth, and W. Vandenbussche (eds) (2007), *Language Histories from Below (1700–2000)* (= Studia Linguistica Germanica 86), Berlin, New York: de Gruyter.

Gardt, A. (ed.) (2000), *Nation und Sprache. Die Diskussion ihres Verhältnisses in Geschichte und Gegenwart*, Berlin, New York: de Gruyter.

Gardt, A., U. Haß-Zumkehr and T. Roelcke (eds) (1995), *Sprache als Kulturgeschichte.* (= Studia Linguistica Germanica 54), Berlin, New York: de Gruyter.

Lass, R. (1997), *Historical Linguistics and Language Change.* (= *Cambridge Studies in Linguistics* 81), Cambridge: Cambridge University Press.

Leyhausen, K. (2005), '"*Vorsicht ist nicht immer der bessere Teil der Tapferkeit*" – Purism in the history of the German language', in: *Linguistic Purism in the Germanic Languages*, edited by N. Langer and W.V. Davies, Berlin, New York: De Gruyter, 302–23.

Nevalainen, T. and H. Raumolin-Brunberg (2003), *Historical Sociolinguistics: Language Change in Tudor and Stuart England*, London, etc.: Longman.

Niedzielski, N. and D. Preston (2000), *Folk Linguistics*, Berlin, New York: De Gruyter.

Paul, H. (1886), *Prinzipien der Sprachgeschichte* (reprint 1975), Tübingen: Niemeyer.

Romaine, S. (1982), *Socio-historical Linguistics. Its Status and Methodology*, Cambridge: Cambridge University Press.

Scardigli, P. (1994), *Der Weg zur deutschen Sprache.* Bern, etc.: Peter Lang.

Schendl, H. (2001), *Historical Linguistics*, Oxford: Oxford University Press.

Trask, R.L. (1996), *Historical Linguistics*, Arnold: London, New York.

Weinreich, U., W. Labov and M.I. Herzog (1968), 'Empirical foundations for a theory of language change', in: *Directions for Historical Linguistics. A Symposium*, ed. W.P. Lehmann and Y. Malkiel, Austin & London: University of Texas Press, 95–195.

Willemyns, R. and W. Vandenbussche (2006), 'Historical Sociolinguistics: Coming of Age?' In: *sociolinguistica. Internationales Jahrbuch für Europäische Soziolinguistik 20.* 146–65.

ROSAMOND MCKITTERICK

A Landmark Figure in the History of German? Charlemagne, Language and Literacy

When Charles, king of the Franks and Lombards, august emperor and governor of the Romans, died in 814, he ruled most of what we now think of as western Europe, that is, the present day countries of France, Germany, Austria, Switzerland, Benelux, part of Catalonia and northern and central Italy. Indeed, as early as 799 one of his court poets had hailed him as *pater Europae*, father of Europe,[1] and in a coin type issued *c.* 806 he is portrayed in the guise of a laureate Roman emperor (looking uncommonly like Vespasian, with a chunky head) and the inscription *imp(erator) aug(ustus)*.[2] The coin and written evidence from the second and third decades of the ninth century suggest that the ideological implications of renewal or *renovatio* of the Roman empire in the west, consequent on Charlemagne's coronation as emperor in Rome on Christmas Day 800, took some years to work out.[3] It has to be said, moreover, that despite the enormous symbolic weight subsequent politicians and historians have put on the events of 800, the imperial title made little difference to Charlemagne's real power and authority at the time.

If one observes the extent of Charlemagne's Frankish empire in 814, it represents the culmination of a steady expansion into Frisia and western France by Charlemagne's great-grandfather Pippin II and grandfather Charles Martel, and into Alemannia and Aquitaine by Charlemagne's father Pippin III.[4] In the thirty or so years from the beginning of his own reign in 768 to

---

1   Hentze (1999: 16) ll. 93–5: *Rex Karolus, caput orbis, amor populique decusque, / Europae venerandus apex, pater optimus, heros, / Augustus.*

2   Fitzwilliam Museum, Medieval European Coinage No. 749, illustrated in Grierson and Blackburn (1986: plate 34, p. 534). I am grateful to Lucy McKitterick for pointing out the parallel with Vespasian.

3   For a discussion with references, see Nelson (1994).

4   See McKitterick (1995b: 80–1, map 4) and *Times Atlas* (1998: 62).

just before 800 Charlemagne or Charles the Great added, both by ruthless political manoeuvering and a series of bloody campaigns, the Lombard kingdom of Italy, Bavaria, the Spanish March, Brittany and Saxony. Certainly he created an empire that proved to be a somewhat unfortunate inspiration to many subsequent European rulers, not least Napoleon Bonaparte who actually thought of himself as another Charlemagne.[5] Certainly too, as I shall explain below, Charlemagne is celebrated for all that he did to promote Latin learning and the Latin language. The Carolingian period saw the consolidation of Latin in education, learning, worship and law, and the secure access thereby established to the knowledge and texts of classical antiquity and the early Christian era. To propose Charlemagne also as a landmark figure in the history of the German language, therefore, exposes the need to consider the implications of the creation of a realm that extended well beyond the bounds of the areas that had once been part of the Roman empire in the west, and thus which had Latin as the common language, into the Germanic speaking areas east of the Rhine.

Another look at the area occupied by the Carolingian empire clarifies this, for the part west of the Rhine and south of the Danube represents areas once within the Roman empire and thus regions in which Latin and subsequently the various Romance languages in antiquity and the Middle Ages were spoken.[6] Everything beyond this area is where the Germanic and Slavic languages are the first language of the native peoples. The linguistic frontier between Romance and Germanic languages in the north of France and western Germany in the middle does not exactly correspond to the bounds of the former Roman territory. It is further west and south and in fact has curious little pockets of Germanic speakers within the Romance area.[7] But everyday speech in any case is not the only issue. Throughout the Carolingian empire, even for those whose mother tongue was a Germanic or Slavic language, Latin was the language of education, law and religion. The greater majority by far of the texts surviving from the Carolingian period are in

5   McKitterick (2002: 30): I have discussed some of these aspects further in that article.
6   For the extent of the Roman empire in late antiquity see the map in Cameron and Garnsey (1998: 18–19) and *The Times Atlas of European History* (1998: 44–5).
7   See the map showing the linguistic frontier in McKitterick (1995b: 122, map 9) or McKitterick (1989: 6): see also Joris (1966: 1–52).

Latin. The Carolingian empire, therefore, was one in which both Romance and Germanic languages were spoken and in which Latin was both spoken and promoted in its written form.

What, then, is Charlemagne's claim to be distinguished as a 'Landmark Figure' in the history of the German language?

Let us first consider the king himself. In what language might he have murmured to his wife in bed or at breakfast, even if at dinner he liked to be read to from the histories of antiquity and one of his favourite books was Augustine's *City of God*?[8]

Charlemagne was a member of an aristocratic Frankish landowning family originating in the late seventh century from the region between the Rhine and the Moselle rivers and who probably therefore spoke a form of Old High German close to Rhenish Franconian. Every written text associated with Charlemagne, however, including letters and legislation, is in Latin. The only indication we get that Frankish was indeed Charlemagne's native language is in Einhard's *Life of Charlemagne*, written in Ciceronian Latin shortly after Charlemagne's death. The date of composition is probably about 817, though many still persist in dating the Life much later, to 829 or 830.[9] Einhard was the son of two minor landowners in the region of Fulda north of the Main river in Germany. He had been educated at the monastery of Fulda, and then spent many years at the court of Charlemagne before retiring from public life and presiding as lay abbot (supported by his wife Imma) over the small communities of Michaelstadt, Steinbach and Seligenstadt. In all three places the churches he had constructed are still standing. The *vita* is the first secular biography of a ruler to be written in the early Middle Ages and is modelled to some degree on the lives of the caesars by the Roman author Suetonius. It gives an engaging account of Charlemagne's career as ruler, his wars and successes, his extensive diplomatic relations with other rulers as far afield as the Caliph of Baghdad and the Emperor of Byzantium, his family life, his activities as a patron and his piety, his personal appearance and tastes. For example, he preferred roast meat to all other food. He liked to hunt and ride

---

8   Einhard, ed. Holder-Egger (1911: c. 24).
9   For a discussion of the dating and the arguments for *c.* 817 see Innes and McKitterick (1994: 203 9), McKitterick (2008. 7-20) and the summary in favour of the later date in Tischler (2001: 151-239).

and to swim in the hot springs at Aachen. Sometimes, Einhard tells us, he invited such a crowd of courtiers and bodyguards to join him in the baths that there might be more than a hundred people bathing together.[10]

Einhard tells us in chapter 25 of the *Vita Karoli* that 'not being content with knowing only his own native tongue, Charlemagne also made an effort to learn foreign languages. Among those, he learned Latin so well, that he spoke it as well as he did his own native language, but he was able to understand Greek better than he could speak it.' Einhard does not specify here what this native language was, but in chapter 29 of the work it becomes clear that it is German:

> But he did direct that the unwritten laws of all the peoples under his control should be gathered up and written down. Charles also ordered that the very old and barbaric poems (*barbara et antiquissima carmina*) in which the deeds and wars of ancient kings were sung, should be written down and preserved for posterity. He also began a grammar of his native language. He even gave names to the months, since before them the Franks were used to referring to them in a mix of Latin and non-Latin/foreign [= Germanic] names (*apud francos partim Latinis, partim barbaris nominibus pronuntiarentur*). He also assigned individual names to the twelve winds, since until then scarcely more than four of them had been named.

January	*Wintarmanoth*	'winter month'
February	*Hornung*	'antler-shedding or mud month'
March	*Lentzinmanoth*	'the month of Lent'
April	*Ostermanoth*	'Easter month'
May	*Winnemanoth*	'month of joy'
June	*Brachmanoth*	'ploughing month'
July	*Heuuimanoth*	'hay month'
August	*Aranmanoth*	'month of ripening wheat'
September	*Witumanoth*	'wind month'
October	*Windumemanoth*	'wine month'
November	*Herbistmanoth*	'harvest month'
December	*Heilagmanoth*	'holy month'

He gave the winds these names

| *Subsolanus* | *Ostroniwint* | 'east wind' |
| *Eurus* | *Ostsundroni* | 'east-south wind' |

---

10   For a useful compendium on Einhard see Dutton (1998).

Euroauster	*Sundostroni*	'south-east wind'
Auster	*Suundroni*	'south wind'
Austro-africus	*Sunduwestroni*	'south-west wind'
Africus	*Westsundroni*	'west-south wind'
Zephyrus	*Westroni*	'west wind'
Chorus	*Westnordroni*	'west-north wind'
Circius	*Nordwestroni*	'north-west wind'
Septentrior	*Nordroni*	'north wind'
Aquilo	*Nordostroni*	'north-east wind'
Vulturnus	*Ostnordroni*	'east-north wind'[11]

Although Einhard only uses the term *nomina barbara*, his list of these names, undoubtedly Germanic in form, establishes without doubt that he meant 'Germanic/Frankish' when he used *barbara*.[12] The versions of the spelling we have received may have been influenced by the degree of familiarity with German of other copyists coping with this passage, let alone Einhard's own family origins in the Fulda region and his education within the monastery of Fulda. Fulda, as we shall see, became a major centre for the production of texts in Old High German from at least the early ninth century onwards. Because of its original foundation within the context of the Anglo-Saxon missionary and reforming enterprise in Hesse, Franconia and Thuringia, moreover, it may well be that the Germanic vernacular and translation of key texts as a means for instructing the laity in the Christian faith were already a concern at Fulda when Einhard was a student there in the 780s.[13]

None of the surviving texts in Old High German which might answer to Einhard's brief description of *barbara et antiquissima carmina*, can be linked securely to the court.[14] But then, there is not much in Old High German surviving at all which does qualify as 'ancient and barbarous song', apart from the *Hildebrandslied*.[15] There is the tantalizing reference in the library catalogue from Reichenau in Lake Constance dated *c.* 821. That lists a collection of

---

11   Trans. Dutton (1998: 34–5).
12   The word barbarian itself originally meant a non-Greek speaker, a man who could only make the sound 'ba-ba'. It came to mean a non-Latin speaker, non-Roman or foreign.
13   On Fulda see Schmid (1978).
14   See the discussion by Dronke and Dronke (1977).
15   For useful surveys of the corpus of Old High German literature see Bostock (1976), Edwards (1994), and the analysis in Haubrichs (1995).

German poems in one volume (*De carminibus Theodiscae volumen I*) in the same section as a copy of the Life of Charlemagne, but no extant manuscript according with this description has been identified (Lehmann 1918: 243). As for the enterprise of collecting and writing down the stories of ancient kings itself, it would be tempting to see a possible inspiration or reminiscence drawn from Cicero's *De oratore*, a text surviving in ninth-century Frankish copies from the Loire region and Corbie, one of which was written by a scholar called Lupus of Ferrières who had spent some time in the school at Fulda in his youth (this manuscript is now London British Library Harley 2736).[16] Cicero recounts the fantasy that Peisistratus, tyrant of Athens, decided to create order among the confusion of texts of the great epic poet Homer.[17] Some scholars, moreover, have suggested that the late eighth-century translations of Isidore of Seville's *De fide catholica* extant in a manuscript of *c.* 800 from the Carolingian heartland of Austrasia, in which there is an attempt to work out a system of orthography, might be linked to the creation of the grammar Einhard describes.[18] Unfortunately, there is no other evidence to enable us to posit such a precise context for the production of this work.

On the other hand there is certainly an indication, in surviving legislation linked with Charlemagne, of an awareness of a need to promote the 'vernacular' as a means of communication. That this is German is implied rather than explicit, owing to the ambiguity and possible alternative interpretations of the first reference to it. This is the decree concerning church reform issued from Tours in 813, one of a series of church councils held in five different venues that year initiated by Charlemagne as part of a more general programme of ecclesiastical and moral reform of the kingdom he had inaugurated a quarter of a century earlier. It advised clerics to translate sermons to the people *in rusticam romanam linguam aut theotiscam.*[19] The references

16   See Beeson (1930) and Reynolds (1983: 102–9).

17   Cicero, *De oratore* (Bk. III, Chp. 34, section 137, p. 109). I owe this comparison to Lucy
       McKitterick.

18   Paris, Bibliothèque Nationale de France lat. 2326, fols 1r–79r and Vienna, National-
       bibliothek Cod. 3093. See Edwards (1994: 145); Bischoff (1981a: 20, note 71) and in
       English translation Bischoff (1994: 35) and compare Bischoff (1981b: 108). The manu-
       script is illustrated in Fischer (1966: no. 4) and there is also a facsimile in Hench
       (1893).

19   Published in *Concilia* (II.i, no. 38, c. 17).

to: *rustica romana* and *theotisca* are generally understood to be a reference to two languages: 'Romance' which in due course became Old French, and 'Deutsch' or German. It is conceivable, however, that *aut theotiscam* is a gloss on *in rusticam romanam linguam* for *theotiscam* can be translated as 'the language of the people' and *aut* can bear the meaning 'or rather, more accurately' as well as 'or at least', and 'or' (antithesis).[20] Given that the correct translation of *theotisca* is 'language of the people', the phrase might be translatable as 'in rustic roman speech or rather, the vernacular'.[21] Against this, the author of the *Annales regni francorum* under the year 788 uses a Germanic word for a gloss and describes it as *theodisca lingua*.[22] That the clause on sermons should first be enunciated at Tours, a former Gallo-Roman town in the depths of the Romance region, is certainly curious. On the traditional interpretation, and given other references to other languages (or, conceivably, language registers) within the Frankish empire, it may also be a crucial thread of evidence for a continuing royal interest and awareness of the needs of Germanic language speakers, or at least the necessity for bi- or even tri-lingual provision (Latin, Romance and German) within the Frankish realm as a whole.[23] Alternatively, the main point surely is that the emphasis is on the oral delivery of the sermons, not their written form, to a mixed population in a rustic or popular rather than learned language which the people can understand. Whatever the case, it has to be said that this clause has caused more excitement and heated debate among historians of Latin and Romance than it has among historians of the German language.[24]

20 Compare the entry on *aut* in Lewis and Short (1879/1969).

21 In the discussion after the lecture in Cambridge in which I first presented this paper, Dennis Green was rightly most insistent upon this point and I am very grateful to him for this. See also Durrell's article in this volume (p. 169).

22 In *Annales* (p. 80) *quod theodisca lingua harisliz dicitur* 'which is called *harisliz* (desertion) in the *theodisca* language.'

23 See also the discussion by Betz (1965: 300–6). Betz points out that the *Admonitio generalis* of 789, in *Capitularia* (p. 59) insists on understanding of the faith, and Alcuin and the Reims reform council of 813 all refer to the use of appropriate languages to enable the people to understand their religion.

24 See, for example Wright (1982: 118–22) and his references.

One might also stress in this respect the famous Strasbourg oaths of 842 recorded by Nithard in his *History of the sons of Louis the Pious* written in Latin.

Thus on the sixteenth of February, Louis and Charles met in the city which at one time was called Argentaria but is now commonly called Strasbourg. There they swore the oaths which are recorded below: Louis in the Roman language and Charles in the language of the people [*Lodhuvicus Romana, Karolus vero Teudisca lingua iuraverunt.*] Before the oath one addressed the assembled people in the language of the people and the other in the Roman language.

[...]

When Charles had spoken the same words in the Roman language,
[*cumque Karolus haec eadem verba Romana lingua perorasset*]
Louis as the elder first swore to uphold the following in the future
[*Lodhuvicus, quoniam maior natu erat, prior haec deinde se servaturum testatus est:*]

'Pro Deo amur et pro Christian poblo et nostro commun saluament, d'ist di in auant, in quant Deus sauir et podir me dunat, si saluarai eo cist meon fradre Karlo et in aidha et in cadhuna cosa, si cum om per dreit son fradra salvar dist, in o quid il mi altresi fazet; et ab Ludher nul plaid numquam prindrai, qui meon uol cist meon fradre Karle in damno sit'

When Louis had concluded, Charles swore the same in the language of the people as follows
[*quod cum Lodhuvicus explesset, Karolus Teudisca lingua sic haec eadem verba testatus est:*]

'In Godes minna ind in thes Christianes folches ind unser bedhero gealtnissi, fon thesemo dage frammordes, so fram so mir Got geuuizci indi mahd furgibit, so haldih tesan minan bruodher, soso man mit rehtu sinan bruodher scal, in thiu thaz er mig sosoma duo; indi mit Ludheren in nohheiniu thing ne gegango, zhe minan uuillon imo ce scadhen uuerhen'

The oath which the followers of the two brothers swore, each in their own language went like this in the Roman language
[*sacramentum autem, quod utrorum populus, quique propria lingua, testatus est, romana lingua sic se habet:*]

'Si Lodhuuigs sagrament, quae son fradre Karlo iurat, conservat, et Karlus meos sendra de suo part non lostanit, si io returnar non l'int pois, ne io ne neuls, cui eo returnar int pois, in nulla aiudha conttra Lodhuuuig nun li iuer.'

In the language of the people it was this
[*Teudisca autem lingua:*]

'Oba Karl then eid, then er sinemo bruodher Ludhuuuige gesuor, geleistit, indi Ludhu-
uuig min herro, then er imo gesuor, forbrihchit, ob ih inan es iruuenden ne mag, noh
ih noh thero nohhein, then ih es iruuennden mag, uuidhar Karle imo ce follusti ne
uuirdhit.' (Nithard, p. 440)

In English translation, these oaths are as follows:

Brothers' oath: For the love of God and for our Christian people's salvation and our
own, from this day on, as far as God grants knowledge and power to me, I shall treat
my brother with regard to aid and everything else as a man should rightfully treat his
brother, on condition that he do the same to me. And I shall not enter into any dealings
with Lothar which might with my consent injure this my brother Charles/Louis.

Followers' oath: If Louis/Charles keeps the oath which he swore to his brother Charles/
Louis, and my lord Charles/Louis does not keep it on his part, and if I am unable to
restrain him, I shall not give him any aid against Louis/Charles nor will anyone whom
I can keep from doing so.[25]

These oaths were sworn by the armies of the two brothers, Louis the
German and Charles the Bald (both grandsons of Charlemagne), sons of
Louis the Pious who had been quarrelling with their brother Lothar about
the division of the Carolingian empire since the death of their father in 840.
The settlement finally reached in 843 with the Treaty of Verdun was the one
which first delineated the lands we know as France and Germany and the
middle kingdom of Lotharingia, the precise boundaries remaining a matter of
dispute until the end of the Second World War. The oaths sworn by the armies
were in 'their own language'. Nithard however, underlines the bilingualism
of the two Frankish rulers as well as the divergence of the spoken from the
written forms of Latin, in that Charles, king of the west Franks, swears the
oath in the language of the people, which is Germanic in form, Louis, king
of the east Franks (known to historians as Louis the German), swears it in
the Roman language, that is, 'Romance'.

25   I follow here, for the convenience of those who may wish to consult the entire text, but
      with a few minor alterations, the translation provided by Scholz (1970: 161–3).

Nithard supplies written texts for these oaths but does not bother to supply a Latin translation. Why not? Did he assume that for the court audience for whom his work was written a Latin version was unnecessary, particularly as the text was probably intended for reading aloud?[26] Here we have the apparent attempt to record in writing what was spoken on a battlefield in a text commissioned by one of the protagonists, Charles the Bald, of whom Nithard was both a cousin and a loyal follower. I have suggested elsewhere that Nithard may here be manipulating conventions of writing. He makes striking use of implied language differences – exchanged by the brothers but maintained by their troops – to enhance both the political difference he wished to stress and the necessity and essential logic of their reconciliation.[27] All the followers of Charles the Bald and of Louis the German could be united symbolically by making them all speak the same language. It is highly unlikely, however, that the oaths are an accurate reflection of the precise linguistic affiliations of the rank and file of the armies of Louis and Charles respectively, even if they may indicate the linguistic range of the gathering as a whole. Equally, Nithard's highly formulaic rendering, similar to many other recorded Carolingian oaths, gives literary form to what may well have been an extempore oral promise.

If we consider texts explicitly linked with royal patronage or dedicated to the rulers Louis the Pious and Louis the German, there are a number of these in Old High German, such as the *Heliand* and Otfrid's *Evangelienbuch*.[28] It is significant to my mind, however, that the *Praefatio* referring to the *Heliand* and one of Otfrid's dedicatory letters were both written in Latin;[29] the latter at least suggests that written German may have been as new to the kings and other patrons as it was to the composers of these poems. The *Praefatio* moreover, also invokes the idea that translations were for the '*illiteratus*', a term

26   On Nithard and his audience see Nelson (1986).
27   See McKitterick (1995a: 11–12) and McKitterick (1991a).
28   See the editions of Behaghel/Taeger (1984) and Erdmann (1973), and a translation of the *Heliand* by Murphy (1992).
29   In *Heliand*, pp. 1–2 and *Otfrid*, pp. 4–7 respectively (Murphy's translation does not include the Praefatio). Otfrid's Latin letter is addressed to Liutbert, archbishop of Mainz and the dedicatory preface, to Louis, although headed in Latin like the sections of the poem in the manuscript from Vienna, *Österreichische Nationalbibliothek* Cod. 2687, is written in German.

which in medieval texts, as Grundmann (1958) established in a classic article, does not simply mean 'unlettered' or 'illiterate' but 'illiterate in Latin'. That is, those who were unable to read Latin might be able to hear a version read out aloud or sung in German. Certainly Otfrid's text and the *Heliand* were designed for recitation or singing, or so what appear to be marks designed to aid recitation or singing in Otfrid manuscripts suggest.[30]

A further royal connection is suggested by the *Muspilli* manuscript where the text was crammed into the margins of pseudo-Augustine's treatise *De symbolo contra iudeos* presented to a young Louis, possibly Louis the German, and originally dedicated to him by Adalram (probably Adalram who was archbishop of Salzburg 821–36).[31] Commentators on this book have come up with various dotty suggestions about who was so bold as to scribble the *Muspilli* poem in the king's book like this. My favourite among these is the opinion, on the grounds that its poor calligraphy is more likely to be that of a woman, that the poem was copied in by Louis the German's wife Imma![32]

The whole corpus of early Old High German texts, with translations of the Lord's Prayer, creeds, baptismal catechisms and confessions, the Rule of Benedict, St Matthew's Gospel, the Gospel harmonies, the *Exhortatio ad plebem christianam*, the *Muspilli* and a number of prayers and charms, comprises texts which were spoken in one context or another. Most, moreover, have been linked both with the royally-promoted missionary endeavours in the pagan Saxon regions as well as the older areas of evangelisation by missionaries from England. These also accord with the insistence on clerical and monastic reform and instruction of the laity which were an intrinsic part of the Carolingian church reforms as a whole (McKitterick 1977). Thus the Merseburg Baptism ritual from Hesse or the Main area in Anglo-Saxon minuscule of the first third of the ninth century provides the priest's questions and answers required of the catechumen,[33] and the Latin–German wordlist in St Gallen

---

30   Vienna, *Österreichische Nationalbibliothek* Cod. 2687, illustrated in Fischer (1966: no. 18).

31   Munich, *Bayerische Staatsbibliothek* Clm 14098, illustrated in Fischer (1966: no. 15).

32   Even Cyril Edwards quotes this theory with apparent acceptance (1994: 149). On the evidence for some women at least as expert scribes in the early Middle Ages see McKitterick (1991b) and the English translation of a revised version as chapter XIII of McKitterick (1994b).

33   Merseburg, *Domstiftsbibliothek*, Cod. 136, illustrated in Fischer (1966: no. 16a).

913, actually written at Murbach at the end of the eighth century, forms part of a handy collection of useful information and short notes on theological issues as well as Jerome's letter (Ep. 53) to Paulinus the Priest.[34] This letter is highly relevant to the contents of the manuscript as a whole. In it, Jerome urges Paulinus to make a diligent study of the scriptures but stresses the virtue of a zeal for learning which sent men on their travels to learn from particular teachers and not just from books. 'Spoken words' he says, possess an indefinable hidden power, and teaching that passes directly from the mouth of the speaker into the ears of the disciples is more impressive than any other.[35]

Other manuscripts containing Old High German texts include books where the German appears as glosses or interlinear translation, as in the copy of the Rule of St Benedict from Reichenau.[36] Oddly enough it is apparently not a translation of the version of the Latin text in which it is written, but rather appears to be a version someone knew by heart. These glosses on Latin texts in Old High German give us some insight into the relationship between reading and understanding written German.[37]

Many Old High German texts were added in space on blank leaves in the book, like the *Hildebrandslied*[38] or the Weissenburg catechism.[39] In the former, the codex contained Biblical books and prayers which left several leaves blank, which were gradually filled in; the Hildesbrandslied was the last text to be added. In the latter the catechism forms part of a mixed Latin and German section of a book comprising a number of once independent *libelli* probably written in Alsace in the first quarter of the ninth century. All the texts in this *libellus* are concerned with the essential elements of the Christian faith and include among others, a German version of the *Quicumque vult* or Athanasian creed. One of the most interesting of these uses of spare pages

---

34   St Gallen, *Stiftsbibliothek* Cod. 913, illustrated in Fischer (1966: no. 1b).

35   In Jerome, § 2, p. 446: also in Labourt (1953: 10).

36   St Gallen, *Stiftsbibliothek* Cod. 916; illustrated in Fischer (1966: no. 3) and see his commentary, pp. 6*–7* and Daab (1959).

37   For a full discussion see Green (1994).

38   Kassel, *Murhard'sche Bibliothek der Stadt Kassel und Landesbibliothek*, Cod. Theol. 20 54, produced at Fulda, in the early ninth century: see Bischoff (1998: 376). Illustrated in Fischer (1966: nos 12 & 13).

39   Wolfenbüttel, *Herzog August Bibliothek* Cod. Weißenburg 91, fols 154r and 154v, illustrated in Fischer (1966: no. 7).

can be found in the codex of the *Apologeticum* of Gregory of Nazianazus, into which were added in *c.* 881/2 both the Old French Eulalia Sequence and the victory poem in Rhenish-Franconian (with some Low German and Middle Franconian forms) celebrating the defeat of a Viking raiding party by a king Louis, son of a king Louis.[40] This Louis is usually identified as the young west Frankish King Louis III who did score a victory over Vikings at Saucourt in 881. It being a puzzle as to why a king in the Romance part of the Frankish realms should be celebrated in a victory poem in German, I have got into some trouble with my colleagues for suggesting that the Louis of the *Ludwigslied* could be Louis the Younger of the east Franks whose main residence was at Frankfurt and who won a battle against the Vikings at Thiméon in 880 (McKitterick 1989: 232–5). This suggestion has at least the merit of resolving the problem of the language of the poem. Louis the Younger's victory at Thiméon itself was also, as the annals of St Vaast make clear, rather more creditable than that of Louis III at Saucourt.[41] On the other hand, the poem and its place in the codex could well be an indication of continuing tri-lingualism in the lower Rhineland at the end of the ninth century.

The manuscript context of much of our Old High German text is therefore opportunistic, with use made of spare space to record texts used in oral contexts. Those which are integrated as part of thematic miscellanies, such as the Weissenburger catechism *libellus* referred to above or the *Wessobrunner Gebet* manuscript would bear further scrutiny.[42] More rarely, in the case of very long texts, do we find Old High German texts as entire codices in their own right. The *Heliand*, Tatian and Otfrid's *Evangelienbuch* produced at Werden, Fulda and Weissenburg respectively, deploy all the skills one is accustomed to observe in Latin books of the period, in presenting the text. The Tatian manuscript presents the Latin facing the German text in a similar way to some surviving Greco-Latin Biblical texts we have from this period,[43]

---

40   Valenciennes, *Bibliothèque municipale*, Ms 150, fols 141v–143r. Illustrated in Fischer (1966: no. 22).

41   In *Annales Vedastini*, s.a 880 and 881, pp. 296 and 300.

42   Munich, *Bayerische Staatsbibliothek* Clm 22053, illustrated in Fischer (1966: no. 14), with a full facsimile in Kraus (1922). On the illustrations to the portion of this codex containing the legend of the True Cross see Bierbrauer (1990: *Textband Kat.* 155, pp. 83–4 and *Tafelband Abb.* 319–36, pp. 92–4).

43   St Gallen, *Stiftsbibliothek* Cod. 56, illustrated in Fischer (1966: no. 9).

and the layout of Otfrid's *Evangelienbuch* resembles Latin poetry books of the same period.[44] The manuscripts, furthermore, make no linguistic differentiation as far as script is concerned. In charters from Anglo-Saxon England, for example, the boundary clauses in Old English are written in a different script from the remaining Latin clauses of the document. In these Old High German texts the same script, caroline minuscule, is used as for all Latin texts, though occasionally a new letter representing a particular sound is inserted, such as the Anglo-Saxon *wynn* rune þ for *w* used in the *Hildebrandslied* manuscript.

The evidence for Old High German texts in the late eighth and the ninth centuries indicates the recording of oral texts, recited or sung. In terms of the promotion of a written Germanic vernacular, it has to be said that the Carolingian rulers, not least Charlemagne himself, compare very unfavourably with the concentrated, even spectacular, achievements of King Alfred the Great of Wessex and the translations into Old English provided at the end of the ninth century.[45] Given the known influence of Einhard's Life of Charlemagne at the court of King Alfred it is not impossible that Alfred was inspired by the description of Charlemagne's own enterprise. But in Old English the translations of Augustine's *Soliloquies*, the first fifty Psalms, Gregory the Great's *Pastoral Care* and Boethius's *Consolation of Philosophy*, by King Alfred himself and Bede's *Ecclesiastical History of the English people*, Orosius's *Seven books of history against the pagans* and many more texts are clearly to be linked with the king.[46] They were certainly designed to be read though could also have been read aloud. There is also a widespread use of English for laws and in legal documents.

Nevertheless, it might be as well to reflect on the context in which these translations were produced in comparison with the situation in Carolingian Europe. In England, the English learned Latin as a second language, a fact underlined by the production of the Latin grammars in England and Ireland in the early Middle Ages specially adapted for those learning Latin as a second language, so marvellously elucidated by the late Vivien Law (1982

---

44   Compare, for example, the ninth-century Vergil codices illustrated in Chatelain (1884–92: Plates LXVII and LXVIII, = Bern, *Burgerbibliothek* MS 165 and Paris, *Bibliothèque nationale de France* MS lat. 7929).

45   See Bately (1980), Bullough (1991) and Pratt (2007).

46   Compare Hummer (2005: 130–54) and Goldberg (2006).

and 1994). On the Continent however, throughout the Frankish realm, the Latin grammars which remained in use during the ninth century were those designed for Latin native speakers by the late Roman grammarians Donatus and Priscian.[47] The Carolingian empire was one in which the vernacular German had a place. But that place has to be carefully defined in relation to literacy and Latin learning more generally as well as to emergent Old French or 'Romance'.

To give some idea of the great contrast between the promotion of written German and the promotion of Latin in the Frankish realms, one could consider the centres of Latin learning and book production within the Frankish realm which are known or suggested to have produced texts or manuscripts containing any of the dialects of Old High German in relation to those without attested or secure links with Old High German texts.[48] It should be stressed that few as the major Old High German text-producing centres are, Freising, Fulda, Reichenau, St Gallen, Weissenburg, Werden, Salzburg and Murbach are all, without exception, famous as centres of Latin learning as well. Fulda in particular is important for the number of copies of works by classical authors copied there, for its Biblical knowledge and for the work of many of its scholars, especially Hraban Maur. Right across the Carolingian Frankish realm there is a common Latin culture in all the monastic and episcopal centres of learning, both old and new. This Latin culture is founded on the works of classical antiquity, on the Latin Bible, on the writings of the church fathers, and on the contributions of such early medieval writers as Boethius, Cassiodorus, Isidore of Seville, Bede and the host of scholars and authors of the Carolingian period. It is also crucial to register that from most of these centres we also have written records and legal documents of one type or another. The St Gallen and Lorsch charters in Latin commissioned by small landholders, and the rich Latin charter material from Agilolfing and Carolingian Bavaria warn us that we should not underestimate the ability of

---

47 I discuss this more fully in McKitterick (1989: 7–22). See also Holtz (1981) and the review by Law (1986).

48 For maps of centres of Latin learning see Bischoff (1994: xvi–xvii) and Contreni (1995: 722–3).

people in Germanic-speaking areas to conduct their business and legal affairs in Latin.[49] These were centres above all of the written word.

Latin culture together with Christianity and Frankish rule expanded to embrace Saxony (and, under Charlemagne's successors and later rulers of Germany) to Denmark, Norway, Sweden, Bohemia, Poland and Hungary. There was undoubtedly, moreover, an accompanying growth in the development of the vernacular, often initially within missionary contexts such as Cyril and Methodius among the Slavs and the creation of Glagolitic script and the writing down of 'Old Church Slavonic'.[50] But common to all the missionary enterprises, and in all the Christian churches of western Europe, including Britain, was a maintenance of the Latin language as the means of formal communication.

It is the Fulda copy which survives of the circular letter sent *c.* 800 by Charlemagne to all his monasteries and bishops known as the *De litteris colendis* ('on the cultivation of letters/learning'):

> We along with our faithful advisers, have deemed it useful that the bishoprics and monasteries [...] should [...] devote their efforts to the study of literature and to the teaching of it, each according to his ability, to those on whom God has bestowed the capacity to learn. Letters have often been sent to us in these last years from certain monasteries [...] in most of these writings their sentiments were sound but their language was uncouth [...] because of their neglect of learning their unskilled tongues could not express it without fault [...] let men be chosen [for the task of improving knowledge] who have the will and ability to learn and also the desire to instruct others.[51]

This letter reinforced directives already given in another crucial text for the Carolingian reform of education, the *Admonitio generalis* of 789 in which Charlemagne decreed:

> and let the clergy join and associate to themselves not only children of servile condition but also the sons of free men. And let schools be established in which boys may learn to read. Correct carefully the Psalms, *notas*, the chant, the calendar, the grammars in each

---

49   On St Gallen, see McKitterick (1989: 77–134); on Lorsch, see Innes (2000); and on Bavaria see Hammer (2002) and Brown (2001 and 2002). See also McKitterick (2000).

50   For the context see Vlasto (1970) and Wood (2001).

51   *Capitularia* (no. 29, 79); English trans. King (1987: 232–3).

monastery and bishopric, and the catholic books; because often some desire to pray to God properly, but they pray badly because of the incorrect books.[52]

Alongside Charlemagne's zeal to encourage everyone in the schools to learn correct Latin was on the one hand an effort to promote uniformity of religious observance and practice. Scholars edited and corrected the text of the Bible; the ruler and his advisers encouraged the use of a standard homiliary or collection of sermons; throughout the empire particular liturgical books for the Mass, chant texts, canon law, and the Rule of Benedict, in versions understood as correct and authorized by the king and his advisers, were copied and distributed with a very considerable degree of success.[53] On the other hand, there was an insistence on the written word in the secular sphere: judges should judge according to the written law and not according to their private opinions; written records of legal transactions and administration had to be made.[54] In Charlemagne's *Capitulare de villis* about the running of his estates, for instance, he stated:

> It is our wish that stewards (*iudices* = judges) should record, in one document, any records, goods or services they have provided, or anything they have appropriated for our use, and, in another document, what payments they have made, and they shall notify us by letter of anything that is left over.[55]

Thirdly it is from the reign of Charlemagne onwards within the Frankish empire that an enormous range of new kinds of texts are produced such as *Libri Vitae*, cartularies, secular biography and many more.

---

52 *Capitularia* (no. 22, 59–60). English trans. King (1987: 217). The translation of *notas* is disputed. Some think it means 'musical notation'; some 'shorthand', and others 'writing'. The position of *notas* between psalms and chant in the list might seem to favour the meaning as musical notation, though no written musical notation, that is, neumes, survive from quite as early as this. See further below, note 57.

53 I explored this in McKitterick (1977 and 1996).

54 See in particular the capitulary for 802 in *Capitularia* (no. 33, 91–100) and English trans. King (1987: p. 233), especially clauses 1, 13, 25, 26, 29, 40. See also Nelson (1990).

55 *Capitulare de villis*, in *Capitularia* (no. 32, 88). English trans. Loyn and Percival (1975: 71).

Lastly we need to reflect on the use of writing in relation to oral communication and its relation to memory. Isidore of Seville said of written letters of the alphabet that:

> they were invented in order to remember things. For lest they fly into oblivion, they are bound in letters. For so great is the variety of things that all cannot be learned by hearing nor contained only in memory. (Isidore: I, iii, 2–3)

It is perhaps significant that in many of the centres where we first get efforts to record Old High German in writing we also observe the earliest use of musical notation, notably at St Gallen and in relation to new compositions of tropes and sequences, for neumes, as musical notes then were called, made possible the precise memory control that is the essence of transmission.[56] It is conceivable that these notational means were devised to augment the aural communication of melodies. Musical notation, like the writing down of Old High German, is to be understood, in other words, in the context of Carolingian attitudes to the written word and to texts. It was also in this period that many dramatic developments were made in the representation and expression of the relationship between texts and images.[57] In exegesis different layers of understanding of a text are unpeeled.[58] Literacy is not just about how many people could read or write. It is the understanding of writing and its meaning, the attitudes towards the written word and the qualitative use of it which are so crucial.

In all of this the role of Charlemagne and his successors as patrons is prominent: there was a systematic patronage of particular centres, there are schools and monasteries associated with the court, there is the a royal role in the dissemination of particular texts to which I have already alluded, along with a direction and impetus provided for the cultivation of contemporary scholarship, a court atelier for the production of fine books for use by the royal family and in the royal chapel, and occasional sponsorship of individual scholars and craftsmen. I have suggested that the development of musical notation as much as the production of texts in the Germanic vernacular is

---

56   For discussion and references see Rankin (1994), Levy (1998) and my review of Levy (2000).
57   See McKitterick (1994 and 2000).
58   See Contreni (1983), reprinted in Contreni (1992).

an important indication of the lively sensitivity on the part of the Franks to the relationship between sound and written symbol. It is as part of the general Frankish energy directed towards the promotion of literacy, writing and the written word that Old High German spoken versions of already existing Latin texts were written down and in due course new texts composed. They served the general aims of Carolingian education and learning.

It is in this context therefore that Charlemagne, a native German speaker himself, has a claim to be recognized as a landmark figure in the history of the German language.

References

Primary sources

Annales
    – *Annales regni francorum*, Kurze, F. (ed.) (1895), *Monumenta germaniae historica, Scriptores rerum germanicarum in usum scholarum* (= *MGH SRG*) 6, Hannover: Hahn.
Annales Vedastini
    – *Annales Vedastini*, in: Rau, R. (ed.) (1972), *Quellen zur karolingischen Reichsgeschichte* 2. Teil, Darmstadt: Wissenschaftliche Buchgesellschaft.
Capitularia
    – Boretius, A. (ed.) (1883), *Monumenta Germaniae Historica. Capitularia regum francorum*, vol. I, Hannover: Hahn.
Cicero
    – Sutton, E.W. and Rackham, H. (eds) (1942), Cicero, *De Oratore*, vol. 2 bk. III. (Loeb Classical Library 349), London: Heinemann.
Concilia
    – Werminghoff, Albert, (ed.) (1906), *Monumenta germaniae historica Concilia aevi Karolini*, vol. II, Hannover: Hahn.
Einhard
    – *Einhardi Vita karoli magni*, Holder-Egger, O. (ed.) (1911), *Monumenta germaniae historica, Scriptores rerum germanicarum in usum scholarum* (*MGH SRG*) 25, Hannover: Hahn.

Heliand
- Behaghel, O. and Taeger, B. (eds) (1984), *Heliand und Genesis* (*Altdeutsche Textbibliothek* 4), 9th ed., Tübingen: Niemeyer.
Isidore
- *Isidori Hispalensis Episcopi Etymologiarum sive originum libri XX*, vol. I, Lindsay, W.M. (ed.) (1911), Oxford: Clarendon.
Jerome
- Hilberg, I. (ed.) (1996), *Sancti Eusebii Hieronymi Epistolae, Part 1.* (*Corpus Scriptorum Ecclesiasticorum Latinorum* 54), 2nd ed., Vienna: Verlag der Österreichischen Akademie der Wissenschaften.
Nithard
- *Nithardi Historiae*, in: Rau, R. (ed.) (1974), *Quellen zur karolingischen Reichsgeschichte*, Teil 1, Darmstadt: Wissenschaftliche Buchgesellschaft.
Otfrid
- Erdmann, O. and Wolff, L. (eds) (1973), *Otfrids Evangelienbuch.* (*Altdeutsche Textbibliothek* 49), Tübingen: Niemeyer.

Bibliography

Bately, J.M. (1980), '*The Literary prose of King Alfred's reign: translation or transformation?*' *An inaugural lecture*, London: King's College, University of London.

Beeson, C.H. (1930), *Lupus of Ferrières as scribe and text critic: A study of his autograph copy of Cicero's 'De Oratore'*, Cambridge, Mass.: The Mediaeval Academy of America.

Betz, W. (1965), 'Karl der Grosse und die *lingua Theodisca*', in: *Karl der Grosse. Lebenswerk und Nachleben*, vol. 2: *Das Geistige Leben*, edited by B. Bischoff, Düsseldorf: Schwann, 300–6.

Bierbrauer, K. (1990), *Die vorkarolingischen und karolingischen Handschriften der Bayerischen Staatsbibliothek*, Wiesbaden: Reichert.

Bischoff, B. (1981a), 'Panorama der Handschriftlichenüberlieferung aus der Zeit Karls des Grossen', in: *Mittelalterliche Studien. Ausgewählte Aufsätze zur Schriftkunde und Literaturgeschichte*, edited by B. Bischoff, Stuttgart: Hiersemann, 5–39.

Bischoff, B. (1981b), 'Paläographische Fragen deutscher Denkmäler der Karolingerzeit', in: *Mittelalterliche Studien. Ausgewählte Aufsätze zur Schriftkunde und Literaturgeschichte*, edited by B. Bischoff, Stuttgart: Hiersemann, 73–111.

Bischoff, B. (1994), *Manuscripts and Libraries in the Age of Charlemagne*, Cambridge: Cambridge University Press. (Translated by M. Gorman).

Bischoff, B. (1998), *Katalog der festländischen Handschriften des neunten Jahrhunderts. Teil I: Aachen – Lambach*, Wiesbaden: Harrassowitz.

Bostock, J.K. (1976), *A handbook on Old High German Literature*, 2nd ed., Oxford: Clarendon.

Brown, W. (2001), *Unjust seizure. Conflict, interest and authority in an early medieval society*, Ithaca: Cornell University Press.

Brown, W. (2002), 'Charters as weapons. On the role played by early medieval dispute records in the disputes they record', *Journal of Medieval History* 28, 227–48.

Bullough, D.A. (1991), 'The educational tradition in England from Alfred to Aelfric: teaching *utriusque linguae*', in: D.A. Bullough, *Carolingian Renewal: Sources and Heritage*, Manchester: Manchester University Press, 297–334.

Cameron, A. and Garnsey, P. (eds) (1998), *The Cambridge Ancient History*, vol. 13, *The late Empire, AD 337–425*, Cambridge: Cambridge University Press.

Chatelain, E. (1884–92), *Paléographie des classiques latins* Part 1, Paris: Librarie Hachette.

Contreni, J.J. (1983), 'Carolingian Biblical studies', in: *Carolingian essays: Andrew W. Mellon lectures in early Christian studies*, edited by U.-R. Blumenthal, Washington, D.C.: Catholic University of America Press, 71–98. Also reprinted in J.J. Contreni (1992), *Carolingian learning, masters and manuscripts*, Aldershot: Variorum.

Contreni, J.J. (1995), 'The Carolingian renaissance: education and literary culture', in: McKitterick, R. (1995), 709–57.

Daab, U. (ed.) (1959), *Die Althochdeutsche Benediktinerregel des Cod. Sang 916*, Tübingen: Niemeyer.

Dronke, P. and Dronke, U. (1977), *Barbara et antiquissima carmina*, Barcelona: Universidad Autónoma de Barcelona, Facultad de Letras.

Dutton, P.E. (1998), *Charlemagne's courtier. The complete Einhard*, Peterborough, Ontario: Broadview.

Edwards, C. (1994), 'German vernacular literature: a survey', in: McKitterick (1994a), 141–70.

Fischer, H. (1966), *Schrifttafeln zum althochdeutschen Lesebuch*, Tübingen: Niemeyer.

Goldberg, E.J. (2006), *Struggle for empire: kingship and conflict under Louis the German, 817–876*, Ithaca: Cornell University Press.

Green D.H. (1994), *Medieval listening and reading. The primary reception of German literature 800–1300*, Cambridge: Cambridge University Press.

Grierson, P. and Blackburn, M. (1986), *Medieval European coinage, with a catalogue of the coins in the Fitzwilliam Museum, Cambridge*, vol. 1: *The early middle ages (5th–10th centuries)*, Cambridge: Cambridge University Press.

Grundmann, H. (1958), 'Litteratus-illiteratus. Der Wandel einer Bildungsnorm vom Altertum zum Mittelalter', *Archiv für Kulturgeschichte* 40, 1–66.

Hammer, C.I. (2002), *A large-scale slave society of the early middle ages. Slaves and their families in early medieval Bavaria*, Aldershot: Ashgate.

Haubrichs, W. (1995), *Geschichte der deutschen Literatur von den Anfängen bis zum Beginn der Neuzeit*. Vol. I: *Von den Anfängen zum hohen Mittelalter*. Part 1: *Die Anfänge:*

Versuche volkssprachiger Schriftlichkeit im frühen Mittelalter (ca. 700–1050/60), 2nd ed., Tübingen: Niemeyer.

Hench, G.A. (1893), *Der althochdeutsche Isidor. Facsimileausgabe des Pariser Codex nebst critischem Texte der Pariser und Monseer Bruckstücke*, Strassburg: Trübner.

Hentze, W. (ed.) (1999), *De Karolo rege et leone papa* (Studien und Quellen zur westfälischen Geschichte 36), Paderborn: Bonfatius. (Text edited and translated by Franz Brunhölzl).

Holtz, L. (1981), *Donat et la tradition de l'enseignement grammatical*, Paris: CNRS.

Hummer, H.J. (2005), *Politics and power in early medieval Europe. Alsace and the Frankish realm, 600–1000*, Cambridge: Cambridge University Press.

Innes, M. and McKitterick, R. (1994), 'The writing of history', in: McKitterick (1994a), 193–220.

Innes, M. (2000), *State and society in the early Middle Ages: the Middle Rhine Valley 400–1000*, Cambridge: Cambridge University Press.

Joris, A. (1966), 'On the edge of two worlds in the heart of the new Empire: the Romance regions of northern Gaul during the Merovingian period', *Studies in Mediaeval and Renaissance History* 3, 1–52.

King, P.D. (1987), *Charlemagne: Translated Sources*, Kendal: P.D. King.

Kraus, C. von (1922), *Die Handschrift des Wessobrunner Gebets. Geleitwort zu der faksimile-Ausgabe von A. von Eckhardt*, Munich: Kurt Wolff.

Labourt, J. (1953), *Lettres. Saint Jérôme*. Vol. III, Paris: Belles Lettres.

Law, V. (1982), *The Insular Latin grammarians*, Woodbridge: Boydell.

Law, V. (1986), 'Review of Holtz (1981)', *Beiträge zur Geschichte der deutschen Sprache und Literatur* 108, 101–9.

Law, V. (1994), 'The study of grammar', in: McKitterick (1994a), 88–110.

Lehmann, P. (1918), *Mittelalterliche Bibliothekskataloge Deutschlands und der Schweiz*. Vol. I. *Die Bistümer Konstanz und Chur*, Munich: Beck.

Levy, K. (1998), *Gregorian chant and the Carolingians*, Princeton: Princeton University Press.

Lewis, C.T. and Short, C. (1879/1996), *A Latin Dictionary*, Oxford: Clarendon.

Loyn, H.R. and Percival, J. (1975), *The reign of Charlemagne: documents on Carolingian government and administration*, London: Arnold.

McKitterick, R. (1977), *The Frankish church and the Carolingian reforms, 789–895*, London: Royal Historical Society.

McKitterick, R. (1989), *The Carolingians and the written word*, Cambridge: Cambridge University Press.

McKitterick, R. (ed.) (1990a), *The uses of literacy in early medieval Europe*, Cambridge: Cambridge University Press.

McKitterick, R. (1990b), 'Text and image in the Carolingian world', in: McKitterick (1990a), 297–318.

McKitterick, R. (1991a), 'Latin and Romance; an historian's perspective', in: *Latin and the Romance languages in the early middle ages*, edited by R. Wright, London: Routledge, 130–45. Reprinted in McKitterick, R. (1995), *The Frankish kings and culture in the early middle ages*, Aldershot: Variorum.

McKitterick, R. (1991b), 'Frauen und Schriftlichkeit im Frühmittelalter', in: *Weibliche Lebensgestaltung im frühen Mittelalter*, edited by H.-W. Goetz, Cologne: Böhlau, 65–118. Revised and translated into English as 'Women and literacy in the early middle ages', in McKitterick, R. (1994), *Books, scribes and learning in the Frankish kingdoms, 6th–9th centuries*, Aldershot: Variorum.

McKitterick, R. (ed.)(1994a), *Carolingian Culture: Emulation and Innovation*, Cambridge: Cambridge University Press.

McKitterick, R. (1994b), '*Testo e immagine nell'alto medioevo*', Settimane di studi del Centro italiano di studi sull'alto medioevo XLI, Spoleto: Centro italiano di studi sull'a to medioevo.

McKitterick, R. (1995a), 'Introduction', in: *The New Cambridge Medieval History. Vol. II c. 700–c. 900*, edited by R. McKitterick, Cambridge: Cambridge University Press, 3–17.

McKitterick, R. (1995b), 'England and the Continent', in: *The New Cambridge Medieval History. Vol. II c. 700–c. 900*, edited by R. McKitterick, Cambridge: Cambridge University Press, 64–84.

McKitterick, R. (1996), 'Unity and diversity in the Carolingian church', in: *Unity and diversity in the church: papers read at the 1994 Summer Meeting, and the 1995 Winter Meeting of the Ecclesiastical History Society* (Studies in Church History 32), edited by R.N. Swanson, Oxford: Blackwell, 59–82.

McKitterick, R. (2000), 'Review of Levy (1998)', *Early Music History* 19, 279–91.

McKitterick, R. (2002), 'Europe and the Carolingian inheritance', in: *The Future of the Past. Big Questions in History*, edited by P. Martland, London: Pimlico 16–35.

McKitterick, R. (2008), *Charlemagne: the formation of a European identity*, Cambridge: Cambridge University Press.

Murphy, G.R. (1992), *The Heliand: the Saxon Gospel*, New York and Oxford: Oxford University Press.

Nelson, J.L. (1985), 'Public Histories and private history in the work of Nithard', *Speculum* 60, 251–93. Reprinted in Nelson, J.L. (1986), *Politics and ritual in early medieval Europe*, London: Hambledon, 195–238.

Nelson, J.L. (1990), 'Literacy in Carolingian government', in: McKitterick (1990a), 258–96.

Nelson, J.L. (1994), 'Kingship and empire in the Carolingian world', in: McKitterick (1994a), 52–87.

Pratt, D. (2007), *The political thought of King Alfred the Great*, Cambridge: Cambridge University Press.

Rankin, S. (1994), 'Carolingian music', in: McKitterick (1994a), 274–316.

Reynolds, L.D. (ed.) (1983), *Texts and transmission. A survey of the Latin classics*, Oxford: Clarendon.

Schmid, K. (ed.) (1978), *Die Klostergemeinschaft von Fulda im früheren Mittelalter* (Münstersche Mittelalterschriften 8), Munich: Fink.

Scholz, B.W. (ed.) (1970), *Carolingian Chronicles. Royal Frankish annals and Nithard's histories*, Ann Arbor: University of Michigan Press.

Times Atlas (1998), *The Times Atlas of European History*, 2nd ed., London: Times Books.

Tischler, M.M. (2001), *Einharts Vita Karoli. Studien zur Entstehung, Überlieferung und Rezeption* (Schriften der Monumenta Germaniae Historica 48), Hannover: Hahn.

Vlasto, A.P. (1970), *The entry of the Slavs into Christendom: an introduction to the medieval history of the Slavs*, Cambridge: Cambridge University Press.

Wood, I.N. (2001), *The missionary life. Saints and the evangelisation of Europe 400–1050*, London: Pearson/Longman.

Wright, R. (1982), *Late Latin and early Romance: in Spain and Carolingian France*, Liverpool: Francis Cairns.

JOHN L. FLOOD

Luther and Tyndale as Bible Translators: Achievement and Legacy

In this increasingly secular age it is perhaps difficult to conceive of the thrill direct access to the Bible in a readable, vernacular translation gave to sixteenth-century readers. Luther's New Testament, we hear, was so widely available 'that even tailors and cobblers, even women and other simple folk who had only learnt to read a little German in their lives, were reading it most avidly as though it were the fount of all truth, while others carried it around, pressed to their bosom, and learned it by heart'.[1] This report, by one of Luther's Catholic opponents, Johannes Dobneck, known as Cochlaeus, (1479–1552), may be exaggerated, but it contains more than a grain of truth, as other contemporary witnesses testify.

Luther's Bible translation in context

Why did Luther's translation generate such excitement? His was by no means the earliest translation of the scriptures into German. Leaving aside the numerous partial renderings in the Middle Ages (see Rost 1939), the German Bible had already been printed entire several times before Luther was even born.

Bible printing began in the early 1450s when the Mainz patrician Johann Gutenberg (c. 1400–68), the inventor of printing with movable type, produced the two-volume Latin Bible now known as the Gutenberg Bible or the 42-line Bible (from the number of lines of text on the page). It was completed by August 1456 at the latest. The earliest known reference to this project is in a

---

1   Cochlaeus (1549: 55). My translation.

letter dated 12 March 1455 from Enea Silvio Piccolomini, the later Pope Pius II but at the time secretary to the Holy Roman Emperor Frederick III, to the Spanish Cardinal Juan de Carvajal. Piccolomini reports that while attending the Imperial Diet at Frankfurt am Main in October 1454 he had seen samples of a printed Bible 'that could be read without glasses', produced for inspection by 'a marvellous man'. Whether this was Gutenberg himself or, perhaps more likely, his associate Peter Schöffer, we do not know.[2]

Gutenberg's 42-line Bible was the first of 94 Latin Bibles printed in Europe in the fifteenth century. Of these no fewer than 57 appeared in German-speaking towns. Soon the Bible became so readily available that already in 1504 the Nuremberg publisher Anton Koberger said of the edition printed for him by Johann Amerbach at Basel between 1498 and 1502, *Es ist warlich ein unkewfflich werck* [...] *der handel der bucher ist so gancz nichtz mer, das ich nicht weiß, was man machen möchte.*[3]

Germany led the way in printing vernacular Bibles too, long before the Protestant Reformers, in asserting 'the priesthood of all believers', contended that all Christians had the right and duty to explore scriptural truth for themselves. The first vernacular Bible ever printed was the German Bible issued by the Strassburg publisher Johann Mentelin before 27 June 1466. Eight editions were already on the market before Martin Luther (1483–1546) was born, and indeed two more had appeared by 1485 when Berthold von Henneberg, Archbishop of Mainz, attempted to ban the printing of Bibles in German.[4] Between 1466 and September 1522 when Luther published his own New Testament translation at Wittenberg fourteen editions of the complete Bible had appeared in High German (at Strassburg, Augsburg and Nuremberg) and four in Low German (at Cologne, Lübeck and Halberstadt). The impact of Luther's translation would be such that none of these earlier versions was reissued.

Luther's translation was innovative, indeed provocative, in that it was based not on the Latin Vulgate, the only version of the Scriptures officially

2   See Davies (1996: 193–215).
3   See Widmann (1965: II, 141).
4   For early reactions to the printing of Bibles in German see Flood (2005).

sanctioned by the Church, but on the Greek and Hebrew sources.[5] His New Testament was based on Erasmus's Greek New Testament, first published in 1516 but known to Luther in the second edition of 1519. For the Old Testament and Apocrypha, on which he worked from 1522 to 1532, Luther used the Hebrew text. When necessary, he availed himself of expert help from his Wittenberg colleagues, especially Philipp Melanchthon and Matthaeus Aurogallus (Goldhahn), who were respectively professors of Greek and Hebrew. Luther was naturally very familiar with the Vulgate, too.[6] The Catholic Church's insistence on upholding the Vulgate, later confirmed by the Council of Trent, was designed to withstand two different threats: on the one hand that emanating from Greek and Hebrew studies, and that posed by vernacular translations on the other.

Luther's Bible translation was first published in its entirety in 1534; he continued to revise it until his death.[7] Since then it has exerted as strong an influence on the German literary language as the Authorized Version, the King James Bible (1611), has on English[8] – in the words of Bluhm (1984b: 112), 'So far as their effect on their national literatures is concerned, the German and English Bibles are in a class by themselves'. Moreover, as this essay will show, Luther's Bible has continued to work through the English, for in some respects it influenced William Tyndale's translation, too.

5   Cochlaeus accused Luther of 'changing many things, omitting, adding, twisting the meaning against the ancient and authoritative reading of the Church' as well as adding marginal notes, 'erroneous and scoffing glosses', and 'leaving out nothing spiteful in his prefaces' (Cochlaeus 1549: 54, 1582: 350).

6   In 1995 a Vulgate printed at Lyon in 1519, containing what may be Luther's own handwritten notes, comments and corrections, was discovered in the Württembergische Landesbibliothek at Stuttgart. See Brecht/Zink 1999, especially the contributions by Sören Widmann (pp. 61–93) and Michael Beyer (pp. 95–116).

7   See Seyferth (2003). For later revisions see Brügger (1983) and Fricke/Meur (2001).

8   See especially Norton (2000).

Tyndale's translation

By the mid-1520s the German Reformation was having two countervailing effects in England: it encouraged pressure for English translations of the Bible, and it caused the bishops to resist such endeavours. In 1523 William Tyndale (*c.* 1494–1536), from Gloucestershire, who had studied at Oxford and possibly Cambridge also, approached Cuthbert Tunstall, Bishop of London, thinking he would be the ideal patron for his plan to print an English translation of the New Testament, based on the Greek text instead of the Latin Vulgate. Though in 1408 Thomas Arundel, Archbishop of Canterbury, had declared it heresy to undertake any new translation of the scriptures or even to own any English version unless both the owner and the translation were formally approved by a bishop, Tyndale imagined that Tunstall, as a classical scholar who in fact had helped Erasmus collate manuscripts in preparation for his 1516 Greek New Testament, would favour reverting to the original texts. Tunstall, however, felt obliged as a bishop to follow the Church's teaching and adhere to the Vulgate. Thus rebuffed, Tyndale went to Germany. One of the principal accounts of what happened next is given in Cochlaeus's biography of Luther (Cochlaeus 1549: 132–5, 1582: 288–94), where he tells how 'two English apostates' (unnamed, but doubtless Tyndale and his amanuensis William Roye, a Cambridge student who had been a Franciscan at Greenwich) who had spent some time at Wittenberg planned to turn the whole population of England Lutheran against the will of King Henry VIII. Wittenberg, then the focus for Biblical scholarship, was a natural destination, and Tyndale seems to have been there for ten months in 1524–5.[9] The Englishmen, Cochlaeus continues, planned to smuggle into England a translation of Luther's New Testament, printed 'in many thousands of copies' at Cologne (a city with strong trading links with England). This was in 1525; the printer was probably Peter Quentel. According to Cochlaeus, the original intention was to print six thousand copies but since the printers were somewhat doubtful about the wisdom of this, they agreed on three thousand, with three thousand more to be produced once the first were sold. Cochlaeus, chancing to discover these plans, plied the

9   See Mozley (1937: 52–3.) Roye enrolled at Wittenberg on 10 June 1525.

printers with wine and learned from them that they had completed the first ten quarto sheets (80 pages) for the first three thousand copies and that the work was being financed by English merchants. Cochlaeus passed this intelligence to Herman Rinck, a Cologne patrician, who investigated the matter and, finding it to be true, reported it to the city council who put a stop to it.[10] Thereupon, Cochlaeus reports, the 'two renegade English monks' fled up the Rhine, taking the printed sheets with them to Worms 'where, alas, the common man has taken up the Lutheran gospel with great lack of sense'. It was here that, in 1526, the first printed English New Testament, now an octavo of 348 leaves, was completed by Peter Schoeffer the Younger (a son of Gutenberg's partner). The Worms edition is mentioned by Luther's friend Georg Spalatin (1484–1545) in his diary on 11 August 1526: 'At Worms six thousand copies of the New Testament in English have been published. This text had been translated by an Englishman who is staying there with two other British citizens [...].'[11] Meanwhile, Rinck had reported the matter to Henry VIII, Cardinal Wolsey, and John Fisher, Bishop of Rochester. A watch was kept on English ports to intercept the book. The Archbishop of Canterbury having declared the 'New Testament of Tindall' to contain 'heretical pravity' on 3 November 1526,[12] Bishop Tunstall, who claimed to have found 'more than two thousand heretical errors' in it, had copies publicly burned at St Paul's Cross in London.

The title of the Worms edition reads: *The newe Testame[n]t as it was written / and caused to be writte[n] / by them whiche herde yt. To whom also oure saveoure Christ Jesus commaunded that they shulde preache it vnto al creatures.* This formulation manifestly proclaims that it has been translated from the original Greek sources, not from the Vulgate, and rejects the Catholic Church's

---

10　　A sole copy of just eight sheets (64 pages) of this 1525 edition, as far as Matthew 22:12, survives in the Grenville Collection in the British Library (G.12179). See Tyndale (1525) edited by Arber (1871), and Herbert (1968): 1, no. 1.

11　　Translated by Popp (1999: 137), note 1, after Mombert (1884 [1967]: 106). Of the three surviving copies of the Worms edition only one, that in the Württembergische Landesbibliothek, Stuttgart, is complete with the title page (see Zwink 1998: 44). The British Library (formerly Bristol) copy lacks the title page, and the third, in the library of St Paul's Cathedral, London, is also imperfect.

12　　See Brewer (1872, IV, 2, p. 1158, no. 2607). For details of the book's importation see Herbert (1968: 2).

claim to the sole right to interpret the Bible. By 1528, or at the latest in 1530, Tyndale went to Antwerp, where he published his Pentateuch. He was finally betrayed to the authorities and imprisoned in 1535 and hanged and burned at Vilvoorde Castle, near Brussels, in October 1536. Tyndale's unfinished translation of the Old Testament was completed by Miles Coverdale who published the first printed complete Bible in English in 1535, *faithfully and truly translated out of Douche* [= Deutsch] *and Latyn*.[13]

Though Tyndale is not as generally well known in the English-speaking world as Luther is in the German, his legacy is nevertheless substantial, for his translation was fed into successive sixteenth-century English Bibles: Coverdale 1535, Matthew's Bible 1537, the Great Bible 1539, the Geneva Bible 1560, the Bishops' Bible 1568, the Rheims New Testament 1582, and especially the Authorized Version of 1611 ('the only literary masterpiece ever produced by a committee', as it has been called). A recent computer-assisted comparison of samples from Tyndale's New Testament and those portions of the Old Testament which he translated with the corresponding passages from the Authorized Version has shown that nearly 84 per cent of the New Testament and approximately 76 per cent of the Old Testament have been transmitted to the Authorized Version unaltered.[14]

Luther and Tyndale as translators

Luther plays a central role in the broader context of translation theory and practice of his day. Some late fifteenth-century German humanists thought that the only way to improve the quality of German writing was to imitate the style of Latin, believing that if only one followed the example of Cicero, elegant Ciceronian German would result. Others took the view that the over-riding aim was to render the sense of the original accurately while the style

---

13   Though Coverdale may have translated from the Zurich Bible of 1524–9 this was essen-
       tially a reprint of Luther's text (Bluhm 1984b: 116).
14   Nielson/Skousen (1998).

was incidental if not immaterial.[15] Luther struck a happy balance between these approaches: he asserted that fidelity to the sense of the original was paramount, most especially in the case of Holy Scripture, and also that it was essential to ensure that it was rendered into clear, natural, idiomatic German. Defending his method in his *Sendbrief von Dolmetschen* (1530),[16] one of several programmatic statements on his approach to translation, he says that Latin, Greek or Hebrew idiom is irrelevant; the important thing is naturalness of expression in the target language, German: [...] *den man mus nicht die buchstaben inn der lateinischen sprachen fragen / wie man sol Deutsch reden / wie diese esel thun / sondern / man mus die mutter jhm hause / die kinder auff der gassen / den gemeinen man auff dem marckt drumb fragen / vnd den selbigen auff das maul sehen / wie sie reden / vnd darnach dolmetzschen so verstehen sie es den / vnd mercken / das man Deutsch mit jn redet* (Luther, *WA*, 30, 2: 637).[17] It is evident that, despite their pettifogging criticisms, even Catholics secretly admired Luther's translation: the 'Catholicized' version which Hieronymus Emser (1477–1527), secretary to Duke George of Saxony, published at Dresden in 1527 was, as Luther to his chagrin immediately recognized, in reality nothing but Luther's own translation with Emser's name on the title-page and a few minor changes to the text.[18] For all that Emser firmly believed, as he stated in his afterword, that reading the Bible was not for the laity but should be reserved for scholars, the pass had been sold: the

15 For contemporary approaches to translation see Schwarz (1986) and my chapter Parallel lives: Heinrich Steinhöwel, Albrecht von Eyb, Niklas von Wyle, in Reinhart (2007).

16 Among the many editions of this the most useful is Arndt (1968). For an English translation of this key document see Luther WK, XXV, 175–202.

17 Hitler's propaganda minister Joseph Goebbels acknowledged Luther's insight when, in 1934, he wrote, 'Wer hier etwas werden und bedeuten will, der muß die Sprache sprechen, die die Masse versteht [...].' See Kegel (2006: 104).

18 See Luther, *WA*, 30, 2: 634. At least eighteen editions of Emser's version were published (predominantly in Catholic towns) between 1527 and 1589. Emser had charged Luther with perpetrating 1400 'heretical' errors in translating the New Testament, one of which was to have rendered the opening words of the Lord's Prayer, *Pater noster*, as *Unser Vater*, using normal German word order, instead of *Vater unser*, the Latinate word order that had been standard in Germany for centuries. For Emser's criticisms see his *Auß was gründ vnnd vrsach Luthers dolmatschung / vber das nawe testament / dem gemeinen man billich vorbotten worden sey*, Leipzig, 1523. Urbanus Rhegius sprang to Luther's defence with his *Ob das new testament ytz recht verteutscht sey* [Augsburg], 1524.

German Bible, Luther's Bible, was here to stay. Its popular success was due not to its being based on the Hebrew and Greek sources instead of the Vulgate but rather to its user-friendly presentation – with pictures (124 woodcuts in the 1534 edition), commentaries and marginal notes –, and above all its accessible, seemingly 'homely' language.[19] For many Protestants it was the language that more or less gave it the status of being equivalent to the original (Karpp 1992: 245). By the time Luther died in 1546, 430 separate editions of his complete Bible or parts of it had been published. It is said that by 1569 800,000 copies were sold.[20]

Tyndale tells us little about his own approach to translation.[21] The brief note 'To the Reader' at the end of the 1526 edition assures us of his *pure entent* and it expresses the hope that *the rudnes off the worke* should not offend. We should *consyder howe I had no man to counterfet* [i.e. he had no model] / *nether was holpe with englysshe of eny that had interpreted the same / or soche lyke thinge in the scriptures before tyme.* Various difficulties *caused that many thynges are lackynge*, hence it was a provisional rather than a finished translation; however, he hopes in due course to be able to *geve lyght where it is requyred / and to seke in certayne places more proper englysshe* as well as to supply a table *to expounde the wordes which are nott commenly vsed / and shewe howe the scripture vseth many wordes which are wotherwyse vnderstonde of the commen people; and to helpe with a declaracion where one tonge taketh nott another.* In sum, this epilogue, couched in the form of a traditional humility formula, acknowledges the translation's imperfections and addresses the needs of 'the commen people'. Indeed, Tyndale's English translation reflects 'the language spoken in the Vale of Berkeley by his parents, brothers, friends, neighbours, by officials and labourers, priests and ploughboys' (Daniell 1994: 18), and thus in effect appeals to the English reader as Luther's translation appeals to the German.

19   His language was not quite as 'popular' as has sometimes been claimed. His style was rather an elevated one influenced by classical rhetoric and the stylistic properties of the original.
20   Neddermeyer (1998, I, 530–6, esp. p. 534). Neddermeyer's figures are sometimes debatable.
21   In his edition of Tyndale (1526), Daniell (1989, xxii), draws attention to Tyndale's remarks about English and the classical languages in his *Obedience of a Christian Man* (1528).

Luther's influence on Tyndale

Luther, however inaccurately, has often been considered 'the father of the German language'. In the same way, Tyndale has been hailed as the maker of English. Thus Daniell – who has been charged with hero-worship[22] – says that he 'made a language for England' (Daniell 1994: 3), 'gave England a Bible language supreme above all other nations (a matter of hard fact, not chauvinism)' (Daniell 1998: 20–1), and describes Tyndale's Bible as 'England's greatest contribution to the world for nearly five hundred years' (Daniel 1994: 280). There is no denying Tyndale's importance, yet it must also be accepted that his English New Testament is not an entirely independent creation: it certainly owes something to Luther's influence.[23]

To begin with the circumstantial evidence, Cochlaeus, as we have seen, was convinced that the Cologne printers were producing a Lutheran version of the English New Testament in 1525. It is telling that Tyndale began with the New Testament – Luther only began translating the Old Testament in November 1522, completing the Pentateuch and the historical and poetical books by October 1524, several months after Tyndale arrived in Germany. By then Luther's New Testament was already available in several editions, some printed at Wittenberg but most of them issued at Basel or Augsburg. Which one Tyndale may have seen is not known. It is no surprise that Tyndale should have followed Luther's example: given his burning ambition to publish an English New Testament, it is entirely reasonable to suppose that he studied Luther's translation – after all, Luther was a figure of international significance and his translation was currently a sensation on the book market. It became the model for all subsequent Protestant Bibles. As Bluhm (1984b: 114) says, it is 'unthinkable' that Tyndale would not have consulted it, and even Daniell (1994: 142) concedes that 'it is safe to assume' that he referred to it.

22 In the review of Daniell (1994) by J. Enoch Powell in the *Times Higher*, 23 September 1994.
23 It is impossible to review this question fully here. Earlier discussions include Trinterud (1962); Bluhm (1965, 1984a, 1984b); Hammond (1980); Daniell (1994); Witzmann (1996); Popp (1999); Zwink (1999).

Even the layout of Tyndale's New Testament shows obvious signs of his indebtedness, for it follows Luther in placing the two Epistles General of Peter and the three Epistles General of John *before* Hebrews, James, Jude, and Revelation, thus separating off these last four books on the grounds that they were written by non-apostolic authors. In the table of contents, Luther and Tyndale[24] numbered only the first twenty-three books, leaving Hebrews, James, Jude, and Revelation unnumbered. (The Authorized Version later restored the Vulgate order, placing the Epistles of Peter and John between James and Jude, while Lutheran Bibles still retain Luther's arrangement.) In the second edition of his New Testament, printed at Antwerp by George Joye in 1534,[25] Tyndale follows Luther in supplying prologues to the books and marginal notes and glosses to the text, and the wording of these frequently shows Luther's influence.[26]

But the influence of Luther's New Testament extended beyond the externals of book design and layout. It is likely that Tyndale consulted Luther's translation and/or consulted his German contacts when wrestling with knotty points, and this may explain the echoes of Luther's translation that have been observed in Tyndale. Of course, the degree to which he may have been guided and influenced by Luther's version begs the question of how much German Tyndale knew. With his background, it is unlikely that he knew any High or even Low German before he went to Germany in 1524. But he was a good linguist: according to Spalatin, he was 'so well versed in seven languages, Hebrew, Greek, Latin, Italian, Spanish, English, French that, in whichever language he speaks, you would think him to be native to it.'[27] There is some suggestion that he enrolled at the University of Wittenberg under an assumed name (these were dangerous times!), for *Guillelmus Daltici* [or *Daltin*] *ex Anglia* [*Tindal*, an accepted variant of Tyndale, being turned into

24 Daniell's statements about this (1994: 120) are demonstrably wrong; see Popp (1999: 143–4).
25 Unique copy: London, British Library: G.12180.
26 Some of the marginal notes in the 1525 fragment are taken directly from Luther. The 1526 edition has no marginal notes, probably because the smaller format (122 x 69 mm) precluded them.
27 Spalatin's diary, 11 August 1526, cited after Popp (1999: 137, note 1). On Tyndale's knowledge of Hebrew see Yates (2002).

Daltin] appears in the records on 27 May 1524,[28] but with the theologians there he would have spoken Latin anyway. English will have been unknown in Wittenberg, though Low German-speakers there may have been a help. We must assume therefore that Tyndale was a quick learner, that he studied Luther's New Testament and perhaps that he had some assistance. He may perhaps even have used Luther's New Testament as his German primer (there were as yet no printed grammars of German).

No convincing 'Germanisms' have been found in Tyndale, yet there is some evidence of Lutheran turns of phrase. Let us examine a few instances, sometimes contrasting Tyndale with Wyclif's translation of *c.*1395 and Luther with the pre-Lutheran printed Bibles of 1466 to 1518.

The most famous textual crux in Luther's New Testament is Romans 3:28, *arbitramur enim iustificari hominem per fidem sine operibus legis* in the Vulgate, which Luther renders as *So halten wyrs nu, das der mensch gerechtfertiget werde, on zuthun der werck des gesetzs, alleyn durch den glawben.* Though admitting that neither the Latin nor Erasmus's Greek text had a word corresponding to *alleyn*, he argued that the word was implicit in the context. 'Justification by faith alone' became the watchword of Lutheranism. Tyndale, not daring to go this far, translated it: *We suppose therfore that a man is iustified by fayth without the dedes of the lawe.* However, in his 1534 edition he added a significant, if still timid, marginal note: *Fayth iustifieth.* It was left to Coverdale to be more explicit: his marginal note read: *Some reade 'By faith onely'.*[29]

A clear indication of Luther's influence is found in Romans 3:25 where the Vulgate has the word *propitiatio*, corresponding to Greek *hilastêrion* Luther in 1522 reads *gnade stuel*, said in Grimm, *Deutsches Wörterbuch*, IV, i, pt. 5, col. 591, to be Luther's coinage. Tyndale likewise refers to *Christ Jesu, whom God hath made a seate of mercy*; Wyclif had had *whom God ordeynede foryyver* (i.e. 'forgiver') while the 1466 German Bible read *den got fürsatzt ein versúner* (Mentelin/Kurrelmeyer, II, 20).[30]

---

28   Thus Mozley (1937: 53). Daniell (1994: 300), is sceptical, but see Popp (1999: 141–2); Flood (2001a: 244).
29   'Some' meaning Luther and also the Zurich Bible based on him. See Bluhm (1984b: 118–9).
30   On this see Popp (1999: 147–9), opposing Daniell (1994: 315). See also Hooker (1997: 135–6).

Another instance is Tyndale's use of *showbread*. In the Vulgate the phrase *panes propositionis*, meaning 'loaves of bread displayed (on the table of the Lord)', first occurs in Exodus 25:30 and then at several other points in the Old Testament, as well as in Matthew 12:4, Mark 2:26, Luke 6:4 and Hebrews 9:2 in the New Testament. At Exodus 25:30 and throughout the New Testament Luther has *Schawbrot*, apparently his coinage (though not specified as such in Grimm, *Deutsches Wörterbuch*, VIII, col. 2302). Tyndale speaks of *hallowed loaves* in Matthew, Mark and Luke, but of *the shewebreed* in Hebrews 9:2.[31] The pre-Lutheran German Bibles read *die brot der fürsetzunge* in Exodus 25:30 (Kurrelmeyer, III, 303) or *die brot der furlegunge* in Matthew 12:4 (Mentelin/Kurrelmeyer, I, 43) and *die fürlegung der brot* in Hebrews 9:2 (Mentelin/Kurrelmeyer, II, 259). Wyclif, too had a literal translation: *looues of proposicioun* in Exodus 25:30 and Matthew 12:4, *looues of settyng forth* in I Samuel 21:6 and I Chronicles 9:32, and *setting forth of looues* in Hebrews 9:2.

A particularly interesting instance of Tyndale's following Luther is found in the Lord's Prayer. In Matthew 6:10 the Vulgate reads *sicut in celo, et in terra* 'as in heaven, so too on earth'. Luther reverses the order of the two components: *auff erden wie ynn dem hymel*, which Tyndale follows with *as well in erth, as hit ys in heven*. Wyclif had had *as in heuen and in erthe*.

Treatment of the Greek colour-term *kokkinos* 'scarlet' is telling. Wherever it occurs, Tyndale parallels Luther exactly: in Revelation 17:3 and 4 Luther has *rosynfarben*, Tyndale *rose colored*; in Revelation 18:12 and 16 Luther has *scharlacken*, Tyndale *scarlett*; in Matthew 27:28 Luther has *purpurn*, Tyndale *purpyll*.

Tyndale sometimes reveals his dependence on Luther through the errors he makes. Most striking is I Corinthians 12:7 where Luther reads *In einem iglichen erzeigen sich die gaben des Geists zum gemeinen nutz*. Tyndale renders this as: *The giftes off the sprete* [i.e. 'spirit'] *are geven to every man to proffit the congregacion*, misconstruing the adjective *gemein* 'common' as the noun *gemeine* (Modern German *Gemeinde*) 'congregation'. In Acts 1:13 Luther in 1522 mistakenly writes *Judas Jacobi son* where the correct reading should be *Judas Jacobi bruder*; Tyndale likewise has *Judas James sonne* (instead of *brother*).

---

31   The New English Bible has *the bread of the Presence*, referring to the fact that the offering was required to be constantly in the presence of God on the table.

Another word of interest in Tyndale is *silverling*, previously not attested in English. This is clearly cognate with *Silberling*, the word Luther uses for the thirty pieces of silver Judas receives for betraying Jesus (Matthew 26:15; 27:3; 27:5; 27:6; 27:9). The 1466 Bible reads *silberin* (Mentelin/Kurrelmeyer, I, 108) while the 1475–1518 German Bibles have *silberin pfenning*.[32] Wyclif's Bible of *c*.1395 read *thretti pans of silver*, and Tyndale has *pieces of silver* or *plates of silver* here. Intriguingly, however, Tyndale reads *fifty thousand silverlings* in Acts 19:19; here Luther reads *funfftzig tausent pfennig*. In the 1545 Bible Luther has a marginal note at this point: *Das machet vber sechsthalb tausent gülden. Ein grossche gilt 30. Lawenpfennig*, which in a sense is anticipated by Tyndale who elucidates: *These silverlings which we now and then call pence the Jews call sickles* [i.e. shekels], *and are worth ten pence sterling*.

Other examples are somewhat less persuasive as parallels. Tyndale's verb *harbour*, meaning 'to show hospitality' in Romans 12:13 perhaps echoes Luther's *herbergt* (2nd pers., pl.); the 1466 Bible has *nachuolgt der herbergung* (Mentelin/Kurrelmeyer, II, 49). In I Timothy 3:2 Tyndale says a bishop should be *harberous* (i.e. hospitable), where, however, Luther in 1522 has *gast frey*; similarly at I Peter 4:9. Tyndale refers to Pontius Pilate as *debyte* (i.e. 'deputy') (Matthew 27:2) and *leftenaunt* (Luke 3:1), rather than 'governor' (*praesidi* in the Vulgate); this may reflect Luther's calling him, at both points, the *Landpfleger* (i.e. someone looking after the country on behalf of another, here the Roman Emperor, as a 'deputy' would) – the 1466 Bible had *richter* and *bericht iude* at these points (Mentelin/Kurrelmeyer, I, 108 and I, 208, respectively), while Wyclif has *iustice*, corresponding to *tetrarcha* in the Vulgate.

Sometimes Tyndale might have done better to follow Luther more closely. In Tyndale, the last of the Four Horsemen of the Apocalypse, Death, rides *a grene horsse* (Revelation 6:8); Luther has *ein falh pferd*, 'a pale horse' (as the Authorized Version also says, as indeed did Wyclif). The Vulgate had *equus pallidus* and the Greek *hippos khlôros* The Greek adjective means both 'grass-green' (as in Revelation 8:7 and 9:4) and 'pale, pallid' – surely the context implies deathly pallor.[33] Another point at which Tyndale might have been well

---

32   Though found in Old High German, *silberling* is not attested in Middle High German. Grimm, *Deutsches Wörterbuch* (X, i, col. 1022–3), suggests that the word may have lived on in tradition until it became firmly established through Luther's use of it.

33   On this and for further examples see Popp (1999).

advised to follow Luther is with the angelic salutation (Luke 1:28) where he
has Gabriel say to Mary, *Hayle full of grace*. One can imagine Luther asking, 'Is
that English?', just as he asked whether *Gegrüsset seistu Maria vol gnaden* was
German. 'What does it mean *full of grace*? A German hearing that will think
of a barrel full of beer or a purse full of money. But I have translated it *Du
holdselige*, even though it would be more natural to say *Du liebe Maria*, but
if I had done that the Papists would have gone berserk and have accused me
of ruining the angel's greeting.'[34] Indeed, as it was, he was accused of making
it sound as though Gabriel were addressing his girlfriend when he had the
angel address her as *Du holdselige*.

Archbishop Runcie summarized Tyndale's aims and achievements in
these words:

> Tyndall simply determined, in a famous phrase, to create a Bible that a ploughboy would
> understand. Ironically, his desire that his Bible should be popular and not literary in
> the classical sense created a simple dialect which by its immediacy, clarity and vigour
> has shaped our culture as no other book or subsequent revision.[35]

In Melvyn Bragg's opinion, 'It is impossible to over-praise the quality of
Tyndale's writing. Its rhythmical beauty, its simplicity of phrase, its crystal
clarity have penetrated deep into the bedrock of English today wherever it is
spoken' (2003: 103). Gavin Bone comments on 'how richly gifted Tyndale was
in his appreciation of spoken idioms' (1938: 67).[36] David Daniell, Tyndale's
foremost champion, praises him for writing 'in the language people spoke,
not as the scholars wrote. At a time when English was struggling to find a
form that was neither Latin nor French, Tyndale gave the nation a Bible language that was English in words, word-order and lilt' (1994: 3) and strongly
believes that 'great and influential exponents of plain style in the middle of
the [sixteenth] century learned [...] their plain technique for addressing the
widest public from Tyndale's Bible' (2005: 15). Yet while there is much truth

---

34   For the original text in the *Sendbrief von Dolmetschen*, see Luther, *WA*, 30, 2: 638.

35   Runcie (1996: 9). The reference to the ploughboy shows how attuned Tyndale was to
     Erasmus who had expressed the hope that the ploughboy would one day read the gospels
     which hitherto been the preserve of the scholar and cleric.

36   See also Jackson (1996), Gordon (1996), The poetics of Tyndale's translation, *Reformation*,
     I, 52–71.

in these assessments, it must be accepted that Luther's example had shown Tyndale the way. 'What Tyndale found in Luther was a way of reaching the popular mind' (Trinterud 1962: 42). The naturalness of Luther's language deserves particular emphasis given the current tendency to idolize Tyndale – Zwink 1999 accuses those who deny the influence of Luther of xenophobic nationalism:

> Über die sprachliche Abhängigkeit Tyndales von Luther könnte man viel sagen. Das ist brisant, weil es die Engländer nicht hören wollen. [...] Nun darf man sich die Abhängigkeiten nicht zu einfach erklären. Nach meiner Einschätzung ist das Problem so vielschichtig, dass es weder mit den Instrumenten des englischen Nationalismus, noch mit deutscher Überheblichkeit und Stolz auf den überragenden Luther, sondern nur durch akribische Textvergleiche [...] zu bewerkstelligen ist.

Meticulous textual comparisons are indeed called for; much of what has been done so far is piecemeal, much more extensive work is required. While the examples cited above clearly demonstrate Tyndale's familiarity with Luther's translation, it is not so much the echoes of particular words and phrases that are important as Luther's example which served Tyndale as a model.

Luther's German was based on living speech, not on written literary style. *Die buchstaben sind todte wörter, die mundliche rede sind lebendige wörter (WA,* 54, 74), he famously said, and he is known to have spoken his translation aloud to test its qualities. Natural German idiom, homely proverbial expressions, alliterative phrases, and above all outstanding rhythmic quality make his Bible language what it is.[37] Compare the woodenness of Matthew 6:26 in the Nuremberg Bible of 1483, the year of Luther's birth: *Seht an die vögel des hymels. wann sy seen noch schneyden nit. noch sameln in den kasten. und ewer hymlischer vater füret sy* with the rhythm and melody of Luther's final version of 1545: *Seht die Vogel vnter dem Himel an / Sie seen nicht / sie erndten nicht / sie samlen nicht in die Schewnen / Vnd ewer himlischer Vater neeret sie doch.* What Luther did for German, Tyndale later did for the English Bible, too: *Beholde the foules of the aier: For they sowe not / neder reepe / nor yet cary into*

---

37   A celebrated 'purple' passage in Luther's translation is I Corinthians 13, whose rhythmic musicality depends to a large extent on the alternation of stressed and unstressed syllables (e.g. *Sie vertreget alles / sie gleubet alles / sie hoffet alles / sie duldet alles*), which has largely been sacrificed in later revisions.

the barnes, and yett youre hevenly father fedeth then. Daniell delights in drawing attention to examples of Tyndale's natural, homely, mellifluous English. For example, he remarks on Luke 2:16 where Tyndale has a succession of a-sounds in *Mary and Joseph and the babe laid in a manger* – yet Luther's *Maria und Joseph, dazu das Kind in der Krippe liegen* is no less effective with its succession of long and short i-sounds and alliteration of *Kind* and *Krippe*. Again, Daniell (1994: 135f.) draws attention to Luke 2:18–19: *And all that heard it, wondered at those things which were told them of the shepherds. But Mary kept all those sayings, and pondered them in her heart.* Daniell praises Tyndale for translating the Greek as *wonder* (rather than *were astonished* or *marvelled*) and for 'echoing' it in *pondered* – but Luther too has *wunderten sich der Rede* and though he does not have the 'echo' *wonder/ponder*, he does have a kind of alliteration in *Maria aber behielt alle diese wort vnd beweget sie in ihrem hertzen.* Then Daniell points to Luke 16:22: *And it fortuned that the beggar died, and was carried by the angels into Abraham's bosom. The rich man also died, and was buried*, declaring that Tyndale's use of native Saxon, not Latin, vocabulary, was 'unusual for high language in 1526 ('beggar', not mendicant, 'died', not deceased, 'carried' not transported)' and praising the 'Greek-like finite verbs, not Latin-like nouns (not "After the death of the rich man, and his burial ..." but "The rich man died and was buried")'. True though this may be, Tyndale's style parallels, emulates, even imitates, exactly Luther: *Es begab sich aber / das der arme starb / und wart getragen von den Engelen in Abrahams schosz / der reyche aber starb auch / vnd wart ynn die helle begraben.*[38] Zwink (1999) likewise stresses such close correspondence. Citing Matthew 26:41, he says of Tyndale's *Watche and praye, that ye fall not into temptacion. The spirite is willynge / but the flesshe is weeke* that it corresponds virtually letter by letter to Luther's *Wachet und betet, auf dass ihr nicht in Anfechtung fallet. Der Geist ist willig, aber das Fleisch ist schwach*, and adds that the phrases *in Anfechtung fallen – fall into temptation* and *willig – willing* are by no means obvious translations of the Greek – but Popp (1999: 152) is doubtless right to say that to assume Tyndale's deliberate emulation of Luther here is 'too close to call'.

38   Luther subsequently deleted the words *ynn die helle.*

The influence of Luther's Bible

The Germanist Hermann Schneider saw Luther's Bible as occupying the same prominent position in German literary history as Dante's *Divine Comedy* in Italian.[39] Luther's language shaped the Protestant sermon of succeeding ages, and many authors cited his Bible translation – in effect, Luther's Bible was *the* German Bible. Sixteenth- and seventeenth-century Biblical drama and devotional literature employed its language, as did J.S. Bach's Passions. Eighteenth-century writers from Hamann and Klopstock to Goethe and the Romantics were influenced by it through the revised version published at Halle by Karl Hildebrand von Canstein early in the century. Ernst Moritz Arndt summed it up well: 'Wenn mir hin und wieder gelungen ist, deutsch zu sprechen, so verdanke ich das mit vielen anderen [...] am meisten der von Kind auf geübten fleißigen Lesung der lutherischen Bibel.'[40] Later Friedrich Nietzsche and Thomas Mann are influenced by it too, while Bertolt Brecht, the Marxist, in 1928 admitted that Luther's Bible was the book that influenced his language most:

> Auf die Frage, welches Buch auf seine Sprache am meisten gewirkt habe, antwortet er 'Sie werden lachen – die Bibel!' Das feierliche Element, das er manchmal der Sprache seiner Figuren beimischt, stammt nämlich aus einer älteren Übersetzung des Alten Testamentes von Martin Luther. Die Inhalte der Religion lehnt der Schriftsteller jedoch ab.[41]

One of the many glowing testimonies to the quality of Luther's Bible translation came from Nietzsche who, as a Professor of Classics, was well able to assess his linguistic achievement. Recognizing Luther's complete mastery of oratory and noting how appropriate it was that the masterpiece of German

---

39 Cited by Burger (1967: 124).
40 Cited by Burger (1967: 131).
41 For Luther's influence on Hans Sachs, Thomas Mann and Bertolt Brecht see the proceedings of the 1983 Martin Luther Quincentennial Conference of the University of Michigan, published in *Michigan Germanic Studies*, 20 (1984); for his influence on Mann also Müller (1983) and Szewczyk (1985); on Goethe Anderegg/Kunz (2005); also Aland (1973).

prose should be the masterpiece of German's greatest preacher, Nietzsche simply declared: 'Luthers Bibel war bisher das beste deutsche Buch.'[42]

As we have seen, however, the influence of Luther's language extended beyond Germany. In his technique and style, even in his phrasing, he clearly left his mark on Tyndale and thus on the English literary language, too.

References

Primary sources

Luther 1522:
  – *Das Newe Testament Deutzsch*, Wittenberg, September 1522. Facsimile: Stuttgart: Deutsche Bibelgesellschaft, 1982.
Luther 1534:
  – Füssel, S. (ed.) (2003), *The Luther Bible of 1534. Complete facsimile edition.* 2 vols and booklet, Cologne: Taschen.
Luther 1545:
  – Roloff, H.-G. (ed.) (1989), *Das Neue Testament in der deutschen Übersetzung von Martin Luther nach dem Bibeldruck von 1545 mit sämtlichen Holzschnitten. Studienausgabe, Bd. 1: Text in der Fassung des Bibeldrucks von 1545. Bd. 2: Entstehungsvarianten, Glossar, Bibliographie, Nachwort.* (Universal-Bibliothek, 3741–2) Stuttgart: Reclam. [With extensive bibliography, II, 299–330].
Luther *WA* = *D. Martin Luthers Werke. Kritische Gesamtausgabe. [Weimarer Ausgabe].* Weimar 1883ff.
Luther WK = *Luther's Works*, ed. Jaroslav Pelikan. St Louis and Philadelphia: Concordia, 1958–67.
Mentelin 1466
  – Kurrelmeyer, W. (1904–15), *Die erste deutsche Bibel*, Tübingen: Litterarischer Verein in Stuttgart.
  – Berndt, E. (ed.) (1987), *Biblia sacra. Deutsche Edition der Bibelausgabe des Hieronymus durch Johann Mentelin 1466 zu Strassburg gedruckt (1. gedruckte deutsche Bibel) nach einer Übersetzung um das Jahr 1350; mit reichhaltigen Summarien und Prologen sowie Anweisungen zur Erarbeitung des Grundtextes*, Berlin: Berndt. [Facsimile of Berlin, Staatsbibliothek. Inc. 2009].

---

42 *Jenseits von Gut und Böse*, §247, in Nietzsche/Schlechta (1973: 715).

Tyndale 1525:
- Arber, E. (ed.) (1871), *The First Printed English New Testament translated by William Tyndale*, London: Selwood.

Tyndale 1526:
- *The New Testament, 1526*, Facsimile: London: David Paradine for the President and Committee of the Baptist College, Bristol, 1976.
- *The New Testament. A Facsimile of the 1526 Edition*. Translated by William Tyndale, with an introduction by David Daniell. Peabody, Massachusetts: Hendrickson, and London: The British Library, 2008. [Colour facsimile of the British Library copy].
- Daniell, D. (1989), *Tyndale's New Testament*, New Haven and London: Yale University Press. [Modernized spelling].

Tyndale 1530:
- Mombert, J.I. (ed.) (1884), *William Tyndale's Five Books of Moses called the Pentateuch*, New York; new edtion (1967) Arundel: Centaur.
- Daniell, D. (1992), *Tyndale's Old Testament being the Pentateuch of 1530, Joshua to 2 Chronicles of 1537 and Jonah*, New Haven and London: Yale University Press. [Modernized spelling].

Wyclif
- Forshall, J. and Madden, F. (eds) (1850), *The Holy Bible ... made from the Latin Vulgate by John Wycliffe and his Followers*, Oxford: Oxford University Press; reprinted New York 1982.

Bibliography

Aland, K. (1973), *Martin Luther in der modernen Literatur*, Witten and Berlin: Eckart.

Anderegg, J. and Kunz, E.A. (eds) (2005), *Goethe und die Bibel*, Stuttgart: Deutsche Bibelgesellschaft. (Arbeiten zur Geschichte und Wirkung der Bibel, 6).

Arblaster, P., Juhasz, G. and Latré, G. (eds) (2002), *Tyndale's Testament*, Antwerp: Brepols [exhibition catalogue].

Arndt, E. (ed.) (1968), *Martin Luther, Sendbrief vom Dolmetschen und Summarien über die Psalmen und Ursachen des Dolmetschens*, Halle: VEB Niemeyer.

Bluhm, H. (1965), *Martin Luther, Creative Translator*, St Louis and London: Concordia.

Bluhm, H. (1984a), *Luther, Translator of Paul: Studies in Romans and Galatians*, New York: Peter Lang.

Bluhm, H. (1984b), 'Martin Luther and the English Bible: Tyndale and Coverdale', *Michigan Germanic Studies* 10, 110–25.

Bone, G.D. (1938), 'Tindale and the English language', in: *The Work of William Tindale*, edited by S.L. Greenslade, London and Glasgow: Blackie, 50–68.

Bragg, M. (2003), *The Adventure of English: The Biography of a Language*, London: Hodder & Stoughton.

Brecht, M. and Zwink, E. (eds) (1999), *Eine glossierte Vulgata aus dem Umkreis Martin Luthers. Untersuchungen zu dem 1519 in Lyon gedruckten Exemplar in der Bibelsammlung der Württembergischen Landesbibliothek Stuttgart*, Bern etc.: Peter Lang (Vestigia Bibliae, 21).

Brewer, J.S. (ed.) (1872), *Letters and Papers, Foreign and Domestic, of the Reign of Henry VIII*, London: Longman.

Brügger, S. (1983), *Die deutschen Bibelübersetzungen des 20. Jahrhunderts im sprachwissenschaftlichen Vergleich*, Bern etc.: Peter Lang (Europäische Hochschulschriften, I, 707).

Burger, H.O. (1967), 'Luther als Ereignis der Literaturgeschichte', in: *Martin Luther. 450 Jahre Reformation*, Bad Godesberg: Inter Nationes.

Cochlaeus, J. (1549), *Commentaria [...] de actis et scriptis Martini Lutheri Saxonis [...]*, Mainz: F. Behem.

Cochlaeus, J. (1582), *Historia Martini Lutheri, das ist Kurtze Beschreibung [...]*, Ingolstadt: Sartorius. (translated by Johann Christof Hueber)

Daniell, D. (1994), *William Tyndale: A Biography*, New Haven and London: Yale University Press.

Daniell, D. (1998), 'William Tyndale and the making of the English churches', *The Tyndale Society Journal* 9, 19–37.

Daniell, D. (2003), *The Bible in English: Its History and Influence*, New Haven and London: Yale University Press.

Daniell, D. (2005), 'No Tyndale, no Shakespeare', *The Tyndale Society Journal* 29, 8–22.

Davies, M. (1996), 'Juan de Carvajal and Early Printing', *The Library*, 6th ser., 18: 193–215.

Eichenberger, W. and Wendland, H. (1977), *Deutsche Bibeln vor Luther*, Hamburg: Wittig.

Flood, J.L. (1998), 'The Book in Reformation Germany', in: *The Reformation and the Book*, edited by Jean-François Gilmont, Aldershot: Ashgate, 21–103. (English edition and translation by Karin Maag). Originally published as: Flood, J.L. (1990), 'Le Livre dans le monde germanique à l'époque de la Réforme', in: *La Réforme et le livre. L'Europe de l'imprimé (1517 – v. 1570)*, edited by Jean-François Gilmont, Paris: Les éditions du cerf, 29–104.

Flood, J.L. (1999), 'Les premières Bibles allemandes dans le contexte de la typographie européenne des xve et xvie siècles', in: *La Bible imprimée dans l'Europe moderne*, edited by B.E. Schwarzbach, Paris: Bibliothèque nationale de France, 144–65.

Flood, J.L. (2001a), 'Ein englischer Reformator als Nothelfer in Lübeck?', in: *Vulpis Adolatio. Festschrift für Hubertus Menke zum 60. Geburtstag*, edited by R. Peters et al., Heidelberg: Winter, 239–48.

Flood, J.L. (2001b), 'Martin Luther's Bible Translation in its German and European Context', in: *The Bible in the Renaissance*, edited by R. Griffiths, Aldershot: Ashgate, 45–70.

Flood, J.L. (2005), 'Hans Folz zwischen Handschriftenkultur und Buchdruckerkunst', in: *Texttyp und Textproduktion in der deutschen Literatur des Mittelalters*, edited by E. Anderson et al., Berlin and New York: de Gruyter, 1–27. (Trends in Medieval Philology, 7).

Fricke, K.D. and Meur, S. (2001), *Die Geschichte der Lutherbibelrevision von 1850 bis 1984*, Stuttgart: Deutsche Bibelgesellschaft. (Arbeiten zur Geschichte und Wirkung der Bibel, 1).

Gerberich, A.H. (1933), *Luther and the English Bible*, Lancester PA: Intelligencer Printing Corporation.

Hammond, G. (1980), 'William Tyndale's Pentateuch: Its relation to Luther's German Bible and the Hebrew original', *Renaissance Quarterly* 33, 351–85.

Herbert, A.S. (1968), *Historical Catalogue of Printed Editions of the English Bible 1525–1961*, London: The British and Foreign Bible Society; New York: The American Bible Society.

Hooker, M.D. (1997), 'Tyndale's "heretical" translation', *Reformation* 2, 127–42.

Jackson, G. (1996), 'The poetics of Tyndale's translation', *Reformation* 1, 52–71.

Karpp, H. (1992), *Schrift, Geist und Wort Gottes. Geltung und Wirkung der Bibel in der Geschichte der Kirche. Von der Alten Kirche bis zum Ausgang der Reformationszeit*, Darmstadt: Wissenschaftliche Buchgesellschaft.

Kegel, J. (2006), *"Wollt ihr den totalen Krieg?' Eine semiotische und linguistische Gesamtanalyse der Rede Goebbels' im Berliner Sportpalast am 18. Februar 1943*, Tübingen: Niemeyer. (Reihe Germanistische Linguistik, 270).

Mozley, J.F. (1937), *Life of William Tyndale*, New York: Macmillan; reprinted 1971 Westport: Greenwood.

Müller, N. (1983), 'Thomas Mann und Luther. Geschichtswirkung und Wirkungsgeschichte', *Wissenschaftliche Zeitschrift der Martin-Luther-Universität Halle-Wittenberg* 32 (5), 45–58.

Neddermeyer, U. (1998), *Von der Handschrift zum gedruckten Buch. Schriftlichkeit und Leseinteresse im Mittelalter und in der frühen Neuzeit. Quantitative und qualitative Aspekte*, Wiesbaden: Harrassowitz. (Buchwissenschaftliche Beiträge aus dem Deutschen Bucharchiv München, 61)

Nielson, J. and Skousen, R. (1998), 'How much of the King James Bible is William Tyndale's? An estimation based on sampling', *Reformation* 3, 49–74.

Nietzsche, F. edited by Schlechta, K. (1973), *Friedrich Nietzsche, Werke in drei Bänden*, 7th ed., Munich: Hanser.

Norton, D. (2000), *A History of the English Bible as Literature*, Cambridge: Cambridge University Press.

Norton, D. (2004), *A Textual History of the King James Bible*, New York: Cambridge University Press.

Popp, M. (1999), 'The Green Horse, or Was Tyndale's Bible translation an independent humanistic achievement?', in: *Anglistentag 1998 Erfurt. Proceedings*, edited by Fritz-Wilhelm Neumann and Sabine Schülting, Trier: Wissenschaftlicher Verlag, 137–57. (Proceedings of the Conference of the German Association of University Teachers of English, 20).

Reinhart, M. (ed.) (2007), *Camden House History of German Literature*, vol. 4: *Early Modern German Literature*, Columbia: Camden House.

Rost, H. (1939), *Die Bibel im Mittelalter. Beiträge zur Geschichte und Bibliographie der Bibel*, Augsburg: Seitz.

Runcie, R. (1996), 'Commemorative Sermon: William Tyndall, 6 October 1994, St Paul's Cathedral', *Reformation* 1, 7–10.

Schwarz, W. (1955), *Principles and Problems of Biblical translation*, Cambridge: Cambridge University Press.

Schwarz, W. edited by Reinitzer, H. (1986), *Schriften zur Bibelübersetzung und mittelalterlichen Übersetzungstheorie*, Hamburg: Wittig. (Vestigia Bibliae, 7).

Seyferth, S. (2003), *Sprachliche Varianzen in Martin Luthers Bibelübertragungen von 1522–1545. Eine lexikalisch-syntaktische untersuchung des Römerbriefes*, Stuttgart: Deutsche Bibelgesellschaft. (Arbeiten zur Geschichte und Wirkung der Bibel, 6).

Spitz, L.W. (1996), *Luther and German Humanism*, Aldershot: Variorum.

Szewczyk, G. (1985), 'Thomas Manns Lutherbild', *Germanica Wratislaviensia* 64, no. 864, 144–57.

Trinterud, L.J. (1962), 'A reappraisal of William Tyndale's debt to Martin Luther', *Church History* 31, 24–45.

Volz, H. (1960), *Bibel und Bibeldruck in Deutschland im 15. und 16. Jahrhundert*, Mainz: Gutenberg-Gesellschaft.

Volz, H. (1978), *Martin Luthers deutsche Bibel*, Hamburg: Wittig.

Widmann, H. (1965), *Der deutsche Buchhandel in Urkunden und Quellen*, Hamburg: Hauswedell.

Witzmann, M. (1996), 'On translating the Old Testament: The achievement of William Tyndale', *Reformation* 1, 165–80.

Yates, J.P. (2002), 'The time and place of Tyndale's Hebrew learning. A reconsideration.' *Reformation* 7, 23–48.

Zwink, E. (1998), 'Confusion about Tyndale. The Stuttgart copy of the 1526 New Testament in English', *Reformation* 3, 29–48.

Zwink, E. (1999), 'Verwirrspiel um eine Bibel. Die Entdeckung des einzigen vollständigen Exemplars des Erstdrucks von William Tyndales New Testament (1526) in der Württembergischen Landesbibliothek Stuttgart', http://www.wlb-stuttgart.de/referate/theologie/tyndvor1.html (accessed 23.11.2006).

NICOLA MCLELLAND

Understanding German Grammar Takes Centuries ...

The earliest evidence of materials for learners of German are vocabulary lists for Romance learners, dating from the ninth century. Yet the earliest known German grammars date from just 500 years or so ago, a very short time compared to the many centuries during which people have been speaking and learning (or trying to learn) German. We shall see in this paper that even once people started examining German grammar, understanding it took a good two or three centuries (and some bits are still debatable today!). The paper begins with the question of why studying German grammar suddenly began to seem like a good idea in the sixteenth century. We then look at how scholars gradually got to grips with describing German grammar, and at some of the garden paths they wandered up before arriving at today's accepted explanations. We will consider examples from the following areas: the parts of speech and numbers of cases; noun group endings; verb conjugation and strong verbs; morphology and word order.

Why study German grammar? The awakening of interest in the sixteenth century

In the European Middle Ages, Latin was the language of power and authority. It was the language of the church, of law, of record-keeping. German had little status – a ninth-century translator of the Gospels into Old High German, Otfrid von Weißenburg, was convinced that German was 'not accustomed to be held by the reins of grammar' (cited e.g. in Percival 1975: 248, n. 28). A rich flowering of medieval literature in German was not accompanied by an equal interest in studying the structures and rules of the language itself. Some authors did comment on questions of good and bad style – perhaps most

famously, Gottfried von Straßburg passed judgement on his contemporaries
and predecessors in his *Tristan*, l. 4619–4818 – but the idea that German (or
the other vernaculars) obeyed fixed rules, as everyone agreed was the case for
Latin and Greek, had not occurred to them.

A number of inter-related factors changed this. First, the invention of
moveable type printing (from about 1450) meant that written texts, previously
laboriously copied by hand, were more readily available and could circulate
more widely. People rapidly became aware of the different conventions followed by the different printing centres of, for instance, Nuremberg, Augsburg,
Wittenberg and Cologne. Commentators were initially most struck by variation in spelling, and called for greater uniformity – a first step in the process
of language standardization.

Second, the growth of towns and the associated rise in commercial trading in the later Middle Ages increased the need for record-keeping outside the
church and court chanceries. More ordinary townspeople needed to read and
write in their own language in order to keep the records of their businesses,
their societies and their town councils. A further important motivation for
learning to read and write German was furnished by the Reformation, sparked
off in 1517 by Martin Luther's attacks on abuses within the Catholic Church,
and the vigorous polemical debates between Reformers and their opponents
which followed. Debates were carried out in cheap, rapidly prepared pamphlets
that were aimed at ordinary people, inviting readers to decide for themselves
the rights and wrongs of the theological controversies. One source of con-
troversy was Luther's translation of the Bible itself, in particular his German
New Testament, which appeared in 1522; the Old Testament followed in
1534. Luther's new translation, though not the first, reflected the importance
that he and his followers laid on believers having access to the holy scriptures
themselves, rather than relying on the priest as intermediary, but certain passages in his translation were hotly disputed as inaccurate (see Flood's article
in this volume, p. 35). Valentin Ickelsamer (1527) explicitly referred to the
issues raised by Lutheranism: 'Reading was never so useful as it is now, when
everyone learns so that he might read God's word and the interpretation of
it by several God-learned men for himself, and so better make a judgement
about it' (*Lesen können hat inn langer zeit nie so wol seinen nütz gefunden /
als itzo / dweyls seer ein jeder darumb lernet / das er Gottes wort und etlicher*

Gotgelerter menner außlegung / darüber selbs lesen / und desto bass darinn
urteylen möge (cited in Müller (1969 [1882]: 53).

This combination of factors meant that by the sixteenth century, many
more people than ever before were starting to take an interest in the written form of their language and in how to teach it. Meanwhile, amongst
the educated elite, humanists were also thinking about education, react-
ing against what they viewed as the backward educational practices of the
Middle Ages, where young boys learnt Latin by reciting chunks of text by
rote. Now, rather than seeking to apply grammatical concepts straight to the
mysteries of Latin – which amounted to 'explaining' an unknown with the
help of another unknown – new approaches to teaching Latin began apply-
ing elementary notions of grammar to pupils' native German too (Puff 1995a,
1995b). For instance, children learnt to distinguish adjectives from nouns by
testing whether one could preface them to the words *Mann, Weib* or *Ding*:
ein weißer Mann, ein weißes Weib, ein weißes Ding are possible, hence *weiß* is
an adjective (Puff 1995b: 228–43).

Another key feature of humanism was an emerging patriotic pride in
one's own culture and language. Across Europe, champions of the various
vernaculars began to argue that their mother tongue was of no less intrinsic
value than Latin and Greek: though long neglected by their speakers, the
vernaculars merely needed to be cultivated as Latin and Greek had been for
centuries, in order to reach a similar state of perfection. One eloquent way
of asserting the worth of a vernacular, therefore, was to show that it obeyed
the same grammatical rules as did Latin. The first users of these grammars
were not Germans themselves, but foreigners – whether travellers or travelling tradesmen – who needed to learn German. Hitherto they had had
to content themselves with vocabularies, phrase-books, and collections of
dialogues in which regularities of grammar were at best implicit in group-
ings of words of similar types in vocabulary lists (McLelland 2003: 293–4;
2004). Now the European travelling elite versed in Latin grammar could
study German through a grammatical framework already familiar to them.
The first three such grammars of German appeared all within a few years of
each in the 1570s, a few decades after the first such grammars in French (e.g.
Garnerius 1558), whose model German scholars sought to emulate: Albertus
(1573), Ölinger (1574), and Clajus (1578). Clajus's little grammar – which had
the advantage of being able to take the best bits from his two predecessors

– was not only useful for foreigners, but became the most popular text used within Germany too, right into the seventeenth century, when it was superseded only by Schottelius (1641, 1651, 1663, 1676), who was in turn surpassed by Gottsched (1748) and Adelung (1781). These 1570s grammars were all in Latin, and were aimed at an international elite readership. It was not until the early decades of the seventeenth century that the first elementary German grammars for German schoolchildren appeared *in* German (e.g. Ratke's work, published anonymously = Anon. 1619; Kromayer 1618; Olearius 1630). But by the mid-seventeenth century, determining and specifying in detail the rules of the written language was an important goal for Germans: the process of 'language standardization' was well underway, as grammarians debated how to select and then codify the norms of the language. Let us now examine some of the problems that German grammar presented to those who first had the task of describing it.

How many parts of speech? How many cases?

To all those working to raise the prestige of their vernacular language, 'grammar' meant in practice 'Latin and Greek grammar'. According to long-established tradition, Latin and Greek had eight different parts of speech and five (Greek) or six (Latin) cases. So, therefore, must German, or so the pioneer grammarians thought. For the parts of speech, the first three grammars of German from the 1570s followed the Greek model, listing pronoun, verb, adverb, participle, conjunction, preposition and article, but Ritter (1616) omitted the participle and instead listed the interjection as a separate item.[1] Not until Schottelius (1651) was the ideal of eight parts of speech dispensed with for German: Schottelius listed both the interjection and article as separate parts of speech, making nine in total. Three and a half centuries later, the same nine are now listed by Eisenberg (1999: 14) in his authoritative grammar of German. It is worth noting that there is a difference, however. Eisenberg

---

1   In Greek grammar, the interjection was subsumed under the adverb.

(1999: 21–3) also gives considerable importance to 'syntactical categories', i.e. sentence constituents that can contain more than one word or part of speech, such as the nominal phrase, prepositional phrase, adjectival phrase, or adverbial phrase. This is a point we shall return to when we are considering word order.

Besides the number of parts of speech, the boundaries between them were also (and still remain) problematic. The adverb is a good example. Even in standard reference grammars today, there is disagreement about whether or not the words underlined in the following sentences are adverbs:

Sie arbeitet <u>schön</u>

Eisenberg (1999: 207), a linguist's grammar of German, would classify *schön* as an adjective, not an adverb.

Das Kind ist der Mutter <u>ähnlich</u>. Wir sind <u>stolz</u> auf uns.

Dreyer and Schmitt (1999), a widely used grammar for foreign learners of German, would say that each underlined word is an adverb (as would Funk (1763); cf. Jellinek 1914: 101).

The adverb arguably overlaps with the adjective (*sie singt <u>schön</u>*), with particles (*komm <u>schon</u>!*), with conjunctions (*<u>deshalb</u> kommt er nicht*), and with the participle (*dies ist <u>dringend</u> erforderlich*) (Eisenberg 1999: 204–9).

Earlier grammarians had still other difficulties. They struggled to distinguish the adverb from prepositions, particles and prefixes (for instance, in *er kletterte hinauf*, Schottelius viewed *hinauf* as an adverb), and often viewed interjections as adverbs. Even some nouns looked to earlier grammarians like adverbs, or perhaps vice versa. In *er kam abends*, for example, *abends* might be seen as the genitive of the noun *Abend*. In other words, the boundaries of the adverb to virtually every other part of speech were as much in doubt in the sixteenth and seventeenth centuries as today (McLelland 2008).

The apparently basic question of the boundaries between the parts of speech still remains topical today, and answers vary depending on the linguistic theory followed. But at least the question of case has now been solved for German, with the four cases of nominative, accusative, dative and genitive (see Jellinek 1914: 190–2). For early grammarians, case too was a problem. In addition to the nominative, accusative, genitive and dative, Latin had two further cases: the vocative (a case used for addressing someone), and an ablative (used after some prepositions and in a number of other constructions). Shouldn't

German have these six cases like Latin, or at least five cases like Greek? Of the first three grammarians of German, Ölinger (1574) omitted the ablative but kept the vocative (as in Greek), while Albertus (1573) and Clajus (1578) found all six cases in German. The vocative could be recognized by the addition of *o____!* (e.g. *O Vater!*) while the ablative looked identical to the dative but was recognizable because it was preceded by *von*. In the seventeenth century, both Olearius (1630) and Schottelius (1663) persisted in their belief in the ablative in German. After all, the *dative* meant the 'giving' case; patently *von* ('from') could not be followed by the giving case, and must govern the 'taking-away' case (the literal meaning of *ablative*) (Schottelius 1663: 229). It was Aichinger (1753: 128–9) in the eighteenth century who first made the important decision that the fact that the *forms* were the same (i.e. the same ending after *von* as after prepositions like *mit*) was sufficient evidence that we are dealing with the *same* case. For Aichinger these visible signs – and not the semantics of the relationships between entities – were definitive (though not all later grammarians agreed). Adelung (1782) did agree with Aichinger, but allowed for a vocative case in a few limited instances only. By the mid-nineteenth century, however, grammarians assumed four cases for German.

Adjective endings

A German grammar today contains tables of declensions, such as the adjective declensions with strong and weak endings found in Durrell (2002: 126–31). This 'tabular' way of conceptualizing endings is now so natural to us that Eisenberg (1994: 56) even describes the paradigm (i.e. the set of possible forms) for the article as having '16 positions': each 'position' is imagined as a box in a table where the four cases are the rows, while the three genders and the plural are the columns. Yet it was not always so: students were learning Latin case endings by rote for centuries before the notion of the table came into existence. Pupils typically learnt to recite an elementary grammar such as Donatus's *Ars Minor* ('small art [of grammar]') from beginning to end, and learnt to list off words written in running text, if they saw the words written at all, rather than having them dictated to them by the teacher. Tabular layouts of sorts (often using curly brackets rather than a grid to structure the space on the page) were well-established by the sixteenth century (see Puff 1996), but even assuming one had decided how many rows and columns there should be (i.e. how many cases and genders), the question of which forms to put in them was far from clear. Adjective declension was particularly difficult to grasp. For one thing, Latin had nothing like the German strong and weak endings (as we call them today). For another thing, there were generally two or three competing endings in Early New High German. The variants were not obviously regionally distributed; rather, such 'polyflection' is found throughout Early New High German (Ebert, Reichmann, Solms and Wegera 1993: 192), for the language was far from fully standardized. Vestiges of this variation survive today after certain quantifiers – do we say *manche andere Ansichten* or *manche anderen Ansichten*, for instance? We might think that German adjective inflection today is difficult, but Table 1 shows an even more complex picture. To keep things simple, Table 1 summarizes the range of adjective inflections just in the nominative singular in Early New High German, as presented by Ebert, Reichmann, Solms and Wegera (1993: 190ff.):

	M	F	n
attributive: 'determinierend' (strong)	gelert(e)r / gelert / gelert(e) > gelert(e)r	gelert(e) / gelert / gelertiu > gelert (e)	gelert(e)s / gelert
'indeterminierend' (weak)	**gelert(e)**	**gelert(e)**	**gelert(e)**
predicate (e.g. *Er ist gelert*)	generally no ending, but an ending was still possible up to the end of the sixteenth century		

Table 1: Adjective endings in the nominative case in Early New High German
(following Ebert, Reichmann, Solms and Wegera (1993: 190ff.)
Alternatives are separated by '/'; '>' precedes the form which gradually
became dominant.

For an adjective of a particular case and gender in attributive use, there
were routinely three possible endings, and there was always the additional
possibility that it might remain uninflected (Ebert, Reichmann, Solms and
Wegera 1993: 199). In predicate use (e.g. *er ist alt*), there was generally no
ending – but this was not always the case either. It is not surprising that the
first grammarians of German did not agree fully in their accounts of this
complex system, nor even in how they tried to capture it: Albertus (1573)
sees two types of endings, Ölinger (1574) three sets. And both Albertus and
Ölinger reduce the complexity for their learners by listing just a subset of
possible forms.

Table 2 shows Albertus's two-way straightforward distinction between
adjectives that do decline and those that do not. Note that his model, according to which adjectives used attributively after *der/die/das* do not decline,
produces a perfectly legitimate subset of the possible forms.

	M	f	n
1) the adjective used i) after the definite article (e.g. *der gelert man*) or ii) in 'absolute' (predicate) use as in *Er ist gelert*, 'he is learned'	gelert gelert i.e. does not decline.		gelert
2) the adjective i) before a substantive (with no definite article, however), or ii) after *ein*, or iii) both	Gelert+er	gelert+e	gelert+es

Table 2: Summary of Albertus's account of adjective inflection in the
nominative singular.

In contrast, Ölinger (Table 3) makes a three-way distinction, between
absolute use, with no inflection, and the *articulatus* adjective and *inarticulatus*
adjective, both of which do inflect. Ölinger's model produces a different, but
equally acceptable subset of the possible forms. (Compare the bold sections
of Tables 2 and 3 to see the differences).

	M	f	n
absolute (i.e. predicate) use, as in *Er ist gelert*, 'he is learned'	gelert _i.e. does not decline_	gelert	gelert
articulatus (where the article *der, die, das* precedes or is understood)	gelert+e	gelert+e	gelert+e
inarticulatus (after *ein, kein, mein, tein, unser, ewer* or 'some other similar addition' (*aliquod simile additamentum*)	*articulatus* + r, i.e. gelert+e+r	*articulatus* + s i.e. gelert+e+s	*articulatus* + Ø i.e. gelert+e

Table 3: Summary of Ölinger's account of adjective inflection in the nominative singular.

This brief example illustrates how the writers of the earliest German grammars had to *create* a system, and that it involved choosing to privilege certain forms over others, so that the resultant grammar was an account of only a subset of possible forms. Adjective inflection in Early New High German sums up the task of language standardization: not just codifying, but also selecting the forms to be codified.

Verb conjugation

When earlier generations of grammarians examined German verbs, many of their difficulties were caused by the fact that there was still quite a lot of variation in the system. For instance, Clajus (1578) was aware of a present indicative form *keuffe* rather than *kaufe*; some verbs still had two different vowels in the singular and plural preterite (e.g. *finden, fand, funden, gefunden*). There was also much variation between the north and south regarding the presence (in the north) or absence (in the south) of unstressed *-e* endings.[2] Here, we discuss just one example of how Germans struggled to recognize the patterns in their own verbal system, and how they puzzled over how best to group the forms once they had determined them. The analysis here relies on Jellinek (1914: 342–56) except in the discussion of Albertus (1573) and Durrell (2002). It may be helpful to begin by summarizing Durrell's account.

Durrell (2002: 234–5) provides two categories of verbs, weak and strong. Weak verbs form their perfect participle in *-t* and their preterite in *-te* (*kaufen, kaufte, gekauft*); strong verbs form their perfect participle in *-en* and undergo vowel changes in both this participle and in the preterite (*finden, fand, gefunden*) and may have a vowel change in the present too (*laufen, läuft, lief, gelaufen*). There are, however, 'irregular weak verbs'.[3] Examples are *nennen, nannte, genannt* and *bringen, brachte, gebracht*. There are also some irregular strong verbs, with consonant changes as well as vowel changes, as in *leiden, litt, gelitten*. The vowel change is known as *Ablaut*. Durrell draws attention to ten different patterns of vowel changes, but does not list the strong verbs according to these groups, just alphabetically (Durrell 2002: 254–60).

Coming from Latin, German grammarians were expecting to find four classes of verbs (known as 'conjugations'), distinguished by different vowels in the infinitive and in the endings added to the verb stem. Examples of the four conjugations in Latin are *amare, sedēre, currere, audire* 'to love, to sit, to run, to hear'. So spare a thought for Albertus (1573). Because German verbs all follow a similar pattern in the infinitive and in the endings of the present tense (*-(e)n, -e, -(e)st, -(e)t, -(e)n, -(e)t, -(e)n*), Albertus declared that German had just one conjugation. Poor Albertus evidently wrestled with, and was ultimately defeated by, the complexities of the German verb system. He could not even fathom the mystery of when the past participle ends in *-en*, and when in *-t*

---

2   To complicate things further, Habermann (1997: 440) notes for the seventeenth century at least that the so-called paragogic (i.e. additional) *e* is 'recht häufig' in the first and third person singular preterite indicative (e.g. *ich ginge* where we would expect *ich ging*) and later refers to the young Goethe's use of these 'hyperkorrekte[n] Präteritumsformen bei den starken Verben der süddeutschen Schriftsprache' (1997: 462).

3   Since Durrell has just defined weak verbs a couple of paragraphs earlier by saying 'Most German verbs are weak; they are the regular verbs' (2002: 234), this amounts to saying 'they are the irregular regular verbs'. But we know what he means: weak verbs all follow the same pattern. Strong verbs follow a different pattern, with some sub-divisions.

(strong and weak verbs respectively), and only hoped that, *volente Deo* 'God willing', he might be able to explain it later. For the time being, however, it could be learnt and understood by practice alone (*solo vsu*). He noticed what amounts to the system of *Ablaut* (vowel-change in strong verbs through the tenses, e.g. *singen, sang, gesungen*), but concluded with touching honesty that his account only 'seems to explain this whole business moderately well' (*hoc totum negotium mediocriter explicare videtur*). He wrote that he had 'not yet sufficiently ascertained how [the vowel mutations] can be grasped by rules' (*non satis iam perspectum habeam, quomodo regulis comprehendi possint*) (all citations from Albertus 1895 [1573]: 104).

The most practical way to divide German verbs into useful classes (to us today, at least) is to use the formation of the past participle and the preterite as criteria. Ritter (1616) was the first to notice two groups of verbs, of which the second (which he called 'regular') had -*te* and -*t* in the preterite and past participle. Ritter excluded what are known for historical reasons as preterite-presents (the more irregular of the modal verbs, plus *wissen*) altogether, treating them separately as 'anomalies'. Irregular verbs were listed alphabetically. Ritter (1616) is thus already quite close to current practice as exemplified by Durrell (2002: 234–5 and 254–60), but it remained to get to grips with the classes of the 'irregular' (strong) verbs. Schottelius (1663) – the most ambitious grammar for Germans of the seventeenth century – followed Ritter, but emphasized the vowel changes in the stem as the defining characteristic of the strong verbs, as had Becherer (1596), who called his two conjugations mutating or non-mutating. This led grammarians down a new path, as they attempted to establish order in the sea of changing vowel stems that had so addled Albertus. Steinbach (1724) identified five classes of strong verbs, according to which of the five vowels was found in the past participle: *a* (incl. *au*), *e*, *i*, *o*, or *u*. Gottsched (1748) also opted for five conjugations, but on the opposite criterion, that of the vowel in the preterite. Both these systems looked simple and attempted to make use of Schottelius's insight about changes to the root vowel, but were obviously not that helpful to the learner. Knowing with Gottsched that *blasen* and *bleiben* belonged to the same class (*blies, blieb*) did not tell one anything about how to form the past participle (*geblasen*, but *geblieben*!). Aichinger (1753) finally combined the two criteria of past participle and preterite vowels, to come up with nine classes, which are similar to those in Durrell (2002: 234), though not identical.

As a curiosity, we might note that in his *Umständliches Lehrgebäude* of 1782, Adelung divided his irregular (our 'strong') verbs into three classes, as in Table 4. In each class, there are three different vowel change patterns. Proper names containing the relevant vowels in the right order served as memory aids. (Note that for Adelung, the order is infinitive, past participle, then preterite. My examples in Table 4 follow that order, rather than the more usual order today of preterite before perfect participle.) Such memory aids remind us that the authors of German grammatical texts were usually not solely concerned about understanding the structure of German grammar, but also about packaging it to help learners master it. But it took three centuries to get from Albertus's first doomed attempt to find any order at all in the German system of *Ablaut* to Adelung's clear presentation with mnemonic aids for learners.

1. Infinitive and past participle have same vowel; preterite has different vowel
Paradies [*fallen, gefallen, fiel*] Faramund [*fahren, gefahren, fuhr*] Engelhard [*sehen, gesehen, sah*]
2. preterite and past participle have same vowel
Heinrici, [*kneiffen, gekniffen, kniff*] Diodor [*frieren, gefroren, fror*] Theopomp [*scheren, geschoren, schor*]
3. all have different vowels:
Theona [*helfen, geholfen, half*] Sirona [*spinnen, gesponnen, spann*] Virgulta [*singen, gesungen, sang*]

Table 4: Adelung's (1782) sub-classes of 'irregular' verbs
(examples in [ ] are NM's)

Word-formation, a German specialty

Compared to Latin and Greek, German has a very rich facility for word-formation, both by derivation and by compounding: the impressive *Donau-dampfschifffahrtsgesellschaftskapitänsmütze* is a compound beloved of teachers of German as a foreign language. The possibility of forming such long compounds in German prompted the American writer Mark Twain (1880) to comment that '[s]ome German words are so long that they have a perspective' – they were not words, but 'alphabetical processions.' As Mark Twain found to his frustration, 'many such words will not be listed in a dictionary; [...] The various words used in building them are in the dictionary, but in a very scattered condition; so you can hunt the materials out, one by one, and get at the meaning at last, but it is a tedious and harassing business.'

Twain's perplexity is that of an outsider looking in at the language – but it was only in the seventeenth century that Germans themselves learnt to understand and describe the details of how the 'building blocks' could be assembled to make new words. The study of word-formation is now an established branch of German linguistics, but it owes its beginnings to Schottelius (1641, 1651, 1663). Derived words (e.g. adding suffixes to *Freund* yields *Freund+lich+keit*) and compounded words (e.g. *Haus + Tür > Haustür*) had generally been noted under two of the traditional headings used to describe the noun, adjective, verb and some other parts of speech: the *figura*, i.e. whether words were simplex – *Haus, Tür* – or compound (*Haustür*), and *species* (i.e. whether a word was primitive, e.g. *blind*, or derived by suffixation, e.g. *Blindheit*). There was no place in this framework for talking about the *mechanisms* by which new compounds were formed, new derivates derived. Schottelius (1641) was the first to offer an explanation of German derivation and compounding, and this aspect of German finally achieved its full recognition in the nineteenth century, when Jacob Grimm treated word-formation as a separate aspect of grammar, between inflection and syntax (Barbarić 1981: 1176–80).

For the first time, Schottelius distinguished clearly between rootwords (very like our 'base morphemes' today), derivational endings (which he called *Hauptendungen*) and inflectional endings (*zufällige Endungen*). He then described in principles, and showed by examples, how they could be combined with one another:

Ungehorsamkeit / alhie ist die Wurtzel oder das Stammwort **/ hör; ge** / ist ein Vor-
wörtlein / daraus wird **gehör: sam** / aber die Hauptendung verändert nicht den wes-
entlichen Verstand des Wortes **gehör** / sondern gibt jhm eine zufällige Eigenschaft
gehorsam / welcher gerne Gehör gibt / das ist / gehorsamet: **keit** / die andere Hauptendung in **Gehorsamkeit** / enderet gleichfals durch jhren Hinterstand die wesentliche
Deutung nicht / sondern veruhrsachet den Verstand eines anderen Zufalles / nemlich
der **Gehorsamkeit: un** / aber ist ein verneinendes Vorwort / und also wird aus diesen
fünf Wörteren* / **Un ge=hor=sam=keit.**

Ungehorsamkeit [*Disobedience*] Here the root or trunk-word is *hör* 'hear'; *ge* is a little
pre-word. Out of that *gehör* is made. Now, the derivative ending *sam* does not change the
essential meaning of the word *gehör*, but gives it the contingent characteristic *gehorsam*,
'who gladly hearkens', that is 'obeys' ['*gehorsamet*']. The second derivative ending *keit*,
placed at the end, also does not change the essential sense, but causes the meaning to
have another contingency, namely *Gehorsamkeit*. Now, *un* is a negating pre-word, and
so out of these five words* we get *Un-ge-hor-sam-keit*.

*Note that in this account Schottelius does not distinguish clearly between words and
word-elements that cannot stand alone.

The sections on *figura* and *species* in German grammars before Schottelius
had ranged from collections of more or less interesting and/or useful curiosi-
ties (as in Albertus 1895 [1573]: 74), who emphasized the 'almost inexhaustible
abundance' of compounds and derivations), to little more than bare repetition of traditional definitions (as in Kromayer 1618). Schottelius's innovation,
which drew on the ideas of a Dutchman, Simon Stevin (1548–1620), was to
make 'rootwords' and their combination in derivation and compounding the
very essence of the language.

Stevin had already made the large number of monosyllabic rootwords he
found in Dutch a measure of the richness of the language, so setting his vernacular clearly ahead of its nearest rival, Greek (Stevin in Dijksterhuis 1955: 83).
Stevin had also made a first stab at analysing internal word-structure: he recognized in a compound like *putwater* ('well-water') a headword (*Grondt*),
water, and its attribute (*Ancleuing*), *put* ('well'). The two terms are rendered
by Schottelius as *Grund(wort)* and *Beyfügige* (e.g. Schottelius 1663: 75).

Schottelius added to Stevin's thinking (cf. Barbarić 1981: 1176–423).
First, he recognized and carefully defined three distinct types of 'word' as
the elements of language: rootwords, inflectional endings and derivational

endings. Two fundamentally different processes were now identified as distinct for the first time. One process generates a finite set of word-forms of individual words or lexemes (inflection, e.g. *Kind, Kind-es, Kind-er, Kinder-n*); the other is infinite, generating new lexemes (derivation by suffixation, and compounding).

Second, Schottelius stated rules governing the combination of these basic elements, going well beyond the basics of head-word and attribute outlined by Stevin. For instance, he listed the different combinations of rootwords that were possible in compounds, such as Noun + Noun (*Haustür*), Noun + Adjective (*nagelneu*), etc.

Matthias Kramer, a German language teacher who wrote many dictionaries and manuals for learners of German, adopted and made important refinements to Schottelius's word-structure theory in his *I veri Fondamenti della Lingua Tedesca* (1694) (Subirats-Rüggeberg 1994). Schottelius had provided a descriptive account of compounds in the German lexicon. For example, he had described *-lich* as a derivational suffix found on adjectives with a meaning of *Eigenschaft/Zugehör/Besitzung/Stand usw.* ('characteristic, belonging, property, state, etc.' 1663: 364). Kramer (1694: 246–7) not only indicated the meaning of the suffix, he also specified exactly how it could be used. It can be added to a substantive, adjective or verb, to yield an adjective or verb; and Kramer also noted that a change may be made to the vowel in the stem, as in *Bruder > brüderlich*. Schottelius provided the terminology for conceptualizing Twain's 'building blocks' of morphology; Kramer spelled out the morphological *process*.

Kramer also added two important compound types not recognized by Schottelius: 1. adding a verbal imperative to a noun or adjective base, as in *Fecht+boden*, and 2. the possibility of verbal (infinitival) base words, to which a substantive is added, e.g. *Fisch+fangen* (Subirats-Rüggeberg 1994: 307). This additional possibility was not recognized within the German-for-native-speakers tradition until twenty years later, by Longolius (1715).

In addition, Kramer clarified the structure of compounds consisting of more than two roots (or base morphemes, as we would say), such as the legal terms *Landfriedbruch* (three roots, 'breach of the peace') or *Erbmannstammgut* (four roots, 'inherited property') (cf. Schottelius 1663: 399). Schottelius had not recognized their internal hierarchical structure, describing such words simply as a succession of root-words. Kramer instead recognized them as binary compounds, where one or both of the two elements is already a compound, represented graphically by Kramer as follows:

Über-zug ⎫ Bett-über-zug
Bett   ⎬
          ⎭

Feuer-werck ⎫ Feuer-werck-zeug-meister
Zeug-meister ⎬
             ⎭

That is, Kramer made explicit an abstract level of word-structure, between the level of the rootwords and the finished compound, which had not previously been described. It is a similar leap – at the level of word structure – to that achieved much later in sentence structure (syntax) by recognizing constituent units above the level of the part of speech (e.g. noun phrase, verb phrase, etc.). Kramer's 1694 *Veri Fondamenti* was for Italian learners of German, but it was published in Latin by the Jesuit Andreas Freyberger in 1733, and so Kramer's insights ultimately found their way back into the native German grammatical tradition, some four decades later.

Word order and syntax

I noted above that an important development in grammatical theory is the notion of the sentence constituent, a unit greater than a single word. Let us return in this context to the problem of defining the adverb. As a 'part of speech', an adverb was expected to be a single word. But taking traditional Latin examples of adverbs – which in Latin were uncontroversial one-word adverbs – and translating them into German often yielded whole phrases, so that supposedly 'model' adverbs were in fact already more than one-word units. This was obviously tolerated because the phrases *behaved* like adverbs – as adverbial phrases, in short. When Aichinger (1753: 349–50) criticized Gottsched and others for allowing adverbs to have more than one word, even chunks that contain their own verb, such as *so wahr ich lebe, seit Adams*

Zeiten, so lange es dauert (Jellinek 1914: 359), he was merely criticizing what had been well-established practice of overlooking the definition in many grammars for over a century. It is odd, though, that the problem still existed in these mainstream grammars, for some of the *foreign* language grammars had found ways round it a good deal earlier – and how they did so reveals to us that they recognized the need for sentence constituents. I consider here two examples: Anchinoander (1616) and Kramer (1689).

Comparing Italian and German, Anchinoander (1616: 500) used the notion of *quasi-adverbia*, to allow both for adverbials of more than one word, and for other parts of speech which might act as adverbs (Anchinoander 1616: 500):

> Es sind noch etliche andere die man Quasi adverbia nennen möchte / deren etlichen von vielen anderen zusammen gesetzet werden / als in questro mentre under deß / perlo adietro fürs vergangene / etc.
> Etliche auch nur ein Wort begreiffen / daß sonst ein ander theil der Rede sey / als dolce für dolcemente süssiglich.
> Letzlich werden auch die Praepositiones für Adverbia gerechnet / wenn sie ihre gewöhnliche Casus nicht bey sich haben / als Sù auff / dinanzi zuvor &c.

> There are still several others which one could call quasi-adverbs ['like-adverbs'], of which several are composed of many others, as in *questro mentre, under deß* ['meanwhile'], *perlo adietro, fürs vergangene* ['for the past'], etc. Several also consist of just one word which is otherwise a different part of speech, as *dolce* ['sweet'] for *dolcemente, süssiglich* ['sweetly']. Finally, prepositions are also counted as adverbs when they don't have their normal case with them, as *Sù auff; dinanzi zuvor* ['thereupon, before'].

Kramer (1689: 121–2) arrived at a different solution. He managed neatly to treat the aberration of multi-word adverbs as a simple extension of the characteristics of the adverb already allowed for under the headings of *species* (primitive or derived) and *figura* (simple or compound). Kramer noted that most adverbs are *derived* from other parts of speech, and then extended this well-accepted traditional point to note that indeed many *are* in fact other parts of speech and phrases with an adverbial meaning:

> Der Herkunfft nach / gibts wenig Adverbia Radicalia, die meiste sind entweder von andern Partibus Orationis abgeleitete / oder es sind gar andere Partibus Orationis und Phrases welche eine Adverbialischen Bedeutung bekommen.

As regards their origin, there are few radical [i.e. root, non-derived] adverbs. Most are derived either from other parts of speech, or indeed they are other parts of speech and phrase which get an adverbial meaning.

Similarly, viewed morphologically, most adverbs are compounds, or indeed combinations of words acting as adverbs:

> Der Figur nach / gibts wenig Adverbia Simplicia, die meiste sind Composita und Decomposita; ja viel aus einer Praeposition und Nomine, Praeposition und Adverbio, Nomine und Verbo & c. gemachte Phrases haben Adverbialische Bedeutung / dieweil sie aus Mangel der eigentlichen und einfachen Wörter / müssen umschriben werden.
> Nota. Wir wollen allhier die Adverbia Primit. Derivativa, Simplicia und Composita setzen; item die Simplices Partes Orationis und Phrases Convenientiae deroselbigen

> As to their *figura*, there are few simplex adverbs. The majority are compounds or are derived from compounds. Indeed many phrases consisting of a preposition and a noun, of a preposition and adverb, of a noun and verb, etc. have adverbial meaning, which must be circumlocuted because of the lack of fitting and simplex words. Here we shall list the adverbs both primitive and derived, simplex and compound; and also the simple parts of speech and the phrases of convenience.

Both Anchinoander and Kramer arrived at different ways of allowing for what they needed – an intermediate constituent that acts like an adverb but that is longer than a single word. But the generalization to the existence of constituents in sentences had not yet been made. And that in turn made it very difficult for German grammarians to grasp what is a basic rule to the most elementary student of German today: the 'verb second' rule. In this final section, we shall see how grammarians of the late seventeenth century groped their way towards it.

The requirement that there be only one constituent before the inflected verb in a main clause (as in *Heute arbeite ich* vs. the ungrammatical **Heute ich arbeite*) is a very salient difference between German on the one hand, and English and Romance languages on the other. Considering how central it is to German as a Foreign Language teaching today, it is something of a surprise to discover how late it comes to prominence in learner grammars. Yet it was quite difficult to express as a general principle in the traditional word-based dependency grammars, which is all that German grammarians had at their disposal until the late seventeenth century. Grammarians described the syntax – chiefly the case relations – not of clauses, but of each part of speech in turn.

For instance, a section on the syntax of the adjective would note structures like *stolz + auf +* accusative, *jdm* (dative) *ähnlich sein,* etc. Obviously it is difficult to generalize rules of sentence structure if one is concentrating only on one part of speech at a time. The first mainstream German grammar to offer *general* rules about word order in addition to syntax for each part of speech was Stieler (1691). Since he mentioned specifically that his observations might be of interest to foreign learners (Stieler, 1691: 196, also cited in Jellinek 1914: 373), Jellinek suggested that Stieler probably drew on German as a Foreign Language grammars for his innovation. Jellinek noted that Pierre Canel's grammar of German (Canel 1689) showed some affinity with Stieler's treatment of the topic. But Canel is far from the only 'German as Foreign Language' grammar to offer general rules on syntax. At least three other grammars written for foreigners to learn German and published in the 1680s ahead of Canel's have some general rules for sentence construction. They are an anonymous one in French from 1682, and Aedler (1680) and Offelen (1687), both for English speakers.

Let us begin with Offelen (1687: 116). Here a traditional but overly simplistic definition of the adverb as having to follow the verb lingered on. Under the syntax of the adverb, Offelen stated:

> 1. *Adverbs* <u>follow always the</u> *Verbs* <u>in a</u> *Sentence,* and precede commonly the *Oblique* [i.e. non-nominative, NM] *Cases,* especially if we speak with *Emphasis,* which *Emphasis* is laid upon the *Adverb. As,* Gehet geschwind mit der artzney zum krancken, Go quickly with the Physick to the sick Body. Er war gestern mit mir im Schauspiel, he was at the Play with me yesterday. [my underlining, NM]

But Offelen also had a general section on sentence structure where he identified eight basic sentence types: affirmative, negative, interrogative and negative interrogative, each in present and perfect tenses. In this general section (1687: 96) we find inversion dealt with:

> 1. *Rule,* The *Accusative* goes regularly after the *Verb,* but sometimes before the *Verb* in this Language, and then the *Nominative* must go after the *Verb,* especially if we speak of a thing with an *Emphasis. As,* Wen liebt ihr? who do you love? R. Ich liebe meinen Bruder, or Meinen Bruder liebe ich, I love my Brother.
> 2. <u>The same holds if an</u> *Adverb* <u>is put in the beginning of a phrase. As,</u> Ich wohne hier, or Hier wohne ich, I live here. [my underlining, NM]

So Offelen did realize on some level – contrary to the first passage cited – that adverbs can occur before the verb, at the head of a clause. He also realized that this affects the order of the following verb and subject, but the rule is awkwardly stated, and conflicts with the basic definition of the adverb given elsewhere in the same book.

Even in the eighteenth century, the Schwanwitz grammar (anon./Schwanwitz 1745) used by Russian learners in St Petersburg pointed out inversion only implicitly:

> 2. Die Adverbia müssen nach den Verbis, und nicht vor denselben gesetzet werden, es sey denn, daß es einen Nachdruck in sich habe, als:
> Dieser Schreiber schreibet **schön**.
> **Kündlich** groß ist das gottselige Geheimniß. [my underlining, NM]

> The adverbs must be placed after the verbs, and not in front of them, unless it is for emphasis, as in: This writer writes nicely [vs.] Manifestly great is the blessed secret.

Aedler (1680) dealt with a different instance where the adverb precedes the verb:

> R.2 when as before verbes there comes an adverbe either medially or immediately; then the verbes come before the pronouns in the later part of the sentence, as we have seen [...] *so bald ich eweren brief empfangen hatte, shikkete ih eine antwort zurükke* as soon as I had received your letter I returned an answer

This is (to me) a novel way of stating what my students of German call the 'verb-comma-verb' rule for inversion in a main clause with a preposed subordinate clause, but the supposed triggering 'adverb' *so bald* would be viewed as a conjunction today, and the inversion would be explained rather differently.

An anonymous 1682 grammar for French learners of German is the first to offer general rules about sentence structure as a whole – and it is seven years earlier than the Frenchman Canel's grammar mentioned by Jellinek. Under a section headed 'De la construction' (1682: 205–28), the author enumerates eight different constructions in German, but not the same eight as Offelen (1687). Offelen's types – affirmative, negative, interrogative and negative interrogative – were handy divisions by semantic function, but the anonymous French grammar is rather more sophisticated, recognizing subordinate clauses as different sentence types. The account begins with the generic sentence type.

This generic sentence structure begins with a nominative, which is followed immediately by the verb (or auxiliary verb in the case of compound tenses), then dative or ablative (!) of person, then adverb, then the object of the verb (which, if a person, will come before the adverb). Example: *Ich habe euch heut meine büecher geliehen* 'I lent you my books today'. The author then presents a second sentence type which is 'almost as much in use as the first' (*presque autant en usage que la premiere*, Anon. 1682: 207). It begins with an adverb, followed by verb, then nominative, then the dative of the person, the object of the verb, and then the participle or infinitive, as in: *Alsdan hat sich der feund zuruck begeben* 'At once the enemy retreated'. This second type is, in effect, a generalized rule for inversion after an adverb. Type 3 presents a similar rule for inversion where the first sentence element is the object of the verb.[4] This whole-sentence approach, though it may still look eccentric in its details to us today, is far ahead of any accounts of syntax to be found in the 'mainstream' native German grammars available up to the 1680s.

Conclusion

It was not until the late sixteenth century that German became the focus of grammatical study. Quite apart from learning to think about language visually (in tables and boxes, thanks to innovations in printing), the early grammarians of German were faced with many challenges that were specific to German, in every area of grammar: from the fundamental questions of identifying the parts of speech and the cases, to the finest details of the language, such as whether to include or omit an -*e* here and there. Contributing to the process of language standardization, grammarians had to select which forms of German were permissible, as we saw when we considered adjective inflection and verb conjugation. But it was not just the raw data of the language

---

4   Type 4. is interrogative, 5. and 6. are subordinate clauses followed by a main clause, of the type *So ich euch heut mein buech gelihen hab, Hab ich es wol thuen wollen*, which the author describes as conditionals; 7 and 8 deal with relative clauses and indirect questions.

itself that presented difficulties. Grammarians also had to find a suitable framework for talking about the forms of German, once decided upon. The unsolved problem of constituent structure hovered in the air and meant that one of today's most elementary rules – the 'verb second' rule – was very, very difficult to uncover. Grammarians had to adjust or invent a suitable grammatical theory, and it took centuries to get it right for German (or as nearly 'right' as it is today, and rightness in any case depends on your standpoint – recall the continued disagreements about defining adverbs amongst leading grammars today, reflecting different theoretical positions). In instances where grammarians relied on established Latin grammar, adjusting the model and learning to reject what was unsuitable (reducing the number of cases or finding new criteria for verb classes), seems to have been even more difficult and time-consuming than inventing a whole new theoretical framework from scratch, as Stevin, Schottelius and Kramer did for the theory of word-formation. It is encouraging for anyone studying German as a foreign language that it is frequently the grammarians writing for foreign learners who make breakthroughs that only filter back into the mainstream grammatical tradition a bit later. Examples are early attempts at general rules for word order in sentences, and Kramer's refinements to describing word-formation processes. It may be heartening too to discover that there is a foundation for the suspicion that grammar is not quite as straightforward as teachers make it out to be. Understanding German grammar really did take centuries, and continues today.

References

Note: Glück (2002) surveys the history of learning German up to the eighteenth century; Penzl (1984) and McLelland (2004) discuss early materials for learners of German. McLelland (2006) considers how the Reformation influenced the way people started thinking about their vernacular. Jellinek (1913–14) – old, but still unbeaten for coverage and detail – and Naumann (1986) survey the history of German grammar up to 1856. Rössing-Hager (2000) and Moulin-Fankhänel (2000) give detailed scholarly overviews of grammars of German up to the eighteenth century; note also Moulin-Fankhänel's (1994–7) bibliographies of German grammars up to 1700. Müller (1969 [1882]), Ising

(1966, 1970), and Puff (1995a, 1995b) provide extracts from some of the very earliest materials for teaching German grammar. A very accessible introduction to the wider context of the history of ideas about language in Europe is Law (2003) – Robins (1997) and the four-volume series edited by Lepschy are more scholarly, but very readable. Gardt (1999) is a history of studying language, grammar, and linguistics in Germany, aimed at German students. On language standardization in German and other Germanic languages, see Linn and McLelland (2002), and Deumert and Vandenbussche (2003).

Primary sources

Adelung, Johann Christoph (1781), *Johann Christoph Adelungs Deutsche Sprachlehre. Zum Gebrauche der Schulen in den Königl. Preuß. Landen*, Berlin: Bey Christian Friedrich Voß und Sohn. (Reprinted in other editions 1792, 1795, 1800, 1806, 1816).

Adelung, Johann Christoph (1782), *Umständliches Lehrgebäude der Deutschen Sprache, zur Erläuterung der Deutschen Sprachlehre für Schulen. Von Joh. Christoph Adelung*, 2 vols, Leipzig: Breitkopf.

Aedler, Martin [anon.] (1680), *The Hig [sic] Dutch Minerva // a-la-mode // or // A Perfect Grammar // never extant before // whereby // The English // may both // easily and exactly // learne // the Neatest Dialect of the German // Mother-Language // used throughout all Europe; // most humbly dedicated*, London: Printed for the Author. (Facsimile reprint Menston, England: Scolar Press, 1972).

Aichinger, Carl Friedrich (1753), *Versuch einer teutschen Sprachlehre, anfänglich nur zu eignem Gebrauche unternommen, endlich aber, um den Gelehrten zu fernerer Untersuchung Anlaß zu geben, ans Liecht gestellt*, Frankfurt and Leipzig: Kraus. (Reprinted (1972), *Versuch einer teutschen Sprachlehre*, edited by M. Rössing-Hager, Hildesheim: Olms).

Albertus, Laurentius (Ostrofrancus) (1573), *Teutsch Grammatick oder Sprach-Kunst. Certissima ratio discendae, augendae, ornandae, propagandae, conservandaeque linguae Alemannorum sive Germanorum, Grammaticis Regulis et exemplis comprehensa & conscripta*, Augsburg: Michaël Manger. (Reprinted (1895), edited by C. Müller-Fraureuth, Straßburg: Trübner).

Anchinoander, Heinrich Cornelius (1616), *Henrici Cornelii Anchinoandri Grammatica Italica: Das ist gründliche Unterrichtung, wie die Italiänische oder Welsche Sprach von den Deutschen in ihrem Land gnngsam kan gelernet werden; sampt einem zu Ende angehengten Nahmenbuch*, Hamburg: Carstens.

anon. (1619), *Allgemeine Sprachlehr: Nach der Lehrart Ratichii*, Köthen.

anon. (1682), *La véritable et unique Grammaire alemande. Exactement corrigée et augmentée de plus d'un tiers dans cette nouvelle édition*. Strasbourg: Schmuck.

anon./Schwanwitz, Martin (1745), *Teutsche // Grammatica // Aus unterschiedenen Auctoribus // ehmahls // zusammen getragen // nunmehro aber von neuem übersehen //*

*und // viel verbessert // Zum Gebrauch // des // St Peterburgischen // Gymnasii //
herausgegeben*, St Petersburg: Kayserl. Academie der Wissenschaften.

Becherer, Johann (1596), *SYNOPSIS GRAMMATICÆ TAM GERMANICAE QVAM
LATINAE ET GRAEC-ae, in usum jubentatis scholasticae conscripta à Johanne
Becherero*, Jena: Typis Tobiae Steinmanni.

Clajus, Johannes (1578), *Grammatica Germanicae Linguae M. Iohannis Claij Hirtzen-
bergensis: Ex Bibliis Lutheri Germanicis et aliis eius libris collectis. Leipzig: Johannes
Rhamba, 1578.* (Reprinted (1895), with an introduction by F. Weidling, Strassburg:
Trübner.

Dijksterhuis, E.J. (eds) (1955), *The Principal Works of Simon Stevin*, vol. I, Amsterdam:
C.V. Swets & Zeitlinger.

Dreyer, Hilke and Schmitt, Richard (1999), *Practice Grammar of German*, New edition,
Ismaning: Verlag für Deutsch.

Durrell, M. (2002), *Hammer's German Grammar and Usage. Fourth edition*, London:
Arnold.

Eisenberg, Peter (1994), *Grundriss der deutschen Grammatik*, 3rd ed., Stuttgart:
Metzler.

Eisenberg, Peter (1999), *Grundriss der deutschen Grammatik, vol. II: Der Satz*, 4th ed.,
Stuttgart: Metzler.

Funk, Gottlieb Benedikt (1734–1814), *J.H. Schlegels Professors bey der Universit:at zu
Kopenhagen Abhandlung über die Vortheile und Mängel des Dänische, verglichen mit
dem Deutschen und Französischen. Aus dem Dänischen, nebst einigen Anmerkungen und einer Abhandlung des Uebersetzers*, Schleswig: bey Joachim Friedrich
Hansen.

Gottsched, Johann Christoph (1748), *Grundlegung der deutschen Sprachkunst, Nach
den Mustern der besten Schriftsteller des vorigen und jetzigen Jahrhunderts abgefasst
von Johann Christoph Gottscheden*, Leipzig: Verlegts Bernh. Christoph Breitkopf.
(Reprinted: 2nd ed. 1749; 3rd ed. 1752. From 4th ed. onwards with title: *Vollstän-
digere und Neuerläuterte Deutsche Sprachkunst, Nach den Mustern ...*, 5th ed. 1762;
6th ed. 1776.

Ickelsamer, Valentin (1527), *Die rechte weis aufs kürtzist lesen zu lernen.* Reprinted (1971),
edited by K. Pohl, Stuttgart: Klett.

Kramer, Matthias (1689), *Vollständige italiänische Grammatica: Das ist: Toscanisch-
romanische Sprach-Lehre, nunmehr aus ihren untersten Fundamentis und Füglichkeit
bis zu der höchsten Perfection und Zierlichkeit, Der Deutschen Nation zum besten
Aufs klärlichst-ordentlichst- und fleissigst ausgeführt und vorgetragen*, Nuremberg:
Endter.

Kramer, Matthias (1694), *Die richtige Grundfeste der deutschen Sprache*, Nuremberg:
Endter.

Kromayer, Johannes (1618), *Deutsche Grammatica um newen Methodo der Jugend zum
besten zugerichtet.* Reprinted (1986), Hildesheim: Olms.

Longolius, Johann Daniel (1715), *Einleitung zur gründtlicher Erkäntniß einer ieden, insonderheit aber der Teutschen Sprache*, Budissin: Richter.

Offelen, Heinrich (1687), *A Double Grammar for Germans to Learn English and for English-men to learn the German Tongue. Zwey-fache gründliche Sprach-Lehr, für Hochteutsche, englisch, und für Engelländer hochteutsch zu lernen*, London: Old Spring Garden by Charing Cross.

Olearius, Tilmann (1630), *Deutsche Sprachkunst. Aus den allergewissesten / der Vernunfft und gemeinen brauch Deutsch zu reden gemässen / gründen genommen. Sampt ange-hengten newen methodo, die Lateinische Sprache geschwinde und mit lust zu lernen*, Halle: Melchior Oelschlegel.

Ölinger, Albertus (1574), *Underricht der Hoch Teutschen Spraach: Seu Institutio Verae Germanicae Linguae, in qua Etymologia, Syntaxis & reliquae partes omnes suo ordine breviter tractantur. In usum iuventutis maximè Gallicae, ante annos aliquot conscripta, nunc autem quorundam instinctu in lucem edita, plaerisque vicimis nationibus, non minus utilis quàm necessaria*, Straßburg: Nicolaus Vuyriot. Reprinted (1975) Hild-esheim: Olms.

Ritter, Stephan (1616), *Grammatica Germanica Nova*, USUI OMNIUM ALIARUM NATIONUM [...], Marburg: Hutwelcker.

Schottelius, Justus Georg (1641) *Teutsche Sprachkunst / Darinn die Allerwortreichste / jhren Gründen erhoben / dero Eigenschafften und Kunststücke völliglich entdeckt / und also in eine richtige Form der Kunst zum ersten mahle gebracht worden. Abgetheilet in Drey Bücher*, Braunschweig: Gruber.

Schottelius, Justus Georg (1651), *Justi-Georgii Schottelii Teutsche Sprach Kunst: viel-faltig vermehret und verbessert, darin von allen Eigenschaften der so wortreichen und prächtigen Teutschen Haubtsprache ausführlich und gründlich gehandelt wird*, Braunschweig: Zilliger.

Schottelius, Justus Georg (1663), *Ausführliche Arbeit von der teutschen Haubtsprache*, Braunschweig: Zilliger. Reprinted (1967), (1995), edited by W. Hecht, Tübingen: Niemeyer.

Schottelius, Justus Georg (1676), *Kurtze und gründliche Anleitung Zu der RechtSchreibung Und zu der WortForschung In der Teutschen Sprache. Für siw Jugend in den Schulen / und sonst überall nützlich und dienlich.* Braunschweig: Zilliger.

Steinbach, Christ. Ernst (1724), *Kürtze und gründliche Anweisung zur Deutschen Sprache. Vel succincta et perfecta Grammatica LINGVAE GERMANICAE Nova methodo tradita*, Rostochii et Parchimi: Apug Georg Ludw. Fritsch.

Stieler, Kaspar (1968) [1691], *Der Teutschen Sprache Stammbaum und Fortwachs [...]*, Nürnberg: Johann Hoffman. Rpt. mit einem Nachwort von Stefan Sonderegger, München: Kösel.

Straßburg, Gottfried von (1977) [*c.* 1210], *Tristan, ed. Karl Marold*, with a new apparatus by Werner Schröder, Berlin: De Gruyter.

Twain, Mark (1880), 'The awful German language', in: *A Tramp Abroad*, London : Chatto
& Windus. Available online at http://www.crossmyt.com/hc/linghebr/awfgrmlg.
html

Bibliography

Barbarić, S. (1981), *Zur grammatischen Terminologie von Justus Georg Schottelius und
Kaspar Stieler: mit Ausblick auf die Ergebnisse bei ihren Vorgängern*, Bern: Peter
Lang.
Deumert, A. and Vandenbussche, W. (eds) (2003), *Germanic Standardizations. Past to
Present*, Amsterdam: Benjamins. (IMPACT Studies in Language and Society 18).
Ebert, R.P., Reichmann, O., Solms, H.-J., and Wegera, K.-P. (eds) (1993), *Frühneuhoch-
deutsche Grammatik*, Tübingen: Niemeyer. (Sammlung kurzer Grammatiken ger-
manischer Dialekte. Hauptreihe 12).
Gardt, A. (1999), *Geschichte der Sprachwissenschaft in Deutschland vom Mittelalter bis
ins 20. Jahrhundert*, Berlin: de Gruyter.
Glück, H. (2002), *Deutsch als Fremdsprache in Europa vom Mittelalter bis zur Barockzeit*,
Berlin: de Gruyter.
Habermann, M. (1997), 'Das sogenannte "Lutherische e". Zum Streit um einen *armen
Buchstaben*', *Sprachwissenschaft* 22, 435–77.
Ising, E. (1966), *Die Anfänge der volkssprachlichen Grammatik in Deutschland und
Böhmen. Dargestellt am Einfluss der Schrift des Aelius Donatus. De octo partibus
orationis ars minor* (Teil I: Quellen), Berlin: Deutsche Akademie der Wissenschaf-
ten zu Berlin.
Ising, E. (1970), *Die Herausbildung der Grammatik der Volkssprachen in Mittel- und
Osteuropa. Studien über den Einfluß der lateinischen Elementargrammatik des Aelius
Donatus. De octo partibus orationis ars minor*, Berlin (DDR): Veröffentlichungen
des Instituts für deutsche Sprache und Literatur.
Jellinek, M. (1913–14), *Geschichte der neuhochdeutschen Grammatik von den Anfängen
bis auf Adelung*, vol. I (1913); vol. II (1914), Heidelberg: Carl Winter.
Law, V. (2003), *The History of Linguistics in Europe from Plato to 1600*, Cambridge:
Cambridge University Press.
Lepschy, G. (ed.) (1994–8), *History of Linguistics*, vol. I (1994), vol. II (1994), vol. III
(1997), vol. IV (1998), London: Longman.
Linn, A.R. and McLelland, N. (eds) (2002), *Standardization. Studies from the Germanic
Languages*, Amsterdam: Benjamins. (Current Issues in Linguistic Theory 235).
McLelland, N. (2001), 'Albertus (1573) and Ölinger (1574). Creating the first grammars
of German', *Historiographia Linguistica* 28, 7–38.

McLelland, N. (2003), 'Die Anfänge der deutschen Grammatikschreibung im 16. Jahrhundert – und davor?', in: *Jahrbuch für internationale Germanistik. Reihe A. Bd. 63*, edited by Peter Wiesinger, Bern: Peter Lang (*Akten des X. Internationalen Germanistenkongresses Wien 2000, Bd. 11*).

McLelland, N. (2004), 'Dialogue & German language learning in the Renaissance', in: *Printed Voices. The Renaissance Culture of Dialogue*, edited by D. Heitsch and J.-F. Vallée, Toronto: University of Toronto Press, 206–25.

McLelland, N. (2006), 'Reformation, Northern European', in: *Encyclopedia of Language and Linguistics, 2nd ed.*, edited by K. Brown, Oxford: Elsevier, 464–8.

McLelland, N. (2008), 'Approaches to the semantics and syntax of the adverb in German foreign language grammars', *Beiträge zur Geschichte der Sprachwissenschaft* 18, 37–58.

Moulin-Fankhänel, C. (1994 and 1997), *Bibliographie der deutschen Grammatiken und Orthographielehren. I. Von den Anfängen der Überlieferung bis zum Ende des 16. Jahrhunderts; II. Das 17. Jahrhundert*, Heidelberg: C. Winter.

Moulin-Fankhänel, C. (2000), 'Deutsche Grammatikschreibung vom 16. bis. 18. Jahrhundert', in: *Sprachgeschichte. Ein Handbuch zur Geschichte der deutschen Sprache und ihrer Erforschung*, 2nd ed., vol. II, edited by W. Besch, A. Betten, O. Reichmann and S. Sonderegger, Berlin: de Gruyter, 1903–11.

Müller, J. (1969) [1882], *Quellenschriften und Geschichte des deutschsprachlichen Unterrichts bis zur Mitte des 16. Jahrhunderts. Mit einer Einführung von Monika Rössing-Hager*, Hildesheim: Olms.

Naumann, B. (1986), *Grammatik der deutschen Sprache zwischen 1781 und 1856. Die Kategorien der deutschen Grammatik in der Tradition von Johann Werner Meiner und Johann Christoph Adelung*, Berlin: Schmidt.

Penzl, H. (1984), 'Gimer min ros. How German was taught in the ninth and eleventh centuries', *The German Quarterly* 57, 392–401.

Percival, W.K. (1975), 'The grammatical tradition and the rise of the vernaculars', in: *Current Trends in Linguistics, vol. 13, Historiography of linguistics*, edited by T.A. Sebeok, The Hague and Paris: Mouton, 231–75.

Puff, H. (1995a), 'Grammatica latina deutsch. Zum Funktionswandel der Volkssprache im 16. Jahrhundert', *Daphnis* 24, 55–78.

Puff, H. (1995b), '*Von dem schlüssel aller Künsten / nemblich der Grammatica. Deutsch im lateinischen Grammatikunterricht 1480–1560*', Tübingen: Francke Verlag.

Puff, H. (1996), 'Exercitium grammaticale puerorum. Eine Studie zum Verhältnis von pädagogischer Innovation und Buchdruck um 1500', in: *Schule und Schüler im Mittelalter. Beiträge zur europäischen Bildungsgeschichte des 9. bis 15. Jahrhunderts*, edited by Kintzinger et al., Cologne: Böhlau, 411–39.

Robins, R.H. (1997), *A Short History of Linguistics*, London: Longman.

Rössing-Hager, M. (2000), 'Frühe grammatische Beschreibungen des Deutschen', in: *History of the Language Sciences. An International Handbook on the Evolution of the*

Study of Language from the Beginnings to the Present. (HSK 18:1–2), 2 *vols*, edited by S. Auroux, K. Koerner, H.-J. Niederehe and K. Versteegh, Berlin: de Gruyter, 777–84.

Subirats-Rüggeberg, C. (1994), 'Grammar and lexicon in traditional grammar. The work of Matthias Kramer and Johann Joachim Becher', *Historiographia Linguistica* 21, 297–350.

WILLIAM JERVIS JONES

Dictionaries and their Role in the Formation of German (1500–1900)

Introduction

From about 1500, the German vocabulary was in ferment as it responded to cultural changes of all kinds. New words were being adopted or created to denote new discoveries and concepts; old words denoting outdated concepts were disappearing; and regional differences in vocabulary were being reduced in favour of a standardized language. But gradually this lexical turmoil came to be catalogued, ordered and codified, by generations of lexicographers working individually and creatively within a many-stranded tradition. As with grammar, so too with the more open and flexible systems of lexis, the linguistic habits of society at large were being shaped and regulated by an educated minority.

In German-speaking countries the production of dictionaries reached a very high level, in quality as well as quantity. German lexicographers drew especially on the achievements of dictionary makers in Italy, France and the Low Countries. In German dictionaries, Latin held on to its role as the international language of learning until about 1700. But alongside this outward-looking internationalism we find a widespread concern for the status and purity of German itself. Not for the first time in its history, but now with renewed intensity, the German language was being cultivated and emancipated.

Dictionaries of the period 1500–1900 are of value in that they reflect older stages of the language, as well as showing us how linguistic theory and method have evolved. But their importance is also that in their day they acted as powerful instruments – helping to stabilize the language, and often promoting changes in everyday usage, as well as in formal education, philosophy, science and technology. Overtly or tacitly, every dictionary is an ideological creation, a reflector of current political, social, cultural and ethical values, which can be detected in definitions and examples, often in the choice of headwords (lemmata), and sometimes even in format and typography.

Dictionaries were most definitely a publisher's commodity – good business, apart from a few famous flops – and historians of the book are led to enquire into commercial aspects: the selling price, the market, and the intended function, whether in schools, in the home, or elsewhere: lexicography as experienced by the recipient rather than the originator. The reception and influence of a dictionary can sometimes be judged indirectly, by the number of editions printed, the format used, the state of surviving copies, the use made of it by later lexicographers, and anecdotal remarks of all kinds.

Approaching this subject, we are aided not only by classic contributions such as the work of Helmut Henne from the 1970s, but also by some very helpful recent studies and surveys. Stanisław Piotr Szlęk (1999), for example, has provided an informative survey of lexicographical programmes up to and including the Grimms, with extensive documentation. Across a wider chronological range, the 'Studienbuch' of Ulrike Haß-Zumkehr (2001) offers much detailed discussion, illustrative material, and references to secondary literature. Highly relevant too are some of the articles contained in the three-volume collection edited by Franz Josef Hausmann and others (1989–91) under the title *Wörterbücher*. Further suggestions for reading are given at the end. My aim in this introductory article is to present a historical outline, much indebted to research done by others, and to provide some examples drawn from my own experiences in the bibliographical description of seventeenth-century dictionaries and from another current project on German colour terms.

Historical outline (to 1850)

At no point in its history can German lexicography be isolated from its European context. Its roots are firmly multilingual. Already in a mid eighth-century Bavarian monastery at Freising somebody was compiling a Latin–German dictionary of synonyms, known from its first entry as the *Abrogans* ('humble'). The earliest surviving German book: a bilingual dictionary. Latin–German lexicography, as an essential instrument in literacy and education, remained highly active through the Middle Ages, propagated in its later stages by the invention of printing. The classic example of this is the fifteenth-century *Vocabularius ex quo*, an alphabetical Latin–German vocabulary which survives in over 250 manuscripts and 40 early printed editions. Throughout the Middle Ages, equivalents needed to be found or coined, to enable the smaller vocabulary of German to match the rich resources of Latin. We can see a similar process happening at various times in other European vernaculars (e.g. Italian, French, Spanish, Dutch, English), creating a shared debt to Latin, and assisting in the convergence of their semantic structures. As Jonathan West has shown (1989), the Lutheran schoolmaster Peter Dasypodius in the 1530s emerges as a particularly creative German lexicographer, inventing new compounds and derivatives in a Latin–German, German–Latin dictionary which with many revisions went on being used for the next 200 years in schools, later especially in Catholic ones. In the wake of Humanism, with its dual emphasis on the cultivation of Classical languages (Latin and Greek) and of the modern vernaculars, the 1500s also saw German no longer simply serving to explain the Latin words, but slowly gaining status of its own, as in Josua Maaler's German–Latin lexicon of 1561, with approximately 27,000 headwords. This case, incidentally, sheds some light on early lexicographical methods: Maaler (1529–1599) seems to have created the basis for his work by systematically reversing the Latin–German dictionary of Petrus Cholinus and Johannes Frisius (editions of 1541 and 1556), which was itself based closely on the Latin–French dictionary of Robert Estienne (Stephanus) (Paris, 1538).

Lexicographers across Europe were already thinking big. The massive polyglot dictionaries published under the name of Ambrosius Calepinus (1435–1511) had been appearing in five-language editions including German since 1545 and were expanded to include eleven languages in handsome but cumbrous folio editions printed at Basel from 1590 onwards. Also conceived on a grand scale, but destined to remain unfinished, was the specifically German dictionary of Georg Henisch (1549–1618), *Teütsche Sprach vnd Weißheit* (1616), comprising over 900 pages. Based partly on Maaler and other sources, this provided equivalents in Czech, English, Flemish, French, Greek, Hebrew, Hungarian, Italian, Latin, Polish and Spanish. More particularly it brought together a wealth of German vocabulary, phraseology and proverbs, these last being primarily the 'wisdom' of its title, though it also contains some encyclopaedic information. Henisch's work was long remembered as an example of what might be technically possible for German, but disastrously stranded for all time in letter G. It is assumed that his advanced age prevented him from finishing it.

During the seventeenth century, lexicography was driven by three main factors:

- practical, educational needs (notably the still very low levels of literacy) which called for authority and, if necessary, prescription in matters of German language

- the need to teach Latin as an educational tool, giving access to the international world of learning

- a desire to achieve for German the prestige and copiousness of a cardinal language (*Hauptsprache*), and to raise it to a status previously reserved for Hebrew, Greek and Latin.

German was felt to need standards of correctness like those that applied to the Classical languages. Achieving this ideal was highly problematic in a pluricentric language community where the written norm might be variously felt to lie in some specific regional variety (like Saxony or Silesia), or in some canon of 'good' writers (Martin Luther, Martin Opitz, Johann Christoph Gottsched) or institutions (the chanceries), or might stand in an abstract sense 'above' the common dialects and be discoverable by logic and analogy, as Justus Georg Schottelius (1612–1676) contended. Many lexicographers were ready to arbitrate in cases of doubt, and even to invent new words where these were lacking in German, a process already prefigured in that early age of lexical experimentation, Old High German (750–1050). Contemporaries in the seventeenth century were mostly not averse to the normative type of grammar or dictionary which legislated on what is correct or incorrect, rather than necessarily always describing actual usage – though it should be stressed that the second aim, description, was generally central to their aims and needs.

Socially, the linguistic theoreticians of the seventeenth century were aspiring members of the educated middle classes (*Bildungsbürgertum*), for example clerics, physicians, lawyers and teachers, often eager to detach themselves from the localized speech of the populace (*Pöbel*), but also ready on occasion, even in an age of absolutism, to differentiate themselves from the high nobility by questioning or rejecting the foreign (French, Italian) influences which most of the aristocracy had by then embraced.

Educationally, people were trying to secure stability and permanence by selective indoctrination of the young on Classical models. And politically, as if to compensate for the national fragmentation and subjugation in this, the period of the Thirty Years War (1618–48), German was being promoted in the spirit of *Kulturpatriotismus*, as a repository of supposedly Germanic virtues, a language for heroes, a *Hauptsprache* genetically at least the equal of Greek or Latin, and certainly superior to the Romance bastardized offshoots Italian, French and Spanish.

Under this powerful combination of influences, the aim of a comprehensive German dictionary was realized with the masterpiece of Kaspar Stieler (1632–1707), *Der Teutschen Sprache Stammbaum und Fortwachs* (1691), based upon a programme mapped out by the grammarian Schottelius some 30 years earlier. Both were members of the *Fruchtbringende Gesellschaft* or Fructifying Society which had been founded in 1617 for the cultivation of German language, literature and morals. Stieler exploited generously (contemporaries said too generously) the many techniques of word formation available to the German Baroque. He had derived from Henisch and Schottelius the key concept of the *Stammwort*, the irreplaceable, mainly monosyllabic root, which was a core concept in the justification of German as a *Hauptsprache*. From these base-forms it was believed that the vocabulary could be multiplied through *Verdopplungskunst* (compounding and derivation) to equal or exceed the resources of Latin or Greek.

In his dictionary of 1691 Stieler applied the principle of the *Stammwort* systematically to the whole of German vocabulary. This work is arranged alphabetically by these roots (about 500 are used), bringing together compounds and derivatives under their respective base-forms (so *entkleiden* is to be found under *Kleid*). The language's capacity to grow and spread is symbolized by the engraving of an Indian fig tree which adorns the frontispiece of this typographically elegant work. With over 2,000 pages and some 68,000 headwords, it far outstrips any previous German dictionary, still using Latin for definitions and comments (as a metalanguage), but with the emphasis decidedly on German itself. Though not exclusively basing himself on any one dialect, Stieler has warm praise for Meißnisch, referring to 'die Richtschnur

der Hochteutschen Sprache', namely 'das prächtige Dreßden / das heilige
Wittenberg / und das Süßeste aller Städte / Leipzig'. On the debit side, his
work as yet lacks precise references to German sources, and the etymologies
ventured are sometimes accurate by modern standards, but sometimes well
wide of the mark: for example, he correctly relates *Gift* to *Gabe*, and *Kunst* to
kennen; but he mistakenly considers *Ader* 'vein' to be derived from a hypothetical *Ahader* (with the root *Aha-* meaning 'water', as indeed it did in Old
High German).

Since Gerhard Ising's study (1956) it has been customary to contrast the
work of Stieler with that of his contemporary Matthias Kramer (1640–1729?).
Kramer worked in Nürnberg as a teacher of languages (Italian, French, Spanish, Dutch). Thousands of students, male and female, passed through the
hands of this talented teacher. Kramer's energy and stamina must have been
colossal: he completed a new Dutch dictionary at the age of 79, and was then
planning a lexicon of Spanish. What especially appeals about Kramer is his
sheer practicality, which is well represented in his finest achievement, the great
German–Italian dictionary of 1700–2. A vast compilation (the dictionary
itself comprises 2,482 pages and approximately 75,000 German headwords),
its stated aim is to describe good oral usage of the day, not too literary, not
too dialectal. But its chief glory is that it consistently looks beyond the word,
to the phrase, and includes countless German and Italian idioms on a scale
previously unknown in German lexicography. Ising argued that Kramer, the
popular language teacher of Nürnberg, was more closely attuned to the fast-
developing everyday language of his time than the Thuringian court poet
and administrator Stieler. This may be too simple a conclusion. Stieler had
had a wide formative experience as a student, soldier and traveller. And historical lexicologists still need to judge on a wide basis (1) how far Kramer's
German and Italian idioms are typical of real usage of their day, (2) to what
extent Stieler filled his dictionary with words of his own invention (as Kramer
claimed), and (3) how much material Kramer took over from Stieler. What is
certain is that, in the number of words cited, and in the detail provided, both
lexicographers far exceeded any of their predecessors in German.

The eighteenth century brought new landscapes and new landmarks,
providing much to support Ulrike Haß-Zumkehr's bold generalization:
'Sprache als Instrument des bürgerlichen Handels und Wandels statt
Sprache als Gedächtnis vergangener nationaler Größe und als Instrument

zur Wiederherstellung dieser Größe' (2001: 86ff.). Inspired by Gottfried Wilhelm Leibniz (1646–1716), and working under the aegis of the *Preußische Societät der Wissenschaften* in Berlin, the teacher and natural scientist Johann Leonard Frisch (1666–1743) is credited with having conceived at age 25, and brought forth at age 75, the first scholarly dictionary of German (Powitz 1959). Published in 1741 with approximately 60,000 word-articles, Frisch's German–Latin dictionary was epoch-making for German in its citation of textual examples from several hundred medieval and early modern sources – a method of linguistic documentation inherited from Classical lexicography and later to be developed to the full by the brothers Grimm and their successors. A transitional work, and organized still by *Stammwörter*, Frisch's dictionary is noteworthy also for its inclusion of some items from dialect and technical language. This, taken with the historical component, quite strongly reflects the recommendations made by Leibniz in his influential and elegantly written *Unvorgreiffliche Gedancken betreffend die Ausübung und Verbesserung der Teutschen Sprache* (Hannover, 1717).

From the 1770s, another major landmark is reached with the publication of the celebrated, standard-setting dictionary of Johann Christoph Adelung (1732–1806). In its historical richness and its detailed semantic analysis a finer achievement than Dr Samuel Johnson's *Dictionary of the English Language* of two decades earlier, Adelung's work was consulted by writers of the quality of Johann Heinrich Voss (1751–1826) and Christoph Martin Wieland (1733–1813), as well as Goethe and Schiller. In its fullest edition it runs to about 5,000 pages and lists over 50,000 headwords, considerably fewer than Stieler or Kramer, but Adelung's individual entries are much more substantial in their documentation and discussion. Though his work is in many ways indebted to Kramer, Frisch and others (Dill 1992: 205), the older practice of ordering by *Stammwörter* is now superseded: the arrangement envisaged here is strictly alphabetical. Another obvious difference is the virtual absence of Latin: this is very much a German–German dictionary.

But what kind of German? Adelung picked his way cautiously between lexical archaism and neologism, internationalism and provincialism, all of which he stigmatized as forms of barbarism. For him in the 1770s–90s, the chief modern classics were Johann Christoph Gottsched (1700–1766) and Christian Fürchtegott Gellert (1715–1769) from one or two generations earlier, when Meißnisch as a model was dominant. His dictionary's declared basis is the German of the upper class in southern Saxony, which he describes as the fatherland of true German (Jellinek 1913–14: I, 360ff.). This seems a bizarre restriction when we recall that at the time German had reached or was reaching new heights of creative expression elsewhere: with Johann Jakob Bodmer (1698–1783) and Johann Jakob Breitinger (1701–1776) in Switzerland, Friedrich Gottlieb Klopstock (1724–1803) in Hamburg, Johann Wolfgang von Goethe (1749–1832) in Frankfurt and Weimar, Friedrich Schiller (1759–1805) and Friedrich Hölderlin (1770–1843) in Swabia. Adelung's view also conflicts with that of most modern historical linguists of German, namely that all regions contributed historically to the formation of the standard language, some clearly more than others. It has been noticed, however, that in Adelung's lexicographical practice the regional restriction (to southern Saxony) is less obvious than the social one. He is certainly giving us upper- and middle-class German, and he despises vulgarity. Vertically, he divides German lexis into five *Classen* (socio-stylistic levels or registers), using the criterion of *Würde*. He defines his first three classes as: '1. die höhere oder erhabene Schreibart; 2. die edle; 3. die Sprechart des gemeinen Lebens und vertraulichen Umganges'; the fourth class he calls 'die niedrige' and marks it with symbols; and the fifth ('die ganz pöbelhafte') he will admit only for special reasons, since it lies 'tief unter dem Horizonte des Sprachforschers' (*Wörterbuch, 1. Ausgabe* (1774), Vorrede, XIV).

Adelung had reasons for locating the source of 'true' German so precisely. He was firstly aware that Meißnisch had acted as a model, and in his own view it had spread 'über das ganze aufgeklärte Deutschland', becoming less and less pure as it went (Jellinek I, 361). In his *Umständliches Lehrgebäude der Deutschen Sprache, zur Erläuterung der Deutschen Sprachlehre für Schulen* (1782: I, 85) he wrote:

> Die herrschende Schriftsprache ist an keine Provinz gebunden, sondern die allgemeine Sprache des Geschmackes und der feinern Sitten in ganz Deutschland, in Obersachsen aber ganz natürlich mehr und reiner als anderwärts, indem sich immer mehr von dem Provinzial-Dialecte mit einmischt, je weiter man sich davon entfernet.

In Adelung's theoretical approach, moreover, Germanic myth and Schottelian metaphysics had no part to play. For him, either a language exists and functions in reality, or it does not; standardized High German as an abstraction is meaningless; and it is hopeless to think of total unification, because diversity of function will always drive a language apart. The mood and perceptions of the age had clearly changed, and the alleged linguistic tyranny of a Gottsched had become insufferable. No longer could grammarians and lexicographers be welcomed or even tolerated as authoritarian legislators; linguists needed to function rather more democratically, in Adelung's words to do no more than count the votes and ensure an accurate return (Jellinek I, 358). A kind of linguistic returning officer, though with suffrage (as we have seen) still far from universal. German, Adelung felt, had been harmed by too much decision-taking: it now required understanding, based on careful analysis: 'Es ist bisher in der deutschen Sprache nur zu viel entschieden worden; es ist Zeit, daß man einmal anfange, zu prüfen und zu untersuchen' (*Wörterbuch, 1. Ausgabe* (1774), Vorrede, XIII).

Adelung's chief contribution to that analysis, in the lexical field, is his close attention to semantic aspects. For each word he lovingly garners its meanings, and typically presents them in a continuum, beginning by defining the primary concrete sense and proceeding outwards to more general, abstract and transferred uses. He is sensitive to semantic nuances and structures, aware of historical developments, and keen to capture the full spectrum of those developments. Where steps seem to be missing from what he calls the 'Leiter der Bedeutungen' (Vorrede, XIV), he tries to supply them, even drawing if necessary on archaic usage, or provincialisms, or vulgarisms. When writing of the 'primary sensuous meaning' ('die erste sinnliche Bedeutung') (Henne ed. 1975: 127), he reveals himself as a cautious disciple of Johann Gottfried Herder (1744–1803) (*Abhandlung über den Ursprung der Sprache*, 1771), concerned to trace each item back to a primitive use from which all the rest can be derived. Adelung cites examples partly drawn from Kramer, Frisch and others, but mostly of his own finding (Dill 1992: 361). The historical dimension, not as sophisticated nor as thoroughly pursued as later with the Grimms, is nonetheless substantial. He quotes from the Gothic Bible, from such Old High German and Middle High German sources as were then available, from Luther and certain Baroque writers, but above all from the early *Aufklärung*. Exact references are provided only in the case of the Bible.

Adelung is difficult to place historically. He has been seen as representing the close of the *Aufklärung* and as strongly anticipating the nineteenth century. Jellinek (I, 332) referred sarcastically to his 'meisterhafte Technik verschweigenden Zitierens' and labelled him a pedant, a conservative, but also an empiricist hitherto unequalled in his knowledge of linguistic facts old and new; an *Aufklärer* keen to differentiate and clarify meanings and concepts in the name of reason, but also a post-Enlightenment figure speaking still the language of the Enlightenment. Adelung appears to us today outmoded in his belated promotion of Meißnisch, his rejection of lower-class variants, his neglect of eminent contemporaries, his naive view of language origins, and his still dubious etymologizing. The more acceptable face of Adelung is to be found elsewhere: in the exclusion of Latin from the description of German, in his sensitivity to word semantics, his respect for the spoken idiom, his development of the historical dimension, his sober concern for linguistic facts and functions, and his curbing of the legislative role.

As we enter the nineteenth century I can do little more than mention the weighty contribution made by Adelung's leading opponent, Joachim Heinrich Campe (1746–1818) (see Orgeldinger 1999). The most famous or notorious of German purists, Campe was motivated mainly by educational considerations: he saw foreign borrowings as erecting an internal barrier to communication, because they would be understood mainly by an educated élite (those trained in Latin, Greek, French, Italian and English), whereas, he argued, a German compound or derivative is relatively transparent, and so more generally accessible to the people. In his *Wörterbuch zur Erklärung und Verdeutschung der unserer Sprache aufgedrungenen fremden Ausdrücke: ein Ergänzungsband zu Adelungs Wörterbuche* (1801), Campe sought to mini-mize this supposed social danger by supplying about 11,000 German words (many of his own invention) to serve as replacements for foreign (largely Latin and French) vocabulary. Probably with his activity in mind, contem-poraries complained of lexicographers setting up their own word-factories (Henne ed. 1975: 130). In Adelung's anti-authoritarian view, no one person had the power to give direction in matters of linguistic usage. In contrast, this 'impotence of the individual' ('Ohnmacht des Individuums') (Jellinek I, 355) held no attraction for the linguistically and politically proactive Campe. Time is perhaps the best judge: some 200–300 of Campe's invented words still survive in regular use (probable examples include *altertümlich, auswerten, einschließlich, Ergebnis, Glühwein*) – a considerable achievement for any indi-vidual in any language. Relying heavily on the unacknowledged assistance of Theodor Bernd, Campe went on to publish a dictionary of German as a whole (1807–11), which far exceeded Adelung's work in the number of its headwords, but with considerable sacrifice of detail. Campe consciously moved away from Adelung's narrow regional, social and cultural basis to a more inclusive policy, employing, however, some dozen symbols as socio-stylistic markers ('der höhern Schreibart', 'veraltet', 'pöbelhaft', 'landschaftlich' etc.), including one to cover words newly invented by himself. Again in contrast with Adelung, he avoided etymological descriptions, but there is frequent (if inexact) citation from a good range of eighteenth-century authors (Henne ed. 1975: 145ff.).

The Grimms and Sanders

And so to the mid-nineteenth century. In lexicography, the saga of what has come to be known as *Grimm Deutsches Wörterbuch* is unique, and mercifully so. Begun in 1838 by those pioneers of German studies Jacob Grimm (1785–1863) and his brother Wilhelm (1786–1859), following their expulsion from Göttingen as members of the *Göttinger Sieben*, the *Deutsches Wörterbuch* was completed only in 1960. In its 32 bound volumes, this work remains the greatest German dictionary on historical principles, and a huge storehouse of textual examples. Planned at the cutting edge of nineteenth-century historical philology, it was also intended by this pair of liberals as a deeply political statement, offered 'auf des geliebten vaterlandes altar', with the aim of uniting the still highly fragmented German-speaking peoples, and so defining a nation. 'Was haben wir denn gemeinsames als unsere sprache und literatur?', Jacob himself asked. He even quaintly saw the dictionary as a popular work, for reading perhaps of an evening within the family circle: 'warum sollte sich nicht der vater ein paar wörter ausheben und sie abends mit den knaben durchgehend zugleich ihre sprachgabe prüfen und die eigne anfrischen? die mutter würde gern zuhören' (Vorrede (1854), XIII).

 Grimm Deutsches Wörterbuch has been labelled a product of German Romanticism and thus a reaction to the dry rationalism of the *Aufklärung*. The labelling is in some ways apt, but not sufficiently precise. Supposedly Romantic features include the Grimms' interest in the Middle Ages and in modern dialects, their partly intuitive approach to linguistic questions, and their reliance on metaphor, especially the nowadays outdated metaphor of language as a living organism. It could easily be argued that all these features are essentially pre-Romantic. In any case, the simple label 'Romantic' fails to do justice to the Grimms' massive intellectual achievement, notably in the development of historical-comparative philology.

Their emotional engagement cannot be denied. There was so much for people to discover: 'die sprache ist allen bekannt und allen ein geheimnis' (Vorrede, XII). The new dictionary was intended to reveal and celebrate the historical and regional richness of the German national language. Jacob is sometimes seen as an antiquarian of language, and indeed he could claim nostalgically in his preface: 'Den leuchtenden gesetzen der ältesten sprache nachspürend verzichtet man lange zeit auf die abgeblichenen der von heute'. But in an equally significant balancing statement the 'washed-out' modern German language is seen as having its attractions too: 'sie bietet [...] einen ohne alles verhältnis gröszern, in sich selbst zusammenhängenden und ausgeglichenen reichthum dar, der schwere verluste, die sie erlitten hat, vergessen macht' (Vorrede, IV).

From the start, the Grimms' dictionary had its quirks: a selective antipathy to foreign words (XXVIff.); a dismissive attitude towards derivatives and especially compounds ('jedes einfache wort wiegt an gehalt funfzig ableitungen und jede ableitung zehn zusammensetzungen auf' (XLIII)); the choice of modern-seeming roman type and non-capitalization; and the adoption of a strictly alphabetical order which disrupted word-families. Contemporaries also complained about the Protestant bias – Jacob's all too forthright response being that, in their use of German during the period in question, Protestant writers had achieved more than Catholics: 'dasz dabei die protestantische färbung vorherscht folgt aus der überlegenheit der protestantischen poesie und sprachbildung' (XXXVIII). He could be equally withering about the hallowed German classics: Friedrich Schiller is 'poor in words [...] no true master of our language' (Kirkness 1980: 70).

Conceived as a six- or seven-volume work, this 'sanctuary of language' (as Jacob described it) was based on the excerption of texts from Luther to Goethe. This task was delegated to over 80 part-time readers, with predictable variations in approach and thoroughness. By the late 1840s, with over 600,000 quotation slips sorted and ready, Jacob began the redaction of letters A, B and C, reserving D for his brother Wilhelm. They were covering four centuries of literature, rather than the seven centuries which the *Oxford English Dictionary* was later to span, but it seems that they were doing so with only one-eighth of the material at the disposal of the *OED*. The dictionary lay like a leaden weight across the Grimms' later years. Wilhelm completed only letter D, and Jacob died (in his own words) still 'ploughing in F' (Kirkness 1980: 251). It is clear from the strained correspondence with his publisher Hirzel that the ageing Jacob had refused to bring in additional helpers, still less to hand over to a team of assistants trained in his method – a method which was in any case never fully and explicitly stated, our best sources being the extensive preface of 1854 and the documentation as presented in particular by Alan Kirkness (1980 onwards).

After Jacob's death in 1863, the project passed into many other hands. The four distinct institutional phases of its production were to absorb the energies of generations of Germanists, as well as reflecting a series of political upheavals: the founding of Bismarck's Germany, the Wilhelmine period, First World War, Weimar Republic, the Nazi dictatorship, the post-war division of Germany. The work was completed only in 1960, comprising nearly 34,000 pages and nearly half a million headwords. The dictionary was mocked journalistically by Eckehard Boehlich as a 'Pyrrhic victory': parodying *Look back in anger* he gave another of his articles the title 'Blick zurück im Grimm' (quoted in Haß-Zumkehr 2001: 139). Criticism focused on some indefensible gaps (no entries for *Kultur, Literatur, Logik* etc.), the work's politically and linguistically conservative character in its choice of headwords, definitions and examples (after a century how could it possibly be otherwise?), and the extreme unevenness of method across the alphabet.

With all its defects, Grimm remains a primary source in historical German lexicology, the supreme metatext, based on about 25,000 textual sources, of which admittedly only about 10% have been fully searched. I recently came to know its strengths and weaknesses intimately as I scoured it from end to end in search of German colour terms, and found many thousands of them. But the unevenness of treatment was all too apparent. The adjectives *blau* and *braun*, as published in 1860, are covered in barely two columns each, but *grün* (1932–3) takes up 20 columns, and *grau* (1958) 25 columns. In general, the longest entries of *Grimm Deutsches Wörterbuch* are probably unique in lexicography world-wide: some amount to small monographs in themselves.

'Zwei spinnen sind auf die kräuter dieses wortgartens gekrochen und haben ihr gift ausgelassen', wrote Jacob Grimm in 1854. He was referring partly to a reasoned critique of the *Deutsches Wörterbuch* which Daniel Sanders (1819–1897) had recently published. As Ulrike Haß-Zumkehr has shown, Sanders deserves closer attention for his own lexicographical achievement. I would myself rank his *Wörterbuch der deutschen Sprache* (1860–5) as (within its own limited terms of reference) the most perfectly designed and executed German dictionary of the nineteenth century – despite its typography, which is partly in an unkind 9-point Fraktur. There are many points of contrast with Grimm. Sanders has fewer examples, drawn from a more restricted chronological range. Semantically, he is not interested in diversity of meaning as a diachronic process, but rather as a synchronic state: the range of meanings as he felt they existed in the 1860s. He is much more receptive to contemporary vocabulary, including specialized and technical terms; and words of foreign origin are admitted, running at about 6% of the total. Under the noun *Blau*, for example, he lists over 60 compounds including *Äther-*, *Azur-*, *Cyanen-*, *Indigo-*, *Louisen-*, *Solid-*, *Turnbull-* and *Ultramarin-Blau*. This is an extensive work comprising ca. 220,000 headwords, usually bound as three volumes, and essentially the brainchild of a modern educator: Sanders taught privately for many years in his native Mecklenburg. He avoids rigid alphabetization, instead nesting many compounds and derivatives under their base word, so *Milchweiß* must be sought under *Weiß*, and *verbleichen* under the simplex verb *bleichen*. His evaluative comments are restrained and non-dictatorial. But above all, this dictionary can be admired for consistency of method and uniformity of execution, across the entire alphabet.

Sanders can be further credited with an extensive dictionary of foreign words, and a uniquely copious German thesaurus, the *Deutscher Sprachschatz* (1873–7). This was the first cumulative synonymic dictionary of German, 'ein unschätzbares Zeitdenkmal für den Sprachstand des 19. Jahrhunderts' (Peter Kühn, introduction to vol. 1 of the reprint (1985)). Based on the English *Thesaurus* ('treasury') (1852) of Peter Mark Roget (1779–1869), Sanders's *Sprachschatz* surpassed its model in richness, offering many more items of vocabulary, including archaic, colloquial, dialectal, specialized and foreign words, orthographical variants, ad-hoc compounds, and other types. Following Roget, he presents his colour terms (sections 306–19), using parallel columns and the headings *Farbe/Farblosigkeit*, *Einfarbigkeit/Buntheit*,

Weiß/Schwarz, Grau/Braun, Roth/Grün, Gelb/Violett, Blau/Orange (Hüllen 2003). In each article, again following Roget, word-classes are presented in the order: nouns, verbs, adjectives/adverbs; one effect of this is to emphasize the abstract terms, which Sanders generously provides (e.g. *Blau; das Blaue; Bläue; Blauheit; Blaulichkeit; Bläulichkeit*). His lists are peppered with markers like *z.B., etc., u.ä.m., u.s.w.*, and this open-endedness is again evident in combinatory sequences such as '*purpur-; rosen-; rubin- etc. -farb(en), -farbig* [...]', the multiplying effect of which is considerable. As synonyms under *blau* Sanders lists over 60 nouns, ten verbs and no fewer than 125 adjectives. In quantity and range, and in its sense of open lexical productivity, Sanders's *Sprachschatz* lies well ahead of later synonymic dictionaries. We again receive a humbling picture of enormous lexicographical industry and dedication, compounded in Sanders's case by his exclusion as a Jew from many walks of life including that of a university academic or a grammar school teacher. It could be claimed that, in their quieter way, the successive editions of his works influenced a wider range of people than any of the other dictionaries which I have so far mentioned.

The appended diagram may help to illustrate the growth of German lexicography and of the German vocabulary itself during the period in question, with some later examples for comparison. These estimates of the number of headwords should be treated with caution for a number of reasons; and naturally the figures themselves say nothing about the quality of individual entries.

Some newer landmarks

Many further landmarks are to be found in German lexicography since the late nineteenth century, and I would like to touch on a few, notably in the fields of dialect, language history, spelling and foreign words.

German dialect had been valued already in the seventeenth century (for example by Leibniz) as a treasury or museum of the past, as a key to etymologies, and as a source of enrichment for the modern language. From the eighteenth century, vocabularies were compiled to assist professional users of standardized German in communicating with dialect speakers. As the status of the standard language became assured, dialect too was approached more positively: in the late eighteenth, nineteenth and early twentieth centuries scholars sensed the need to document rural forms of speech now under threat from increasing urbanization and standardization. On this basis, German dialect materials were systematically collected, leading to a range of big dialect dictionaries unique for any language. Most areas are now covered lexicographically; a few dialect dictionaries are still in progress. The great dictionary of Swiss dialects, the *Schweizerisches Idiotikon* (*Wörterbuch der schweizerdeutschen Sprache*), begun in 1862, is now somewhere in letter W with completion foreseen round about 2015, totalling 17 volumes.

For older historical periods, German lexicography is notoriously incomplete. The Old High German dictionary begun in 1935 by Theodor Frings, Elisabeth Karg-Gasterstädt and others, a work of the highest scholarship, has now reached letter J. The much more recent Early New High German dictionary (too modestly described by one of its editors as 'ambitious, foolhardy and desperate') has been farmed out to a team of compilers, with perhaps one third of the alphabet so far published. Deplorably, our best Middle High German dictionaries date from the 1850s and 1870s and reflect the incomplete coverage of sources and dubious editorial practices of those years. From highly important initiatives in Trier and Göttingen (Kurt Gärtner and Klaus Grubmüller), we are promised a fine new MHG dictionary – by 2030.

Next, we come to a single volume which has served the needs of five political epochs. The authoritative dictionary of German spelling, founded by Konrad Duden in 1880, has since appeared in some 25 revised editions. Adopted as the basis for spelling reform in Wilhelmine Germany, the Duden *Rechtschreibung* gradually expanded over the years; in 1934 it was quickly Nazified; in the postwar years we find it grotesquely divided between east and west, with rival Dudens of divergent character appearing in Leipzig and Mannheim; and eventually in the 1990s it was in a sense reunified, but largely on a Western basis. And for another example of how language and ideology condition one another, we turn to the East German *Wörterbuch der deutschen Gegenwartssprache (WDG)* produced in six volumes under the editorship of Ruth Klappenbach and others from the 1950s. The tortuous evolution of this work clearly illustrates the external pressures acting upon a lexicographer whose role has been changed by circumstances, in this case the East German regime's insistence on the alignment of the dictionary, its definitions and its examples, to the Marxist-Leninist world-view.

The name Duden was developed commercially in an ever-growing series of publications by the Duden-Verlag, which would be a study in itself. Space allows us here only to mention the controversial history of Duden, *Das Große Wörterbuch der deutschen Sprache* in its alleged early dependence on *WDG* and in its growth from six to ten volumes in successive editions from 1976 to 1999 (see in particular Haß-Zumkehr 2001: 233–50). Likewise, we must pass rapidly over

- major individual and cumulative achievements in bilingual (especially German–French and German–English) lexicography from the eighteenth century onwards: names such as Muret-Sanders, Langenscheidt and Sachs-Villatte have been familiar to generations of learners across the twentieth century and beyond

- the advent of etymological dictionaries (notably the successive editions of Friedrich Kluge's work)

- the lengthy tradition of Hermann Paul, *Deutsches Wörterbuch* (many revisions since 1897, 10th edition 2002), noted for its selective incorporation of historical data into a modern dictionary, and for its sensitivity to semantic and morphological relationships between lexical items (Haß-Zumkehr 2001: 183–201)

- the lexicographical cataloguing of synonyms, for example Daniel Sanders, Franz Dornseiff, Wehrle-Eggers (outlined by Haß-Zumkehr 2001: 264–90), as an escape from alphabetical fragmentation into the more integrated world of semantic structures and relationships.

Nor would our sketch approach adequacy without a mention of that specially German product, the *Fremdwörterbuch*, to which few parallels exist in other languages. Foreign-word dictionaries, with various functions, have been appearing since 1571. The category itself is linguistically debatable, because the words concerned are no longer strictly foreign (aliens), but immigrants of varying linguistic status, leading some modern scholars to deplore the ghettoization of so-called foreign vocabulary in a separate work. Two examples of the genre are worth highlighting here as works of scholarship. The *Deutsches Fremdwörterbuch* was in preparation from the early years of the twentieth century and completed in 1984 at the Institut für deutsche Sprache (Mannheim) as a selective historical dictionary of established loanwords, tracing changes of form, function and meaning on the basis of cited textual examples from all periods. A second edition is in progress, the plan being to re-work letters A to Q to the same standard as letters R–Z. More specialized again is the *Anglizismen-Wörterbuch* edited by the late Broder Carstensen and others, an important scholarly tool in three volumes published between 1993 and 1996 (now also in a paperback version), and dealing with approximately 3,500 Anglicisms judged to be most current in modern German. This work is complete, but only in one sense, because like all contemporary lexicography it was chasing a fast moving target.

Meanwhile, *Grimm Deutsches Wörterbuch* has been born again, in three distinct forms.

- The original edition was successfully reprinted in 1984 as 33 paperback volumes.

- A new edition, covering the oldest and weakest portion, letters A–F, has been gestating since 1957, its redaction earlier shared between East and West (Berlin and Göttingen). There are probably now some 20 people working full-time on it, and the plan is to complete letters A–F in ten projected volumes rather than the original three and a half. But even in pursuit of this aim, drastic and damaging reductions in the extent and detail of the work have been imposed, implying cuts of well over 25%.

- Thanks to the initiatives of Kurt Gärtner and others in Trier, the whole of the first edition became available in 2004 on CD-ROM at an affordable price (and is now accessible online) – answering, incidentally, the Grimms' early hope that their dictionary might truly become a household book. Its 33 volumes (some 300 million characters) were transcribed manually twice over in China, using two independent data entry bureaux from 1998 onwards, and collated and further corrected in Trier. This is a priceless resource: the standard of transcription is generally high, though not entirely flawless, and the accompanying search engines are helpful, if still limited by many of the shortcomings and inconsistencies of the original work.

Grimm Deutsches Wörterbuch continues to stimulate discussion, as in Volker Harm's article (2005): he notes its inability to deal adequately with word-families, word-fields and sociological aspects, and himself indicates some new paths in historical lexicography, notably a post-1700 dictionary or 'Wissensspeicher', to be made available electronically as a database.

In search of dictionaries

Since the work of Helmut Henne and others, a canon of German lexico-graphical landmarks has rightly come to be recognized, and so far I have mainly tried to evoke a series of 'great names'. Several years ago I decided to look systematically beyond the canon, and to compile a descriptive biblio-graphy of seventeenth-century dictionaries of German, hoping to unearth perhaps 50 such works. My baby grew alarmingly, if also excitingly, and in the book that was published (Jones 2000), I found myself describing over a thousand items from the seventeenth century alone, in the knowledge that many more still await discovery. I now hope to see this work continued into the eighteenth, nineteenth and twentieth centuries, where there are still huge gaps in bibliographical research of this kind.

Mostly these works were bilingual or multilingual dictionaries, com-bining German with one or more languages, occasionally ten or more at a time, including Latin, Greek, Hebrew, French, Italian, Spanish, Portuguese, Dutch, English, Danish, Swedish, Polish, Czech, Sorbian, Croat, Slovene, Russian, Latvian, Lithuanian, Estonian, Finnish, Hungarian, Arabic, Persian and Turkish. This international dimension is a key feature of the period. Latin vocabulary is found in nearly all the works listed and, next to this, German is most likely to be found alongside French and Italian.

The variety of types came as a surprise: already before 1700 there were German dictionaries of synonyms, idioms, rhymes, dialect, criminal jargon,

'foreign' words, and a range of specialized vocabulary (theological, philosophical, musical, administrative, legal, military, nautical, mathematical, commercial, medical, pharmaceutical, mining, zoological, botanical, etc.). Even
at that stage, the vocabulary of German was too diversified for most practical lexicographers to treat it comprehensively as a unity. The bibliography
contains some monumental tomes, justly respected as landmarks in German
lexicography. But there are many humbler, and perhaps more representative
and influential, works which met specific needs of language users, including
learners and teachers, traders, travellers, administrators, and specialists in
many fields.

Most of these dictionaries are arranged more or less alphabetically, an odd
exception being the rather inaptly named *Lexique François–Allemant tresample*
(Frankfurt am Main, 1631), which is sectionalized by parts of speech, but also
lists words in the intricate, phonetically motivated order A E I O U Y S L R M
N F V W H B P D T C K G Q Z X J. Other works are ordered semantically
by subject, structuring knowledge in many different ways. These classified
(topical) dictionaries are the most extreme departure from the alphabetical
principle. Over 20 different classificatory systems can be illustrated from my
seventeenth-century material, occasionally with several hierarchical levels;
some of these topical systems are rooted in antiquity (notably Aristotle),
whilst others were evidently home-made. Several systems are based on 50
categories, and were designed to fit the weeks of the year (one topic a week)
in a crowded school curriculum with maybe two weeks allowed for holidays!
There are some curious insights into educational practice, for example the
rhymed Latin–German dictionaries: to assist learners in schools, a work of
1616 presents Latin vocabulary in semantically classified sections, with the
simple rhymed lists of the type *Bellum – Krieg; Victoria – Sieg*.

German bibliography is tantalizing for this entire period. The pluricentric
nature of German, Austrian and Swiss politics, society and culture, which persisted well into the nineteenth century and beyond, caused book production
to be spread over many locations, and library collections to be established in
many different places. Two world wars and their aftermath led to the destruction or dispersal of exceptionally large collections, for example in Heidelberg,
Darmstadt and Hamburg. Visiting Dresden in 1999, I was thankful to find
about 60% of their dictionary holdings still preserved, but in some of their
other subject areas virtually nothing survived the Allied bombing raids of 1945.

In Berlin during the 1940s, the contents of the Staatsbibliothek were dispersed in haste to 29 sites, and only about one-fifth of the older stock is now available. Many items were destroyed in their new, supposedly safe havens, many books were improperly disposed of, and some are only gradually becoming accessible in Polish, Czech and Russian libraries.

Searching for copies has been revolutionized by the availability of library catalogues on Internet, but coverage is still patchy and sometimes inaccurate. Many of the works are great rarities, surviving only in a very few copies. Of the items known to me from the years 1600–1700, only about 50% survive in one or other of the four leading libraries for this purpose, in Wolfenbüttel, Munich, Vienna and London. The remaining 50% have needed to be located elsewhere, in over 200 libraries across 20 or more countries. Designed often for use in practical circumstances, dictionaries were apt to disappear from libraries through wear and tear as well as theft, and older editions, if not worn out, were discarded, or passed into private hands, as newer editions became available. School texts and other modest publications probably suffered more in this way than the monumental works, which are relatively well preserved: of Kaspar Stieler's dictionary (1691) there are upwards of 80 copies surviving world-wide, but of an anonymous 568-page *Nomenclator latino-germanicus* (1693), compiled for use in Hamburg schools and selling at perhaps one-tenth of the cost of Stieler, only one copy came to light in my searches.

Dictionaries form a special case bibliographically, with patterns of publication which are in some ways different from other text types. There is a high proportion of anonymous works (about 15% of the total) and sometimes a series of posthumous editions with the names of the continuators gaining ascendancy over the originators of the work. Practical (as opposed to monumental) lexicography was often seen as low-grade, mechanistic, collective work, perhaps performed obscurely within the family or with unpaid student help – assistance not always felt to merit recognition on the titlepage or in the preface, and certainly not attracting the respect for copyright which we would nowadays attach to intellectual property. Dead or alive, the lexicographer was fair game to the vulture plagiarism, and complaints about this are commonly found. Occasionally already, a dictionary becomes known under the name of its publisher, a tradition familiar to us today with corporate names like Collins, Harrap, Langenscheidt, Duden, though the aim nowadays is to convey an impression of impersonal authority and permanence.

In the seventeenth century we find as yet little attempt to convey pronunciation within the dictionary. There is some interest already in German
etymology (sometimes accurate, sometimes undisciplined), also in dialect: for
High German, it seems that the Bavarians got there first with Johann Ludwig
Prasch's glossaries (1686–9); and arguments developed by Sheila Watts (2001)
suggest that Schottelius, the leading German linguist of his century and an
advocate of a supraregional High German, may in his heart of hearts have
been a dialectologist *manqué* of his native Low German.

From about 1600, bilingual dictionaries appeared, linking German
directly with modern European languages: French from 1596, Italian from
1605, Spanish from 1634, English from 1686, Dutch from 1719. But the modern
ideal of the symmetrical bilingual dictionary is scarcely to be found at this
time. More often the parts vary in the amount and nature of information supplied, with the German-based works naturally giving emphasis to the foreign
language in question. Levinus Hulsius's *Dictionarium teutsch und frantzösisch*
(Frankfurt am Main, 1607) is typically lop-sided, with a German–French
section about 35% longer than the French–German one.

The still pivotal position of Latin is well shown in the case of Peter Lode-
recker's *Dictionarium septem diversarum linguarium* (Prague, 1605), which
contains a seven-language Latin–French–Italian–Czech–Polish–German–
Hungarian section; then sections pairing each of these modern languages
with Latin (Italian–Latin, Croatian–Latin etc.). As a result in this work,
equivalences between pairs of modern languages can only be found indirectly,
via the Latin section.

In a highly important study, Peter Müller (2001) has stressed the continuities that connect lexicography of the sixteenth and seventeenth centuries:
several sixteenth-century dictionaries went on being revised and re-issued after
1600. My findings in part endorse that view as far as practical (rather than
scholarly) lexicography is concerned, at least in the first half of the century,
and I would claim something similar for the eighteenth century, where we
find many re-issues of works launched well before 1700. This momentum is
typical of the genre, and would be obvious wherever the chronological cut
was made. Dictionaries are rarely if ever written from scratch; their makers
build on traditions, perhaps critically, perhaps mindlessly; and the *Wortschatz*
or word-hoard becomes just that: a cumulative investment of time, labour
and money, which later practitioners are reluctant to disregard, even when

paradigms and ideologies have changed. But to balance this partial image of unending repetition we should note also

- the demonstrable impact of external forces (e.g. Schottelius's and Leibniz's new programmes as realized by Stieler and (in part) Frisch respectively)

- the creation of new dictionaries as a conscious, even hostile, reaction to what has gone before (e.g. Kramer's dictionary as a response to Hulsius, or Campe's as an alternative to Adelung)

- the massive injection of labour and other resources by individuals and their supporters (Kramer, Adelung, the Grimms, Sanders and many others).

The commitment of certain publishers and the number of editions show that, in general, dictionary publishing made excellent commercial sense, though it is very noticeable that until Adelung most of the dictionaries focusing on German (Maaler, Henisch, Stieler, Frisch) never went into a second edition, whereas the Latin–German, French–German and other dictionary types regularly did, catering typically for educational markets, fashionable cross-cultural links, and the needs of travel and commerce.

The labour involved must have been enormous for all concerned. Perhaps the most humbling aspect arises from the practicalities of printing during the early modern period. Typesetting a large dictionary would have had to be interrupted countless times in the print shop by more urgent work. In any case, a printer before about 1700 only had enough metal type in stock to print perhaps 16 pages of an average-sized quarto volume at a time, after which the type had to be manually distributed and then re-used for the next 16 pages. Maintaining accuracy and consistency in these circumstances would be a challenge to any compositor. And naturally every new edition had to be re-set from scratch, because no printer could afford to keep even part of a work in standing type from one printing to the next.

It was commonplace among practitioners to label dictionary-making 'the toil of the damned'. In fact, we know as yet little about the process of creating dictionaries in earlier times: there are many detailed questions regarding the use of sources, methods of compilation and revision, and the habits and demands of dictionary users. We certainly know of people who read dictionaries from cover to cover as if they were normal books. A copy of Heinrich Decimator's *Thesaurus linguarum* (Magdeburg, 1614) in Halle University Library, comprising some 1,500 pages, has on its titlepage a proud handwritten note, 'Perlegi' ('I have read this through') and the date, 1707. I am always intrigued by the position of the lexicographer, whether damned or not in his vocation, but sometimes blessed by a wife and children who assisted and carried forward his work. Hulsius's pioneering French and German dictionary re-appeared posthumously in 1607, published at the expense of his widow, and with the dedication signed by his two sons. Kramer's work was supported and continued by his son. Lexicography was a part-time activity for the compilers of all these seventeenth-century dictionaries. How did they find the time? How did they compile, store and edit their material? How did you set about converting a Latin–French into a Latin–German dictionary? or worse, turn a Latin–German into a German–Latin dictionary? How much were they paid? and so on.

In the history of German lexicography, there are many practical questions of this kind, to which researchers are only gradually finding the key.

References

Primary sources

Ordered chronologically (for other works, see the bibliography of Haß-Zumkehr (2001)).

Dasypodius, Petrus (1536), *Dictionarium Latinogermanicum* [...], Straßburg: Rihel (reprinted Hildesheim, New York: Olms, 1974).

Maaler, Josua (1561), *Die Teütsch spraach* [...], Zürich: Froschauer (reprinted Hildesheim, New York: Olms, 1971).

Henisch, Georg (1616), *Teutsche Sprach vnd Weißheit. Thesaurus linguae et sapientiae Germanicae*, Augsburg: Franck (reprinted Hildesheim, New York: Olms, 1973).

Schottelius, Justus Georg (1663), *Ausführliche Arbeit Von der Teutschen HaubtSprache* [...], Braunschweig: Zilliger (reprinted Tübingen: Niemeyer, 1967).

Stieler, Kaspar (1691), *Der Teutschen Sprache Stammbaum und Fortwachs / oder Teutscher Sprachschatz* [...], Nürnberg: Hofmann (reprints: Hildesheim, New York: Olms, 1968; Munich: Kösel, 1968).

Kramer, Matthias (1700–2), *Das herrlich Grosse Teutsch–Italiänische Dictionarium* [...] [2 vols], Nürnberg: Endter (reprinted Hildesheim, Zürich, New York: Olms, 1982)

Frisch, Johann Leonhard (1741), *Teutsch–Lateinisches Wörter-Buch* [...], Berlin: Nicolai (reprinted Hildesheim, New York: Olms, 1977).

Adelung, Johann Christoph (1774–86), *Versuch eines vollständigen grammatisch-kritischen Wörterbuches Der Hochdeutschen Mundart, mit beständiger Vergleichung der übrigen Mundarten, besonders aber der Oberdeutschen* [5 parts], Leipzig: Breitkopf.

Adelung, Johann Christoph (1782), *Umständliches Lehrgebäude der Deutschen Sprache, zur Erläuterung der Deutschen Sprachlehre für Schulen* [2 vols], Leipzig: Breitkopf.

Adelung, Johann Christoph (1793–1801), *Grammatisch-kritisches Wörterbuch der Hochdeutschen Mundart* [...] [4 parts], Leipzig: Breitkopf (reprinted Hildesheim, New York: Olms, 1970) (transcription on CD-ROM, Digitale Bibliothek, 40 (Berlin, 2001).

Campe, Joachim Heinrich (1801/13), *Wörterbuch zur Erklärung und Verdeutschung der unserer Sprache aufgedrungenen fremden Ausdrücke. Ein Ergänzungsband zu Adelungs Wörterbuche*, Braunschweig: Schulbuchhandlung, 2nd edition 1813 (reprinted Hildesheim, New York: Olms, 1969).

Campe, Joachim Heinrich (1807–13), *Wörterbuch der Deutschen Sprache* [5 parts], Braunschweig: Schulbuchhandlung (reprinted Hildesheim, New York: Olms, 1969).

Grimm, Jacob and Wilhelm (1854–1960), *Deutsches Wörterbuch* [33 vols], Leipzig: Hirzel. *Elektronische Ausgabe*, Verlag Zweitausendeins, 2004. *Neubearbeitung* (1965ff.).

Sanders, Daniel (1860–5/1876), *Wörterbuch der deutschen Sprache. Mit Belegen von Luther bis auf die Gegenwart* [2 vols in 3], Leipzig: Wigand, 2nd edition 1876 (reprinted Hildesheim, New York: Olms, 1969).

Sanders, Daniel (1873–7), *Deutscher Sprachschatz, geordnet nach Begriffen zur Auffindung und Auswahl des passenden Ausdrucks. Ein stilistisches Hilfsbuch für jeden Deutsch Schreibenden* [2 vols], Hamburg: Hoffmann & Campe (reprinted Tübingen: Niemeyer, 1985).

Kluge, Friedrich (1883 onwards), *Etymologisches Wörterbuch der deutschen Sprache*, Straßburg: Trübner 1883; 24th edition revised by Elmar Seebold, Berlin, New York: de Gruyter 2002.

Paul, Hermann (1897 onwards), *Deutsches Wörterbuch*, Halle a. S.: Niemeyer 1897; 10th edition revised and extended by Helmut Henne, Heidrun Kämper and Georg Objartel, Tübingen: Niemeyer 2002.

Deutsches Fremdwörterbuch. Begründet von Hans Schulz, fortgeführt von Otto Basler, weitergeführt im Institut für deutsche Sprache [Mannheim], bearbeitet von Alan Kirkness, Gerhard Strauß u. a. Straßburg: Trübner 1913; Berlin [etc.]: de Gruyter 1942, 1977–84; 2nd edition Berlin [etc.]: de Gruyter 1995ff.

WDG = Klappenbach, Ruth, and Wolfgang Steinitz (1961–77), *Wörterbuch der deutschen Gegenwartssprache*, Berlin: Akademie.

Duden (1976–81), *Das große Wörterbuch der deutschen Sprache in sechs Bänden*, Mannheim [etc.]: Bibliographisches Institut, Dudenverlag.

Carstensen, Broder et al. (1993–6). *Anglizismen-Wörterbuch. Der Einfluß des Englischen auf den deutschen Wortschatz nach 1945*, begründet von Broder Carstensen, fortgeführt von Ulrich Busse unter Mitarbeit von Regina Schmude. Berlin, New York: de Gruyter.

Bibliography

Dill, G. (1992), *Johann Christoph Adelungs Wörterbuch der 'Hochdeutschen Mundart'. Untersuchungen zur lexikographischen Konzeption*, Frankfurt am Main [etc.]: Peter Lang (Europäische Hochschulschriften I/1303).

Dückert, J. (ed.) (1987), *Das Grimmsche Wörterbuch. Untersuchungen zur lexikographischen Methodologie*, Leipzig: Hirzel.

Gardt, A. (1999), *Geschichte der Sprachwissenschaft in Deutschland. Vom Mittelalter bis ins 20. Jahrhundert*, Berlin, New York: de Gruyter (pp. 252–67 on Adelung and Grimm).

Harm, V. (2005), 'Perspektiven auf die sprachhistorische Lexikographie *nach* dem deutschen Wörterbuch', *Zeitschrift für germanistische Linguistik* 33, 92–105.

Haß-Zumkehr, U. (1995), *Daniel Sanders. Aufgeklärte Germanistik im 19. Jahrhundert*. Berlin, New York: de Gruyter (Studia Linguistica Germanica 35).

Haß-Zumkehr, U. (2001), *Deutsche Wörterbücher – Brennpunkt von Sprach- und Kulturgeschichte*, Berlin and New York: de Gruyter.

Hausmann, F.J. et al. (eds) (1989–91), *Wörterbücher. Ein internationales Handbuch zur Lexikographie* [3 vols], Berlin and New York: de Gruyter (Handbücher zur Sprach- und Kommunikationswissenschaft 5.1–3) (in particular, the articles by Oskar Reichmann, 'Geschichte lexikographischer Programme in Deutschland' (230–46), Klaus Grubmüller, 'Die deutsche Lexikographie von den Anfängen bis zur Beginn des 17. Jahrhunderts' (2037–49); Peter Kühn and Ulrich Püschel, 'Die deutsche Lexikographie vom 17. Jahrhundert bis zu den Brüdern Grimm ausschließlich' (2049–77), and Kühn/Püschel, 'Die deutsche Lexikographie von den Brüdern Grimm bis Trübner' (2078–100)).

Henne, H. (ed.) (1975), *Deutsche Wörterbücher des 17. und 18. Jahrhunderts. Einführung und Bibliographie*, Hildesheim and New York: Olms; reprinted 2001.

Hüllen, W. (2003), 'Die Adaptation von Rogets *Thesaurus* in Daniel Sanders' *Sprachschatz*', in: '*Vir ingenio mirandus*'. *Studies presented to John L. Flood*, edited by

William J. Jones, William A. Kelly and Frank Shaw, Göppingen: Kümmerle (Göppinger Arbeiten zur Germanistik 710), 897–919.

Hundt, M. (2000), *'Spracharbeit' im 17. Jahrhundert. Studien zu Georg Philipp Harsdörffer, Justus Georg Schottelius und Christian Gueintz*, Berlin and New York: de Gruyter (Studia Linguistica Germanica 57).

Ising, G. (1956), *Die Erfassung der deutschen Sprache des ausgehenden 17. Jahrhunderts in den Wörterbüchern Matthias Kramers und Kaspar Stielers*, Berlin: Akademie.

Jellinek, M.H. (1913–14), *Geschichte der neuhochdeutschen Grammatik von den Anfängen bis auf Adelung*, [2 vols], Heidelberg: Winter. (I, 329–85 on Adelung).

Jones, W.J. (2000), *German Lexicography in the European Context. A descriptive bibliography of printed dictionaries and word lists containing German language (1600–1700)*, Berlin and New York: de Gruyter (Studia Linguistica Germanica 58).

Kirkness, A. (1980), *Geschichte des Deutschen Wörterbuchs 1838–63. Dokumente zu den Lexikographen Grimm*, Stuttgart: Hirzel.

Kirkness, A. et al. (eds) (1991), *Studien zum Deutschen Wörterbuch von Jacob Grimm und Wilhelm Grimm* [2 vols], Tübingen: Niemeyer.

Müller, P.O. (2001), *Deutsche Lexikographie des 16. Jahrhunderts. Konzeptionen und Funktionen frühneuzeitlicher Wörterbücher*, Tübingen: Niemeyer (Texte und Textgeschichte 49).

Orgeldinger, S. (1999), *Standardisierung und Purismus bei Joachim Heinrich Campe*, Berlin and New York: de Gruyter (Studia Linguistica Germanica 51).

Polenz, P. von (1994), *Deutsche Sprachgeschichte vom Spätmittelalter bis zur Gegenwart. Band II: 17. und 18. Jahrhundert*, Berlin and New York: de Gruyter (pp. 126–33 and 181–99).

Powitz, G. (1959), *Das deutsche Wörterbuch Johann Leonhard Frischs*, Berlin: Akademie.

Schneider, R. (1995), *Der Einfluß von Justus Georg Schottelius auf die deutschsprachige Lexikographie des 17./18. Jahrhunderts*, Frankfurt am Main [etc.]: Peter Lang (Theorie und Vermittlung der Sprache 21).

Strohbach, M. (1984), *Johann Christoph Adelung. Ein Beitrag zu seinem germanistischen Schaffen mit einer Bibliographie seines Gesamtwerkes*, Berlin, New York: de Gruyter (Studia Linguistica Germanica 21).

Szlęk, S.P. (1999), *Zur deutschen Lexikographie bis Jacob Grimm. Wörterbuchprogramme, Wörterbücher und Wörterbuchkritik*, Bern [etc.]: Peter Lang.

Watts, S. (2001), '"Wer kan wider eines gantzen Landes Gewohnheit?" Justus Georg Schottelius as a dialectologist', in: *'Proper Words in Proper Places'. Studies in Lexicology and Lexicography in Honour of William Jervis Jones*, edited by M.C. Davies, J.L. Flood and D.N. Yeandle, Stuttgart: Heinz, 101–14. (Stuttgarter Arbeiten zur Germanistik 400).

Wells, C.J. (1985), *German: a Linguistic History to 1945*, Oxford: Clarendon (pp. 332–41 on Adelung).

Wells, C.J. (2001), 'Aspects of archaism in Adelung', in: *'Proper Words in Proper Places'. Studies in Lexicology and Lexicography in Honour of William Jervis Jones*, edited by M.C. Davies, J.L. Flood and D.N. Yeandle, Stuttgart: Heinz, 133–63.

West, J. (1989), *Lexical Innovation in Dasypodius's Dictionary. A contribution to the study of the development of the Early Modern German Lexicon based on Petrus Dasypodius' Dictionarium Latinogermanicum, Straßburg 1536*, Berlin and New York: de Gruyter (Studia Linguistica Germanica 24).

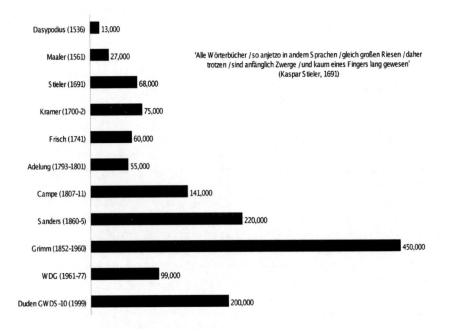

Headwords in German dictionaries (estimated)

Dictionary	Headwords
Dasypodius (1536)	13,000
Maaler (1561)	27,000
Stieler (1691)	68,000
Kramer (1700-2)	75,000
Frisch (1741)	60,000
Adelung (1793-1801)	55,000
Campe (1807-11)	141,000
Sanders (1860-5)	220,000
Grimm (1852-1960)	450,000
WDG (1961-77)	99,000
Duden GWDS-10 (1999)	200,000

'Alle Wörterbücher / so anjetzo in andern Sprachen / gleich großen Riesen / daher trotzen / sind anfänglich Zwerge / und kaum eines Fingers lang gewesen' (Kaspar Stieler, 1691)

Diagram of Headwords in German dictionaries

MARIA B. LANGE

Texts and Text Types in the History of German

Text linguistics: introduction, history, and problems

The term *text linguistics* in its widest sense refers to the interdisciplinary study of texts and their use and, in this sense, text linguistic research can take place in a wide range of fields, such as psychology or sociology. In a more strictly linguistic sense, text linguistics is the discipline devoted to establishing the general principles of text constitution. Its central concepts are those of text and textual coherence.

Coherence is understood to be the underlying organizational principle of a text, which accounts for its functional connectedness or textuality (Halliday/Hasan 1976).[1] Sequences of sentences are defined as being coherent if they are syntactically and/or thematically connected. It is a fundamental task of text linguistics to specify the conditions under which textual coherence is achieved.

The existence of coherence is one of the prerequisites for the identification of text, which can be defined as a coherent sequence of linguistic signs with a communicative function (cf. *Textkohärenz* and *Textlinguistik* in Lewandowski 1994). As *text* and *textuality* are used differently according to tradition and focus, a generally accepted definition of the terms is still considered to be one of the central aims of text linguistics (cf. Schoenke 2000: 126).

While text linguistics evolved in the 1960s as an independent discipline, from the 1990s onwards it has often been seen as a tool of other linguistic disciplines such as pragmatics, conversation analysis, communication studies,

---

1   Textuality also considers a variety of extralinguistic concepts, such as the language users' knowledge of the world, their inferences and assumptions, and the way they communicate (in other words, textuality is culturally dependent). For a concise definition see Finch (2000: 210ff.).

media studies, and intercultural linguistics. Within the field of linguistics text linguistics is important for the study of a host of other subjects, such as conversational and discourse analysis, pragmatics, special languages, semiotics, aphasia, foreign language studies.[2]

The first part of this paper will give an overview of the history of text linguistics as a discipline, explaining the interest of text linguistics in text typologies and describing the range of attempts towards a definition of the term text type that has been made over the years. The differences in approach between text linguistics in German-speaking and English-speaking countries will be discussed, and a prominent approach to text linguistics within the German-speaking tradition will be introduced. In the second part of this paper we will focus on historical text linguistics, outlining specific problems of this area and summarizing tendencies in the development of Middle High German, Early New High German, and New High German text types. Despite the problems, the conclusion offers strong support for the evolving discipline of historical text linguistics.

Text typology

Knowledge of different text types such as letters, news reports, or recipes is an integral part of speakers' intuitive knowledge about texts. On the basis of everyday language use, speakers acquire a vague but complex knowledge of frequently occurring text types, especially when these are clearly standardized. Thanks to their experience with communication, they not only identify relevant text types but can also react to them according to situation and social context and they can usually reproduce the relevant text types adequately. This intuitive knowledge of text types is expanded more or less systematically

---

2   Kalverkämper (2000: 10) identifies the following characteristics of texts as the reason for this interest: the importance of the medium for communication, the importance of linguistic, situational, and factual contexts, the specific use and functions of texts, and the ability to create specific texts addressing individual aspects of the communication situation (or to deal with them respectively).

by schooling and in the work context, especially in text types relevant for interpersonal communication, but also in literary and journalistic text types. It has been shown that once speakers have been trained in some text types, the recognition and handling of new text types becomes much easier (Heinemann 1991, 2000: 507).

The observation that certain structures and expressions are recurrent in some texts while they are absent in others has led linguists to the conclusion that texts are governed by certain rules which are determined by their belonging to a certain category (*Textsortengeprägtheit*; Heinemann 2000: 508; cf. de Beaugrande/Dressler 1981, 188 and Brinker 2005: 138ff.). Three features have been determined as being decisive for the categorization of texts: their function (e.g. instruction, news report, promise), the communicative situation (e.g. telephone conversation, letter, newspaper article) and their content (e.g. weather report, marriage certificate, recipe; cf. Brinker 2005: 141f.). The study of text types is one of the fundamental aims of text linguistics, which according to Heinemann (2000: 508) strives to understand the intuitive knowledge of speakers about text types, to define the term text type and to recognize its relevant constituents, to describe the specific way text types use linguistic signs to fulfil certain communicative functions, to grasp any existing systematic links between individual text types, using them to develop a typology of text types, and to develop didactic recommendations for the everyday use of relevant text types and the expansion of text-type-related knowledge in specific areas.

Definitions of text type

Despite a great number of publications in the field (see Adamzik 1995 for an overview up to that date; cf. further articles in Brinker et al. 2000), text linguists have not yet reached agreement on more than a very basic definition of the term text type. An early definition had already been stated in 1964 by Peter Hartmann (1964b: 23), who said that text types were 'groups of texts sharing certain characteristics'. But this general statement or even Hartmann's revised definition of text types as 'sets of texts which can be characterized and distinguished by certain relevant features' (1971: 22 and in Heinemann 2000: 509) does not function as a satisfactory tool for the categorization of texts.[3]

A great number and variety of approaches trace the evasive characteristics that allow the differentiation of text types (for details see Heinemann 2000: 509ff. and Schoenke 2000: 125ff.). After unsatisfactory attempts to characterize text types by focusing on one dimension only, such as a text's structure, content, situational context, or function, it became clear that phenomena as complex as texts were not to be understood using one-dimensional models only. Therefore, a multitude of models were developed which combined several dimensions. These were based on the view that different text types are characterized by a combination of varying factors (Heinemann 2000: 513). Depending on the perception and evaluation of these dimensions, they led to models of text types with three to six dimensions (for examples see ibid. 513f. and cf. also Schuster 2004: 43ff.).

Despite the differences in definitions, most linguists will agree that the following aspects are necessary to determine the concept text type (cf. Heinemann, ibid. 513ff.):

i) Text types are limited sets of samples of actual texts with specific shared characteristics.

ii) The shared characteristics of textual samples of one text type occur in several dimensions at the same time:

– the physical form of the texts
– the characteristic structure, i.e. the use of linguistic means in the texts
– the situational conditions, including the medium of the texts
– the communicative function of the texts.

The characteristics of all dimensions are connected with each other in a complex correlation, the exact character of which is controversially debated. The dimensions carry different weight for different text types.

---

3   As Heinemann points out, such a general definition could also include nonsensical types such as 'texts beginning with A or text on sheets of the same format' (ibid.).

iii) The individual dimensions can be described as bunches of elemental characteristics in the form of cognitive and cotextual variables.[4]

iv) Text types (*Textsorten*) are sets of texts defined by more criteria than the supercategory of text class (*Textklasse*) and by fewer criteria than the subcategory of textual variant (*Textvariante*). The level of abstraction and the range of the respective category diminishes according to the number of criteria applied in their definition.

v) Text types are the result of communicative actions based on the conventions of a speech community. As these conventions are, in turn, results of the speakers' experiences, they allow for a relatively wide range of variations in the actual realization of text types. This is why the borders between text types are floating, with the result that text types form open sets where overlapping is possible (i.e. text types can belong to several categories), and the exact number of sets is impossible to determine (the historical development of text types can illustrate the open character of these sets of text types and account for their ambiguity, as will be seen in the second part of this article).

vi) Often the term text type still refers to written texts, excluding oral texts (types of conversations) and literary/poetic texts (genres).[5]

As will become clear in the second part of this article, for historical text linguistics it will often be linguistic-structural dimensions that dominate text linguistic investigation, since pragmatic features or knowledge about the author(s)/reader(s) of a text can be hard to reconstruct. Apart from the mere definition of text types, tasks for historical linguistics are the description of the evolution of text types, the location of individual texts within their historical development, and – if possible – the reconstruction of the

---

4   The term *cotext* is sometimes used to refer to linguistic context, to exclude the implications of extralinguistic contexts.

5   Heinemann (2000: 515) is among those who advocate the extension of the term text type to all spheres of language. Only a few years on, today the term is already increasingly used to include spoken texts.

contemporary knowledge about text types that would have facilitated production and reception of a historical text.

Terminological jungle

Terminological difficulties arise from the large number of different aspects
of text linguistics and the resulting variety of approaches. In German alone
there is a wide range of terms used synonymously with that of text type,
e.g. *Textklasse, Textart, Texttyp, Textform, Textmuster, Äußerungssorte, Kom-
munikationssorte* (Rolf, quoted in Heinemann 2000: 509).[6] This unclear
terminology is a major problem in text linguistics and stands in the way of
unambiguous academic discourse. Different traditions in English and German
text linguistics account for further confusion.

For German text linguistics, Heinemann with Adamzik (1995: 14) suggests the use of the term *Textklasse* (text class) as an unspecific umbrella term
for any group of texts. Furthermore, he suggests the term *Textmuster* (textual
pattern) as a cognitive term for the abstract concept (more ibid. 515ff.; see
also Schoenke 2000: 127) while *Textsorte* (text type) should be used for actual
samples of concrete texts. The terms *Textsortenklasse, Textsorte,* and *Textsorten-
variante* for him are tools to differentiate hierarchically within the umbrella
term *Textklasse*.[7] He reserves the terms *Gattung* and *Genre* for texts with a
dominant aesthetic function.

---

6   Heinemann himself quotes seventeen German terms that can be found as synonyms or
     in close relation with the term text type (2000: 515; cf. also Pfefferkorn 1998: 414).
7   The term *Texttyp* is often used synonymously with that of *Textklasse*. However, as *Texttyp*
     is also frequently found to denote a great variety of other concepts (cf. Heinemann
     2000: 519f.), it is perhaps best avoided.

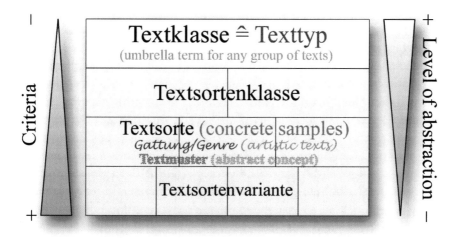

Overview of the most frequent and/or preferable uses of terms for the classification of texts according to Heinemann (2000: 514ff.).

Differences between German and English text linguistics

It was Peter Hartmann and his collaborators (1964a, 1968, 1971) who provided the initial impulse for text linguistics in Germany in the late 1960s (Schoenke 2000: 123). The term *Textlinguistik* itself was coined by Harald Weinrich (1967: 109). Apart from these West German attempts, East German linguists made key contributions at the same period (e.g. Isenberg 1974, 1976, 1977; Viehweger 1976; for further examples see Schoenke 2000: 123). The close co-operation of the *Ostberliner Zentralinstitut für Sprachwissenschaften* and the *Prager Institut für tschechische Sprache* (e.g. Daneš 1970) was both influential and productive.

However, German text linguistics was influenced not only by the Prague School, but also took guidance from French semantics (Greimas 1966), and from publications in English and Dutch investigating the spoken language (e.g. by Halliday/Hasan 1976 and van Dijk 1972, 1980; for further examples, see Schoenke 2000: 123).

Despite the roots of text linguistics in ancient rhetoric, in the German-speaking tradition text linguistics is still seen as a discipline evolved from the study of written (literary) texts. By contrast, in the English-speaking tradition text linguistics is largely seen as part of the analysis of spoken discourse (Thiele 2000: 123).[8] As a consequence of the focus on discourse analysis, the analysis of texts in these traditions is undertaken within a sociolinguistic and functional framework and with an emphasis on the interactive aspect of written texts. In these pragmalinguistic approaches, texts are seen as communication between addresser and addressee and speech as a social activity, following suggestions in the teachings of Herbert P. Grice, John L. Austin and John R. Searle (cf. Thiele 2000: 134). The analytic tools used in textual analysis are usually those developed for spoken communication. A distinction between discourse analysis and text linguistics is rarely made in English-speaking countries.

A current trend in text linguistics, both in German- and in English-speaking countries, is the investigation of intercultural communication (cf. Thiele 2000: 136). For historical text linguistics it is only natural that its focus is on the study of written texts, as we shall see in the next section of this article However, insights gained through the study of spoken language can be helpful for historical research, if the necessary information is accessible (e.g. the investigation of the relationship between addresser and addressee).

Historical text linguistics: problems, trends, and outlook

Until recently text linguistics has focused its attention mainly on the study of modern texts, but this neglect of older material is increasingly attracting criticism. It has been argued for some time now that for a deeper understanding of language change it is necessary to include text types into the study of language change (e.g. Pfefferkorn 1998: 399f. and Endermann 2000: 1918f.). As the change of text types includes both the change of the grammatical

---

8   For a summary of research representative of important schools within the English speaking tradition see Thiele (2000: 132ff.).

and thematic structure of language itself and the change of the pragmatic functions of language, incorporating text types into the theory of language change would provide a valuable link between the change of external factors and the change of language systems (Pfefferkorn, 1998: 399f.). At the same time, tracking the change of text types through history could also serve as an indicator for the underlying changes of communication systems (Endermann 2000: 1921) and, even more generally, of human interaction (cf. Schank 1984: 762). Technological progress has only relatively recently made it possible to record spoken language for posterity, therefore it is written language that is at the heart of historical text linguistics. Nevertheless, attempts have been made to trace 'reflexes of spoken language' in historical texts (e.g. Bischoff 2000 and cf. Endermann 2000: 1918).

It is thought that linguistic change starts in individual text types and individual communicative areas from where it spreads through the language system (Pfefferkorn 1998: 400; Endermann 2000: 1921). In order to recognize and describe the processes of language change through time, it is necessary to begin by taking stock of the text types of a language era and subjecting them to detailed analysis. Historical linguistics has only recently begun this process (see Pfefferkorn 1998: 400 for individual studies and see below).[9] In this endeavour, a basic problem arises from the nature of text preservation. Traditionally, a distinction between works worth preserving and works not preserving is made (e.g. novel vs. shopping list). Contemporary catalogues, inventories, sales documents etc. – that is, the material used for the investigation of quantitative and regional distribution of texts – usually only mention works designed for publication. As a result, the area of everyday texts is dramatically underrepresented. Research is thus limited by the nature of inventorial documentation (cf. Kästner/Schütz/Schwitalla 2000: 1613 and Endermann 2000: 1918). Unfortunately, the lack of agreement on standards and methods in text linguistics mentioned in the first section of this paper is also a source of difficulties in the area of historical text linguistics.

---

9   It may seem like an impossible task to even roughly classify the multitude and variety of ENHG texts (cf. Kästner/Schütz/Schwitalla 2000: 1605f.). However, any attempt to go beyond the study of individual texts will contribute to our understanding of the historical communication situation and thus improve our understanding of the texts produced within its parameters.

Apart from the general problems of text linguistics, there are more specific difficulties which arise from the nature of historical research itself. Oliver Pfefferkorn, whose work has had a key role in defining the discipline (1998), identifies seven problems of historical text linguistics which are summarized here (1998: 401–14).

1. Missing context

There is a consensus that the function of a text type is an important, if not the central, concern of textual analysis. The textual function can be distinguished by examining the language of a text and by determining its illocutionary structure. As Pfefferkorn shows, the further analysis of the context can sometimes lead to the specification or even change of the function established by text-immanent analyses, namely when it becomes clear that the two do not coincide. However, in the case of historical texts, the situational context and linguistic co-text are often partly if not wholly unknown. How severely this lack of context can limit the interpretation of the textual function is shown by Pfefferkorn who cites a number of texts which, judged on formal aspects, seem to be unequivocally directive (e.g. cooking recipes). His analysis of their context shows, however, that some of them are included in educational compilations merely to provide material for discussions. In some cases, the instructions are clearly unrealistic so that the texts' contents already provide a clue to their true function (e.g. Pfefferkorn quotes an instruction to transform lead into copper and another one to recreate a herb out of its ashes). In other cases, only the context of the compilations reveals their function as a stimulant for discussion.[10]

---

10   It has been argued that texts contain markers which indicate their function and which can be historically reconstructed (Lerchner 1990: 317). Pfefferkorn dismisses this option, since such markers do not appear in all text types and thus their analysis only provides a limited analytic tool (ibid. 403f.). See also Endermann (2000: 1918) about the problem of missing text-external characteristics in historical research.

2. Polyfunctional character: multiple intentions/addressees

When it comes to historical texts, Pfefferkorn questions a frequently found paradigm in text linguistics which states that each text has only one dominant illocution (i.e. meaning or function). He describes historical text types which he considers polyfunctional, since they have several intentions and are directed to several addressees at the same time. In the case of texts that are copies of lost originals (e.g. medieval manuscripts) there is the added difficulty of possible alteration by the copyist, who might have tried to adapt the text to his own intentions.

3. Polyfunctional character: entertainment/usefulness

Modern texts are typically divided into non-literary texts on the one hand and literary/poetic texts on the other. While non-literary texts serve certain practical functions, literary and poetic texts cannot be as easily linked to such specific use. Instead, they are designed to be heard or read for pleasure. This distinction is relatively modern. Up to the early eighteenth century, useful texts could also be poetic and poetic texts could very well serve practical purposes In this way, they can also be considered polyfunctional.

4. Lack of perspective in individual studies

Pfefferkorn has doubts about the adequacy of the isolated study of individual historical text types. He points out that the analysis of individual text types, while able to supply detailed descriptions of single text types, does not make it possible to divide the wealth of characteristics into those features which are text type specific, those which are specific to the area of communication, or those which are typical for texts of the particular era. Ultimately, the isolated study of historical text types only provides a list of characteristics that can be excluded from the studied text type. Only through the contrastive study of text types of larger contrasting communication areas can the specific features of individual text types be understood. As Kästner/Schütz/Schwitalla (2000: 1616ff.) point out, it is often also necessary to take foreign communication traditions into account if one is to understand the development of a text type, its rise, potential restructuring, and demise.

5. Fuzzy boundaries

Historical text types seem to be generally less standardized and show fewer specific characteristics than modern text types, although it seems to be the case that historical text types from institutions and public areas are relatively more standardized than those from private areas. Also, traditional text types have developed more specific characteristics than text types that are only just emerging in the era under investigation. Generally, it can be said that historical text types are (in accordance with a lower complexity of social structures in former times) likely to be less specified and also more tolerant of variation of illocutionary structure and choice of linguistic means. As a result, boundaries between text types and even between whole communication areas in historical eras are blurred. Nevertheless, there are text types which appear to be prototypical for what we nowadays (often retrospectively) perceive as distinct text types. Many texts, however, can be located at the periphery of these text types where they overlap with others and where they can be interpreted as belonging to a variety of different text types (alternatively, they can be interpreted as belonging to mixed text types). In the historical development of text types it is often difficult to say if a text with varying characteristics is a deviation from an existing text type, a mix of several text types, or an early form of an emerging new text type (see the example below).

6. Lacking contemporary awareness of text types

It has already been noted that knowledge about text types belongs to the speakers' intuitive linguistic knowledge. For most historical text types the linguistic intuition of the speakers is impossible to establish retrospectively. Thus we have to be aware of the fact that most names for historical text types are not contemporary and may therefore be highly artificial. It appears that it is only relatively recently that clearly defined text types have come to be linked with certain intentions and functions, as a consequence of the growing complexity of human communication, and that in eras of simpler communication situations the number of possible textual functions would have been limited.

7. Lack of definitions as well as problematic terminology

Pfefferkorn points out that there are historical terms for groups of texts which do not necessarily denote text types.[11] Delineating the boundaries between terms for individual textual phenomena and terms for text types is not made any easier by the problematic nomenclature of text linguistics in general. Ideally, as in all research, there should be generally accepted methods and terminology for text type analysis: the desirable methodical and terminological transparency in text linguistics is not yet in sight.

An example of historical text linguistics in practice

To illustrate the difficulties in appreciating form and function of historical texts, we can use the following example from Kaspar von Stieler's *Secretariat=Kunst* from 1673. The book is a *Briefsteller*, a compilation of sample texts, provided as a basis for writing practice, both for professional scribes and for lay people. It is important for the understanding of the example that unlike earlier *Briefsteller*, Stieler's *Secretariat=Kunst* contains detailed passages on the theory of text production and can therefore be considered an early textbook rather than a traditional collection of sample material: that is, the book itself can be considered an example of an emerging new text type. The following passage is entitled *Von den Bildern* (p. 1072):

---

11   A separate issue is that of paratexts. Paratexts are texts which cannot function by themselves and which only have a communicative function in relation with the text they belong to (e.g. dedications, tables of content, etc.; Pfefferkorn 1998: 413).

WEil die Kinder schône Bilder und Kupferstûcke sehr lieben / so kan man ihnen durch nichts beßers / als dieselbe den ganzen Grund des Christlichen Glaubens einbilden / auch ihnen die Tugend angenehm und die Laster gehâßig machen. Hierzu ist die Gota- ische Bilderschul sehr dienlich: Dann die Catechismus= und Evangelienbilder: Letzlich der *orbis pictus* des *Comenii*, zum Verstândnûß der weltlichen Hândel. Es muß sich aber ein Lehrmeister nicht verdrießen laßen / ihnen die Sachen oft und vilmal / doch allezeit vernehmlich zu erzehlen. Solches faßen die Kinder leichtlich und mit Lust / reden oft darvon / und schârfen damit den Verstand und das Urteil gewaltig / werden auch daher stracks Anfangs zur Liebe gegen Gott / und alle Christliche Tugenden angewehnet. Wann nun dieses also vernûnftig und fleißig getrieben wird / so ist das hârteste ûberwunden / und kan man so dann auf diesen Grund ferner nach Beliebung bauen / gestalt ich hierbey einen unmaßgeblichen Vorschlag zur beliebten Nachfolge ûbersende / und den Herrn Gottes Schutz ergebe.

The fact that we are considering *Briefsteller* and the chapter heading *XXII. Von den Unterredungs= Lehr= und Streitschreiben* (p. 1063, my emphasis) are suggestive of the text type *letter* (function: to maintain contact) as a fitting category for our example. This seems to be confirmed by the formulaic ending of the text (lines 12f.), which also contains a reference to the sending of the letter and to an appendix containing further suggestions for the education of children. From the same heading, however, we can expect a discussion or an instructional text type on the use of images in education (functions: to influence or to teach). Also, the fact itself that there is a heading instead of an address seems to imply this categorization.

Considering the wider context (further texts on education, e.g. on home schooling, learning how to pray), the question arises whether it is justified to consider the text as an independent unit, or whether the whole collection of texts on education and childhood should be considered as one text. Here, it could be discussed whether in addition to the concept of polyfunctional- ity mentioned above in the summary of Pfefferkorn, one should allow for a polyidentity of texts as both independent parts and as parts of larger units.

It is worth considering whether the innovative character of Stieler's whole approach (commented textbook instead of mere compilation) might not account for a lower degree of standardization encountered in the constitu- ent texts (e.g. lower definition of boundaries between the sample texts). An important question here would be to establish how far Stieler edited existing material or whether he also created (some of) the texts he used.

Detailed analyses of the example's linguistic features (e.g. on the lexical and on the syntactical level) and a comparison with other texts of the time (e.g. 'real' letters, texts from other compilations, texts that are clearly instructive/educational) would be the next step towards a definition of the example's textual function(s) and text type. Ideally, the catalogue of examined features would be specific enough to allow for a clear characterization of the example while at the same time being general enough to facilitate the comparison with the analyses of other texts.

Tendencies in the development of Middle High German text types

The emergence of Middle High German (MHG) text types is thought to have occurred at the beginning of the MHG period, just after 1050 (cf. Kästner/ Schirok 2000: 1365). Their existence, use and effects reach far beyond the end of the MHG period in the mid fourteenth century well into the sixteenth century, creating a considerable period of overlap with New High German text types (Kästner/Schirok 2000: 1366). While it is clear that there are groups of texts that can be perceived as typical MHG text types, research is still very far from a typology of these.

Kästner and Schirok (2000) summarize attempts towards a typology of MHG text types and outline ideas for a new text typology. As they show, the typology of medieval texts has so far been almost entirely a task of literary studies (ibid. 1368f.). Their summary of relevant research on medieval text types mentions linguistic attempts to establish medieval text types only in passing (ibid. 1368f.). The fact that only three authors of linguistic research into MHG text types are named demonstrates the scarcity of linguistic research up to the turn of the twenty-first century (works cited by Kästner/Schirok 2000 are Kuhn 1956, Jauss 1972 and Köhler 1977).

The other approaches referred to by Kästner/Schirok are those which rely on tools designed for the study of literature and, not surprisingly, their subject matter is exclusively literary and poetic language. Like many text linguistic approaches mentioned in the first section of this paper, these approaches towards a typology of (literary) MHG texts suffer from the complexity of their object of study: text type models with too many factors do not establish clear categories while models with too few factors are not able to categorize the variety of texts. The difficulties pointed out by Pfefferkorn can also be observed here.

The authors attempt a rough stock-taking of written medieval texts using such parameters as subject areas (e.g. religion, everyday life, poetry, science) or features of the production of texts (e.g. groups of authors, patrons, literary centres) as well as their reception. For highly artistic texts they continue to use the established generic terms from literary studies.

Kästner/Schirok's summary demonstrates the need for a more elaborated linguistic typology of medieval texts. However, despite the tentative character of their suggestions and the need for further research, they come to a set of observations on medieval text types, summarized as five tendencies in the MHG period (Kästner/Schirok 2000: 1366 and 1380):

- oral text types turn into written text types

- Latin text types appear in vernacular form

- new text types emerge

- there is a general increase in the production of vernacular text types

- there is a transition from verse to prose.

Furthermore, Kästner/Schirok observe an evolution of many text types from the early to the late Middle Ages. Like modern text linguists, they consider the reconstruction of medieval communication processes by means of inter-disciplinary research an important aim of text linguistics (ibid. 1369).

Tendencies in the development of Early New High German text types

Kästner/Schütz/Schwitalla (2000: 1605) give an overview of text types of the fifteenth and sixteenth centuries, the core of the Early New High German (ENHG) period if this is taken to be *c.* 1350–1650. In view of the vast quantity of texts from the ENHG period and their heterogenous character, the authors consider it an impossible task to classify ENHG texts up to the actual level of text types. Instead, to cope with the multitude and variety of material, they propose as a first approach towards a classification a rough distinction into general areas of text types and their functions, using the terms *Funktionsbereiche, Textsortenfelder,* and *Textsortengruppen,* ibid. 106–7 and 1612). For detailed descriptions of ENHG texts they refer to existing research on literary text types.

For their own approach, Kästner, Schütz and Schwitalla try to distinguish areas of text types with special relevance for future developments which are indicative of social and communicative change. They take up Alfred Schütz's (1971) *phenomenology of the social world* and distinguish five spheres of reality and their respective social functions: everyday life, institutional life, religious life, scientific life, and poetic life.[12] Like Kästner/Schirok 2000, the authors also recur to existing genre terms in their descriptions of exemplary texts for each sphere.

Within the investigated social spheres Kästner, Schütz and Schwitalla look at dominant functions performed by the typical texts. They also look at preferred topics, participants in the relevant types of communication, samples of typical text types, special features of these, and important developments. They do not claim that all historical texts can be assigned to exactly one area (i.e. one corresponding function) but they think that despite the overlapping of the investigated social spheres in some cases such assignment is possible. In order to add information about the communication practices and the

12   They are aware that it is problematic to apply a modern understanding of these spheres, since the contemporary understanding and interaction of these spheres were different to ours. The boundaries between the distinct fields were much more transparent which caused an overlapping of functions of these texts (2000: 1606; cf. the summary of Pfefferkorn above).

quantitative and regional distribution of text types to the investigation of functional groups, they also investigate groups of authors and readers and the distribution of text types.

In their description of ENHG spheres of text types Kästner, Schütz and Schwitalla observe certain trends. Generally, they find that text types become increasingly differentiated and distinguishable over time, as was already noted for MHG above. They note a number of important factors for the development of text types in the early modern period, related to the general historical developments.

Firstly, new developments in trade and commerce require new text types (e.g. manuals for new techniques or equipment in mining or agriculture). Due to an increase in alphabetization, the fifteenth century sees the rise of a new, profane written culture that joins the existing religious traditions and slowly begins to replace it. Printing has a lasting impact on text production and reading preferences, and, as in MHG, there is a shift from Latin to German text types. The involvement of the wider population in social and political events like the Reformation or the Peasants' War gives rise to new political text types. At courts and universities, translations into German increase the number of German text types. In general, indeed, a rising interest in information promotes the development of informative text types, and there is an increase in the production of prose texts which reflects the rising interest in factual information on one hand and the increased use of written media in both cultural and everyday life on the other (summarized from Kästner, Schütz and Schwitalla 200: 1615ff).

Tendencies in the development of New High German text types

An overview of important developments concerning New High German (NHG) text types of non-literary language from the seventeenth century up to the middle of the twentieth century is provided by Heinz Endermann (2000).[13] Endermann (2000: 1920) divides the NHG era into two periods:

13   Endermann promotes the separate study of poetic/literary and non-literary text types (2000: 1930).

a first part up to around 1800, in which the development of a literary language and a standard language was concluded (although see Davies in the present volume), and a second part from around 1800 to the present, in which the development of a wider awareness of language, a new way of dealing with texts, and the development of technical media took place. In his summary he shows how the complex relationships between historical developments (of society, technology, the media etc.) are reflected in the resulting communication forms which condense into constantly changing text types.

Endermann uses a choice of relevant text types to demonstrate the kind of changes which are characteristic of NHG. His early examples from the seventeenth to the early eighteenth century are text types which are products of the study of ancient rhetoric: poetry, speeches, book reviews, theatre and music reviews (2000: 1926ff.). For the slightly longer period from the seventeenth to the end of the eighteenth century he concentrates on pamphlets and newspapers The emergence of the school essay in the eighteenth century is used to discuss the development of older text types related to the growing importance of the German language as a tool for and a subject of teaching (ibid. 1929f.). Letters, both texts that use the format of letters and really are reports, pamphlets, or novels, and real letters, are discussed in the context of the eighteenth century and up to the mid twentieth century (2000: 1924ff.). For these text types, characteristics and examples are provided and details of their development, their interrelation with other text types, conditions for their development, problems and interrelation with other types are outlined.

Among the points of interest for further research suggested by Endermann (passim) are:

– the continuity or discontinuity of text types (with special attention to mixed forms, where the existence of text types temporarily overlap)

– the openness of text types for influences from other languages (these are hardly investigated but there seem to be striking differences

and

– the use of the phonic versus the graphic medium (i.e. speech vs. writing, especially the interrelation of the two, e.g. the replacement of oral text forms by written forms).

Conclusion

When approaching historical texts, it is only with a thorough knowledge of the historical context that one can fully appreciate their content and function. For linguists, the character of the communicative situation and the state of the language at the time of text production are part of this multi-faceted historical context, the knowledge of which is imperative for the appreciation of a text's linguistic structure. Since for the understanding of complex communication situations a detailed reconstruction of the context is necessary, historical linguistics is a highly interdisciplinary field. Using as much available background knowledge as possible, research can begin to reconstruct the linguistic and social norms that would have applied to a given text form in order to appreciate the conditions of its production and reception and to undertake its analysis. After establishing the norms relevant for a text, it also becomes possible to perceive its deviations from these norms (e.g. speaker's lack of skill, use of humour etc.).

The difficulty in reconstructing historical context when there is little or no information available and coping with the wealth and diversity of material from some eras are grave problems in historical linguistics. The representativity (or lack thereof) of the existing historical sources is something of which historical linguists have to be aware. Despite the fact that large-scale contrastive studies of both a synchronic and a diachronic nature would be ideal to establish historical text typologies, it is realistically possible to work only on comparatively small areas at a time. There are risks of misinterpretation or of simply missing important information until enough knowledge is accumulated to form a larger picture. As some texts – depending on period, text type, or situation – allow for high degrees of variation in which their structure, content, and function can have several interpretations, this risk cannot be underestimated. In some cases many individual studies are necessary until a larger picture can be created.

The complex nature of communication as subject matter and the variety of approaches provide further sources of difficulties and finding exhaustive, yet generally applicable, clear text typologies is, and probably will always be, difficult. Even the most optimistic text linguist will admit that a general agreement on text linguistic standards and nomenclature is still far away.

Despite all these problems, studying trends in historical text type developments has already proved successful. As further research adds to existing islands of knowledge, an ever finer net of knowledge is slowly being created, allowing a more sophisticated understanding of historical text types. As with all models, there must remain a certain degree of fuzziness: after all, models are there to allow quick access to complex knowledge and not to provide a one-to-one copy of the studied subject.

Contributing to the knowledge of historical text types is an exciting task, as it furthers our understanding of processes of linguistic change and of historical communication itself. Due to the interlocking nature of the subjects, this works both ways, as research on linguistic change and historical media, in turn, help to explain historical text types. Historical text linguistics also focuses on facilitating improvement of the theoretical tools for further research. Interdisciplinary co-operation and use of both traditional methods (as derived from rhetoric and stylistics) and modern research tools (as developed by modern discourse analysis) make it an area of research that is as fascinating as it is challenging.

References

Primary Source

Stieler (Der Spahte), Kaspar von. 1673. *Teutsche Secretariat=Kunst / [...] mit grundrichtigen Sätzen zuverläßigen Anweisungen und reinen teutschen Mustern / nach heutigem durchgehendem Gebrauch / [...]*. Nürnberg. HAB A: 35.1 Rhet.

Bibliography

Adamzik, K. (1995), *Textsorten – Texttypologie. Eine kommentierte Bibliographie*, Münster: Nodus.
Bischoff, K. (2000), 'Reflexe gesprochener Sprache', in: *Sprachgeschichte. Ein Handbuch zur Geschichte der deutschen Sprache und ihrer Erforschung, 2. Teilband*, edited by

W. Besch, A. Betten, O. Reichmann, S. Sonderegger, Berlin, New York: de Gruyter, 1491–5.

Beaugrande, R.A. de and Dressler, W.U. (1981), *Einführung in die Textlinguistik*. Tübingen: Niemeyer.

Brinker, K., Antos, G., Heinemann, W. and Sager, S.F. (2000), *Handbücher zur Sprach- und Kommunikationswissenschaft. Band 16.1: Text- und Gesprächslinguistik*, Berlin, New York: Walter de Gruyter.

Brinker, K. (2005), *Linguistische Textanalyse. Eine Einführung in Grundbegriffe und Methoden*, 6th ed., Berlin: Erich Schmidt.

Daneš, F. (1970), 'Zur linguistischen Analyse der Textstruktur', in: *Folia Linguistica IV*, 72–8.

Dijk, T.A. van (1972), *Some Aspects of Text Grammars. A study in theoretical linguistics and poetics*, The Hague and Paris: Mouton. (Jana linguarum, Series maior; 63).

Dijk, T.A. van (1980), *Textwissenschaft. Eine interdisziplinäre Einführung*, Tübingen: Niemeyer (Dutch original 1978).

Dudenredaktion (eds) (2005), *Duden. Die Grammatik. Duden Band 4*, Mannheim, Leipzig, Wien, Zürich: Dudenverlag.

Endermann, H. (2000), 'Die Textsorten des Neuhochdeutschen bis zur Mitte des 20. Jahrhunderts', in: *Sprachgeschichte. Ein Handbuch zur Geschichte der deutschen Sprache und ihrer Erforschung. 2. Teilband*, edited by W. Besch, A. Betten, O. Reichmann, S. Sonderegger, Berlin and New York: de Gruyter, 1918–32.

Finch, G. (2000), *Linguistic Terms and Concepts*, Houndmills and New York: Palgrave.

Greimas, A.J. (1966), *Sémantique structurale*, Paris: Larousse.

Halliday, M.A. K. and Hasan, R. (1976), *Cohesion in English*, London: Longman.

Hartmann, P. (1964a), 'Text, Texte, Klassen von Texten', in: *Strukturelle Textanalyse – Analyse Du Récit – Discourse Analysis*, edited by W.A. Koch, (1972), Hildesheim, New York: Georg Olms, 1–22.

Hartmann, P. (1964b), 'Text, Texte, Klassen von Texten', *Bogawus Zeitschrift für Literatur, Kunst und Philosophie* 2, 15–25.

Hartmann, P. (1968), 'Textlinguistik als neue linguistische Teildisziplin', *Replik* 2, 2–7.

Hartmann, P. (1971), 'Texte als linguistisches Objekt', *Beiträge zu Textlinguistik*, edited by W.D. Stempel, München, 9–30.

Heinemann, W. (1991), 'Textsorten/Textmuster – ein Problemaufriß', in: *Textsorten – Textmuster in der Sprech- und Schriftkommunikation*, edited by R. Mackeldey, Leipzig: Universität Leipzig, 8–16.

Heinemann, W. (2000), 'Typologisierung von Texten I: Kriterien', in: Brinker et al. (2000), 507–23.

Isenberg, H. (1974), 'Überlegungen zur Texttheorie', in: *Lektürekolleg zur Textlinguistik. Bd. 2*, edited by W. Kallmeyer, W. Klein and R. Meyer-Hermann, Frankfurt: Athanäum, 193–212.

Isenberg, H. (1976), 'Einige Grundbegriffe für eine linguistische Texttheorie', in: *Probleme der Textgrammatik*, edited by F. Daneš and D. Viehweger, Berlin: Akademie Verlag, 47–145.

Isenberg, H. (1977), '"Text" versus "Satz"', in: *Probleme der Textgrammatik 2*, edited by F. Daneš and D. Viehweger, Berlin, Akademie Verlag, 119–46.

Jauß, H.R. (1972), 'Theorie der Gattungen und Literatur des Mittelalters', in: *Grundriß der romanischen Literaturen des Mittelalters*, Bd. 1, edited by H.R. Jauß et al., Heidelberg: Winter, 107–38.

Kalverkämper, H. (2000), 'Vorläufer der Textlinguistik: die Rhetorik', in: Brinker et al. (2000), 1–17.

Kästner, H., Schütz, E. and Schwitalla J. (2000), 'Die Textsorten des Frühneuhochdeutschen', in: *Sprachgeschichte. Ein Handbuch zur Geschichte der deutschen Sprache und ihrer Erforschung. 2. Teilband*, edited by W. Besch, A. Betten, O. Reichmann and S. Sonderegger, Berlin and New York: de Gruyter, 1605–23.

Kästner, H. and Schirok, B. (2000), 'Die Textsorten des Mittelhochdeutschen', in: *Sprachgeschichte. Ein Handbuch zur Geschichte der deutschen Sprache und ihrer Erforschung. 2. Teilband*, edited by W. Besch, A. Betten, O. Reichmann and S. Sonderegger, Berlin and New York: de Gruyter, 1365–84.

Klosa, A., Wermke M. et al. (eds) (1998), *Duden Grammatik der deutschen Gegenwartssprache. Duden Band 4*, Mannheim, Leipzig, Wien and Zürich: Dudenverlag.

Köhler, E. (1977), *Ideal und Wirklichkeit in der höfischen Epik. Studien zur Form der frühen Artus- und Graldichtung*, Tübingen: Niemeyer.

Kuhn, H. (1956), 'Zur Typologie mündlicher Sprachdenkmäler', 5th reprint (1969) in: *Text und Theorie*, Stuttgart: Hugo Kuhn, 10–27.

Lerchner, G. (1990), 'Kontextualisierung historischer Texte. Zum Markiertheitsprinzip in einer textsortenbezogenen Sprachhistoriographie', *Zeitschrift für Phonologie, Sprachwissenschaft und Kommunikationsforschung*, 43/3, 315–26.

Lewandowski, T. (1994), *Linguistisches Wörterbuch Bd. 1–3*, Heidelberg, Wiesbaden: Quelle & Meyer.

Pfefferkorn, O. (1998), 'Möglichkeiten und Grenzen einer Analyse historischer Textsorten', *Zeitschrift für deutsche Philologie 117*, Heft 2 und 3: 399–415.

Riecke, J., Hünecke, R., Pfefferkorn, O., Schuster, B.M., and Voeste, A. (2004), *Einführung in die historische Textanalyse*. Göttingen: Vandenhoeck & Ruprecht.

Rolf, E. (1993), *Die Funktionen der Gebrauchtextsorten*, Berlin, New York: Walter de Gruyter.

Sanders, W. (2000), 'Vorläufer der Textlinguistik: die Stilistik', in: Brinker et al. (2000), 17–28.

Schank, G. (1984), 'Ansätze zu einer Theorie des Sprachwandels auf der Grundlage von Textsorten', in: *Sprachgeschichte. Ein Handbuch zur Geschichte der deutschen Sprache und ihrer Erforschung*, edited by W. Besch, O. Reichmann and S. Sonderegger, Berlin, New York: de Gruyter, 761–8.

Schmidt, W. (2000), *Geschichte der deutschen Sprache. Ein Lehrbuch für das germanistische Studium*, Stuttgart: S. Hirzel.

Schoenke, E. (2000), 'Textlinguistik im deutschsprachigen Raum', in: Brinker et al. (2000), 123–31.

Schütz, A. (1971), *Das Problem der sozialen Wirklichkeit. Gesammelte Aufsätze. Band 1*, The Hague: Nijhoff.

Schuster, B.M. (2004), 'Textsortenbestimmung', in: *Einführung in die historische Textanalyse*, edited by J. Riecke, R. Hünecke, O. Pfefferkorn, B.-M. Schuster and A. Voeste, Göttingen: Vandenhoeck & Ruprecht, 43–65.

Thiele, W. (2000), 'Textlinguistik im englischsprachigen Raum', in: Brinker et al. (2000), 132–9.

Viehweger, D. (1976), 'Semantische Merkmale und Textstruktur', in: *Probleme der Textgrammatik*, edited by F. Daneš and D. Viehweger, Berlin: Akademie Verlag, 195–206.

Weinrich, H. (1967), 'Syntax als Dialektik' (Bochumer Diskussionen), *Poetica 1*, 109–26.

FALCO PFALZGRAF

Linguistic Purism in the History of German

Introduction

The phenomenon of linguistic purism is particularly fascinating because it reveals long-held and ever-recurring beliefs about language by laypeople. As recently as July 2007, the well-respected newspaper *Die Zeit* ran a series of articles about the perceived decline of the German language (see Jessen 2007). The aim of this paper is to give a brief overview of linguistic purism in the history of German. According to Jones (1995: 4), written purist statements were made as early as in the thirteenth century. For the purpose of this paper, however, we will examine purism from the Baroque period in the seventeenth century up to the beginning of the twenty-first century, almost two decades after German unification. Purism is a phenomenon that appears not only in connection with the German language, but in so many other languages that it can be regarded as almost universal; it can even 'come up in societies where literacy is heavily restricted and institutions which would organize purist movements are largely missing' (Boeder et al. 2003: viii). We will therefore first define the term in a general sense, then look at discourses which manifest themselves especially with regard to German *Fremdwortpurismus*, which is to say that we will focus mainly on lexical purism. Next, the question of how linguistics should deal with foreign lexical influences will be discussed. After that, a brief overview of six phases of linguistic purism in the history of German will be given, and we will suggest possible reasons for the emergence of linguistic purism during those six phases, with particular attention to current purist activities in Germany.

Definitions

What is purism? Linguists have examined the phenomenon in detail at least since the 1960s, but nonetheless there is scarcely any intellectually satisfying definition to be found in the relevant literature. As George Thomas rightly points out, 'purism has simply not been terminologized' (1991: 10). Nils Langer and Winifred Davies, after discussing three definitions, provide a summary of 'what purism is: an (influential) part of the speech community voices objections to the presence of particular linguistic features and aims to remove them from their language' (2005: 4). Among those discussed by Langer and Davies is a definition by David Crystal who describes purism in a rather general way as 'a school of thought which sees a language as needing preservation from external processes which might infiltrate it and thus make it change' (2006: 381). For the purpose of this paper, however, we will draw on George Thomas, who gives an overview of various available definitions, points out their strengths and weaknesses, and eventually delivers what he calls a 'working definition':

> Purism is the manifestation of a desire on the part of a speech community (or some section of it) to preserve a language from, or rid it of, putative foreign elements or other elements held to be undesirable (including those originating in dialects, sociolects and styles of the same language). It may be directed at all linguistic levels but primarily the lexicon. Above all, purism is an aspect of the codification, cultivation and planning of standard languages. (1991: 12)

This is probably the best general definition of linguistic purism currently available, as it 'does not restrict itself to foreign influences but includes varieties such as dialects and particular styles of a language' (Langer and Davies 2005: 3). In this account, however, we will mainly focus on the *Fremdwortfrage*, on metalinguistic reactions to exogenous elements in German lexis.

Although Thomas's definition of purism is very useful, a more practical approach is required in order to analyse a text with the intention of establishing whether or not its content can be considered to be of a puristic nature. As the theoretical basis for such an approach, Andreas Gardt's research into attitudes to foreign words in German offers a valuable starting point. Gardt (2001a) has analysed an open corpus of texts ranging from the sixteenth century to

World War II and provides an overview of what German authors thought and wrote about foreign words, how these were defined or characterized, and what was regarded to be their nature for different authors at different times. For the four centuries in question, Gardt has identified four major discourses about attitudes towards foreign words.

Firstly, a discourse about foreign words relating to the structure of the language (*sprachstruktureller Fremdwortdiskurs*), which is concerned mainly with questions relating to grammar, syntax and lexis. It is characteristic for that discourse that there is no understanding of the fact that a 'pure' language is merely a hypothetical construct, and that language contact has always influenced the vocabulary; the inevitability of this is not acknowledged. When foreign words are discussed, they are hardly ever defined, and not even a systematic nomenclature or concept exists. Therefore, language protectors often hold opposing views to the question of which words can be regarded as being German and which should be rejected as foreign. Concerning the latter, those of Greek or Latin origin are usually accepted, whereas others, often those of French or English origin, are not. The problem is similar when technical terms of foreign origin are discussed. However, these are more easily accepted than foreign words in everyday German, which are regarded as superfluous, as having a damaging effect on German grammar, and as having a negative impact on lexis (*Bastardwort, Mischmasch*). Consequently, demands for the substitution of foreign words are made.[1] To do so, it is believed to be best to reinstate archaisms, to adopt dialectalisms, and to form new words on the basis of German or Germanic words.

Secondly, an ideological discourse about foreign words (*sprachideologischer Fremdwortdiskurs*), which is connected to nationalist or cultural-patriotic purism. Characteristic of this discourse is an emphatic praise of one's own language and the assumption that it is characterized by age and a genetic/genealogical purity. Therefore, foreign words are regarded not as being an enrichment of the language, but rather as a danger to it. Furthermore,

---

[1] For the German verbs *eindeutschen* or *verdeutschen* we will not use 'to germanise' but 'to substitute' as the latter is a more precise and well-established linguistic term which covers: loan coinage (*Lehnprägung*), loan meaning (*Lehnbedeutung*), loan formation (*Lehnformung*), loan creation (*Lehnschöpfung*), loan translation (*Lehnübersetzung*), and loan rendering (*Lehnübertragung*), see Duckworth (1977).

language is often perceived as being part of one's own culture, and foreign words are consequently seen as a threat to one's own identity. There is often a tendency to attach value to one's own language in a naively defiant way and, at the same time, to degrade other languages. Sometimes, the predominant tenor of argumentation can be blatantly nationalistic.

Thirdly, a pedagogical/sociological discourse about foreign words (*sprach-pädagogisch-sprachsoziologischer Fremdwortdiskurs*) which assumes a correlation between cognition and the ability to deal with foreign words, that is, the speakers' education and their ability to use and process foreign words. It is assumed that when foreign words are used, less educated people are excluded from political and social life, which is seen as a danger for democracy, since a language which contains foreign words might hinder the process of enlightenment of the people and therefore slow down or even stop processes of democratization. Consequently, the substitution of foreign words is seen as a means to break down language barriers. Regarding lexical substitution, language protectors often express completely opposing positions: some people assume that the use of foreign words enriches the language, while others are of the opinion that foreign words impoverish the language. Some perceive certain foreign words as more comprehensible than the German equivalent, whereas others are of the opposite opinion. Individual taste plays an important role here.

Fourthly, a discourse about foreign words relating to language criticism for stylistic or rhetorical reasons (*sprachkritischer Fremdwortdiskurs*) which in turn shows three main further characteristics, as follows. When the use of foreign words is criticized, this is often an expression of the language protectors' individual taste where questions of style and aesthetics constitute the centre of argumentation. The use of foreign words is judged as superficial, merely fashionable participation in current social trends, as an expression of pseudo-intellectual behaviour, as an attempt to impress people, an effort to gain social prestige, or simply as thoughtlessness. The language of previous ages, in contrast, is always considered to be the better language: language and literature of medieval times is named as being exemplary. It is assumed that the use of foreign words leads to a divergence between the word and the world (*mehr Schein als Sein*). A perversion of 'actual reality' is perceived and the use of foreign words is regarded as absurd and offensive.

Purism and Linguistics

Language matters are discussed and commented on not only by profession-
ally trained linguists, but also by laypeople who have no deeper insight into
the subject. In fact, it is notable that language matters, in our case questions
related to linguistic purism, are often discussed in the mass media, alas most
often without the participation of professional linguists, but rather within a
circle of politicians, journalists, writers, singers, editors, or the like.[2] As Langer
and Davies point out, '[l]anguage is distinguished from other academic disciplines such as astronomy, Roman mythology, or physics because all speakers
consider themselves to be experts in the field of language' (2005: 1).

It is also noteworthy that self-appointed guardians of the German language often complain about linguists' attitudes to current foreign lexical
influences. The *Verein Deutsche Sprache* (VDS), for example, criticizes the
alleged somnolence of many linguists in the face of anglicization and accuses
linguists of failure and inability to meet their responsibilities.[3] Dieter E.
Zimmer, journalist, translator and one of Germany's best-known language
protectors, complains in a similar vein:

> Die Sprachwissenschaften haben ohnehin längst allem 'Normativen' abgeschworen und
> die bloße Beschreibung des Vorgefundenen zum Programm erhoben: Das Volk spricht,
> die Wissenschaft beobachtet es beim Sprechen und erklärt dann, wie es spricht. Wie es
> sprechen sollte, will sie unter keinen Umständen mehr sagen. (1997: 7–8)

It is the view of Zimmer and other language protectors that the function
of linguistics should be to give advice to people concerning the proper use

2   To name one of many possible examples: in *Sabine Christiansen*, a German talk show
     (ARD, 29.07.2001), the subject 'Man spricht deutsch – aber wie?' was discussed by poli-
     tician and theologian Annette Schavan, writer Walter Jens, politician and lawyer Klaus
     von Dohnanyi, singer Wolfgang Niedecken, journalist and editor Florian Langenscheidt,
     journalist and writer Feridun Zaimoglu, and Gerd Schrammen, Professor of Romance
     Literature and vice chair of the Verein Deutsche Sprache (VDS). For a very recent
     example, see Jessen (2007).
3   The VDS calls this the 'Dämmerschlaf vieler Sprachwissenschaftler angesichts der
     öffentlichen Anglisierung', Verein Deutsche Sprache, 'Argumente zur deutschen Sprache'
     (accessed February 2007), <http://www.vds-ev.de/denglisch/>.

of the German language: *Sprachkritik*. The role of linguists is best explained
by Hans-Martin Gauger, Emeritus Professor of Romance Linguistics at
Freiburg University, who states the following about the different branches
of linguistics:

> In *einem* aber sind sie alle sich einig: alle wollen nur beschreiben, wollen nur wissen, was
> in der Sprache *ist* oder in ihr *war*. [...] Alle diese Richtungen betrachten *dies* als eine der
> unabdingbaren – nicht hinreichenden, aber notwendigen – Voraussetzungen ihrer Wis-
> senschaftlichkeit: keine Wertung, Verzicht auf Orientierung; keine dieser Richtungen
> will Orientierungen vermitteln im Blick auf sogenannten 'guten' Sprachgebrauch. [...]
> 'Wissenschaftlich' stellt sich also dem 'Präskriptiven' entgegen. (1999: 88)

At the same time, Gauger does not deny that norms are necessary. He does
not claim, however, that it is the role of linguists to advise on 'good' usage:

> Die Sprechenden selbst unterscheiden, bewerten und bemühen sich, unter bestimmten
> Umständen 'richtig' oder 'gut' oder 'schön' zu sprechen. Und die Sprachwissenschaft
> [...] *kann* [...] die Bewertungen verzeichnen. [...] Nochmals: der Sprachwissenschaftler
> wertet nicht, aber er verzeichnet Bewertungen, die er – gänzlich unabhängig von ihm
> selbst – schon vorfindet, und die in der Sprachgemeinschaft und also in der Sprache
> selbst sind. (1999: 98–9)

To sum up, one can say that linguistics as such does not provide a basis to
judge what might or might not be regarded as 'good' usage. Such judgments
must be made elsewhere.

One example for the discussion of 'good' usage is the current – rather
emotional – debate about anglicisms in German, and most speakers of the
language have a view on the subject. Linguists may take the opportunity
to analyse and describe this discussion, and to draw conclusions. This of
course also applies to purism and its history: linguists will follow a descriptive
approach, they do not judge the movement as 'good' or 'bad' in itself. This
is particularly true because – and as will be seen below – purist movements
have differed over the centuries with respect to why they came into existence
and what their declared aims were.

Six Phases of Purism in the History of the German Language

I. The Baroque Era

In the early seventeenth century, religious discord and a weak empire led to the Thirty Years War (1618–48), resulting in the devastation of the German countries and culture. At this time, German was heavily influenced by Latin, the language of national and international communication for scholars and the clergy, and by French, which played a similar role for the nobility. German 'lacked the traditional (if not unquestioned) status of Hebrew, Greek and Latin; and it was functionally the inferior of French, Italian, and Spanish' (Jones 1999: vii). With the Bible considered as an accurate historical source for academic writing in Europe at the time, it was generally agreed that Hebrew was the language closest to the one spoken by Adam and Eve (and maybe even by the snake) in paradise; all other languages were younger. Among German scholars, German was increasingly regarded as an ancient and dignified language which supposedly had not changed much since the Biblical incident known as the 'Confusion of Languages': it was seen as a sister of Hebrew and as not necessarily junior to the Biblical languages Latin and Greek. Italian, Spanish and French, in contrast, were regarded as no more than adulterated versions of Latin and therefore inferior to the German, which was an '*Ur- und Hauptsprache*' (Jones 1999: 1–24). It was consequently thought to be important to cultivate the German language and keep it pure and unadulterated from foreign influences. The concept of purity, however, referred not only to foreign lexical influences; it also applied to the correctness of syntax and word formation, as well as a usage which abstained from offensive and ambiguous words and expressions (Leweling 2005). This was the first step towards the development of an autonomous German literature, borne by a standardized, supra-regional language, to fend off the cultural dominance of French and Latin. As the latter were still the languages of the court and the scientific world respectively, the use of German was to be encouraged. This, among other activities such as the translation of Italian and French literature into German which was to serve as an example of good style for German authors, was the main aim of the so-called *Sprachgesellschaften*, and it was during the Baroque era that they first appeared in Germany.

The most important and most influential of these language associations was the *Fruchtbringende Gesellschaft* which was founded in 1617 by Prince Ludwig von Anhalt-Köthen (1579–1650) and which lasted until the end of the century. It was understood as the German equivalent of the Italian Language Academy, *Accademia della Crusca*, established in 1582, of which Prince Ludwig was a member. Even though membership in the *Fruchtbringende Gesellschaft* was not restricted to the nobility, the latter constituted 75% of the members, the remaining quarter being the educated bourgeoisie who contributed by far the most to the achievements of the association. All members were male and mostly Protestants, but religious denomination and even nationality were regarded as secondary to a strong, genuine interest in the German language. The symbol of the association was the palm tree, and each member was given an emblem and an emblematic name: Prince Ludwig was called *Der Nährende* (The Nurturer) and used a loaf of baked wheat bread as an emblem. Caspar von Teutleben (1576–1629), who suggested the foundation of the association to Ludwig, was called *Der Mehlreiche* (Rich in Flour), his emblem being freshly-milled wheat flour falling out of a sack, with the words *hierin find sichs* (here's where you'll find it). Both the names and the emblems of members relate to the name of the Italian academy, with *crusca* meaning 'chaff'. The metaphor of separating the grain from the chaff expresses the idea that there are both desirable and undesirable words, phrases, grammatical constructions, etc., in every language, the former being worth taken care of, whereas the latter should be abolished.

Other *Sprachgesellschaften* of the Baroque were the *Aufrichtige Gesellschaft von der Tannen* (founded in 1633), the *Deutschgesinnte Genossenschaft* (founded in 1643), the *Elbschwanenorden* (founded in 1656), and the *Pegnesischer Blumenorden* which was founded in 1644 and has existed without interruption to the present day.[4]

The most influential members of Baroque *Sprachgesellschaften* in terms of puristic activity were Andreas Gryphius (1616–1664), Georg Philipp Harsdörffer (1607–1658), Martin Opitz (1597–1639), Justus Georg Schottelius (1612–1676) and Philipp von Zesen (1619–1689). It was their love of the fatherland and of the heroic German language which motivated them:

4   Pegnesischer Blumenorden (ed.), 'Pegnesischer Blumenorden' (accessed February 2007), <http://www.irrhain.de/>.

> Die Deutschen hätten [...] sich selbst dadurch geschändet und entehrt, daß sie ihre Sprache vernachlässigt und verachtet hätten. Sie müßten sich aber jetzt eines besseren besinnen und sich der Pflege der Muttersprache befleißigen. Zuallererst müßten sie dazu gebracht werden, ihre [sic] übermäßige Fremdwörtersucht abzuschwören. (Kirkness 1975: 18)

The fashionable, so-called *Einflicken* (insertion, mixing in) of foreign words, especially by what were seen as fawning courtiers and bourgeois fops, was perceived as superficial and pseudo-cultured and consequently criticized, for example in satirical verse by Sigmund von Birken, a member of the *Deutschgesinnte Genossenschaft*, *Pegnesischer Blumenorden* and *Fruchtbringende Gesellschaft*:

> Ich bin nun *deschargirt* von dem *maladen* Leben. / Mir hat der Maur *facon* genug *disgousto* gegeben. / Wo Einfalt *avanciert*, und Vnschuld mit *raison*, / Die *retrogarde* hat, da ist die Sache *bon*. (1645: 86)

The replacement of French and Latin terms was the main means used to rid German of unwanted lexical items. Gryphius is credited with successfully replacing many words, among them *Port* with *Ufer*, *Parlament* with *Herrenhaus*, *Ade* with *Fahrt wohl*. Harsdörffer replaced *Akt* with *Aufzug*, *observieren* with *beobachten*, *Korrespondenz* with *Briefwechsel*, *Gusto* with *Geschmack*, *Chronographicon* with *Zeitschrift*. Harsdörffer was not fiercely opposed to all foreign words but mainly to the *Alamodewesen* which led to a fashionable intermingling of French and German words. Schottelius was probably the most outstanding and influential language researcher of the Baroque. In 1641, he published his *Teutsche Sprachkunst*, and 1663 he wrote the influential *Ausführliche Arbeit von der Teutschen Haupt-Sprache*. For him, as for others, language cultivation was a moral and patriotic issue:

> Eine reine natürliche Sprache deute auf ein gesundes kräftiges Volk hin. [Schottelius] verwirft die Sprachmengerei nicht nur aus sprachlichen Gründen, sondern auch aus patriotischen, sittlichen und religiösen. Hinzu kommt auch noch sogar das politische Moment [...]. (Kirkness 1975: 38)

Schottelius is also credited with the successful replacement of a great number of foreign words, such as *Kolon* with *Doppelpunkt*, *signum interrogationis* with *Fragezeichen*, *Säkulum* with *Jahrhundert*.

The above-mentioned Philipp von Zesen was a translator, writer and poet of great reputation, and he also coined a great number of replacements for foreign words such as *Glaubensbekenntnis* for *Konfession*, *Bücherei* for *Bibliothek*, *Lehrling* for *Disciple*, *Oberfläche* for *superficies*, *Vertrag* for *conventio*, *Vollmacht* for *Plenipotenz*. Zesen was often subject to ridicule, even during his own time, because some of the replacements he suggested were deemed ridiculous, the most infamous being *Jungfernzwinger* for *Frauenkloster*, *Tagleuchter* for *Fenster*, *Sattelpuffer* or *Reitpuffer* for *Revolver* and *Löschhorn* or *Gesichtserker* for *Nase*. One should, however, not forget that Zesen's successful terms which sound perfectly normal to us today were in his own time probably not much less unusual than all his other coinages. As far as the Baroque is concerned, Kirkness states that the concept of a 'pure' language was rather broad; not only foreign words were targeted, but also obsolete or dialectal words and ungrammatical expressions:

> Der Begriff 'Sprachreinheit' wurde weit aufgefasst: Die Sprachreinigung im mittleren 17. Jahrhundert zielte auf ausländische, veraltete, mundartliche und im besonderen grammatisch unrichtige Ausdrücke in der Hochsprache. Trotz vieler Mißgriffe und Übertreibungen haben die barocken Sprachreiniger ganz wesentlich dazu beigetragen, den deutschen Wortschatz zu reinigen und zu bereichern, eine hochsprachliche Norm herauszubilden und der Vorherrschaft des Lateinischen und des Französischen entgegenzuwirken. (1975: 44)

Gardt shows that all of his four purist discourses appear in the Baroque Age, though quite differently in their intensity. The cultural patriotic discourse was the most widespread; however the chief criticism was not of foreign languages and cultures as such, but of the uncritical adoption of those languages and cultures. In fact, the great number of works translated from French rather proves that this language and culture was in fact admired and regarded as a model or even an ideal.

II. *The early eighteenth century / the Age of Enlightenment*

The main concern of the eighteenth century was to establish German as a language of science to replace the widely-used Latin language. There are four names which must be mentioned in dealing with standardization and puristic tendencies in the German language during the Age of Enlightenment:

Gottfried Wilhelm Leibniz (1646–1716), Johann Christoph Gottsched (1700–1766), Johann Christoph Adelung (1732–1806) and Friedrich Gottlieb Klopstock (1724–1803).

Leibniz argued that a language which was based on the principles of referential exactness, that is, similar to mathematics where every signifier refers to only one concept signified, would enable all reasonable beings to understand the world intellectually, and that this would serve the development of the human community as a whole. He assumed that German was threatened by decay or even extinction, since the intellectual elite much preferred French and Latin to German. Where German was used, Leibniz was in favour of a moderate cleansing of the language from foreign elements but he did not condemn all foreign influences *per se*, foreign words should be avoided, but so should rude, obscene, indecent and colloquial expressions. Common everyday German should, if possible, contain no foreign words at all, whereas writings of especially the government and the intellectual elite could contain them.

Gottsched and Adelung were both grammarians and contributed considerably to the establishment of the High German standard variety. Naturalness, rationality, the search for a middle way, and the avoidance of extremes are characteristic of Gottsched's enlightened language concept. In his German grammar, he insisted that one ought to abstain from the use of archaisms, provincialisms, and rude, obscene or indecent expressions. Gardt points out that the qualities of the German language which Gottsched mentioned are very much in tradition with classical rhetoric: 'Reichtum bzw. Überfluß and Ausdrucksmitteln, Deutlichkeit und Kürze bzw. Nachdruck [...] (copia, perspicuitas, brevitas)' (1999: 174). Concerning Gottsched's attitude towards foreign lexical influences, Kirkness states:

> Gottsched [nimmt] eine gemäßigte Stellung ein und wendet sich gegen die schlimmsten Auswüchse der barocken Sprachreinigung sowie zugleich gegen die affektierte und geschmacklose, daher unvernünftige Sprachmischung des 17. und 18. Jahrhunderts. (1975: 57)

Gottsched tolerated foreign influences, as he understood the communicative function of language. He did not think that German was in a bad condition and he disagreed with the traditional claim that an excessive use of foreign words would lead to the demise of the language. As Gardt puts it:

> Auch der traditionelle Vorwurf, nach dem exzessiver Fremdwortgebrauch zum Untergang einer Sprache [...] führt, kann Gottsched nicht vom negativen Zustand des Deutschen überzeugen [...] Die extremen fremdwortpuristischen Forderungen der Fruchtbringenden Gesellschaft sind für ihn 'Grillen'. (1999: 175)

Johann Christoph Adelung, in contrast, was very much opposed to the use of foreign words, a fact which must be understood as part of his aim to develop a linguistic norm. He tried to distinguish between necessary and objectionable foreign influences – and, as with many purists, fell into the definition trap. For him, as for Gottsched, a pure language meant an absence of archaisms and provincialisms, as well as rude, obscene or indecent expressions. For his famous dictionary, Adelung rejected these as well as substitutes which, in his opinion, expressed ideas either in a wrong or in an incomplete way. He assumed a correlation between language and intellect and categorized languages according to their complexity, believing that only grammatically complex languages were capable of expressing complex concepts. He therefore concluded that Chinese, which he regarded as 'stiffly monosyllabic', was a hindrance to the development of cultured thought. Gardt points out that it is dangerous to assume that language determines the cognitive processing of reality, as this would lead to the incorrect interpretation that certain lexical or grammatical features of a language are a barrier for the development of a speech community (1999: 187). He furthermore emphasizes that this assumption of a correlation between language and cognition is a vital part of the *sprachstruktureller Fremdwortdiskurs* and common among linguistic purists.

Friedrich Gottlieb Klopstock was, according to Kirkness (1998: 409), the most extreme language protector of the Enlightenment, his resolute opposition to foreign linguistic influences grounded in his lifelong love of Germany and everything German. Klopstock's language work can be regarded as very much in the tradition of the purists of the Baroque, it had nationalistic aims and pursued primarily the 'patriotic pride in the mother tongue' (*vaterländischer Stolz auf die Muttersprache*: Kirkness 1975: 54). He endorsed an extreme, nationalistic fight against foreign words and hoped to activate a German national pride and to make the German *Volk* aware of its strength and honour (*Kraft und Ehre*).

III. From the French Revolution to the Carlsbad Decrees (1789–1819)

Kirkness refers to the time between the French Revolution and the Carlsbad Decrees (*Karlsbader Beschlüsse*, 1819) as a transitional phase in which Standard High German was not only established to the greatest possible extent as the language of writing, but also mastered as a spoken variety all over the German-speaking countries (1998: 409–10). It was the basis for a feeling of cultural and philosophical unity of a nation with no political unity. Von Polenz (1999: 266) highlights for this period that German established itself completely as a language of prestige in place of French and Latin, with the result that the problem of a written norm was solved and that the existence of German was no longer in any danger. However, the French Revolution in 1789, the end of the Holy Roman Empire of the German Nation in 1806 and the victory over the French in the Napoleonic Wars led to the foundation of the *Deutscher Bund* (German Confederation) in 1814/15. It now appears to have been, as, Kirkness sees it, necessary for Germany to disassociate and distinguish itself from France:

> Diese Entwicklungen spiegelten sich zwangsläufig in der puristischen Bewegung wider, deren Motivation und Zielsetzung zunehmend eine (national-)politische wurde, deren Hauptinteresse fortan eindeutig den nichtdeutschen Wörtern aus der Fremde, den Fremdwörtern galt. (1998: 410)

Linguistic purism, however, was limited to educated, academic circles. The most prominent names of the time are Joachim Heinrich Campe (1746–1818), Karl Wilhelm Kolbe der Ältere (1757–1835), Karl Christian Friedrich Krause (1781–1832) and Friedrich Ludwig Jahn (1778–1852).

J.H. Campe was one of the most influential supporters of the Enlightenment, who, after the French Revolution, worked nearly exclusively on the German language. He was of the opinion that only a pure German language, comprehensible to every citizen, would lead to the general enlightenment of the German people. He compiled five volumes of his *Wörterbuch der Deutschen Sprache* (1807–11) as well as the *Wörterbuch zur Erklärung und Verdeutschung der unserer Sprache aufgedrungenen fremden Ausdrücke* (1813). Gardt points out that Campe's work, although puristic in nature, was clearly motivated by the Enlightenment (1999: 206). According to Kirkness, Campe coined almost 3,500 new words himself, of which only 10% are still used today

(1975: 148–59). That Campe's suggestions were not very successful might be connected to the fact that his knowledge of linguistic matters was not particularly deep, and that his methods were superficial. He was aware of that the distribution and circulation of his suggestions were very much dependent on the style of the recognized writers of his time and consequently tried to correct the style of some contemporary classical writers, but his exaggerations made him the subject of their ridicule. Johann Wolfgang von Goethe (1749–1832), for example, wrote in his *Xenie Nr. 25* 'An des Eridanus Ufer umgeht mir die furchtbare Waschfrau / Welche die Sprache des Teut säubert mit Lauge und Sand', and in *Xenie Nr. 39* he writes 'Sinnreich bist du, die Sprache von fremden Wörtern zu säubern / Nun, so sage doch, Freund, wie man Pedant uns verdeutscht';[5] both refer to Campe and his purist efforts. Many other famous eighteenth-century writers too, such as Johann Gottfried Herder (1744–1803), Christoph Martin Wieland (1733–1813), Jean Paul (Johann Paul Friedrich Richter, 1763–1825) and Friedrich Schiller (1759–1805) were familiar with Campe's work.

The Berlin artist Karl Wilhelm Kolbe had an aesthetic approach to language and regarded it as a complete unity (Kirkness 1998: 411). He was of the opinion that foreign lexical influences on German could potentially lead to a change in its structure, to the abandonment of its singularity, and finally to its extinction. He assumed a strong connection between language and nation, and his books *Über den Wortreichthum der deutschen und französischen Sprache* (1806) and *Über Wortmengerei* (1812) are characterized by an extreme tone and frequent exaggerations which were common during the time he was writing. They must be understood as a patriotic act against the fear of French domination in general, which is a very common manifestation of Gardt's *sprachideologischer Fremdwortdiskurs*, where the purist does not criticize a foreign language, but rather a foreign culture.[6]

The philosopher Christian Friedrich Krause, an extremist among linguistic purists (Kirkness 1975: 236), aimed to develop a new, rational language which was systematically constructed of supposedly Germanic forms only. He regarded it as a patriotic duty to conserve the German language

5   Goethe (1948: 211–13). For a more detailed account of Goethe's attitude towards purism, see Kirkness (1975: 267–82).
6   Pfalzgraf (2006: 158). See also pp. 222, 239, 280, 310.

and to eliminate all foreign elements, as in his view the German people would damage itself through random borrowing. Krause tried to achieve greater clarity of expression and translated 'dieser Mensch ist Gottes Sohn' as 'dieses orendliche [sic!] Geistleibinvereinswesen ist durch Wesen als gleich-wesentliches Nebenausserwesen miteigenlebverursacht' (quoted in Kirkness 1975: 230–6).

Friedrich Ludwig Jahn was probably the most extreme purist of his time. His love of everything German and his hatred of everything foreign – espe-cially French – strongly influenced his views on language. He rejected the use of almost all foreign words in German and was of the opinion that contact with foreign countries could only be destructive for German language and culture. In his view, the influence of foreign countries on Germany had a demoralizing effect on the Germans, and should therefore be eradicated. Von Polenz points out that the term *Fremdwort* was first used by Jahn:

> Nachdem im älteren Sprachreinigungsdiskurs bis ins frühe 19. Jh. nur von *fremdes / ausländisches / undeutsches Wort, Welschwort* usw. die Rede war, finden sich die beiden frühesten Belege für die Zusammensetzung *Fremdwort* 1816 und 1819 bei einem der Ide-ologen des frühen deutschen Nationalismus in der Napoleonzeit, Friedrich Ludwig Jahn [...]. In beiden Erstbelegen wird Fremdwort bereits als Kampfwort kontextuell definiert; mit biologischer und rechtsgeschichtlicher Metaphorik wird bereits 'Ausgestoßensein' und 'Vertilgung' thematisiert, was für den (ebenfalls durch Jahn angeregten) rassistischen Diskurs in Deutschland typisch ist. (1999: 265)

Renowned as the German *Turnvater*,[7] Jahn naturally introduced numer-ous new terms within the area of gymnastics. However, he was also engaged in the coining of military and other terminology. His wish for purity often led to exaggerations and an incomprehensible style: the perception that he went too far when it came to the replacement of foreign words led to his being ridiculed by his opponents. Kirkness (1998: 412) holds the view that for Jahn, purism was a means with a cultural-political end: foreign words were seen as symptoms of a ruinous foreign – especially French – influence on Germany, an evil which needed to be removed.

---

7   Jahn is known as the *Turnvater* because he initiated many gymnastics associations. His aim was to restore the spirits of the Germans by the development of their physical and moral powers through the practice of gymnastics.

In summarizing the period from the French Revolution to the Carlsbad
Decrees, Kirkness (1998: 411) distinguishes four different movements: the
educative-enlightening approach of Campe (*volksaufklärerisch-bildungs-*
politisch), the language structural approach of Kolbe (*sprachstrukturell*), a
radically rational approach of Krause (*radikal-vernünftelnd*), and the political-
nationalistic approach of Jahn (*politisch-nationalistisch*). It is remarkable that
three of these four movements identified by Kirkness are almost identical
with three of the four *Fremdwortdiskurse* which Gardt distinguishes for the
period between the Baroque age and the Second World War. In the nineteenth
century, the structurally-orientated purists assumed that foreign words could
endanger the structure of the German language, which they assumed would
result in a collapse of the entire language. Purists who were influenced by the
Enlightenment regarded the use of foreign words as a barrier between the
educated and uneducated classes, a barrier that would have to be overcome
in order to enable the people to participate in democratic processes. Other
purists had nationalistic motives and assumed that language was a part of the
German culture which was at least equivalent – if not superior – to foreign
cultures, especially that of France. For them, language criticism was cultural
criticism.

IV. The early nineteenth century

The nationalistically motivated purist movement outlined in the previous section came to a sudden end with the Carlsbad Decrees in 1819, but re-emerged
when the urge for national unity became stronger in the mid-nineteenth
century. It was now members of the academic community who criticized the
use of foreign words and who, as Kirkness (1975: 417–18) points out, acted
not as linguists but as conscious German patriots: for them, an unadulterated standard German was seen as an indication of German national unity
and emancipation.

Kirkness argues that the efforts of Josef Dominicus Carl/Karl Brugger
(1796–1865) must be understood within this context (1975: 342). Brugger
was involved in the foundation of the short-lived and unsuccessful *Verein der
Deutschen Reinsprache* in 1848, and from 1850 edited *Die Eiche*, a fortnightly
publication dealing with issues related to the German language, German

literature, art, and culture. Both the association and the publication shared the same fate: after an enthusiastic beginning, practically nothing was achieved. Brugger suggested to the 1848 *Nationalversammlung* that all words of foreign origin should be translated, and that only German words should be used: he aimed to thoroughly cleanse the German language from everything foreign, mainly by replacing lexical items with coinages supposedly based on Germanic roots. But although Brugger tried to address the public authorities, government institutions, teachers, writers, journalists and editors, his work was known almost exclusively to academics. Brugger was regarded as overeager, even in his time, and was not at all qualified for either linguistic research or language cultivation, as his knowledge of linguistic structures was at best superficial.

Many other language protection organizations were founded around the same time, but all of them published little or nothing, had no impact on the German language at all, and ceased to exist soon after they came into existence. Georg Heinrich Otto Volger (1822–1897) was one of the founders of the *Freies Deutsches Hochstift* which does still exist today.[8] The purpose of the *Hochstift* was to unite all sciences, arts, and general educational institutions, and the purification of the German language was mentioned as one of its aims. Volger was, however, alone in his interest in linguistic purism and sometimes criticized by other leading figures of the *Hochstift*, and for Kirkness (1975: 357), it comes as no surprise that its purist activities ceased when Volger left for Lüneburg in 1866.

To sum up, one can say that the *Fremdwortpurismus* of the early to mid nineteenth century was an academic movement which failed to convince or even attract the public and which, despite the foundation of various *Sprachschutzvereine* and publications, had no perceivable success. The movement was exclusively patriotic and, according to Gardt, both an ideological discourse about foreign words and a discourse concerning stylistics and rhetoric prevailed. Despite some differences from earlier phases of purism, language criticism was once again used as a means of cultural criticism.

---

8 Freies Deutsches Hochstift (ed.), 'Freies Deutsches Hochstift' (accessed February 2007), <http://www.goethehaus-frankfurt.de/hochstift/>.

V. From 1871 to World War II

The establishment of the German Empire in 1871 can be seen as the beginning
of the institutionalization of linguistic purism. During the re-organization
of the state administration, many officials with a critical approach towards
foreign words came to office, and this led to a great number of substitutions
of foreign – and especially French – words. The General Postmaster Heinrich
von Stephan, for example, issued a decree which replaced some 800 French
words with German equivalents, such as *Couvert* with *Briefumschlag, poste
restante* with *postlagernd* and *recommandiert* with *per Einschreiben*. Another
official, the Senior Building Officer (*Oberbaurat*) Otto Sarrazin successfully
translated and substituted around 1,300 technical terms from the areas of civil
engineering and the railways, including *Barriere* with *Schranke, Perron* with
Bahnsteig and *Retourbillet* with *Rückfahrkarte*. Such efforts were supported
by the Prussian King Wilhelm IV, for example, regarding the language of the
army where *Charge* was substituted by *Dienstgrad, Avancement* by *Beförderung*
and *Anciennität* by *Dienstalter*.

Simultaneously with this official support, the hunt for foreign words
became a widespread movement among ordinary people. Of great importance
in this respect is the foundation of the *Allgemeiner Deutscher Sprachverein*
(ADSV) in 1885 by Hermann Riegel (1834–1900), Director of the Brunswick Museum and Professor of Art History at Brunswick Polytechnic, in co-
operation with Hermann Dunger (1843–1912), a grammar school teacher in
Dresden.[9] In the first issue of the periodical of the ADSV Riegel stated the
society's three aims: to encourage the purification of the German language
from unnecessary foreign elements; to cultivate the preservation and restora-
tion of the true spirit and the genuine character of the German language; and
thus to strengthen the national awareness of the German people:

> Der 'allgemeine deutsche Sprachverein' ist ins Leben getreten, um 1) die Reinigung
> der deutschen Sprache von unnöthigen fremden Bestandtheilen zu fördern, – 2) die
> Erhaltung und Wiederherstellung des echten Geistes und eigenthümlichen Wesens der
> deutschen Sprache zu pflegen – und 3) auf diese Weise das allgemeine Bewußtsein im
> Deutschen Volke zu kräftigen. (1886: 1)

9   Dunger was not, as often claimed, Professor of German at Dresden University but a
     teacher at two Dresden grammar schools, see: Viereck (1989: 3*).

Obviously, the notion of the beauty and purity of the German language was highly valued by the ADSV, but it is important to point out that the aims of the association were not primarily concerned with language, but with issues related to culture and nation. This is also apparent in the ADSV slogan 'Gedenke auch, wenn du die deutsche Sprache sprichst, daß du ein Deutscher bist!'[10]

Commenting on the first of the main aims of the ADSV, Bernsmeier notes that it was the ADSV's goal to eliminate foreign words from German (1980: 117). This was mainly aimed at French influences; however, English words were also targeted (Dunger 1909). In theory, the ADSV distinguished between useful or good and unnecessary or bad foreign words, and the latter were to be replaced by German equivalents. The terms 'good' and 'equivalent', however, were interpreted quite differently within the ADSV as no criteria had been developed for distinguishing between, for example, 'good' and 'equivalent' (Kirkness 1983: 19).[11] One's knowledge of the German language was not important; it was more important to speak German, to think in a German way, and to be German – not to put forward good linguistic arguments:

> Beim Fremdwortpurismus kam es also nicht auf Wissen über Sprache, [...] sondern darauf an, deutsch zu sprechen, deutsch zu denken und deutsch zu sein. [... Es ging] dem Sprachverein nicht darum, sprachwissenschaftlich zu argumentieren. (Kirkness 1983: 20)

In practice, the ADSV did not follow its own theoretical approach to combat only those foreign words which were regarded as superfluous and to exclude those which had long been fully integrated into German. The names of the months and their Latin origin, for example, were always a matter of concern for the association – consequently, old terms such as *Hornung* for *Februar* or *Scheidling* for *September* were used in ADSV publications.

The German language was regarded as a 'House of Treasures' (*Schatzhaus*), a monument (*Denkmal*), a sanctuary (*Heiligtum*), a national symbol (*Nationalsymbol*) and a cultural heritage (*kulturelles Erbe*) (von Polenz 1999: 271), In order to protect these, the ADSV expected people to fight for them, and this *Kampf* was seen as an act of national education (*nationalerzieherisches*

---

10   See e.g. Lohmeyer (1917: 198).
11   Kirkness (1983: 19).

Werk) (Kirkness 1983: 20). Foreign words were metaphorically described as a flood (*Fremdwortflut*) and as a cancerous wound on the body of German traditions ('krebsige Wunde am Leibe deutschen Volkstums'), while their use was regarded as spiritual treason ('geistiger Landesverrat') or as a sign of national lethargy and leading to a 'linguistic swamp' ('Zeichen nationaler Stumpfheit und sprachlicher Versumpfung'). In addition to these metaphors of water, flood and mud, metaphors of illness and disease, of moral decline (*Sittenverfall*), crime (*Verbrechen*), or decay (*Verfall*) of the sick German language ('kranke deutsche Sprache'), characterize ADSV discourse (von Polenz 1999: 276).

The prevailing topic of language deterioration shows that the ADSV believed in the former existence of a perfect language which has always been subject to decay. Some members of the ADSV praised the medieval language of the *Nibelungenlied* or of Walther von der Vogelweide, others pointed to Old High German (750–1050). But no matter what was recommended, all ADSV members believed in a formerly unadulterated, healthy and strong, perfect language which had been degenerating and would continue to do so. The language was likened to a plant or flower, which grows and develops, then comes into full bloom and eventually decays and dies; thus the normal phenomenon of language change is understood as language decay.

Concerning supposedly superfluous and unnecessary foreign words, the ADSV claimed that these had a negative influence on the beauty and originality of German, that they would prevent German from fully developing its means of word formation, and that this would lead to an impoverishment of the lexis; furthermore that such words were often unclear, ambiguous and incomprehensible and that their use would lead to a communication barrier between members of the language community:

> dass sie die Schönheit und Ursprünglichkeit des Deutschen beeinträchtigten [...], daß sie das Deutsche daran hinderten, die eigenen, vom Germanischen stammenden Wortbildungsmittel [...] voll einzusetzen, und somit eine Verarmung des Wortschatzes darstellten; daß sie häufig unklar, mehrdeutig oder unverständlich wären und deshalb Verwirrung stifteten und eine Bildungsbarriere quer durch die Sprachgemeinschaft errichteten. (Kirkness 1983: 19)

To remedy this, the ADSV published so-called 'language corners' (*Sprachecken*) in its journal, the aim of which was to sharpen the readers' feel for language, their *Sprachgefühl*. They also issued numerous *Verdeutschungsbücher* which offered German 'equivalents' in order to substitute the vocabulary in different areas of language such as schooling, sports, or restaurant menus. As mentioned above, some substitutions by ADSV members were so successful that these words are still used today, as is the case in the areas of the postal service and the railways. On the other hand, some unfortunate suggestions were made, such as *Kahlkopfverlegenheitsabhelfer* for *Perücke* or *Starkschwach-fingerschlagtonkasten* for *Klavier* or *Piano*.

As far as the use of foreign words was concerned, the ADSV ascribed this to negative character attributes such as slothfulness, laziness of thought, vanity, arrogance and snobbery. Furthermore, it believed that users of foreign words suffered from an exaggerated respect for everything foreign and a con-current self-disregard. Although language was the ADSV's primary concern, it repeatedly subordinated language matters to non-linguistic political objectives, particularly during the First World War. 'The war cleanses the language' (*Der Krieg reinigt die Sprache*), rejoiced the ADSV (1914: 305) when the war broke out. Later, when Hitler came to power, the ADSV expressed itself in increasingly political terms: as the 'SA of the mother tongue', violently protesting against the disfigurement and mutilation of the 'holy blood heritage' by 'vermin of the nation' (1934: 146). Initially, the ADSV regarded the outbreak of German fascism as an opportunity to gain support from the highest governmental authorities to do away with all foreign words in German. It soon turned out, however, that the leading Nazis did not share the association's interests: Goebbels expressed a great disapproval for the ADSV's work during a meeting of the Cultural Chamber of the Reich, (*Reichskulturkammer*), in 1937, and two years later the ADSV periodical was taken from the association and put under different editorship; the ADSV was henceforth allowed only to publish a report about its work. Eventually, in an edict of 1940, Hitler personally turned against the translation and substitution of foreign words. This was de facto the end of the association, and with it the end of the hounding of foreign words as a widespread movement among ordinary Germans.

VI. After the Second World War

It is generally agreed that no significant purist activity took place between the abolition of the ADSV in the 1940s and German unification in 1990. Kirkness (1998: 414–15) points out that the foreign words in German were still an issue, but all in all, they were better tolerated, and nationalist linguistic purism appeared only infrequently. Von Polenz emphasizes that public criticism of foreign words was mostly ignored, while more extreme ideas were simply ridiculed:

> Die durchaus geäußerte öffentliche Kritik am Überhandnehmen von Anglizismen [...] im westlichen Nachkriegsdeutschland wurde ohne erkennbare Wirkung registriert: extreme Verdeutschungsvorschläge wurden als Randerscheinungen belächelt oder verspottet. (1999: 287)

Since the early 1990s, however, the debate about the use of foreign words in German has increased in intensity. While only a few German politicians commented on the subject between the Second World War and the 1990s, since 2001 numerous high-profile politicians from all parties have criticized the alleged overuse of anglicisms, e.g. the then Federal President Johannes Rau (SPD), the Speaker of the German Parliament Wolfgang Thierse (SPD), the leader of the FDP Wolfgang Gerhard, the Bavarian Interior Minister Hans Zehetmair (CSU), and the Governing Mayor of Berlin Eberhard Diepgen (CDU). For the first time since the 1930s there have been demands for laws to protect the German language.

Closely related to this is the fact that, since the early 1990s, an increasing number of organizations for the protection of the language have emerged in Germany. Some have a remarkably large number of members and regularly voice their opinions in the media, while others are much smaller and less influential, although their aims are similar. The most influential associations are the *Verein Deutsche Sprache* (VDS),[12] the *Verein für deutsche Rechtschreibung und Sprachpflege* (VRS),[13] the *Verein für Sprachpflege* (VfS) with its

---

12   Verein Deutsche Sprache, 'Verein Deutsche Sprache' (accessed February 2007), <http://www.vds-ev.de/>.

13   Verein für deutsche Rechtschreibung und Sprachpflege, 'Startseite' (accessed February 2007), <http://www.vrs-ev.de/>.

publication *Deutsche Sprachwelt* (DSW),[14] and the *Bund für deutsche Schrift und Sprache* (BfdS).[15] Pfalzgraf (2003a, b) has shown that both the VfS and the BfdS have contacts with political right-wing organizations and individuals, while the others have more or less successfully eliminated such connections in recent years. However, one must be aware of the fact that the issue of foreign words in general and anglicisms in particular is sometimes consciously used to support right-wing propaganda.[16]

The largest and best-known language protection organization, the *Verein Deutsche Sprache* (VDS), was founded under the name *Verein zur Wahrung der deutschen Sprache* (VWdS) in Dortmund in 1997 by the mathematician and statistician Prof. Walter Krämer. According to its website, the VDS has 30,000 members in almost 100 countries. Using similar metaphors to the puristically-inclined ADSV, the VDS claims that there is currently an ugly flood of unnecessary anglicisms. The VDS criticizes a perceived mixture of languages (*Sprachgemisch*) which it refers to as 'Denglisch' and 'Imponierge-fasel' (drivel which aims to impress). They oppose superfluous English bits and pieces (*die überflüssigen englischen Brocken*) and perceive a disdainful treatment of German (*verächtliche Behandlung der deutschen Sprache*). Language is regarded by the VDS as an entity that deserves respect. The aim of the VDS is to oppose the anglicization of the German language and to remind the Germans of the value and the beauty of their mother tongue.[17]

The academic advisory board (*Wissenschaftlicher Beirat*) of the VDS consists almost entirely of university professors – hardly any of them an expert linguist – who state its aim to defend the German language in the face of acute danger:

> Der für alle Völker selbstverständliche Sprachpatriotismus ist in Deutschland und Österreich angesichts ihrer jüngsten Geschichte belastet. Trotzdem macht es die aktuelle

14 Verein für Sprachpflege, 'Deutsche Sprachwelt' (accessed February 2007), <http://www.deutsche-sprachwelt.de/>.

15 Bund für deutsche Schrift und Sprache, 'Bund für deutsche Schrift und Sprache' (accessed February 2007), <http://www.bfds.de/>.

16 See Pfalzgraf and Leuschner 2006.

17 Verein Deutsche Sprache, 'VDS vorgestellt' (accessed February 2007), <http://www.vds-ev.de/verein/>.

Gefährdung der deutschen Sprache als Kulturgut notwendig, jetzt für ihre Verteidigung einzutreten.[18]

The similarities of the views of VDS and ADSV are striking: language is regarded as a cultural heritage (*kulturelles Erbe*) and an essential part of the cultural wealth to be preserved at all costs (*unverzichtbares Kulturgut*), it is seen as the primary resource for literary art (*Rohstoff für sprachliche Kunstwerke*), and it is endangered (*in Gefahr*) and on the verge of becoming unusable (*droht unbrauchbar zu werden*). Anglicisms are judged as a development which came into existence because of bad taste and linguistic, cultural, and political indifference. The advisory board further holds the view that the language has been severely damaged and that German will become sick because of overfeeding (*Überfütterung*) with anglicisms. The advisory board claims that the perceived anglicization of German is caused by the political and cultural dominance of the USA, together with a lack of loyalty to the German language and the willingness of Germany to adopt US values.[19]

To fight English influence on German, the VDS publishes its quarterly *Sprachnachrichten*[20] and various books;[21] it also organizes a number of activities, such as the *Tag der deutschen Sprache*, which is intended to promote German linguistic consciousness and prevent the 'crazy' use of 'Denglisch':

> Der Tag der deutschen Sprache soll ein Sprachbewußtsein schaffen und festigen, das den unkritischen Gebrauch von Fremdwörtern, insbesondere die Sucht, überflüssige englische Ausdrücke zu benutzen, den Englisch- und Denglischwahn, eindämmt bzw. verhindert.[22]

---

18   Verein Deutsche Sprache, 'Gründungserklärung des Wissenschaftlichen Beirats des Vereins Deutsche Sprache (VDS)' (accessed February 2007), <http://vds-ev.de/verein/wissenschaftlicher_beirat_grundsatz.php>.

19   Ibid.

20   Verein Deutsche Sprache, 'Sprachnachrichten' (accessed February 2007), <http://www.vds-ev.de/verein/sprachnachrichten/>.

21   Verein Deutsche Sprache, 'VDS-Buchversand' (accessed February 2007), <http://www.vds-ev.de/buchversand/>.

22   Verein Deutsche Sprache, 'Tag der deutschen Sprache' (accessed February 2007), <http://www.vds-ev.de/verein/aktionen/tag-der-deutschen-sprache/>.

Together with the Eberhard-Schöck Foundation, the VDS awards the annual *Kulturpreis Deutsche Sprache* to people who work to preserve the German language and help its development. This prize has been awarded to, amongst others, writer Rolf Hochhuth and humorist Vicco von Bühlow (alias 'Loriot').[23] In addition, the VDS regularly launches campaigns such as *Deutsche Sprache ins Grundgesetz* or *Sprachlicher Verbraucherschutz* in order to fight supposedly harmful anglicisms.[24]

Like other purist organizations, the VDS also calls for the translation and substitution of anglicisms with what is believed to be their German equivalent. Their *Anglizismen-Index* is a words list which offers alternatives for the use of anglicisms:

> Der Anglizismen-Index ist ein aktuelles Nachschlagewerk für Anglizismen mit einer Auswahl deutscher Entsprechungen, die eine Alternative für solche Anglizismen sein können, die deutsche Wörter verdrängen und vornehmlich Bedeutungserklärung für solche, die als ergänzend oder differenzierend gelten dürfen.[25]

This index offers evaluations of whether an anglicism is regarded as being additional (*ergänzend*), differentiating (*differenzierend*), suppressive (*verdrängend*) or a proper noun (*Eigenname*). Like other purist organizations, the VDS has no criteria for these distinctions: it is a matter of taste. Like the ADSV, the VDS is trying to substitute long-established words such as *T-Shirt* with *T-Hemd* or with the Gallicism *Trikothemd*.[26] On their website, *T-Shirt* is translated as *Leichthemd*, a word which few Germans would understand.[27] The VDS states that they would accept certain anglicisms: 'Gegen fair, Interview,

23 Verein Deutsche Sprache, 'Kulturpreis Deutsche Sprache' (accessed February 2007), <http://www.vds-ev.de/verein/aktionen/kulturpreis.php>, and <http://www.kultur-preis-deutsche-sprache.de> (accessed February 2007).

24 Verein Deutsche Sprache, 'Arbeitsgruppen im Verein Deutsche Sprache' (accessed February 2007), <http://www.vds-ev.de/verein/aktive/arbeitsgruppen.php>.

25 Verein Deutsche Sprache, 'Der Anglizismen-Index' (accessed February 2007), <http://www.vds-ev.de//anglizismenindex/>.

26 Verein Deutsche Sprache, 'Wörterliste: T-Shirt' (accessed February 2007), <http://www.vds-ev.de/anglizismenindex/suche2.php?str=t-shirt>.

27 Verein Deutsche Sprache, 'VDS- Buchversand' (accessed February 2007), <http://www.vds-ev.de/buchversand/>.

Trainer, Doping, Slang haben wir nichts einzuwenden.'[28] However, all these words are on its substitution list, and *Training* is regarded as being *verdrängend*. The difference between puristic theory and practice is evident.

Conclusion

If we compare the purist movement since German unification with the purists before 1990, there are apparent similarities. However, a thorough analysis has shown major differences concerning the constitution of the four discourses which are typical of linguistic purism: the almost complete absence of the pedagogical/sociological discourse about foreign words (*sprachpädagogisch-sprachsoziologischer Fremdwortdiskurs*) and the concurrent strength of ideological discourse (*sprachideologischer Fremdwortdiskurs*) (Pfalzgraf 2006: 303–12). The strong presence of the latter shows that the motivation for the criticism of anglicisms – other foreign words are often less criticized or even accepted, especially if these stem from classical Greek or Latin – is of an ideological nature. This discourse essentially expresses the fear of a linguistic and cultural 'colonization' by the USA, a fear which in extreme cases can manifest itself as a right-wing political position. Language criticism is a substitute for cultural criticism and instead of the USA itself, Anglicisms – and sometimes people who use them – are criticized, insulted, harassed, or attacked vicariously. This also explains the almost complete absence of a pedagogical/sociological discourse: while the motives of education or enlightenment were of great importance for Campe, as it was his principal aim to improve the democratization of Germany, such motives no longer prevail. Whether Gardt's four discourses are present or not can be explained by cultural criticism aimed against the USA. Because of this particular form of purism with its distinct constitution of puristic discourses, Pfalzgraf (2006) has suggested the use of the term *Neopurismus* (neo-purism) to describe it.

28   Verein Deutsche Sprache, 'VDS vorgestellt' (accessed February 2007), <http://www.vds-ev.de/verein/>.

The phenomenon of anti-Americanism must be understood within the socio-economical context of Germany since its unification. Soon after the *Wende* it became clear that the German government would not be able to solve the problems which came with it. The economic situation in Germany worsened, with an increase in unemployment resulting in the deterioration of the social security system and a new economic and emotional division between East and West Germany. Furthermore, the collapse of the Soviet Union, the resulting fall of the Berlin Wall, and the end of the separation of the world into East and West forced the Germans – once more – to define what it means to be German, especially with regard to its relationship with the USA. 'Now, are we Germans or just bad copies of Americans'[29] is the core question repeatedly asked by purists.

The neo-puristic tendencies which have occurred since German unification could consequently be understood as the result of a German identity crisis similar to the one after the Thirty Years War, after the Napoleonic War, and during the establishment of the *Kleindeutsches Reich*. Despite such similarities, however, the situation is different today. Certainly, many linguists believe that German purism has always coincided with nationalism and/or war. Von Polenz describes purism as a development which is strongly related to the history of German national emotions and nationalism. He points out that linguistic purism in Germany has always been connected to peaks of political activation of nationalist feelings. As examples, von Polenz (1967: 79–80) names the historical events mentioned above and the outbreak of the First World War, as does Keller who adds 'the time of the Nazi take-over of power' (1978: 611–12). This is true at least as far as the development of purist movements in the German past is concerned. However, the strongly related issue of language and identity seems to be underrated. As Claudia Law (2002: 82–3) states, one can hardly speak of German nationalism today, and even less of the danger of a war, as Germany is a stable, democratic nation with an exemplary social system. She agrees that current purism is not based on a crisis of the German state or the nation, but is related to a deeply-rooted crisis of a psychological nature: Germany, the second largest language area in Europe,

---

29   See, for example, Michael Geisberger. 'Das Ärgernis' (accessed April 2003). <http://www.denglisch.com/aergerniss.htm>.

is currently trying to define itself and its position in Europe and the world in terms of culture and politics.

References

Adelung, J.C. (1808), *Grammatisch-kritisches Wörterbuch der hochdeutschen Mundart. Mit beständiger Vergleichung der übrigen Mundarten, besonders aber der Oberdeutschen. Mit D.W. Soltau's Beyträgen. Rev. und berichtiget von Franz Xaver Schönberger*. Wien: Pichler, Reprographic reprint (1990), Hildesheim. CD-ROM Berlin (2001), available online, http://www.ub.uni-bielefeld.de/diglib/adelung/grammati/ (accessed February 2007).

ADSV = Allgemeiner deutscher Sprachverein. *Zeitschrift des Allgemeinen deutschen Sprachvereins* (1886); *Zeitschrift des Allgemeinen deutschen Sprachvereins* (1914); *Zeitschrift des Allgemeinen deutschen Sprachvereins* (1934).

Bernsmeier, H. (1977), 'Der Allgemeine Deutsche Sprachverein in seiner Gründungsphase', *Muttersprache* 87, 369–95.

Bernsmeier, H. (1980), 'Der Allgemeine Deutsche Sprachverein in der Zeit von 1912 bis 1932', *Muttersprache* 90, 117–40.

Bernsmeier, H. (1983), 'Der Deutsche Sprachverein im "Dritten Reich"', *Muttersprache* 93, 35–58.

Birken, S. von (1645), *Fortsetzung Der Pegnitz-Schaeferey*, Nürnberg: Wolffgang Endter.

Boeder, W., Brincat, J. and Stolz, T. (2003), 'Preface', in: *Purism in Minor, Regional and Endangered Languages*, edited by J. Brincat, W. Boeder and T. Stolz, Bochum: Brockmeyer, vii–xiv.

Bund für deutsche Schrift und Sprache: http://www.bfds.de/ (accessed February 2007).

Campe, J.H. (1807–11), *Wörterbuch der deutschen Sprache*, 5 vols, Braunschweig. Reprographic reprint (1969–70), 6 Vols, Hildesheim.

Campe, J.H. (1813), *Wörterbuch zur Erklärung und Verdeutschung der unserer Sprache aufgedrungenen fremden Ausdrücke*, Braunschweig: Schulbuchhandlung.

Crystal, D. (2006), *A Dictionary of Linguistics & Phonetics*, 5th ed., Oxford: Blackwell.

Duckworth, D. (1977), 'Zur terminologischen und systematischen Grundlage der Forschung auf dem Gebiet der englisch-deutschen Interferenz. Kritische Übersicht und neuer Vorschlag', in: *Sprachliche Interferenz – Festschrift für Werner Betz zum 65. Geburtstag*, edited by H. Kolb and H. Lauffer, Tübingen: Niemeyer, 36–56.

Dunger, H. (1882/1909), *Wörterbuch von Verdeutschungen entbehrlicher Fremdwörter / Engländerei in der deutschen Sprache*. Reprint (1989) of Leipzig (1882) and Berlin (1909) editions, Hildesheim: Olms.

Eisenberg, P. (1999), 'Stirbt das Deutsche an den Internationalismen? Zur Integration von Computerwörtern', *Der Deutschunterricht* 51:3, 17–24.

Eisenberg, P. (2001), 'Die grammatische Integration von Fremdwörtern. Was fängt das Deutsche mit seinen Latinismen und Anglizismen an?', in: *Neues und Fremdes im deutschen Wortschatz. Aktueller lexikalischer Wandel*, edited by G. Stickel, Berlin: de Gruyter, 183–209.

Freies Deutsches Hochstift: http://www.goethehaus-frankfurt.de/hochstift/ (accessed February 2007).

Gardt, A. (1999), *Geschichte der Sprachwissenschaft in Deutschland*, Berlin: de Gruyter.

Gardt, A. (2001a), 'Das Fremde und das Eigene. Versuch einer Systematik des Fremdwortbegriffs in der deutschen Sprachgeschichte', in: *Neues und Fremdes im deutschen Wortschatz. Aktueller lexikalischer Wandel*, edited by G. Stickel, Berlin: de Gruyter, 30–58.

Gardt, A. (2001b), 'Zur Bewertung der Fremdwörter im Deutschen (vom 16. bis 20. Jahrhundert)', *Deutsch als Fremdsprache* 3, 133–42.

Gardt, A. (ed.) (2000), *Nation und Sprache. Die Diskussion ihres Verhältnisses in Geschichte und Gegenwart*, Berlin: de Gruyter.

Gauger, H.M. (1999), 'Die Hilflosigkeit der Sprachwissenschaft', edited by C. Meier, *Sprache in Not? Zur Lage des heutigen Deutsch*, Göttingen: Wallstein, 85–101.

Geisberger, M. (2003), *Das Ärgernis*: http://www.denglisch.com/aergerniss.htm. (accessed April 2003).

Goethe, J.W. von, edited by Trunz, E. (1948), *Goethes Werke. Hamburger Ausgabe*, vol. 1, Hamburg: Christian Wegner.

Greule, A. and Ahlvers-Liebel, E. (1986), *Germanistische Sprachpflege. Geschichte, Praxis und Zielsetzung*, Darmstadt: Wissenschaftliche Buchgesellschaft.

Hohenhaus, P. (2001), '"Neuanglodeutsch" – Zur vermeintlichen Bedrohung des Deutschen durch das Englische', *German as a foreign language* 1, 57–87 available online: http://www.gfl-journal.de/1-2001/hohenhaus.pdf. (Accessed February 2007).

Hohenhaus, P. (2002), 'Standardization, language change, resistance and the question of linguistic threat. 18th century English and present-day German', in: *Standardization. Studies from the Germanic languages*, edited by A.R. Linn and N. McLelland, Amsterdam: Benjamins, 153–78 (Current issues in linguistic theory, vol. 235).

Jessen, J. (2007), 'Die verkaufte Sprache', *Die Zeit* 31 (26.July).

Jones, W.J. (ed.) (1995), *Sprachhelden und Sprachverderber. Dokumente zur Erforschung des Fremdwortpurismus im Deutschen (1478–1750)*, Berlin: de Gruyter (Studia Linguistica Germanica 38).

Jones, W.J. (1999), *Images of Language. Six Essays on German Attitudes to European Languages from 1500 to 1800*, Amsterdam: Benjamins.

Keller, R.E. (1978), *The German Language*, London: Faber & Faber.

Kirkness, A. (1975), *Zur Sprachreinigung im Deutschen 1789–1871. Eine historische Dokumentation*, 2 vols, Tübingen: Narr.

Kirkness, A. (1983), 'Fremdwort und Fremdwortpurismus: Lehren aus der Sprachgeschichte für den Deutschunterricht', *Sprache und Literatur in Wissenschaft und Unterricht* 51, 14–29.

Kirkness, A. (1998), 'Das Phänomen des Purismus in der Geschichte des Deutschen', in: *Sprachgeschichte. Ein Handbuch zur Geschichte der deutschen Sprache und ihrer Erforschung*, edited by W. Besch, A. Betten, O. Reichmann and S. Sonderegger, (HSK), 2nd, fully revised edition, vol. 2.1, Berlin: de Gruyter, 407–16.

Kolbe, K.W. (1806), *Über den Wortreichthum der deutschen und französischen Sprache und beider Anlage zur Poesie: nebst andern Bemerkungen, Sprache und Litteratur betreffend*, 2 vols, Leipzig: Reclam.

Kolbe, K.W. (1812), *Über Wortmengerei. Anfang zu der Schrift. Ueber den Wortreichthum der deutschen und französischen Sprache*, 2nd, completely revised edition, Leipzig: Reclam.

Langer, N. and Davies, W. (2005), 'An Introduction to Linguistic Purism', in: *Linguistic Purism in the Germanic Languages*, edited by N. Langer, and W. Davies, Berlin: de Gruyter, 1–17 (Studia Linguistica Germanica 75).

Law, C. (2002), 'Das sprachliche Ringen um die nationale und kulturelle Identität Deutschlands. Puristische Reaktionen im 17. Jahrhundert und Ende des 20. Jahrhunderts', *Muttersprache* 1/112, 67–83.

Leweling, B. (2005), *Reichtum, Reinigkeit und Glanz – Sprachkritische Konzeptionen in der Sprachreflexion des 18. Jahrhunderts*, Frankfurt am Main: Peter Lang.

Lohmeyer, E. (1917), *Unsere Umgangssprache. Verdeutschung der hauptsächlichsten im täglichen Leben und Verkehr gebrauchten Fremdwörter*, 3rd, fully revised edition, Berlin: Verlag des ADSV (Verdeutschungsbücher des Allgemeinen Deutschen Sprachvereins III).

Neue Fruchtbringende Gesellschaft: http://www.fruchtbringende-gesellschaft.de. (accessed February 2007).

Otto, K.F. (1972), *Die Sprachgesellschaften des 17. Jahrhunderts*, Stuttgart: Metzler.

Pegnesischer Blumenorden, *Anfangsseite*: http://www.irrhain.de/ (accessed February 2007).

Pfalzgraf, F. (2003a), 'Fremdwortdiskussion und Rechtsextremismus', *German Life and Letters* 1/LVI, 102–16.

Pfalzgraf, F. (2003b), 'Recent Developments Concerning Language Protection Organizations and Right-Wing Extremism in Germany', *German Life and Letters* 4/LVI, 397–409.

Pfalzgraf, F. (2005), 'Auffassungen von Laien zum Gebrauch von Anglizismen im Deutschen', in *Field Studies. German Language, Media and Culture*, edited by C. Fehringer and H. Briel, CUTG Proceedings, vol. 5, Oxford: Peter Lang, 29–49.

Pfalzgraf, F. (2006), 'Neopurismus in Deutschland nach der Wende', in: *Österreichisches Deutsch. Sprache der Gegenwart, vol. 6*, edited by R. Muhr and R. Schrodt, Frankfurt am Main: Peter Lang.

Pfalzgraf, F. and Leuschner, T. (2006), 'Einstellungen zu Fremdwörtern und Anglizismen. Anmerkungen zu einer Repräsentativerhebung des Instituts für Deutsche Sprache', *Germanistische Mitteilungen* 64/2006, 85–107.

Polenz, P. von (1968), 'Sprachpurismus und Nationalsozialismus. Die "Fremdwort"-Frage gestern und heute', in: *Nationalismus in Germanistik und Dichtung. Dokumentation des Germanistentages in München vom 17.–22. Oktober 1966*, edited by B. von Wiese and R. Henß, Berlin: Erich Schmidt, 79–112.

Polenz, P. von (1999), *Deutsche Sprachgeschichte*, vol. 3, Berlin: de Gruyter.

Stoll, C. (1973), *Sprachgesellschaften im Deutschland des 17. Jahrhunderts*, München: List.

Stukenbrock, A. (2005), *Sprachnationalismus. Sprachreflexion als Medium kollektiver Identitätsstiftung in Deutschland (1617–1945)*, Berlin: de Gruyter (Studia Linguistica Germanica 74).

Thomas, G. (1991), *Linguistic Purism*, London: Longman.

Verein Deutsche Sprache, '*Arbeitsgruppen im Verein Deutsche Sprache*', http://www.vds-ev. de/verein/aktive/arbeitsgruppen, (accessed February 2007).

Verein Deutsche Sprache, '*Argumente zur deutschen Sprache*', http://www.vds-ev.de/ denglisch/ (accessed February 2007).

Verein Deutsche Sprache, '*Der Anglizismen-Index*', http://www.vds-ev.de//anglizismenindex/ (accessed February 2007).

Verein Deutsche Sprache, '*Gründungserklärung des Wissenschaftlichen Beirats des Vereins Deutsche Sprache (VDS)*', http://vds-ev.de/verein/wissenschaftlicher_beirat_grundsatz.php (accessed February 2007).

Verein Deutsche Sprache, '*Kulturpreis Deutsche Sprache*', http://www.vds-ev.de/ verein/ aktionen/kulturpreis.php (accessed February 2007).

Verein Deutsche Sprache, '*Sprachnachrichten*', http://www.vds-ev.de/verein/sprachnachrichten/ (accessed February 2007).

Verein Deutsche Sprache, '*Tag der deutschen Sprache*', http://www.vds-ev.de/verein/ aktionen/tag-der-deutschen-sprache/ (accessed February 2007).

Verein Deutsche Sprache, '*VDS-Buchversand*', http://www.vds-ev.de/buchversand/ (accessed February 2007).

Verein Deutsche Sprache, '*VDS vorgestellt*', http://www.vds-ev.de/verein/ (accessed February 2007).

Verein Deutsche Sprache, '*Verein Deutsche Sprache*', http://www.vds-ev.de/ (accessed February 2007).

Verein Deutsche Sprache, '*Wörterliste: T-Shirt*', http://www.vds-ev.de/anglizismenindex/ suche2.php?str=t-shirt (accessed February 2007).

Verein für deutsche Rechtschreibung und Sprachpflege, '*Startseite*', http://www.vrs-ev.
de/ (accessed February 2007).

Verein für Sprachpflege, '*Deutsche Sprachwelt*', http://www.deutsche-sprachwelt.de/
(accessed February 2007).

Viereck, W. (1989), 'Zum Nachdruck zweier Werke Hermann Dungers', in: *Wörterbuch
von Verdeutschungen entbehrlicher Fremdwörter / Engländerei in der deutschen
Sprache*, H. Dunger, reprint of the Leipzig 1882 and Berlin 1909 editions, Hildesheim: Olms, 1*–11*.

Zimmer, D.E. (1997), *Deutsch und anders – die Sprache im Modernisierungsfieber*, Reinbek bei Hamburg: Rowohlt.

MARTIN DURRELL

Deutsch: Teutons, Germans or Dutch?
The Problems of Defining a Nation

The question of German identity is one of the more intractable questions in European sociolinguistics and politics, principally because the conflict between linguistic and political criteria ultimately does not allow of resolution, despite the fact that the political unification of the majority of the German states in 1871 had an explicit ethno-linguistic motivation. The dimension and some of the essence of the problem can be perceived from the unique variety of designations for the people and their language among their European neighbours, cf. Reiffenstein (1985: 1724) and Dann (1993: 31). They are variously called *Germans* (by the Romans, the Irish, the Greeks and, since the seventeenth century, the British), *Allemans* (by the Welsh, French, and in most other Romance languages), *Saxons* (by the Finns – but that is what the Celtic peoples of the British Isles call the English), *Nemtsy* (by the Slavonic peoples and the Hungarians), and in the international Latin of the Middle Ages and later they were referred to as *Teutonici*, which has itself been quite frequent in English usage since the seventeenth century to refer to (High) Germans, especially in a pejorative sense. They call themselves *Deutsche*, but this appellation is only used for them by the Italians, the Scandinavians and the Dutch – who used the term (in the form *dietsch*) to designate themselves until fairly recently and who are themselves called this by the English – although until at least the seventeenth century (and much later in America) the term was also widely used of what we now usually call 'Germans'.[1]

A name is of course a crucial component of identity, for a people as for an individual. It is inevitable that the origin and history of a name will be

---

1   Much of the information in this paragraph was collated from the entries in the *Oxford English Dictionary* (2001) under the head-words *Almain*, *Dutch*, *German* and *Teutonic*, where further information may be found.

seen as giving clues towards answering the questions 'where did we come from?' and 'what are we?', and, crucially, the answers to these can form an important constituent of national mythologies about the origin and descent of a people. German scholars began asking questions of this kind about the names given to their people from the period of late medieval humanism. The first printed German edition of Tacitus' *Germania* in 1473 equated *deutsch* with his *germanicus* or *teutonicus*, cf. Beck (1990: 445), and associated the virtues of the Germanic tribes he described with the modern Germans. The *Deutsche* were associated with the earth-god *Tuisco* (or *Tuisto*) mentioned in *Germania*, chapter 2, as the ancestor of their race, cf. Beck (1990: 446) and Gardt (1999: 11), so that Ickelsamer writes in 1534 that 'die teutschen [werden] nach dem Kaiser Tuiscon genandt' (cited in Beck 1990: 446). An association was then also made with Ascenas, a descendant of Noah, and German was thus confirmed as one of the *Hauptsprachen* which derived directly from the confusion of tongues at Babel, as maintained consistently by Schottelius (1663: 48): 'Also ist gleichfals unsere jtzige Teutsche Sprache / eben dieselbe uhralte weltweite Teutsche Sprache'. As the identity of the Celtic and Germanic peoples had been long assumed by the sixteenth and seventeenth centuries – as early as the ninth century, according to Zeuss (1837: 64) – the name was equated with the ancient Celtic *Teut*, if not also with Latin *deus* and Greek ϑεός (*theos*), as the perceived origin of *teutonicus* and justifying the spelling *teutsch*. Schottelius (1663: 36) thus says, 'also Teut, Teutisch, Teutsch: welches denn die rechte unfehlbare Uhrankunft und Wurtzel des Teutschen Nahmens ist, nemlich der Nahme des wahren Gottes selbst, daß also Teutisch so viel heisset als Göttisch oder Göttlich'.[2]

In this way, the various names of the people had already been incorporated in the age of Baroque cultural patriotism into an incipient national mythology, emphasizing the age of the German people, confirming their history as a single people, their divine origin, their inherited virtues and the antiquity of their language. Like all such myths, although purporting to represent

---

2   Some of the information in this paragraph derives from McLelland (2003), which was originally given as a paper in Manchester in November 2000 at a meeting of the Forum for Germanic Language Studies. I am grateful to Dr McLelland for sending me a copy of this paper prior to publication. An excellent concise survey of early ideas about the origin and ancestry of German is to be found in Jones (1993).

history, it is ultimately a-historical in its projection into the past of contemporary notions and aspirations, in this case the perceived need to confirm national self-esteem and the independent value of German culture. By the end of the eighteenth century, though, the wishful thinking of what Grimm (1848: I, 415) was to call 'wilde etymologie' became unsustainable because of improved knowledge of texts in the older Germanic languages. In the 1770s both Adelung and Friedrich Karl Fulda already recognized that *deutsch* was not connected with the Latin word *Teutonicus* or the Celtic god *Teut*, but was derived from the Germanic root *thiod* 'people', cf. Beck (1990: 448). In later work Adelung (1806: 150–5) gives an extensive justification for this etymology, with the assumption that the name of the Germans goes back ultimately to this word simply meaning 'people', and this is now generally accepted as correct.

The modern word *deutsch* is thus an adjectival derivation from the Germanic noun **þeud* (Old High German (OHG) *thiod*) 'people'. However, tracing the origins and development of this adjective is fraught with difficulties which have baffled scholars for two centuries, cf. Weisgerber (1953: 98–102). First of all it is unclear how and why an adjectival derivation which presumably meant something like 'popular', 'of the people' *'volkstümlich'* came to be used to designate a specific people. This means that the self-designation of the Germans differs from that of all other European peoples, whose names typically derive from a tribal entity or the territory they inhabit. Secondly, its first attestations are not in German texts, but in the Latin form *theodiscus*, which first appears in the eighth century, occurring, for example, in the Straßburg oaths of 842, where (in the form *teudisca*) it is contrasted with the *romana* spoken in the western portion of the Carolingian Empire. The German form *diutisc*, which is clearly the ancestor of our modern word – aside from one or two problematic and controversial occurrences – only appears two centuries later in the works of Notker. Thirdly, the root vowel *eo* of these Latin forms does not represent the regular phonological development from the presumed Germanic adjective **þeudiskaz*; OHG *diutisc*, with *iu*, on the other hand, can be clearly traced back to this Germanic etymon. Fourthly, the Latin word, and the OHG attestations, are used almost exclusively with reference to a language, not a people – and not exclusively to German, but possibly to any Germanic language. Indeed, and this is the fifth problem, the first attestation of the word *theodiscus* is used with reference to Old English in a text of 786, where we are told of a synod in Mercia that the decisions were proclaimed 'tam latine quam theodisce quo omnes intellegere possent' ('both in Latin and in *Deutsch*, so that everyone could understand').[3]

The literature on these problems is described in a recent edition of Kluge's *Etymologisches Wörterbuch* (Kluge 1995: 175) as 'fast unübersehbar'. However, a generally accepted solution has still not been found, and it is not the intention here to review this literature fully or propose any new solutions. Rather, the focus here will be on the linguistic historiography of this problem, in particular in the nineteenth and the first half of the twentieth centuries, and the light which this throws on the development of myths of German nationhood and German identity over the period in question. During this period a narrative became established of how the German people came to be as they are, and, for a people defined primarily on an ethno-linguistic basis, the history of the language plays a vital role within this. The study of the history of the German language from the early nineteenth century onwards is inextricably linked with the political history of Germany and the development of German nationalism. Aspirations towards national unity in nineteenth-century Germany were commonly justified by reference to national identity based on ethnic-linguistic criteria, i.e. that the speakers of German constituted a distinct group which was taken to legitimize demands for a single political entity which would include all 'Germans', defined in terms of the language which they spoke. A primary objective of nationalist linguistic historiography was thus to demonstrate the historical unity of the language and the peoples who spoke it, and, characteristically, this was undertaken by members of the *Bildungsbürgertum* who were in the forefront of moves towards political unification and the supporters of the new national state after its establishment in 1871, cf. Haß-Zumkehr (1998: 351). Of course, such motivations for linguistic historiography were not unique to Germany in this period, as (Crowley 1991) has convincingly demonstrated for English. Leith, too, points out that:

> [T]he story of the English language, as customarily told by linguistic historians, was mainly constructed in the nineteenth century, and [...] it draws particularly on nineteenth-century ideas of national identity. Indeed, the very idea of national identity is largely a construct of nineteenth-century nationalism [...]. Such nationalism assumes

3   See the summary in Harting-Correa (1995).

the existence of an unchanging national 'essence', residing in a shared ethnic origin, a fixed territory and a common language. (1996: 95)

Of course, the same is true of Germany, but it took on a more urgent dimension in the light of the political fragmentation of the German lands. Essentially, what was required was a history of the language which would provide a historically based justification for aspirations towards national unity in terms of the language which was the most important (or even the only) symbol of the nation. The requirements placed upon such a linguistic history are not essentially different from the characteristic features of national history as described by Sheehan: 'In order to establish its identity, every nation must seek to create a national history. As official versions of the nation's origins these histories forge a nation's links to its past, provide justifications for its present, and establish guidelines for its future. Because national histories tell the story of how a nation had to become what it is, they are all both deterministic and teleological' (1992: 48).

In this context, an account of the origin and development of the name of the people was of primary importance in the establishment of a myth of national unity and national identity. If it could be clearly demonstrated that the name *deutsch* had always been used as a designation for the totality of this people, who had had a clear perception of their separate identity as a distinct ethnic group speaking what they perceived as the 'same' language from the earliest times, this could be instrumentalized as a legitimization of contemporary aspirations to a national state or, after 1871, of its nature and its policies. A similar motivation – albeit cultural rather than specifically political – had obviously underlain attempts to explain the various names of the people in the seventeenth and eighteenth centuries, but it was made more intense by the changed political situation, the older views needed to be revised in the light of new evidence, and, significantly, the conclusions could be underpinned by the new science of philology. The success of this enterprise, however, depended crucially on satisfactory answers being given to the questions outlined above concerning the origin and development of the word *deutsch*, and the remainder of this paper will sketch briefly how this was done and show how the various solutions proposed parallel the course of German nationalism over the past two hundred years.

The connection between this topic and German nationalist ideologies has, of course, been seen before. Ehrismann observes that 'Die Forschungen über die Anfänge des Wortes *deutsch* sind schon früh in besonderem Maße politisch-ideologisch belastet worden' and showed 'die Wortgeschichts-schreibung als Spiegel und Bedingung der Nationalgeschichte', whereby 'Ein Großteil der Wissenschaftler sah es dabei augenscheinlich als patriotische Pflicht an, die nüchterne Haltung des Forschenden aufzugeben' (1990: 293). And Wells (1985: 32) says that 'the vague nature of the word *deutsch* pan-dered to the nationalistic feelings of some less critical scholars who sought to project into the past a national unity and a national language which never existed' (1985: 32). However, these 'less critical scholars' who abandoned their 'nüchterne Haltung' read like a roll-call of the leading figures in Germanic philology from the early nineteenth century on, including Jacob Grimm, Karl Luick, Wilhelm Braune, Friedrich Kluge, Otto Behaghel, Viktor Michels, Theodor Frings, Louis L. Hammerich and many others, aside from admit-tedly less well known (or less able) scholars. It is easy from the perspective of the present, with the hindsight provided by the knowledge where extreme varieties of German *völkisch* nationalism led, to see more clearly the ideologi-cal motivation for the narrative they established,[4] but the historiographer has to maintain a perspective and show how the story of *deutsch* reflects the motives and concerns of those who wrote it in the context of their times – it is worth recalling again the parallels with how the 'story of English' is still traditionally presented, cf. Gardt (2000: 250).

By the early nineteenth century the correct origin of the adjective had become clear. As Jakobs (1968: 86) shows, Fichte, who is quite explicit about language as the defining characteristic of a people, effectively equates *thiod* with modern *Volk* in his seventh *Rede an die deutsche Nation*, and hence con-siders *deutsch* to refer simply to the people. So did Jahn, who coined the word *volkstümlich* on the basis of his understanding of the etymology of *deutsch*, cf. Dove (1898: 319). Jacob Grimm (1840) took up this idea from Jahn, seeing *deutsch* as, effectively, meaning 'the language of the people', and his explana-tion, in the *Excurs über Germanisch und Deutsch* in the third edition of his *Deutsche Grammatik*, remained the accepted account until towards the end

---

4   Hutton (1999) shows in admirable detail the links between Germanic philology and
     National Socialist ideologies, but it would be facile to see a necessary teleological pro-
     gression between nationalistically motivated accounts of the history of the German
     language and the rise of National Socialism.

of the nineteenth century. For Grimm, like Fichte, it was self-evident that a people should be defined on ethno-linguistic principles, as in the well-known definition in his address to the *Germanistenversammlung* held in Frankfurt in 1846: 'ein volk ist der inbegriff von menschen, welche dieselbe sprache reden' (Grimm 1884: 557). He thus interpreted *deutsch* as having the meaning 'volks-gemäß', and was only too willing to convince himself that the German peoples had defined themselves from the outset in terms of a common language. He assumed that the Latin form *theodiscus* and OHG *diutisc* went back to a Germanic adjective *þeudiskaz*, despite the fact that the reflexes of this are barely attested in other early Germanic languages. For Grimm, like Schottelius (1663: 33) and Adelung (1806: 151) before him, this word was used to designate the Germanic tribes as a collectivity and thus what in his view was the whole people. It equated in this way with the contemporary Latin use of *germanicus* and corresponded both to Latin *gentilis* and *popularis* or *vulgaris*, referring both to an ethnic group and the commonalty, and similar ideas are widespread in Grimm's contemporaries, e.g. in Brugger (1847: 14). Grimm quite explicitly rejected the notion that the unity of these peoples only dated back to Carolingian times: 'Wer nun aus diesen stellen folgern wollte, erst im neunten jh., seit Carl der große die deutschen stämme stärker vereinte, sei die allgemeine benennung entsprungen, würde fehlen' (1840: 7). In this way, Grimm is as concerned as the writers of the seventeenth and eighteenth centuries to demonstrate the antiquity of this people as a single ethnic group. Grimm's account belongs very much to the age of Romantic nationalism, cf. Hughes (1988), with typically rather unclear (or unrealistic) notions of the possible political implementation of their aspirations. Grimm's notions of political unification were often remarkably unfocussed; he wrote to the Danish scholar Carl Christian Rafn in 1849: 'ich [...] halte aber eine scandinavische und deutsche einheit für das endziel aller patriotischen wünsche. in solcher einheit wird sich der Däne, Norwege, Schwede erst vollständig fühlen' (cited in Janota 1980: 141).

Jacob Grimm's vague and ultimately a-historical views of what constituted *deutsch* found broad acceptance through the second half of the nineteenth century, with a persistent confusion of German and Germanic. Rückert (1875: 23) saw Theoderich as having united 'alle deutsche Völkerschaften von den Alpen bis zum Nordmeer' (1875: 23) and speaks (Rückert 1875: 53) of 'Deutsche' settling England. Scherer (1878: 11–12) similarly postulates three epochs of the 'deutsche Sprache' before Carolingian times. However, although this confusion on the central question of national identity (i.e. 'What is a German?') was to persist even longer, especially outside philological circles, notably with the emergence of racial theories, the focus of interest in this topic shifts with the establishment of a German Empire which is identified as a the national state of the Germans (with all the ambiguities that involves). We can see this already in Rückert (1875: 82–3), who considers the use of *theodiscus* as signalling the emergence of an awareness among the elite of the Carolingian empire of a common nationhood going beyond tribal divisions, that is, that this self appellation 'die Gemeinsamkeit des Blutes und der Herkunft aller Deutschen zu einem Volke verbinde'. This notion that German national consciousness, an awareness of the underlying unity of all the German people as shown in the language which they have in common and call *deutsch*, emerges under Charlemagne, who created the first German state, becomes the dominant element in all later explanations of the origin and development of the word *deutsch* into the nineteen-sixties, despite many differences in detail. This marks a decisive break with the earlier ideas of Jacob Grimm, who, as we saw, considered that such unity long predated the Carolingian period. This ideological construct is seen – sometimes implicitly, sometimes explicitly – to legitimize the new German Empire and its ethno-linguistic foundation, with the particularism of the individual tribes being overcome.[5] The continuity of the people is thereby established, so that Luick could already write that 'Es kann somit nicht bezweifelt werden, dass unsere heutige bedeutung "deutsch" bereits für das ix. jh. feststeht' (1889: 137), and now, from 1871, the people have an Empire again as they did at the beginning of their history, cf. Schrader (1896: 156–7).

The first detailed and systematic attempt to establish this construct on the basis of the early history of the word *deutsch* was made by Alfred Dove in a number of publications from 1893 on, notably in the essays collected in Dove (1898) and the posthumously published and summative Dove (1916). Dove was primarily a historian, a pupil of Ranke's and very much influenced by Droysen's ideas on the importance of *Stamm* and *Volk* as historical participants,

5   This is particularly clear in Dove (1898: 316), and this construct also underlies the notion of Müllenhoff and Scherer (1864: ix) of a Carolingian *Hofsprache* as the first reflection of this linguistic unity, an idea already foreshadowed in Mone (1830: 261).

cf. Jakobs (1968: 87). Dove (1916: 7–9) rejected Grimm's views as 'ein unge-schichtlicher Traum', which projected a Romantic concept of the *Volk* into the past, and concentrated on what he saw as the central problem of how an adjective meaning 'of the people' (i.e. *volkstümlich*) came to be employed as the name of that people. His starting point is given by the title of his *akademische Festrede* of 1890, i.e. *Der Wiedereintritt des nationalen Prinzips in die Weltgeschichte*, as he saw the re-emergence of individual peoples (*gentes*) as a characteristic consequence of the collapse of the Roman Empire, cf. Dove (1916: 17–25). The word *deutsch* (OHG *diutisc*), meaning 'of the people', which derived from Germanic **þeuda* (meaning *gens*), must have existed in Germanic before emerging in the Latin form *theodiscus* and being applied to the language. To outsiders, specifically Christian missionaries like Boniface, the languages of the continental Germanic tribes must have all appeared the same, and they adopted this German word to designate the language of the heathen population, indeed Dove (1898: 323) conjectures that Boniface may have known the cognate Old English word *geþéode* as a designation for 'language', since it is widely attested in this meaning. This usage in the church was taken over by the Germanic peoples, who realized it represented what they had in common by contrast to the other peoples with which they were coming into contact, cf. Dove:

> Die Angehörigen jedes dieser sechs Stämme mußten daher den Ausdruck *theodisk*, sobald er ihnen in Bezug auf das eigene Volksthum in Opposition zu einem fremden entgegengehalten ward, in gerader Linie auf das bayerische, thüringische, friesische *theod* u. s. w. beziehen. Aber alle diese anscheinend divergirenden *theodisk* trafen, wenn damit auf die angestammte Sprache gezielt ward, bei der wesentlichen Einheit sämmtlicher Mundarten in der Sache dennoch zusammen. So ward gleichsam schlummernd in die Volksseele, gebettet in den nachgiebig dehnbaren Namen Volkssprache, der Gedanke eines größeren *theod*, als einer sechsfältig einheitlichen Nation, hineingetragen, um in den folgenden Menschenaltern durch den stetig wiederholten Ruf 'so weit die deutsche Zunge klingt' zum hellen Bewußtsein des Deutschthums erweckt zu werden. (1898: 316)

In this way the dawning awareness of the common language effectively created a national consciousness, above tribal particularism, which came with the first Christian German empire. In this way Dove could claim: 'ich [wage] den Namen Deutsch für den geschichtlichen Taufnamen unseres Volkes zu erklären' (1898: 324).

Dove's view is ultimately a positivist one, of a people formed through becoming conscious of its common language, rather than on the basis of supposedly ancient (and untraceable) genetic origins. It also emphasizes the semantic problems in attempting primarily to solve the problem of how an adjective becomes a name. It involves suppressing some of the other problems, in particular the cases where *theodiscus* is used to refer to other Germanic languages, notably the awkward first attestation in England, although this was actually discovered by him, cf. Dove (1898). However, he finds an explanation for it in terms of the transference to England by German monks of continental ideas about languages and peoples, so that in Dove (1916: 314) he can finally describe it as 'eine irreführende Erscheinung'.

In practice, this example is a problem for many subsequent accounts, too, like that of Rosenstock (1928), who sought to locate the origin of the word even more clearly in the Carolingian period, and saw many of Dove's basic assumptions as unnecessarily speculative. He is also concerned to disprove the notion that it was coined by outsiders before being taken over by the Germans. This is of course unwelcome for nationalist ideological assumptions. He concentrates on the second attestation of 788, which relates to the desertion of the Bavarian duke Tassilo from Charlemagne's forces, and sees the word as arising as a legal term in Charlemagne's army to designate the official language of the army, of what he refers to as the 'unverwälschte Franken' (Rosenstock 1928: 43).[6] It is the 'Königssprache', not the language of the *vulgus*. In this way Rosenstock (1928: 86) claims that 'Karl der Große hat zuerst das weltgeschichtliche Bewußtsein der deutschen Völker geschaffen' and that

> Die Sprache des Heeres wird Herr über die Zersplitterung der deutschen Stämme. Das Reich des Heeres ist immer umfassender als das des Zivil. Das sind die Grundsätze deutscher Geschichte geblieben seit dem Tage, an dem Karls Heer Bayern und Sachsen aufnahm. [...] Kriegsgemeinschaft hat das deutsche Volk geschaffen. Der deutsche Militarismus ist kein leerer Wahn. (1928: 100–1)

This defiant restatement in 1928, from the pen of a Jewish scholar, of conservative notions of the essence of German nationhood in military values

---

6   Jakobs (1968: 90) points out that J. Brüch had suggested as early as 1913 that *theodiscus* had its origin in the legal Latin of the Carolingian period, although Rosenstock (1928) does not appear to have known this and does not refer to it.

gains immense potency through its linkage with the origin of the name of the people, and in its clear consciousness of the catastrophe of 1918 it is fully typical of the period.

Krogmann (1936), on the other hand, tried to rescue Grimm's notion of *deutsch* as reflecting the inherited unity of the Germanic peoples and tried, unlike many others, to provide a coherent explanation for the problematic attestation of *theodiscus* to designate Old English in 786. Not unlike Dove, he saw it as a scholarly creation by non-German clerics who heard the word *thiodisk* being used of themselves by Germanic speakers and assumed mistakenly, because of the apparent similarity with Latin *teutonicus*, that it was their general self-appellation. This meaning was then taken over from clerical jargon into the native word *diutisc*, which is then finally attested two centuries later in Notker. This explanation was challenged forcefully in the following years, which saw an explosion of scholarly activity on this topic, as may be seen from the fact that eleven of the eighteen contributions to the collected *Wege der Forschung* volume (Eggers 1970) date originally from the years 1940–4, cf. Thomas (1988: 296). Chief among these was Leo Weisgerber in numerous publications, most of which were republished (largely unchanged) after the war.[7] His basic postulates are those of a popular nationalism, in that he sees it as unacceptable that the name of the Germans should have arisen on the basis of a misunderstanding, claiming typically: 'Ich glaube nicht, daß ein im Sprachgebrauch eines Landfremden irrtümlich gebrauchtes Wort je Aussicht gehabt hätte, sich als Sprachname und schließlich als Volksname durchzusetzen' (1953: 53). Similarly, he opposed any notion that the word was a *Gelehrtenbildung* as suggested by Krogmann (1936) and Lerch (1942), although the latter is as adamant as Weisgerber and many of his predecessors that the word reflects a consciousness of linguistic unity which formed the basis for ethnic unity, cf.Lerch who writes: 'Wir Deutschen waren ein Sprachvolk, lange bevor wir politisch zu einem Volke wurden' (1942: 19). For Weisgerber, the word had to have arisen with the people itself and reflect their sense of national identity. He saw *þiuda* and its derived adjective as denoting, as Frings puts it, 'die Idee der blutmäßigen Zusammengehörigkeit mit der politischen Einheit' (1941: 240). Adhering to the *Mutterspracheideologie*

---

7   In particular the monograph Weisgerber (1949) and the collection of essays Weisgerber (1953), most of which had originally been published between 1936 and early 1945.

which was such a characteristic feature of nationalist ideology in the later Wilhelmine period, he saw the common language as reflecting the essential nature of the people.[8] The Germans were unique among European peoples in naming themselves after their *Muttersprache*, and this language is the very basis of the *Volksgemeinschaft*. He took as his starting point the phonological problem, the apparently irregular vowel of *theodiscus*, which he saw as the original form, explaining it as a West Frankish formation which emerged among the Franks of northern France whose ethnic identity was under threat. It arose as an antonym to *welsch*, the designation for those of the rival ethnic group who were assimilating them.[9] In this way Weisgerber is able to claim that 'Der deutsche Sprachname ist in gewissem Sinne ein Heimatruf der in dem Schicksal der Romanisierung stehenden Franken jenseits der späteren Sprachgrenze, ausgesandt bei dem Bemühen, dieses kaum mehr abwendbare Schicksal aufzuhalten und umzukehren' (1953: 80). It then spread as the focus of the Carolingian Empire spread eastwards, and was adopted in that empire as an expression of its political and cultural goals of the unity of the German people. In Weisgerber's view, the 'einigendes Band der gemeinsamen Muttersprache mußte erst die Bahn frei machen für das Bewußtwerden der volklichen Einheit' (1953: 86), especially after the establishment of the Ottonian empire in 919 and in the light of the new threat from the Slavs in the East, after which the definitive German form *diutisc* takes on its meanings.[10]

Weisgerber's mystical interpretations of the essential and enduring significance of the name *deutsch* need not concern us further here, but the contemporary importance of this ideological construct, with its notion of the

8   An account of the development of this ideology is to be found in Ahlzweig (1994), the eighth chapter of which specifically deals with Weisgerber's work. It is of course dubious in the extreme whether any common German language existed at this time, cf. Wolf (2003).

9   This had already been known in the nineteenth century and is central to the account by Vaas (1924), cf. Krogmann (1936: 65); as already seen above, it is explicit in the notion of Rosenstock (1928: 43) that *deutsch* designated the language of the *unverwälschte Franken*.

10 That the spread in the use of the German word *diutisc* was given significant impetus by the ethnic conflict with Slavonic peoples to the East is claimed particularly by Vaas (1924), cf. Krogmann (1936: 65), and it gains further currency in the twenties and thirties.

name of the people arising as an expression of essential national identity at a
time when that identity is conceived as being under threat, is quite evident,
and Weisgerber's ideas were generally accepted by others who were more
clearly associated with the Nazi regime, like Neumann, who sees Weisgerber
as demonstrating that *deutsch* meant 'das wirklich Angestammte, des Erbechte'
(1940: 220) and testified to a 'germanisch-deutsches Einheitsbewußtsein'
(1940: 206) in the eighth century. More surprising, though, is the fact that
Weisgerber's ideas found general acceptance for a long time after 1945, with
Eggers claiming that 'bis auf Einzelfragen das Problem des Wortes Deutsch
heute als gelöst gelten kann' (1970: VII–VIII). Similar assessments are to
be found in Moser (1961: 65), Rupp (1951) and Weisweiler (1959: 102–4),
although Betz (1959: 124), in the same volume, is one of the first to sound a
note of caution.

By the late 1960s, though, it was becoming clear that Weisgerber's ideas
still essentially constituted an interpretation of the data in the ideology of
'völkisch' nationalism, cf. Jakobs (2000) and Roth (1978: 347–92), and justified the kind of strictures we saw made by Wells (1985: 32). Dieckmann is
clear that the kind of claims made by Weisgerber are untenable: 'das Wort
deutsch hat keine Nation erschaffen' (1969: 113). Betz, too, points out: 'Wäre
die Geschichte anders verlaufen, wenn statt *theodiscus* etwa *germanicus* oder
teutonicus eingeführt worden wäre [...] nicht *theodisc* hat die Entwicklung der
deutschen Geschichte bestimmt, sondern die deutsche Geschichte hat die
Entwicklung von *theodisc* bestimmt' (1968: 20). Roth gives a good account of
the fallacy of the ideological constructs put by Weisgerber on the origin of the
word, pointing out that he is extremely cavalier with the evidence: 'Spezifisch
ausgewählte historische Daten in höchstabstrakter Form setzen den Rahmen
für die Festlegung der Wortwirkungen, deren Weisgerber so sicher ist, daß sie
nicht erst lange an Einzelbeispielen erläutert werden müssen' (1978: 387). The
idea that the 'Germans' were essentially a single people seems barely tenable,
given the later struggle of the Ottonians to enforce their rule, which scarcely
constituted a 'freiwilliger Zusammenschluß der Stämme'. Weisgerber's account,
like so many of his predecessors, is basically a-historical, projecting a contemporary ideological construct into an idealized past, cf. Ehlers (1989: 303–4).
It is quite possible that the widespread use of *deutsch* to refer to themselves
only became widespread in the eleventh century with the rise of feudalism,
which is when we find it in the *Annolied* and the *Kaiserchronik*, cf. Große

(1972: 22) and Thomas (2000: 49), and it this context it seems significant that only in 1020 does the emperor (Henry II) refer to himself as *rex teutonicorum*, cf. Ehlers (1989: 308). If anything, though, this makes the answers to the questions about the origins and early development of *deutsch* and where the Germans got their name from even more obscure, and the most recent research, e.g. Jakobs (2000) and Thomas (2000), seems even further from a definitive and generally accepted answer.

However, it is in the nature of myths that they persist long after scholars have begun to question their fundamental accuracy. As we have seen, historians of the German language from the early nineteenth century on succeeded in establishing the ideological construct of a people whose national consciousness as a single people can be traced back to the beginning of their recorded history with the foundation of their first state. This consciousness was established through their perception that they spoke the common language which they still possess and after which they named themselves, maintaining the awareness of that underlying ethno-linguistic unity despite a long history of subsequent political fragmentation. This construct was an immensely potent national symbol, especially in terms of legitimising the establishment of a German nation state in terms of the past, and it is in many ways not implausible to non-specialists, since it fits in with a number of other related popular constructs of German history. Dann (1993: 31) has pointed out the importance of this account of the history of *deutsch* for the 'deutsche Nationalbewegung', and we see it not only in the accounts of scholars in the nineteenth and early twentieth centuries but also in works written primarily for non-specialists, such as Weise who claims: 'Unsere Altvordern [...] [hielten] die Volkstümlichkeit der Sprache für wichtig genug, die ganze Nation darnach zu benennen' (1912: 45), or Frederking who talks of 'die heimische "Sprache des Volks", wie die Deutschen ihre Muttersprache nannten' (1898: 150).

In practice, this construct remains the accepted view outside specialist philological circles, although some of the more obviously extreme features associated with now discredited forms of nationalist ideologies have been abandoned. The latest edition of Meyers *Lexikon* (Meyer online) still sees Charlemagne as the founder of the German language, as we see under the entry 'Deutsche Sprache': 'Die Voraussetzungen für die Entstehung der deutschen Sprache aus mehreren germanischen Dialekten wurde durch das Frankenreich unter Karl dem Großen geschaffen.' The most recent edition of *Ploetz:*

Deutsche Geschichte claims for the beginning of German history (Conze and Hentschel 1998: 42): 'Das Wort *deutsch*, althochdeutsch *diutisc, theodisk*, mittellateinisch *theodiscus* sowie (in gelehrt-irrtümlicher Angleichung) *teutonicus*, bedeutet im 8./9. Jahrhundert *volkssprachig, nichtlateinisch*. Schon im 9. Jahrhundert wird jedoch die Sprachbezeichnung zum Volksnamen für die Stämme des Ostfrankenreichs [...] die seitdem ein gemeinsames Volksbewußtsein bezeugen.' And Peter Schneider in *Der Mauerspringer* says:

> Wenn ein Vaterland der Deutschen weiterhin existiert, so hat es am ehesten in ihrer Muttersprache überlebt [...]. Das Wort *deutsch* bezeichnete ja ursprünglich weder ein Volk noch einen Staat, sondern bedeutete 'Volk', 'volksmäßig', als Bezeichnung der gemeinsamen Sprache verschiedener Stämme [...]. Diese sprachliche Einheit bestand Jahrhunderte vor der Gründung des Heiligen Römischen Reiches Deutscher Nation, und sie hat die Entstehung und Zerfall aller weiteren unheiligen Reiche uberlebt. In einem bestimmten Sinn scheinen die Deutschen also wieder am Ausgangspunkt ihrer Geschichte angelangt: das Wort 'deutsch' läßt sich unmißverständlich nur noch als Adjektiv gebrauchen, und zwar nicht in bezug auf Staat und Vaterland, sondern, soweit von der Gegenwart die Rede ist, in bezug auf ein einziges Substantiv: Sprache. (1982: 116–17)

Even since Schneider wrote this, political changes have taken place which have again altered perceptions of German identity and its relationship with language, yet it is still not clear whether the question of 'Who is a German?' can be answered with any greater clarity. But Schneider shows us how the myths established by earlier linguistic historiography about the relationship of the Germans, their name and their language are immensely powerful and persistent in popular imagination, and can themselves be interpreted in many ways. As Gardt says: 'die Geschichte der Beschäftigung mit diesem kontroversen Gegenstand [läßt] wie kaum ein anderes Thema erkennen, wie sehr Sprachwissenschaft von gesellschaftlichen und politischen Interessen geprägt sein kann' (1999: 11).

References

Adelung, J.C. (1806), *Aelteste Geschichte der Deutschen, ihrer Sprache und Litteratur, bis zur Völkerwanderung*, Leipzig: Göschen.

Ahlzweig, C. (1994), *Muttersprache – Vaterland. Die deutsche Nation und ihre Sprache*, Opladen: Westdeutscher Verlag.

Ameri, S.M. (1991), *Die deutschnationale Sprachbewegung im wilhelminischen Reich*, New York, etc.: Peter Lang (German Life and Civilization 5).

Beck, H. (1990), '"Deutsch" in den Anfängen der Germanistik', in: *Deutsche Sprachgeschichte. Grundlagen, Methoden, Perspektiven. Festschrift für Johannes Erben zum 65. Geburtstag*, edited by W. Besch, Frankfurt/Main, etc.: Peter Lang, 443–53.

Betz, W. (1959), 'Nachtrag zu "Deutsche Frühzeit"', in: *Deutsche Wortgeschichte*, vol. 1, 2nd. ed., edited by F. Maurer and F. Stroh, Berlin: Walter de Gruyter, 105–33.

Betz, W. (1968), 'Möglichkeiten und Grenzen der Sprachkritik', *Sprache im technischen Zeitalter* 25, 7–27.

Brugger, J.D. C. (1847), *Das Urbild der deutschen Reinsprache, aus der Geschichte, dem Wesen und dem Geiste unserer Sprache dargestellt. Nebst einem Fremdwörterbuche worin viele Wörter neu übersetzt und ausführlicher erklärt sind*, Heidelberg: Julius Groos.

Conze, W. and Hentschel, V. (eds) (1998), *Ploetz: Deutsche Geschichte*, 6th ed., Darmstadt: Wissenschaftliche Buchgesellschaft.

Crowley, T. (1991), *Proper English? Readings in Language, History and Cultural Identity*, London and New York: Routledge.

Dann, O. (1993), *Nation und Nationalismus in Deutschland 1770–1990*, München: Beck. (Beck'sche Reihe 494).

Dieckmann, W. (1969), *Sprache in der Politik. Einführung in die Pragmatik und Semantik der politischen Sprache*, Heidelberg: Carl Winter.

Dove, A. (ed.) (1898), *Ausgewählte Schriftchen vornehmlich historischen Inhalts*, Leipzig: Duncker and Humblot.

Dove, A. (1916), 'Studien zur Vorgeschichte des deutschen Volksnamens', *Sitzungsberichte der Heidelberger Akademie der Wissenschaften. Philosophisch-historische Klasse* 7 (8. Abhandlung), 1–98.

Eggers, H. (ed.) (1970), *Der Volksname Deutsch*, Darmstadt: Wissenschaftliche Buchgesellschaft. (Wege der Forschung 156).

Ehlers, J. (1989), 'Schriftkultur, Ethnogenese und Nationsbildung in ottonischer Zeit', *Frühmittelalterliche Studien* 23, 302–17.

Ehrismann, O. (1990), '*deota/diutisk*. Zur frühen Semantik des Wortes *deutsch*', in: *Sprache in der sozialen und kulturellen Entwicklung. Beiträge eines Kolloquiums zu Ehren von Theodor Frings (1886–1968)*, edited by R. Grosse, Berlin: Akademie-Verlag

(Abhandlungen der sächsischen Akademie der Wissenschaften zu Leipzig, Phil.-Hist. Klasse 73/1).

Frederking, A. (1898), 'Unsere Muttersprache unter Fremdherrschaft', *Wissenschaftliche Beihefte zur Zeitschrift des Allgemeinen Deutschen Sprachvereins*. Heft 14/15, 148–67.

Frings, T. (1941), 'Das Wort Deutsch', in: *Altdeutsches Wort und Wortkunstwerk. Georg Baesecke zum 65. Geburtstage 13. Januar 1941*, edited by F.J. Schneider and K. Wessel, Halle/Saale: Niemeyer, 46–82 (Cited from the reprint in Eggers (ed.) 1970: 209–44).

Gardt, A. (1999), *Geschichte der Sprachwissenschaft in Deutschland. Vom Mittelalter bis ins 20. Jahrhundert*, Berlin and New York: de Gruyter.

Gardt, A. (ed.) (2000), *Nation und Sprache. Die Diskussion ihres Verhältnisses in Geschichte und Gegenwart*, Berlin and New York: de Gruyter.

Gardt, A. (2000), 'Sprachnationalismus zwischen 1850 und 1945', in: Gardt (ed.), 247–71.

Grimm, J. (1840), 'Excurs über Germanisch und Deutsch', in: J. Grimm, *Deutsche Grammatik, Erster Theil*, 3rd ed., Göttingen: Dieterich, 10–20. (Cited from the reprint in Eggers (ed.) 1970: 1–16).

Grimm, J. (1848), *Geschichte der deutschen Sprache*, Leipzig: Hirzel.

Grimm, J. (1884), 'Vorträge auf den germanistenversammlungen zu Frankfurt a. M. und Lübeck 1846 und 1847', in: J. Grimm, *Kleinere Schriften*, Vol. 7, Berlin: Dümmler, 556–63.

Große, R. (1972), 'Zum Begriff der Nationalität in der Geschichte der deutschen Sprache', *Linguistische Arbeitsberichte 6*, 18–25.

Harting-Correa, A. (1995), *Walahfrid Strabo's Libellus de Exordiis Et Incrementis Quarundam in Observationibus Ecclesiasticis Rerum: A Translation and Liturgical Commentary*, Leiden: Brill.

Haß-Zumkehr, U. (1998), 'Die gesellschaftlichen Interessen an der Sprachgeschichtsforschung im 19. und 20. Jahrhundert', in: *Sprachgeschichte. Ein Handbuch zur Geschichte der deutschen Sprache und ihrer Erforschung*, edited by W. Besch, A. Betten, O. Reichmann and S. Sonderegger, 2nd ed., Berlin, New York: de Gruyter, Vol. 1, 349–58.

Hughes, M. (1988), *Nationalism and Society. Germany 1800–1945*, London: Edward Arnold.

Hutton, C.M. (1999), *Linguistics and the Third Reich. Mother-tongue Fascism, Race and the Science of Language*, London and New York: Routledge.

Ipsen, G. (1938), 'Jacob Grimms Begriff des Deutschen', *Zeitschrift für Deutsche Bildung* 14, 301–10.

Jakobs, H. (1968), 'Der Volksbegriff in den historischen Deutungen des Namens Deutsch', *Rheinische Vierteljahresblätter* 32, 86–104.

Jakobs, H. (2000), '*Diot* und *Sprache. Deutsch* im Verband der Frankenreiche (8. bis frühes 11. Jahrhundert)', in: Gardt (ed.) (2000), 7–46.

Janota, J. (ed.) (1980), *Eine Wissenschaft etabliert sich 1810–1870*, Tübingen: Niemeyer.

Jones, W.J. (1993), '"König Deutsch zu Abrahams Zeiten". Some perceptions of the place of German within the family of languages, from Aventinus to Zedler', in: '*Das unsichtbare Band der Sprache.' Studies in German Language and Linguistic History in Memory of Leslie Seiffert*, edited by J.L. Flood, P. Salmon, O. Sayce and C.J. Wells, Stuttgart: Heinz (Stuttgarter Arbeiten zur Germanistik 280), 189–213.

Kluge, F. (1995), *Etymologisches Wörterbuch der deutschen Sprache*, 23rd ed. revised by E. Seebold, Berlin and New York: de Gruyter.

Krogmann, W. (1936), *Deutsch. Eine wortgeschichtliche Untersuchung*, Berlin and Leipzig: de Gruyter (Deutsche Wortforschung 1).

Leith, D. (1996), 'The Origins of English', in: *English: History, Diversity and Change*, edited by D. Graddol, D. Leith and J. Swan, London and New York: Routledge, 95–135.

Lerch, E. (1942), *Das Wort 'Deutsch'. Sein Ursprung und seine Geschichte bis auf Goethe*, Frankfurt/Main: Vittorio Klostermann (Das Abendland. Forschungen zur Geschichte europäischen Geisteslebens VII).

Luick, K. (1889), 'Zur Geschichte des Wortes deutsch', *Anzeiger für deutsches Altertum* 15, 135–40.

Maurer, F. and Stroh F. (eds) (1959), *Deutsche Wortgeschichte*, 2nd. ed., Berlin: Walter de Gruyter.

McLelland, N. (2003), 'Schottelius, the notion of *Teutsch* and sleight of hand', in: '*Vir ingenio mirandus', Studies presented to John L. Flood*, edited by William J. Jones, William A. Kelly and Frank Shaw, Göppingen: Kümmerle, 835–54.

Meyers Lexikon Online, Mannheim: Bibliographisches Institut and F.A. Brockhaus AG. http://lexikon.meyers.de/lexikon/Startseite (Accessed 03.12.08).

Mone, F.J. (1830), *Quellen und Forschungen zur Geschichte der teutschen Literatur und Sprache*, Aachen and Leipzig: Jacob Anton Mayer.

Moser, H. (1961), *Annalen der deutschen Sprache von den Anfängen bis zur Gegenwart*, Stuttgart: Metzler. (Sammlung Metzler 5).

Müllenhoff, K. and Scherer, W. (eds) (1864), *Denkmäler deutscher Poesie und Prosa aus dem viii–xii Jahrhundert*, Berlin: Weidmannsche Buchhandlung.

Neumann, F. (1940), 'Wie entstand das Wort "deutsch"? Bemerkungen zu Joh. Leo Weisgerbers Schrift: Theudisk. Der deutsche Volksname und die westliche Sprachgrenze (1940)', *Zeitschrift für Deutsche Bildung* 16, 201–21.

Oxford English Dictionary (2002), 2nd ed., (CD-ROM version 3.0), Oxford: Oxford University Press.

Reiffenstein, I. (1985), 'Bezeichnungen der deutschen Gesamtsprache', in: *Sprachgeschichte. Ein Handbuch zur Geschichte der deutschen Sprache und ihrer Erforschung*, edited by W. Besch, O. Reichmann and S. Sonderegger, Berlin and New York: de Gruyter, vol. 2, 1717–27.

Rosenstock, E. (1928), 'Unser Volksname deutsch und die Aufhebung des Herzogtums Bayern', *Mitteilungen der Schlesischen Gesellschaft für Volkskunde* 29, 1–66. (Cited from the reprint in Eggers (ed.) 1970: 32–102).

Roth, K.-H. (1978), *'Deutsch', Prolegomena zur neueren Wortgeschichte*, München: Fink (Münchner Germanistische Beiträge 18).

Rückert, H. (1875), *Geschichte der Neuhochdeutschen Schriftsprache*, Leipzig: T.O. Weigel.

Rupp, H. (1951), 'Entstehung und Sinn des Wortes "Deutsch". Ein Forschungsbericht', *Der Deutschunterricht*, Heft 1, 74–9.

Scherer, W. (1878), *Zur Geschichte der deutschen Sprache*, 2nd ed., Berlin: Weidmannsche Buchhandlung.

Schneider, P. (1982), *Der Mauerspringer*, Reinbek bei Hamburg: Rowohlt Taschenbuch Verlag.

Schottelius, J.G. (1663), *Ausführliche Arbeit von der Teutschen Hauptsprache ...*, Braunschweig: Zilliger.

Schrader, O. (1896), '"Deutsches Reich" und "Deutscher Kaiser", eine sprachlich-geschichtliche Betrachtung zum 18. Januar 1896', *Wissenschaftliche Beihefte zur Zeitschrift des Allgemeinen Deutschen Sprachvereins* 10, 153–72.

Sheehan, J.J. (1992), 'State and nationality in the Napoleonic period', in: *The State of Germany. The National Idea in the Making. Unmaking and Remaking of a Modern Nation-State*, edited by J. Breuilly, London and New York: Routledge, 47–59.

Thomas, H. (1988), 'Der Ursprung des Wortes theodiscus', *Historische Zeitschrift* 247, 295–331.

Thomas, H. (2000), '*Sprache* und *Nation*. Zur Geschichte des Wortes *deutsch* vom Ende des 11. bis zur Mitte des 15. Jahrhunderts', in: Gardt (ed.) (2000), 47–101.

Vaas, H. (1924), *Die Entwicklung des Begriffs 'Deutsch'*, Doctoral thesis: University of Berlin.

Weise, O. (1912), *Unsere Muttersprache: Ihr Werden und ihr Wesen*, 8th ed., Leipzig and Berlin: B.G. Teubner.

Weisgerber, L. (1949), *Der Sinn des Wortes 'Deutsch'*, Göttingen: Vandenhoeck and Ruprecht.

Weisgerber, L. (1953), *Deutsch als Volksname. Ursprung und Bedeutung*, Stuttgart: Kohlhammer.

Weisweiler, J. (1959), 'Deutsche Frühzeit', in: *Deutsche Wortgeschichte*, vol. 1, 2nd. ed., edited by F. Maurer and F. Stroh, Berlin: Walter de Gruyter, 50–104.

Wells, C.J. (1985), *German: A Linguistic History to 1945*, Oxford: Clarendon Press.

Wolf, N.R. (2003), 'Gibt es althochdeutsche Sprachregionen? Oder: Warum gibt es keine althochdeutsche Schriftsprache?', in: *Die deutsche Schriftsprache und die Regionen. Entstehungsgeschichtliche Fragen in neuer Sicht*, edited by R. Berthele, H. Christen,

S. Germann and I. Hove, Berlin and New York: de Gruyter (Studia Linguistica Germanica 65), 111–25.

Zeuss, K. (1837), *Die Deutschen und die Nachbarstämme*, München: Ignaz Joseph Leutner.

WINIFRED V. DAVIES

Standard German in the Nineteenth Century

The sociohistorical background

The nineteenth century was a century of great social and political upheaval in many parts of Europe, and this was no different in Germany. At the beginning of the century there was no unified German state and all German territories west of the Rhine were under French rule. Prussia was in such a weak condition that the French armies had little trouble vanquishing it and, after the Peace of Tilsit in 1807, France annexed all the Prussian territories west of the Elbe as well as some in the east (Fulbrook 1990: 98–9). By the end of the century, there would be a German Empire under the domination of Prussia, a state which had recovered so successfully that it had led successful military campaigns against Austria, Denmark and France, and which was convinced that the German Empire under its leadership was destined to be the dominant power in Europe as well as a world power. In the middle of the century, the (failed) revolutions of 1848 added to the social and political upheaval.

Two defining characteristics of the century were nationalism and industrialization (cf. von Polenz 1999: 2–3). The latter was accompanied by the spread of literacy as the school system expanded to serve the growing need for more effective communication, and by greater mobility as people moved to urban areas from the countryside. All these factors had an effect on linguistic usage and attitudes as more people came into contact with standard (written) German in the classroom and as it became necessary for speakers to expand their linguistic repertoires in response to social, commercial and technological pressures (see Elspaß 2005a). Another consequence of the spread of literacy and the growing differentiation of society was the need to increase the register range of standard German, to expand what Warnke calls its 'Polyfunktionalität' (Warnke 1999: 17). However, attempts to open up the norm of standard German, for instance by Daniel Sanders, who drew on specialist and technical registers as well as the usage of prestigious authors when compiling his dictionaries, were often opposed by the educated middle classes (*Bildungsbürgertum*) and his works were criticized because they were not considered normative enough (Haß-Zumkehr 1995: 544). As we shall see below, standard German was an integral part of the group identity of the *Bildungsbürgertum*, and these educated middle classes fought bitterly to retain their authority as gate-keepers of what was to count as standard German. Linking standard German to a particular register, the language of the classical writers, also ensured that only the elite who had received a 'proper' education at a classics-based grammar school could hope to acquire it. Like other high cultural artefacts, its value would be compromised if it were to be too accessible to the 'masses'.

According to Townson (1992: 91), from the second half of the eighteenth century onwards, there was a growing sense of German nationhood and a desire for unity on the part of sections of the middle classes (what he calls the progressive middle classes), which was probably accelerated by, but not the result of the trauma of the French occupation after 1806. Attempts were made to compensate for political and military losses by exalting German culture (literature above all) and language, especially at the expense of French, for example in Fichte's *Reden an die deutsche Nation* (1808). This talking up of German literature and language was part of the project of igniting the consciousness of 'wanting to be a nation' (cf. Stevenson 2002: 17, referring to Alter 1994: 11), that is, it was aimed at generating a national consciousness which would have political consequences. The hope amongst the liberal middle classes was that a sense of cultural and linguistic unity would be the springboard for uniting the Germans as one political entity. However, despite the stress on cultural and linguistic unity, as expressed for example in the concept of *Nationalliteratur* (cf. Townson 1992: 91) and Jacob Grimm's rhetorical question in the preface to the first volume of the *Deutsches Wörterbuch*: 'was haben wir dann gemeinsames als unsere sprache und literatur?' (Grimm and Grimm 1854: iii), and despite the fact that most commentators, claim that 'die Standardsprache zu Beginn des 19. Jahrhunderts etabliert [ist]',[1] as late as 1846 we find a writer, known only as J.F., complaining that there is no 'Gesammtsprache der Gebildeten' and that this was a 'Loch in unserer

---

1   For example, Stukenbrock (2005: 241). See also Gardt (2000: 171).

[i.e. of the Germans] Sprachnationalität, dessen wir uns zu schämen haben'
(cited in Dieckmann 1989: 214). J.F. is referring to the fact that there was
still no standardized spoken German. Pronunciation was not standardized
until the end of the century, after political unification had taken place, but
the codified standard pronunciation, as found for example in Siebs *Deutsche
Aussprache* or Duden *Aussprachewörterbuch*, is even today rarely realized in
practice, and some linguists, e.g. Auer (1990: 2), would claim that there is
still no German standard pronunciation because the gap between the codex
and reality is too large.

  J.F.'s comment illustrates clearly how the German language was seen as
more than just a means of communication, yet not just as a symbol of social
in-group identity (i.e. as a badge of belonging to the educated middle classes).
The communicative demands of modernization and industrialization certainly had a major influence on the development of standard German in the
nineteenth century, but we can not ignore the influence exerted by speakers'
awareness of the various social symbolic functions of language (Mattheier
2003: 218–19), in J.F.'s case as a major component of national identity. During
the first part of the nineteenth century, using 'correct' or 'good' German served
mainly to mark off the *Bildungsbürgertum* from other social classes, including the *Kleinbürgertum* and the *Besitzbürgertum* (Bluhm-Faust 2005: 2). For
the *Bildungsbürgertum*, standard German was a form of symbolic cultural
capital (Bourdieu 1991), which became an important component of their
group identity. During the course of the century, however, standard German
developed more and more into a symbol of German national identity, marking
out the national in-group in opposition to national and ethnic out-groups,
and finally, after 1871, it became a *Staatssymbol* (cf. Stukenbrock 2005: 320).
In the second half of the century and especially after the establishment of the
Second Empire, the symbolic link between Germanness and the (written)
standard variety was ruthlessly exploited in the political project of nation-
state building (cf. Mattheier 2003: 236). Such efforts drew on the theories
of writers like Johann Gottfried Herder and Wilhelm von Humboldt, who
argued that every language was bound up with a particular national world-
view, so speakers of a particular language would see the world in a particular
way, e.g. 'Die Sprachen werden nur von Nationen erzeugt, festgehalten und
verändert, die Vertheilung des Menschengeschlechts nach Nationen ist nur
seine Vertheilung nach Sprachen' (Humboldt 1827–9/1963: 161, cited in Stevenson 2002: 18).

The effects of nationalism can be seen both in the concern for the form of standard German (purist tendencies) as well as in the promotion of its sociolinguistic status, for example in the school system, where the position of German was consolidated at the expense of Latin and French. In 1892, Emperor Wilhelm II exhorted grammar schools to ensure that they turned out young Germans rather than young Greeks and Romans (a sideswipe at the dominance of classical languages in their curricula for much of the century), and German classes were perceived as having a special role to play: 'Der deutsche Aufsatz muß der Mittelpunkt sein, um den sich Alles dreht' (Wilhelm II, quoted in Becker and Kluckert 1993: 75). The discipline of *Germanistik* (German Studies) had been established in the mid-nineteenth century and many of its practitioners saw their role, before 1871, as contributing to the forming of a national consciousness, and, afterwards, to the consolidation, even glorification of the Empire.[2]

As we mentioned above, the place of German in schools changed during the course of the century. In the early years we find complaints such as the following by Theodor Heinsius, himself the author of a grammar for schools:

> Haben die Deutschen, die, nach mühevoller Besiegung der Barbarei, mit ihrer unbestrittenen geistigen Urkraft allen Völkern der Erde vorausgeeilt sind, es verdient, daß ihre reiche, kräftige, bildsame und bildende Sprache den Söhnen ihres Landes nur so neben her gelehrt, oder, was dasselbe ist, vorenthalten werde? (Heinsius 1830: 8, quoted in Straßner 1995: 252)

This is perhaps not too surprising a state of affairs if we consider that German had only become established as a school subject by about 1780. However, according to Townson (1992: 57), between 1856 and 1891, the time devoted to German classes in secondary schools (*höhere Schulen*) was raised by 30 per cent, at the expense of Latin and French (this happened first in Prussia and the central German states; the southern Catholic states clung to the Latin rhetorical tradition for longer, cf. Bluhm-Faust 2005: 10). Furthermore, in Bavaria, Prussia, Saxony and Württemberg, a pass in German in the *Abitur* became a necessary precondition for passing that exam as a whole (cf. Jordan 2000: 184). The strength of the link between the German language and nation at the end of the century is summed up by von See:

2   See Dahle (1969), Townson (1992: 92–6), Hutton (1999).

> Deutsche Sprache gilt hier weniger als Verständigungsmittel denn als Ausdruck deutschen Wesens. Noch immer wird 'Volk' nicht von der Rasse, sondern allein von der Sprache her definiert, und gerade aus solcher Auffassung heraus wird für das Deutsche in der Schule nun ein Anspruch auf totale Herrschaft gestellt. (von See 1984: 250)

The high status accorded to German is also reflected in Weber's rather pathetic claim that 'Das Amt eines deutschen Sprachlehrers ist ein königliches, ein hohepriesterliches Amt' (Weber 1872: 4, in Straßner 1995: 261).

One trend that started in the eighteenth century but became particularly salient after 1871 is the reification of the German standard written variety as a *Kultur-* or *Nationalgut* like art or religion rather than a dynamic means of communication, for instance in the statement 'Der Völkerfrühling kam. Aus den Heldentaten des Jahres 1870 blühte Segen auf für alle Nationalgüter, auch für die deutsche Sprache' (Fischer 1900, column 93, quoted in Cherubim 1998: 66).

Unification was not the only political event to have a major influence on the schools: the revolutions of 1848 also played a role. From the eighteenth century onwards it had been clear that economic and social changes required a better-educated workforce, but the ruling classes were still determined that the emancipation of the lower classes should not go too far. The education provided by elementary schools (*Volksschulen*), which was the only school type attended by most pupils for most of the century (Jordan 2000: 174), was deliberately kept pretty basic, and little money was invested in teacher training or the provision of schoolbooks (Bluhm-Faust 2005: 21). Despite these failings, Bluhm-Faust (2005: 107) claims that the standard of teaching at elementary schools was still higher before the revolutions of 1848/1849 than it was afterwards. After the revolutions, the middle classes were more worried than ever about keeping their privileged position and determined that the lower classes should acquire even less education. One consequence was less stress on the teaching of standard German in elementary schools. For some years in the early nineteenth century, there had been efforts to reform the education system and to provide a better education for every child, regardless of social background, but those efforts were viewed with suspicion after the events of 1848. In Baden, in the 1850s, there was a deliberate lowering of the level to be attained in German classes at elementary schools (Bluhm-Faust 2005: 107). In the grammar books used in grammar schools, on the other hand, 'war die Messlatte grammatischer Normen so hoch gelegt, dass es nur

einer kleinen elitären bildungsbürgerlichen Schicht gelang, sie zu erreichen'
(Elspaß 2005c: 91). As Bluhm-Faust (2005: 548) puts it, 'Damit waren die
Schulen am Offenhalten der Sprachschere beteiligt', in other words, the already
existing dual-track system of elite education at grammar schools and a much
more basic (*volkstümlich*) and mechanistic acquisition of skills at elementary
schools was maintained, along with the concomitant social inequalities.[3]

The sociolinguistic background

By the beginning of the nineteenth century a supra-regional written standard
variety is taken as a given in grammars and textbooks and all school types see
it as their duty to teach this to pupils,[4] although there is disagreement over
the methods to be used and it would take a while yet for German to win its
place as a subject on the curriculum and to oust Latin as the core subject. The
strong position of Latin is illustrated by the fact that, as late as 1899, we still
find arguments that it would be more helpful for pupils to be taught Latin
grammar since this would help them with German and Latin (e.g. J. Keller
1899: 164–5, cited in Bluhm-Faust 2005: 381). There were also some people
who were unconvinced of the value of teaching German to native speakers,
although it must have been the every-day experience of most educators that,
for many pupils, standard German was almost as foreign as an L2.[5] In the
light of this, some of the theorists who were originally unconvinced of the
value of teaching German to native speakers changed their minds (e.g. von
Raumer 1855: 104). A major opponent of teaching German systematically to
native speakers was Jacob Grimm, who believed that formal teaching would

---

3   Hobusch talks of a 'qualifizierende Elitebildung' and a 'minderwertige Massenbildung'
    (Hobusch 1989: 115, in Bluhm-Faust 2005: 38).
4   Cf. Bluhm-Faust (2005: 543): 'Am Anfang des 19. Jahrhunderts war der richtige Gebrauch
    der hochdeutschen Sprachform erklärtes Ziel des deutschen Sprachunterrichts in der
    Volksschule' (she is referring to schools in Baden). See, too, Vesper (1980: 84–5).
5   Hildebrand aimed to change this perception by encouraging teachers to build on the
    child's vernacular when transmitting standard German (Hildebrand 1887: 6).

damage the free development of the children's linguistic abilities (cf. Frank 1973: 452). According to Frank (1973: 454), Grimm's negative judgement meant that German grammar was not taught systematically at Bavarian and Prussian grammar schools until about 1862.

Even by the end of the nineteenth century it was probably the case that, although there was a widespread passive knowledge of standard German, and a substantial number of people, although far fewer, also had active competence in it, and although it was used in a greater range of situations than at the beginning of the century, there were still significant regional and social differences (including urban / rural) as well as gender differences (more boys than girls attended school, Bluhm-Faust 2005: 549) in mastery of and confident use of this variety (Mattheier 2003: 234–8).

Most modern scholars of the history of German are of the opinion that, by the end of the eighteenth century, German grammar (i.e. morphology and syntax) and lexis had been standardized to a great extent:

> Im 19. und 20. Jahrhundert gibt es nur noch wenige variable Bereiche innerhalb der Standardvarietät, die teils kontaktinduziert und teils artikulatorisch-perzeptiv bzw. innersystematisch motiviert sind. (Mattheier 2000: 1953)[6]

Occasionally, however, one hears a dissenting voice. Chorley, for example, claims that usage was still uncertain – or flexible – in areas of morphology (particularly inflection) and syntax (especially agreement and government) as well as orthography, and not merely in the writings of the less well educated, but in the works of the most intellectual too (Chorley 1984: 61).[7]

What seems fairly clear from the available evidence is that there was a great deal of variability in the actual and perceived competence of speakers, whatever the level of codification and standardization achieved. A study of essays written by grammar-school pupils shows a high level of norm competence, measured by the use (or avoidance) of certain variants such as *besser wie* (Ziegler 2007). On the other hand, the large number of language advice works (*Sprachratgeber*) on the market, e.g. Wustmann's *Sprachdummheiten*, which

---

6   See, too, Admoni (1990: 219), Bluhm-Faust (2005: 1), Gardt (2000: 171) and Stukenbrock (2005: 241).

7   I am grateful to Julie Chorley for permission to quote from her unpublished M.Litt. thesis.

went through fourteen editions from 1891 to 1966, indicates that there was a high degree of linguistic insecurity. Hirt (1925: 239) claims that every issue of the *Zeitschrift des Allgemeinen Deutschen Sprachvereins* (which appeared from 1886 to 1924) was full of questions about competing forms.

Elspaß (2005b) shows that the apparent misconceptions regarding the level of uniformity of German in the nineteenth century can be traced back to the way the historiography of the language has tended to focus on only one register when investigating language use, i.e. the variety taught in grammar schools to the middle classes and used by them in formal, mainly written contexts. This has led to the misleading conclusion that variation had been more or less eliminated from writing (except for spelling, which was not standardized until the end of the century) and that written texts were now fully standardized.

Codification and standardization

German is today a highly codified language, that is, there is a range of reference works which German-speakers can consult to check what is correct in grammar, lexis, orthography and pronunciation. However none of these works has official status and the most widely known[8] works are produced by a private publishing house, the *Duden-Verlag* in Mannheim, rather than by any state authority such as an Academy. In the nineteenth century, too, there was a range of reference works in which speakers could look up what was correct grammar and lexis, although orthography and pronunciation were not codified until the end of the century, the former in Theodor Siebs's pronunciation manual, *Deutsche Bühnenaussprache* (first edition 1898), the latter in Konrad Duden's *Vollständiges Orthographisches Wörterbuch der deutschen Sprache* (first published 1880). With regard to grammar, according to Mattheier (2003: 227), 'The developments towards formulation of a general German standard language culminated in the work of Johann Christoph

8   I deliberately say 'widely known' rather than 'widely used' since we know little about how and how frequently reference works are used.

Adelung (1732–1806)'. Adelung wrote a grammar which was widely used in schools (Adelung 1782) as well as an orthography book (Adelung 1788) and a five-volume dictionary (Adelung 1774–86). These works summarized the state of knowledge about the German standard variety at the time as well as contributing to the development of a normative basis which became more widespread in the nineteenth century because of their frequent use in schools (cf. Mattheier 2003: 227).

Codification is not of course synonymous with standardization. In Haugen's well-known model of language standardization, codification is the second stage and is followed by implementation, i.e. 'the gradual diffusion and acceptance of the newly created norm across speakers as well as across functions' (Deumert and Vandenbussche 2003: 7). The importance of acceptance by the speech community is stressed in Haugen's definition of a standard variety:

> Any vernacular language or dialect may be 'standardized' by being given a uniform and consistent norm of writing that is widely accepted by its speakers. It may then be referred to as a 'standard' language'. (Haugen 1994: 4340, in Elspaß 2005b: 134)

Some commentators do claim that a German written standard variety was not only codified but had also been accepted by the end of the nineteenth century (Elspaß 2005b: 134 refers to Besch 1983 and Mattheier 2000 in this context). At the turn of the century, Fischer wrote that

> Wer ein Auge dafür hat, kann mit Freude wahrnehmen, daß namentlich die Fähigkeit, das Hochdeutsche schriftlich zu gebrauchen, auf dem besten Wege ist, Allgemeingut zu werden. Heute sind auch die unteren Klassen, Arbeiter und dienende Personen, imstande, sich innerhalb ihres Anschauungskreises schriftlich auszudrücken. (Fischer 1900, column 95, quoted in Cherubim 1998: 67)

However, on the basis of his study of letters written by German emigrants to the US, Elspaß argues that there were at least two written norms in existence. Since there is no evidence that Fischer's claims are based on any sort of empirical study, we have to assume that widespread literacy does not necessarily mean the same as widespread usage of a shared set of linguistic norms. Elspaß's position can be summed up as follows:

> Die Vielfalt der Formen und Entwicklungen in der Realität der geschriebenen All-
> tagssprache von Menschen, die möglicherweise repräsentativ für die übergroße Mehrheit

der Bevölkerung sind, lässt es zweifelhaft erscheinen, ob man im 19. Jahrhundert schon
von einer deutschen '**Standardsprache**' sprechen kann. (Elspaß 2005b: 470, emphasis
in original)

If we widen the notion of standardized language to include speech, then
we have to conclude that the standardization of German was very far from
having being achieved by the end of the nineteenth century. A standard pronunciation was indeed codified in 1898, but its bias towards northern forms
meant that it found little acceptance in the south of the German-speaking area
(cf. von Polenz 1999: 259). As we saw above, even today it is difficult to argue
that it enjoys wide acceptance and there is still no comprehensive description
of the syntax of standard spoken German. Works like the *Duden-Grammatik*
have usually been orientated more or less explicitly towards the norms of written German (cf. Jäger 1980; *Duden-Grammatik* 2005: 1176).

Grammars and usage guides

Authors and approaches

As we said above, in the nineteenth century there was a range of reference
works in which speakers could look up what was correct or good German,
although none of them had official status. The dominant academic trends
were towards comparative and historical grammar, but such approaches were
not considered particularly helpful for the practical task of transmitting
the norms of standard German grammar in the classroom or for consulta-
tion in order to solve a specific linguistic problem (e.g. was it correct to say
größer wie or *mit großem roten Mund*).⁹ Then as now there was also a tension
between the descriptive approach of academics (often caricatured nowadays

---

9   Schmidt (1985: 175) stresses the gulf between the needs of teachers and the interests
     of academics: he claims that teachers felt at a loss in the face of the stress on historical
     linguistics in the first half of the nineteenth century and could not see its relevance for
     their task of improving German teaching at schools.

as an 'anything goes' approach) and the fact that many speakers felt the need to be able to classify constructions as right or wrong.[10] Hirt (1925: 241–2) makes the point that, because of the reluctance of academic linguists to pass judgement on correct and incorrect or good and bad usage (what Schmidt 1985: 157 calls the 'sprachpflegerische Abstinenz der Linguistik des 19. Jahrhunderts'), it was often teachers and people from outside the discipline who wrote works dealing with linguistic correctness, despite the fact that many of them lacked the necessary academic training in linguistics, even if they took an active interest in language.

A second very practical reason why teachers wrote grammars and usage guides is because schools needed textbooks once German had won its place on the curriculum. Radlof bears testimony to the fact that many such works were produced by the practitioners themselves:

> Seitdem man ... um die Jahre 1780 angefangen, auch noch die vaterländische Sprache zum Gegenstande des öffentlichen Unterrichtes zu erheben, tritt fast jeder Lehrer ... mit einer neuen Teutschgrammatik hervor, zu deren Abfassung er natürlich die dringendsten Beweggründe hat ... (Radlof 1826: 355f., cited in Schmidt 1985: 172)

The level of education of the authors and the extent to which they were familiar with the latest scholarship in the fields of German or linguistics will of course have varied enormously, and different works were produced for different readers. For instance, Elspaß (2005b: 137) points out that German classes at *Volksschulen* would have been based on fairly elementary works like Bohm and Steinert (1851) whereas pupils at grammar schools would have used (or at least their teachers would have used) works like Adelung (1782), Heyse (1838) and Becker (1863), which were much more comprehensive and required a greater familiarity with technical grammatical terms. But, in general, regardless of the intended readership, works produced by authors outside the academy for a lay audience tended to be characterized by an explicitly evaluative and prescriptive stance, and usually had the express aim of teaching the norms of standard German, although the labels *Standardsprache* and *Standarddeutsch* are not amongst the many terms used for the variety promoted within their pages. Amongst the terms that do occur are *Schriftsprache*, *Schriftdeutsch*,

---

10 Cf 'Es wird höchste Zeit, daß neben die beschreibende Grammatik wieder die gesetzgebende tritt' (Wustmann 1896: vii, quoted in Schmidt-Regener 1995: 137).

Literatursprache, Hochdeutsch, gutes Deutsch, echtes Deutsch and *statthaftes Deutsch*, terms which reflect the origins and nature of the variety and its place within the national value system. The bibliography of primary works at the end of this paper contains a comprehensive list of grammars and usage guides produced at this time.

Readership

It is clear from the fact that many of the grammars and guides produced in the nineteenth century were published in several editions that there was a ready market for them. For example, in the preface to the ninth edition of his work (also included in later editions), Heinsius (1829: viii) writes that it the first eight editions were spread over only eleven years), while Chorley (1984: 1) says of J.C.A. Heyse's grammar that it was so popular that it was constantly published and imitated for over one hundred years. According to Schieb (1981: 142), there were 13 editions of Sanders' *Wörterbuch der Haupt-schwierigkeiten in der deutschen Sprache* in ten years, rising to 30 in the twentieth century with the publication of large and small versions of the book. Wustmann's *Allerhand Sprachdummheiten* was first published in 1891, and a second, enlarged edition was already on the market by 1896.

Unsurprisingly, since schools were to some extent a captive audience, some of these works are aimed directly at pupils (the preface to the ninth edition of Heinsius's grammar states that the publisher will give a discount to schools which introduce the book), while others are aimed at pupils through their teachers (K.G. Keller 1879: VI–VII believes his *Deutscher Antibarbarus* will be useful for teachers, who have the task of 'die Jugend vor landläufigen Verirrungen zu bewahren'). In some cases there was a deliberate policy of not distributing grammar books to pupils: for instance, at the First Pomeranian Directors' Conference in 1861, it was resolved that pupils in the middle and upper classes should not be given grammar books, but that the teachers should use one. This was so as not to encourage the pupils to regard their mother tongue as a foreign language like Latin or French (for which they would presumably have their own grammar books) (cf. Vesper 1980: 53). However, schools are by no means the only segment of the population targeted. Many works are aimed at a more general audience, such as Sanders (1882), which can best be described as a self-help manual for adults, and Heyse (1838: v), who makes it clear that his work is aimed not only at school pupils, but also at 'denkenden Geschäftsleuten, denen die Reinheit und Richtigkeit im Sprechen nicht gleichgültig ist'.

The fact that so many grammars and guides were produced (cf. Hirt 1925: 242; Straßner 1995: 272; von Polenz 1999: 299) indicates that there was a widespread demand for them, fuelled of course by the spread of literacy. Whilst some speakers would be prepared to invest in the acquisition of standard German for purely functional reasons, others no doubt wished to acquire it as a sort of social capital (cf. Bourdieu 1991; Linke 1996). Book titles such as *Sprachsünden* testify to the social (even moral) importance attached to its correct use.

Content

Even if the grammar of the standard variety had been codified in theory by the end of the eighteenth century, it is clear from the range of constructions discussed in grammars and usage guides that there were many areas of insecurity (this is also indicated by the frequent use of terms such as *Zweifelsfälle* or *Sprachschwierigkeiten* in the titles of the works), and it seems that the process of selecting variants into the standard was by no means complete. Many of the constructions discussed in these works are still *Zweifelsfälle* today and can be found in works like *Duden–Richtiges und gutes Deutsch*, e.g. *bräuchte / brauchte* (written standard German has no mutation on subjunctive II forms of weak verbs, although the latter form is common in southern Germany); *sie braucht nicht gehen / sie braucht nicht zu gehen* (should *brauchen* be treated as a modal verb or not?); *er starb in 1987 / er starb 1987* (traditionally German does not use the preposition *in* before the year); *sie blieb wegen dem schlechten Wetter / des schlechten Wetters zu Hause* (case selection after *wegen*); *trotz dem Regen / des Regens kam sie mit* (case selection after *trotz*); *diese Kinder sind viel schöner wie / als jene* (which particle to use following the comparative of adjectives?); *wenn er gehen würde / ginge* (when should synthetic forms of the subjunctive II of strong verbs be replaced by analytical forms?); *mit großem blauem Tisch / großem blauen Tisch* (declension of more than one adjective not preceded by an article); *reines / reinen Herzens* (declension of adjective in front of a masculine or neuter noun in the genitive case); *die Onkel / Onkels* (acceptability of *s* plural, especially on 'native' nouns); *ich sah den Held/en* (declension of weak masculine nouns); *der Mann, welcher / der* (choice of relative pronoun); *die Generäle / Generale* (acceptability of mutation to show plural of 'foreign' nouns); *er ging / ist gegangen* (simple present vs. perfect tense); *Schönheits(s)preis* (should one use the joining *s* to link morphemes in compound words if the first part of the compound is a feminine noun?); *er tut gehen / geht* (periphrastic verb forms vs. simple forms); *die Stiefeln / Stiefel* (competing plural forms for native masculine nouns ending in *-el*; gradually *n* becomes restricted to feminine nouns in standard German – with some exceptions, e.g. *Muskel, Pantoffel* and weak masculines); *der Frau ihre Tochter / die Tochter der Frau / von der Frau* (the dative periphrasis as a means of expressing possession is still common in spoken German but is not considered standard, cf. *Duden-Grammatik* 2005: 835). The fact that these are still *Zweifelsfälle* even though in many cases nineteenth-century works (and modern works) come down clearly in favour of one variant rather than another (e.g. *brauchte, er starb 1987, schöner als, die Onkel, den Helden*) illustrates the limitations of codification and standardization when applied to a living language.

Nineteenth-century grammarians do not always provide reasons why one variant is better or more correct than another, relying on their readers to accept their authority unquestioningly. When they do provide reasons, they tend to draw on a set of criteria which have been used for centuries to persuade speakers of the superiority of one variant rather than another. These are summarized in Gloy (1975: 66–79):

(1) Strukturgemäßheit der Sprachvarietäten im Sprachsystem;

(2) traditionalistisch-historische Qualität der Sprachvarietäten;

(3) moralische Qualität der Sprachvarietäten;

(4) Zweckmäßigkeit im Hinblick auf verständliches Sprechen;

(5) Belegbarkeit im faktischen Sprachgebrauch.

A criterion which is not listed here but which is often appealed to in order to justify the selection of one variant rather than another is 'one form, one function' (Chorley 1984: 237). This is often linked to criterion (4) by arguing that using the same form to express more than one meaning (e.g. the use of *nachdem* to express a temporal and a causal relation between clauses, as is common in southern Germany: *Die Kinder gingen ins Klassenzimmer, nachdem die Lehrerin aufgeschlossen hatte* vs. *Nachdem die Lehrerin nicht kommen konnte, mussten die Kinder draußen bleiben*) endangers communication by confusing the hearer / reader. Regarding criterion (5): of course, 'Sprachgebrauch' means the usage of social groups considered worthy models of linguistic behaviour; in the nineteenth century many constructions (e.g. plural *s*, *wegen* with dative case, use of the dative periphrasis to express possession) were classified as non-standard on the basis that they are *volkssprachlich* or part of *Volkssprache*, so they may indeed be present in the usage of speakers, but these are unfortunately not 'the right kind of speakers'. We see this in, for example, Heyse (1868):

> Fehlerhaft ist der Gebrauch der Volkssprache in manchen Provinzen, dem vorangestellten Genitiv des Besitzers noch das mit dem regierenden Substantiv verbundenen Possessivpronomen (sein, ihr usw.) beizufügen, oder auch statt jenes Genitivs den Dativ in Verbindung mit diesem Pronomen zu setzen. Man sage also nicht: das ist meines Vaters (oder meinem Vater) sein Haus, meiner Schwester ihr Buch usw. (Heyse 1868: 298)

Counted amongst the right kind of speakers or, more accurately, writers are usually, according to Meyer (1993: 287), Goethe, Lessing and Schiller, that is, the classical authors of the late eighteenth and early nineteenth centuries.

Criteria (1) and (2) can be used to argue against borrowings from foreign languages, whether in lexis or in morphology (e.g. plural *s*). It can be argued that 'foreign' elements are inauthentic and (consequently) do not fit into the native system. It is obvious that political circumstances play a role in linguistic judgements, although that is rarely openly acknowledged. According to Townson:

> With the growing view of the German language as a symbol of national unity and the move away from the emancipatory concerns of the first generations of *Germanisten*, linguistic purism ceased to be regarded as a means to an end, but became an end in itself. Foreign words were now no longer to be rejected because of their incomprehensibility or because they excluded sections of the population from certain discourses, but solely because of their foreignness, which was seen as detrimental to German 'Geist' as reflected in the language. (Townson 1992: 98)

We see this reflected in the treatment of constructions such as plural *s* and *in 1987*. No one could argue convincingly that these pose comprehension problems for German-speakers and one could even argue that adding *s* to a form like *Onkel* makes the plural form clearer, clarity being a criterion that is often invoked in other contexts. However, we find the plural *s* ending regularly associated with the adjective 'fremd' and a distinction is frequently drawn between its acceptable use with unassimilated word from other languages and its unacceptable use with 'native' German words or even with words of French or English origin which are regarded as having been assimilated into German, e.g. *Offiziere* (cf. Davies and Langer 2006: 137).

Conclusions

Recent research into the attitudes and practices of German teachers in Germany (e.g. Davies 2000; Davies 2005) has shown that, nowadays, standard German as an idea enjoys a high level of support, but it has also shown that there is substantial disagreement over the concrete form of this variety. That is to say, even amongst speakers who are considered norm authorities (Ammon 2003: 3) there is disagreement as to exactly which constructions actually count as standard. The situation at the end of the nineteenth century was not dissimilar. It may well be true that, as Straßner (1995: 288) says, citing Riegel (1885) and Matthias (1892):

> Unter sprachpflegerischem Aspekt wird die Sprache gegen Ende des Jahrhunderts aus national-ethischer Sicht als höchstes Kulturerbe, als das 'unschätzbare und edelste Gut des deutschen Volkes', das 'köstliche Kleinod' und das nationale Bindeglied, das das deutsche Volk in Notzeiten zusammenhält, aufgefaßt

but it is also true that the concrete realization of the norm was still the subject of debate and it is difficult to accept the consensus that the norm of standard German had been fixed more or less definitively by the end of the eighteenth century. Even where the authors of linguistic advice books and grammars were largely in agreement (e.g. that *mit großem blauem Tisch* was preferable to *mit großem blauen Tisch*), this did not ensure acceptance for their judgements (in this particular case, many authors make it clear that speakers are indeed following a rule, but a different rule from the one they themselves are promoting; cf. Davies and Langer 2006: 169ff for a detailed discussion of the treatment of this construction in nineteenth-century works). As long as the *Bildungsbürgertum* were the acknowledged gate-keepers of standard German, that is, as long as it was to a large extent, only a sociolect, and used in a relatively restricted range of domains, it could be relatively homogenous, but as soon as it became a national symbol and was transmitted to larger and more disparate social groups and its use promoted in more and more domains, it was inevitable that the once focused norm would become more diffuse (see Elspaß 2005c). It is therefore difficult to disagree with Elspaß's (2005b: 470) claim that 'Entgegen der herrschenden Meinung kam die Standardisierung der deutschen Sprache im 19. Jahrhundert noch nicht zum Abschluss; sie war vielmehr in vollem Gang(e)'. This view suggests that the nineteenth century is more interesting than hitherto assumed in the historiography of German, and throws a different light on claims that one of the most important developments to affect modern German is destandardization (cf. Mattheier 2003: 239).

References

Primary sources

Adelung, Johann Christoph (1774–86), *Versuch eines vollständigen grammatisch-kritischen Wörterbuches der Hochdeutschen Mundart mit beständiger Vergleichung der übrigen Mundarten, besonders aber der Oberdeutschen*, Five volumes, Leipzig: Breitkopf.
Adelung, Johann Christoph (1782), *Umständliches Lehrgebäude der Deutschen Sprache zur Erläuterung der Deutschen Sprachlehre für Schulen*, Leipzig: Breitkopf.
Adelung, Johann Christoph (1778), *Vollständige Anweisung zur Deutschen Orthographie, nebst einem kleinen Wörterbuch für die Aussprache, Orthographie, Biegung und Ableitung*, Leipzig: Breitkopf.
Andresen, Karl Gustaf (1890), *Sprachgebrauch und Sprachrichtigkeit im Deutschen*, 6th ed., Heilbronn: Verlag von Paul Henninger.
Ausgabe, 13th, expanded edition, Berlin: Langenscheidt'sche Verlag-Buchhandlung (1st ed. appeared as *Kurzgefasstes Wörterbuch der Hauptschwierigkeiten in der deutschen Sprache* 1872).

Becker, Karl Ferdinand (1863), *Schulgrammatik der deutschen Sprache*, revised by Theodor Becker. 8th ed., Frankfurt am Main: Joh. Christ. Hermannsche Verlagsbuchhandlung.

Bohm, H. and Steinert W. (1851), *Kleine deutsche Sprachlehre*, Berlin: K.W. Krüger.

Duden–Aussprachewörterbuch (1990), edited by M. Mangold, 3rd. ed., Mannheim, Leipzig, Vienna, Zürich: Duden Verlag.

Duden–Richtiges und gutes Deutsch, Wörterbuch der sprachlichen Zweifelsfälle (2001), 5th ed., Mannheim, Leipzig, Vienna, Zurich: Duden Verlag.

Duden–Grammatik (2005), 7th. ed., Mannheim, Leipzig, Vienna, Zürich: Duden Verlag.

Götzinger, Max Wilhelm (1836/1839), *Die Deutsche Sprache*, 2 vols, Stuttgart: Hoffmann'sche Verlags-Buchhandlung.

Grimm, Jacob and Grimm, Wilhelm (1854–1960), *Deutsches Wörterbuch*, Leipzig: S. Hirzel.

Heinsius, Theodor (1829), *Kleine theoretische praktische Deutsche Sprachlehre für Schulen und Gymnasien*, 11th ed., Reutlingen: J.J. Mäcken'schen Buchhandlung.

Heintze, Albert (1894), *Gut Deutsch. Eine Anleitung zur Vermeidung der häufigsten Verstöße gegen den guten Sprachgebrauch und ein Ratgeber in Fällen schwankender Ausdrucksweise*, 2nd ed., Berlin: Verlag von C. Regenhardt.

Heyse, Johann Christian August (1838), *Theoretisch-praktische deutsche Grammatik oder Lehrbuch der deutschen Sprache, nebst einer kurzen Geschichte derselben. Zunächst zum Gebrauch für Lehrer und zum Selbstunterricht*, 5th, completely revised and much extended edition, vol. 1, Hannover: Hahn (reprint: Hildesheim: Olms, 1972).

Heyse, Johann Christian August (1849), *Theoretisch-praktische deutsche Grammatik oder Lehrbuch der deutschen Sprache, nebst einer kurzen Geschichte derselben. Zunächst zum Gebrauch für Lehrer und zum Selbstunterricht*, 5th, completely revised and much expanded edition, vol. 2, Revised by Dr K.W. L. Heyse, Hannover: Hahn. (reprint: Hildesheim: Olms, 1972).

Heyse, Johann Christian August (1868), *Deutsche Schulgrammatik oder kurzgefasstes Lehrbuch der deutschen Sprache mit Beispielen und Übungsaufgaben*, revised by Dr K.W. L. Heyse revision, 21st, improved ed., Hannover: Hahn'sche Hof-Buchhandlung.

Keller, K.G. (1879), *Deutscher Antibarbarus. Beiträge zur Förderung des richtigen Gebrauchs der Muttersprache*, Stuttgart: A. Liesching and Comp.

Lehmann, August (1878), *Sprachliche Sünden der Gegenwart*, 2nd ed., Braunschweig: Verlag von Friedrich Wreden.

Matthias, Theodor (1897), *Sprachleben und Sprachschäden. Ein Führer durch die Schwankungen und Schwierigkeiten des deutschen Sprachgebrauchs*, 2nd, improved and expanded edition, Friedrich Brandstetter: Leipzig.

Sanders, Daniel (1880), *Deutsche Sprachbriefe*, 2nd expanded and more comprehensive ed., Berlin: Langenscheidt.

Sanders, Daniel (1882), *Wörterbuch der Hauptschwierigkeiten in der deutschen Sprache. Große Ausgabe*, 13th expanded edition, Berlin: Langenscheidt'sche Verlag-Buchhandlung (1st ed. appeared as *Kurzgefasstes Wörterbuch der Hauptschwierigkeiten in der deutschen Sprache 1872*).

Siebs, Theodor (1969), *Deutsche Aussprache*, edited by H. de Boor, H. Moser and C. Winkler, 19th. ed., Berlin: de Gruyter.

Wustmann, Gustaf (1891), *Allerhand Sprachdummheiten. Kleine deutsche Grammatik des Zweifehlhaften, des Falschen und des Häßlichen. Ein Hilfsbuch für alle, die sich öffentlich der deutschen Sprache bedienen*, 1st ed., Leipzig: Grunow.

Wustmann, Gustaf (1896), *Allerhand Spachdummheiten. Ein Hilfsbuch für alle, die sich öffentlich der deutschen Sprache bedienen*, 2nd, revised and expanded ed., Leipzig: Grunow.

Wustmann, Gustaf (1966), *Allerhand Sprachdummheiten. Ein Hilfsbuch für alle, die sich öffentlich der deutschen Sprache bedienen*, 14th ed., Berlin: de Gruyter (updated by Dr Werner Schulze).

Bibliography

Admoni, W. (1990), *Historische Syntax des Deutschen*, Tübingen: Niemeyer.

Alter, P. (1994), *Nationalism*, 2nd ed., London: Arnold.

Ammon, U. (2003), 'On the social forces that determine what is standard in a language and on conditions of successful implementation', *Sociolinguistica* 17, 1–10.

Auer, P. (1990), *Phonologie der Alltagssprache. Eine Untersuchung zur Standard/Dialekt-Variation am Beispiel der Konstanzer Stadtsprache*, Berlin: de Gruyter.

Beckert, H. and Gerhard K. (1993), *Die Bildung der Nation*, Klett-Cotta: Stuttgart.

Besch, W. (1983), 'Dialekt, Schreibdialekt, Schriftsprache, Standardsprache. Exemplarische Skizze ihrer historischen Ausprägung im Deutschen', in: *Dialektologie*, vol. 1.2, edited by W. Besch et al. (eds), Berlin and New York: de Gruyter. 961–90.

Bluhm-Faust, C. (2005), *Die Pädagogisierung der deutschen Standardsprache im 19. Jahrhundert am Beispiel Badens*, Frankfurt am Main, etc.: Peter Lang.

Bourdieu, P. (1991), *Language and Symbolic Power*, edited and introduced by J.B. Thompson, Cambridge: Polity Press.

Cherubim, D. (1998), 'Kontinuität und Diskontinuität in der deutschen Sprache des 20. Jahrhunderts', in: *Das 20. Jahrhundert. Sprachgeschichte – Zeitgeschichte*, edited by H. Kämper and H. Schmidt, Berlin, New York: de Gruyter. 59–85.

Chorley, J.A. (1984), *J.C.A. Heyse (1764–1829) and K.W.L. Heyse (1797–1855) and German School Grammar in the First Half of the Nineteenth Century*, M. Litt. Thesis, University of Oxford.

Dahle, W. (1969), *Der Einsatz einer Wissenschaft*, Bonn: Bouvier.

Davies, W.V. (2000), 'Linguistic norms at school. A survey of secondary-school teachers in a central German dialect area', *Zeitschrift für Dialektologie und Linguistik* 67, 129–47.

Davies, W.V. (2005), 'Deutschlehrer und Deutschlehrerinnen (in Deutschland) als Geber und Vermittler von sprachlichen Normen' in: *Germanistentreffen: Deutschland – Großbritannien – Irland*, Proceedings of conference organized by German Academic Exchange Service (DAAD), Dresden, October 2004. Bonn: DAAD. 323–38.

Davies, W. and Langer N. (2006), *The Making of Bad Language*, Frankfurt am Main, etc.: Peter Lang.

Deumert, A. and Vandenbussche W. (eds) (2003), *Germanic Standardizations. Past to present*, Amsterdam and Philadelphia: John Benjamins.

Dieckmann, W. (ed.) (1989), *Reichthum und Armut deutscher Sprache*, Berlin and New York: de Gruyter.

Elspaß, S. (2005a), *Sprachgeschichte von unten. Untersuchung zum geschriebenen Alltagsdeutsch im 19 Jahrhundert*, Tübingen: Niemeyer.

Elspaß, S. (2005b), 'Standardisierung des Deutschen. Ansichten aus der neueren Sprachgeschichte, von unten' in: *Standard variation, Wie viel Variation verträgt die deutsche Sprache?*, edited by L. Eichinger and W. Kallmeyer, Berlin: Walter de Gruyter. 63–99.

Fichte, J.G. 'Reden an die deutsche Nation (1808)', in: *Fichtes Werke* vol. 7, edited by I.H. Fichte, Berlin 1845/46. Reprinted Berlin (1971), 257–499.

Fischer, K. (1900), 'Unsere Muttersprache im 19. Jahrhundert', *Zeitschrift des Allgemeinen Deutschen Sprachvereins* 15/4, 90–6.

Frank, H.J. (1973), *Geschichte des Deutschunterrichts. Von den Anfängen bis 1945*, Munich: Carl Hanser Verlag.

Fulbrook, M. (1990), *A Concise History of Germany*, Cambridge: Cambridge University Press.

Gardt, A. (ed.) (2000), 'Sprachnationalismus zwischen 1850 und 1945', in: *Nation und Sprache* edited by A. Gardt, Berlin and New York: de Gruyter. 247–71.

Gloy, K. (1975), *Sprachnormen I. Linguistische und soziologische Analysen*, Stuttgart-Bad Cannstatt: Friedrich Frommann Verlag.

Grimm, J. and Grimm W. (1854–1960 (reprints)), *Deutsches Wörterbuch*, Leipzig: S. Hirzel.

Haß-Zumkehr, U. (1995), *Daniel Sanders. Aufgeklärte Germanistik im 19. Jahrhundert*, Berlin, New York: de Gruyter.

Haugen, E. (1994), 'Standardization', in: *The Encyclopaedia of Language and Linguistics*, vol. 8, edited by R.E. Asher, Oxford: Pergamon, 4340–2.

Hildebrand, R. (1887), *Vom deutschen Sprachunterricht in der Schule und von deutscher Erziehung und Bildung überhaupt. Mit einem Anhang über die Fremdwörter und einem über das Altdeutsche in der Schule*, 3rd, improved and expanded ed., Leipzig, Berlin: Klinkhardt.

Hirt, H. (1925), *Geschichte der deutschen Sprache*, 2nd ed., Munich: C.H. Beck.

Hobusch, J. (1989), *Der Deutschunterricht in den Anfängen der bürgerlichen Reformpäda-gogik*, Frankfurt am Main, etc.: Peter Lang.

Humboldt, W. von (1827–9/1963), *Über die Verschiedenheiten des menschlichen Sprach-baues*, Stuttgart: Cotta.

Hutton, C.M. (1999), *Linguistics and the Third Reich. Mother-tongue fascism, race and the science of language*, London and New York: Routledge.

Jäger, S. (1980), 'Standardsprache', in: *Lexikon der germanistischen Linguistik*, edited by H.P. Althaus, H. Henne and H.E. Wiegand (eds). 2nd ed. Tübingen: Niemeyer, 375–9.

Jordan, A.L. (2000), *Wer sprach wie? Sprachmentalität und Varietätengebrauch im 19. Jahrhundert. Part A*, Dossenheim: Anna-Luise Jordan.

Keller, J. (1899), 'Denken und Sprechen und Sprachunterricht. Eine Studie zur Frage nach der formalen Bildung', in: (1913), *Gesammelte Reden und Abhandlungen von Julius Keller*, vol. 2, Karlsruhe, Leipzig: Gutsch, 83–167.

Linke, A. (1996), *Sprachkultur und Bürgertum. Zur Mentalitätsgeschichte des 19. Jahrhunderts*, Stuttgart and Weimar: Metzler.

Mattheier, K.J. (2000), 'Die Durchsetzung der deutschen Hochsprache im 19. und beginnenden 20. Jahrhundert: sprachgeographisch, sprachsoziologisch', in: *Sprachgeschichte. Ein Handbuch zur Geschichte der deutschen Sprache und ihrer Erforschung*, edited by W. Besch, A. Betten, O. Reichmann and S. Sonderegger, vol. 2.2, 2nd, completely revised ed., Berlin and New York: de Gruyter. 1951–66.

Mattheier, K.J. (2003), 'German', in: *Germanic Standardizations. Past to present*, edited by A. Deumert, and W. Vandenbussche, Amsterdam and Philadelphia: John Benjamins, 211–44.

Meyer, K. (1993), 'Wustmanns "Sprachdummheiten". Untersuchungen zu einem Sprachratgeber des 19. Jahrhunderts', *Sprachwissenschaft* 18, 223–315.

Polenz, P. von (1999), *Deutsche Sprachgeschichte vom Spätmittelalter bis zur Gegenwart. Bd III: 19. und 20. Jahrhundert*, Berlin and New York: de Gruyter.

Radlof, J.B. (1826), *J.G. Radlof's teutschkundliche Forschungen und Erheiterungen für Gebildete*, vol. 2, Berlin: Vossische Buchhandlung.

Raumer, R. von (1855), *Über deutsche Rechtschreibung*, Vienna: Gerold.

Schieb, G. (1981), 'Zu Stand und Wirkungsbereich der kodifizierten grammatischen Norm Ende des 19. Jahrhunderts', *Beiträge zur Erforschung der deutschen Sprache* 1, 134–76.

Schmidt, H. (1985), 'Aspekte der Institutionalisierung. Zur Durchsetzung der neuen Denkmuster', in: *Sprachwissenschaftliche Germanistik. Ihre Herausbildung und Begründung*, edited by W. Bahner and W. Neumann, Berlin: Akademie Verlag, 151–248.

Schmidt-Regener, I. (1995), '"Es giebt ... kein Richtig und Falsch einer Sprachform" – Das Verhältnis der etablierten Germanistik zur öffentlichen Sprachkritik im letzten Drittel des 19. Jahrhunderts', in: *Wie redet der Deudsche man jnn solchem fall? Studien zur deutschen Sprachgeschichte. Festschrift anläßlich des 65. Geburtstages von Erwin Arndt*, edited by G. Brandt and R. Hünecke, Stuttgart: Heinz, 137–49.

See, K. von (1984), 'Politisch-soziale Interessen in der Sprachgeschichtsforschung des 19. und 20. Jahrhunderts' in: *Sprachgeschichte. Ein Handbuch zur Geschichte der deutschen Sprache und ihrer Erforschung*, edited by W. Besch, O. Reichmann and S. Sonderegger, vol. 1, 1st. ed., Berlin, New York: de Gruyter, 242–57.

Stevenson, P. (2002), *Language and German Disunity*, Oxford: Oxford University Press.

Straßner, E. (1995), *Deutsche Sprachkultur. Von der Barbarensprache zur Weltsprache*, Tübingen: Niemeyer.

Stukenbrock, A. (2005), *Sprachnationalismus*, Berlin, New York: de Gruyter.

Townson, M. (1992), *Mother-tongue and Fatherland. Language and politics in German*, Manchester: Manchester University Press.

Vesper, W. (1980), *Deutsche Schulgrammatik im 19. Jahrhundert. Zur Begründung einer historisch-kritischen Sprachdidaktik*, Tübingen: Niemeyer.

Warnke, I. (1999), *Wege zur Kultursprache. Die Polyfunktionalisierung des Deutschen im juridischen Diskurs (1200–1800)*, Berlin, New York: de Gruyter.

Weber, H. (1872), *Die Pflege nationaler Bildung durch den Unterricht in der Muttersprache*, Leipzig: Siegismund and Volkening.

Ziegler, E. (2005), 'Putting standard German to the test. Some notes on the linguistic competence of grammar-school students and teachers in the nineteenth century', in : Germanic Language Histories 'from below' (1700–2000), edited by W. Vandenbussche, S. Elspaß, N. Langer and J. Scharloth, Berlin, New York: de Gruyter, 309–32.

NILS LANGER

Sociolinguistic Changes in the History of Low German

Introduction

One of the most prominent features of linguistic research is the examination, description and explanation of language change. Comparing languages such as English and German makes us realize that their similarities in syntax, phonology and lexis are not accidental, but that some set of changes occurred in the past which can account for the differences between the two modern languages. However, it is not only the systemic properties of a language which can change, for instance changes in the pronunciation or the regular positioning of words in a sentence, but its sociolinguistic properties, such as the geographic area in which a language is spoken, the situations in which the use of a language is acceptable and the folk-linguistic status of a language. In this paper aspects of the history of a particular language are presented to demonstrate how certain sociolinguistic changes can affect the way a language is used and perceived both by its speakers and in the outside world, in particular with respect to the question of whether a linguistic variety is seen to be an independent *language* or 'merely' a *dialect* of a supra-variety. I will focus on Low German (*Niederdeutsch*, *Plattdüütsch*), a language predominantly spoken in Northern Germany which has been subject to a wide range of sociolinguistic changes during its history.[1]

---

1   My gratitude goes to Annelie and Hans Voss who initiated my first encounter with Low German in 1976. Also, I wish to thank Elspeth Buchanan and Rachel Spiller for interesting and illuminating discussion on the subject. Finally, thank you to Geoffrey West for his patience and help in correcting my English.

Low German

Low German is a language variety predominantly spoken in Northern Germany. German dialects are traditionally divided into two major groups, High German (HG) and Low German (LG), with subdivisions of High German into Upper German and Central German. This division was suggested as early as the thirteenth century with Berthold von Regensburg's famous quotation (cited in Glück 2002: 25):

> *Ir wizzet wol. daz die Niderlender und die Oberlender gar unglîch sint an der sprâche und*
> *an den siten. die von Oberlant, dort her von Zürich, die redent vil anders danne die von*
> *Niderlande, von Sahsen, die sint ungelîch an der sprâche.*

Today, the traditional distinction between LG and HG is almost solely based on the absence (in LG) or presence (in HG) of the Second Sound Shift, that is, the shift from voiceless stops to affricates and fricatives which distinguishes High German from all other Germanic languages. This is an important point for our discussion. As we will see below, the 'language or dialect' question has had important political repercussions in the very recent history of LG, in that LG was eligible for protection under the *European Charter for Minority or Regional Languages* only if classified as a language, not a dialect. Hence, knowing the vast range of criteria that distinguish languages from each other (in their phonology, morphology etc.) we should keep in mind that the oldest and most fundamental grouping of German language varieties rests principally on the absence of a sound change that affected a mere three consonants, and that hence it can be argued that LG is not as different from HG as the traditional view claims. This is particularly important for the question of whether LG is an independent language or 'only' a German dialect.

Apart from the Second Sound Shift, there are other systemic differences between LG and HG, such as the lack of the Central German diphthongization (LG *min niewes hus* vs. HG *mein neues Haus*) or the loss of nasals in *fîf* (vs. HG *fünf*), *goos* (vs. HG *Gans*). Syntactically, there is little difference between HG dialects and LG though there are significant differences between the morpho-syntax of Standard German and LG, for example in the much greater use of analytic constructions such as periphrastic possessives or auxiliary *do* in subclauses. With regard to vocabulary, LG texts are by and large comprehensible to a Standard German speaker, not least because of its high degree of borrowing from High German, as shown for example in the following sentence uttered by an Emsland farmer contrasted with its 'pure' LG translation:

> die Ems / di **is** woll nich so **schöön** asn Rhein / **aber** wi Emsländer / wi **sind** doch **einigermaßen** schtolz up unsen fluss
>
> > (actual speech sample; my bolds – NL)

> de Ems / de mag wal nich so moj wern as'n Rhein / men wi Emslänner / wi bint doch orig schtolt up em
>
> > ('correct' Emsland LG: Stellmacher 2000: 94)

> Die Ems, die ist wohl nicht so schön wie der Rhein, aber wir Emsländer, wir sind doch einigermaßen stolz auf unseren Fluss.
>
> > (Standard written German)

Sociolinguistically and historically there are fundamental differences between LG and HG. HG dialects were 'full languages' up until the emergences of supraregional written languages (*Schreibsprachen*) in the fifteenth and sixteenth centuries when a sociolinguistic verticalization of the language varieties in Germany took place (Reichmann 1988). In the seventeenth century, this verticalization resulted in the creation of a prestige standard language, accompanied by an intense metalinguistic discussion about which dialect, if any, would be appropriate to become a national / standard German language. With this, the dialects became restricted to the oral domain so that, by the late seventeenth century, one was no longer able to deduce the regional origin of a text from its language. Today, the use of HG dialects is almost exclusively restricted to oral and private language. Compared to their Northern counterparts, almost all of whom are monolingual Standard German speakers, a much higher percentage of speakers in Central and in particular Southern Germany can comfortably switch between the local / regional dialect and (a regionalized form of) Standard German. However, just as in Northern Germany, dialect use in the South and in particular in Central Germany is on the decline, especially amongst younger speakers.

The early history of Low German parallels the histories of other German varieties in that it was increasingly used as a written language from the eighth and ninth centuries and as the vernacular spoken language of its region at least up until the fourteenth century. From the fourteenth century, HG and LG developed in different ways: LG became the lingua franca of the Hanseatic League and was used as an international written language throughout Northern Europe. From the sixteenth century, LG lost its international importance and its geographical domain became reduced to Northern German territories. Subsequently, the language suffered a loss of prestige and was stigmatized as unacceptable in all public and most private domains for at least four hundred years. It lost its status as a written language and its oral domains became ever fewer so that today, LG as a native language is on the whole restricted to older speakers in rural areas. However, since the 1970s there has been a renewed interest in LG (and German regional varieties as a whole), and public and private initiatives are concerned with promoting both use and awareness of the language. After lobbying, LG became the only German language variety to meet the qualifications for inclusion in the *European Charter of Minority or Regional Languages*.

The beginnings

The first Low German texts to survive date from the ninth century, which marks the beginning of the Old Saxon period (OS, *c.* 800–1100). Before this, all linguistic evidence is in the form of place and personal names; there are no surviving texts as such. During the Old Saxon period, the written language of Northern Germany was almost exclusively Latin (Peters 1998: 113) and the few vernacular texts (literary and theological) that were produced and copied were written in a small number of monasteries. There are no surviving LG texts at all from the twelfth century and consequently the Middle Low German (MLG) period begins in the thirteenth century (*c.* 1200–1550) with legal and business prose texts (documents and charters, legal codices (*Sachsenspiegel*)) but also general prose (*Sächsische Weltchronik*) (Niebaum 1986: 18). Interestingly, poetry was not written in MLG but in the 'poetic language' of the time, Middle High German (MHG), showing that Northern poets such as Heinrich von Veldeke and Heinrich von Halberstadt were aware of the greater prestige and wider geographcial range of the Southern

Dichtersprache. Importantly, this difference in prestige between a MHG and a MLG variety only pertained to *poetry* and did not spread to other text types. Thus so far, we can witness linguistic *processes* in the history of LG in the form of a change from oral to written communication, the range of text types in which the language is used (from none to literary/theological to business/legal/theological) and in the prestige of the language (sufficient prestige to be used in prose but not in poetry).

LG = Hansesprache?

The most distinctive feature of the history of LG is its function as the language of the Hanseatic League from 1370–1500. Recently, scholars have been keen to dispel the myth that Middle Low German can be identified as the *Hansesprache* since there was both a lot of MLG outside the Hanseatic League, and a lot of Hanseatic business that was not transmitted in MLG (Peters 1987: 66), especially since the language reached its peak in the late fifteenth century when the economic power of the Hanseatic league had already been declining for a couple of generations. However, it cannot be denied that without the international success of the Hanseatic League, LG would not have become an international language.

The Hanseatic League (*Hanse*) was the dominant commercial union in Northern Europe from the thirteenth to the fifteenth century. It began when German merchants formed associations with each other to provide protection against robbers and pirates. Using Lübeck as their base, Westphalian and Saxon merchants expanded northwards and eastwards across the Baltic to trade with cities in Scandinavia, Russia and what are now the Baltic states, supporting the foundation of cities such as Riga, Tallinn, Gdansk and establishing permanent trading enclaves (*Kontore*) in many cities such as Brugge (Flanders), Bergen (Norway), Novgorod and London. In the fourteenth century, about a hundred towns and cities were members of the Hanseatic league (Friedland 1991: 203ff.). The organization was always commercial rather than political in nature and had no permanent army, navy or government. However, there were periodic assemblies (*Hansetage*, the last one in 1669) and an authoritative

Law Court in Lübeck, which grew to become the second-largest city in Germany (after Cologne) with 25,000 inhabitants. The prominent position of Lübeck was further strengthened by its central geographic location on the cross-roads between Scandinavia and the Alps, and Russia and England. The League declined when cities' individual interests started to grow apart in the early fifteenth century, with a simultaneous strengthening of the territorial states (Lithuania and Poland merged in 1386, Union of Denmark, Sweden and Norway in 1397, increase of Dutch and later also English powers in controlling the seatrade). The League was never dissolved, but it lost its dominant position by the sixteenth century.

The League's most pre-eminent city was Lübeck whose language was LG. Hence if any language was to replace Latin in international communication, LG would be the first candidate. Most chanceries changed from Latin to LG in the early fourteenth century and the Hanseatic institutions in Lübeck were in fact rather late in their switch, which took place in 1369 with the first writing of the Hanseatic protocols in LG (Peters 2000a: 1413). Why the Hanseatic league abandoned Latin is not clear – it certainly had enough power and prestige to continue with Latin. But the use of LG was probably just much more convenient as it was an easier means of communication for North Germans and speakers of other Germanic languages such as Swedish and Flemish. The foundation of German writing schools (*dudesche scryffscholen*) in the fourteenth century, where future merchants and administrators were trained in accountancy but also the reading and writing of (Low) German, corroborates the impression that Latin was not considered functionally adequate in the trading world. Thus, here we see the continuation of the linguistic process of *extension of functional domain*: the vernacular language continued to replace Latin in an increasing number of text types.

Nonetheless, this is a process that occurred all over Europe. The history of LG and other vernacular languages is similar in this respect. However, LG was so prestigious during the Hanseatic period that it exceeded the prestige of other language in the area. LG was adopted as the primary lingua franca and was used, not just in communications between Hanseatic trading enclaves (*Kontore*) across Northern Europe, but also in correspondence between Hanseatic cities and Scandinavian rulers and Flemish cities (Dollinger 1989: 342). There is some evidence that interpreters were used, especially in *Kontore* which were outside the Germanic world such as Reval (Tallinn) and Novgorod.

Here trade with locals was conducted through intermediaries and it is likely that some merchants learnt Russian,[2] thus showing that the prestige of LG did not extend to making fur or honey traders in Eastern Europe learn the language. Depending on the specialist area of trade, merchants would have a knowledge of French, English, possibly Italian, and certainly Dutch and High German (Peters 2000b: 1502). Anecdotal evidence includes the correspondence from 1375 between two Hanseatic merchants giving advice that when coming to London, one should enlist the services of an interpreter who speaks French (Peters 1987: 79), or the fact that in 1351 the Brugge Hansekontor would use Flemish when corresponding with the city council of Brugge, but Latin (not LG!) when communicating with the Hanse in Hamburg (Peters 2000b: 1499). The use of LG outside the native German areas was particularly prominent in the Baltic, especially in Scandinavia where the use of LG was facilitated by the relative similarity with Scandinavian languages[3] and the general bilingualism of parts of the Danish and Swedish bourgeoisie (Peters 2000b: 1502). However, the idea that 'pure' LG was used as a means of communication has recently been challenged in favour of the suggestion that in Northern Europe a type of semi-communication was employed (cf. articles in Braunmüller and Diercks 1993), as is still the case within Scandinavia today (albeit without LG of course).

With the dominance of Lübeck and the use of LG as its language in supra-regional communication, Lübeck LG gained in prestige and a process of standardization can be observed in the Hanseatic period: 'Im klassischen Mnd. tritt die Variantenvielfalt zugunsten großräumiger Vereinheitlichung zurück. Das bereitet der lübischen Norm den Boden' (Stellmacher 2000: 40). This should not be compared with 'traditional' processes of standardization (cf. Haugen 1984, and Langer 2003 for an application of Haugen 1983 to LG), but rather involved the avoidance of certain non-Lübeck LG variants. Crucially, there is no evidence that Lübeck LG was explicitly taught as a prestige variety, nor is there any substantial metalinguistic evidence for its prestige.

---

2   The importance of learning Russian, but also the continued use of LG as a native language, is attested in foreign language grammars published as late as Tönnies Fenne's *Manual of Spoken Russian* (1607; cf. Hammerich and Jakobson 1970).

3   It is estimated that between 33% and 50% of modern Swedish words are loans from LG (cf. Jahr 1995: 126)!

Nonetheless, during the fourteenth and fifteenth centuries, LG texts show an increasing tendency towards uniformity where in general Lübeck-specific linguistic features – lexical (*vaken* rather than *dicke* 'often'), morphological (<en>-plural) and phonological (*uns*, not *us*) – are preferred over others and used in areas outside the Lübeck language domain (Peters 2000b: 1500f.).

In sum, LG was subject to various processes in the Middle Ages: its use as a written language increased dramatically (*Verschriftlichung*) at the expense of Latin, its geographical range and number of speakers expanded beyond the native area of Northern Germany, and its prestige increased as seen in its use as an international lingua franca as the language of the Hanseatic League. Finally, there was a process of standardization, although this was never completed.

The decline of Low German: From international language to little dialect (1500–1650)

The Hanseatic League went into decline in the fifteenth century and had lost its dominant position as a trading union by 1500 due to a range of factors, including the discovery of new markets in America and India, and the strengthening of territorial powers (Scandinavian countries, Russia, the Netherlands etc.) (cf. Dollinger 1989 or Friedland 1991 for discussion). The language of the Hanseatic league remained relatively unaffected by this, and many scholars see the fifteenth century as a period when LG flourished rather than declined. From 1500 onwards, however, we see a marked decline of LG as a written language, leading to the virtually complete replacement of printed LG by HG by 1650. Whilst MLG was used by everyone, after 1600 LG was a language of the lower classes (Lasch 1926: 422). A number of reasons have been suggested for this change of the 'official' language of the area but overall, scholars are somewhat at a loss to account for its speed and completeness: 'Der vollständig und relativ schnell ablaufende Schreibsprachenwechsel ruft auch heute noch eine gewisse Ratlosigkeit hervor' (Peters 1998: 122).

One frequently cited factor is the invention of printing in 1450 when many HG books were increasingly traded in LG-speaking areas. Whilst it is true that this meant that relatively cheap HG texts became available in Northern Germany, printers had no reservations about publishing in LG, and Lübeck became a major LG printing centre around 1500 when its geographical and economic position as the gateway to Scandinavia became a major factor in the dissemination of books. The sheer number of printed books shows that lack of texts cannot have been a reason for the decline of the language:

> Die große Zahl der nd. Drucke beweist zur [sic] Genüge, daß auch dem Buchdruck keine ursächliche Bedeutung für das Eindringen der hd. Sprache in Norddeutschland beizumessen ist. (Gabrielsson 1983: 137)

Nevertheless, statistics document very clearly the decline of the language in printed, i.e. public, discourse:

Low German Prints:

C15:	359	
C16:	2466	
C17:	1103	
C18:	992	in total: 4920
		(Borchling/Claußen 1931–6: Einführung, no page)

The Reformation was another radical development in the sixteenth century. A key aspect of Lutheran thought was that the Bible should be directly accessible to the believer and hence it was necessary to convey its message in a language comprehensible to the target audience. Luther himself emphasized that for his Bible translation, he was keen to use a type of German that was genuine and not wooden or stilted (cf. his *Sendbrief vom Dolmetschen*). Hence one would expect the Reformation to promote the use of LG as the vernacular language in Northern Germany, and consequently we find the publication of as many as 24 LG Bibles[4] between 1522–1621 and the use of LG in church services (Dollinger 1989: 343). It is not entirely clear why LG ceased to be used in church services but reasons cited in the secondary literature include:

---

4   Incidentally, the first LG Bible was published in 1494 in Lübeck, well before the Reformation. For a discussion of the 'quality' of the most famous LG Lutheran Bible, the Bugenhagen-Bible, cf. Francis (2001).

- the relative lack of LG universities so that vicars had to be trained in the HG universities such as Wittenberg or Erfurt

- the large number of clergymen from HG-speaking areas who occupied important professional positions in the North

- the prestige of Luther's own (HG) German as the 'real' language of the Lutheran Bible.

This list of reasons is not entirely compelling, since one can just as easily imagine the Reformation using LG in the LG areas. After all, the Reformation in Sweden and Denmark used Swedish and Danish respectively as its languages, not HG, so why did the same not happen with regard to LG?

We have descriptions only of what happened, not why it happened. Overall, the sixteenth and seventeenth centuries witnessed the change from LG to HG in many different stages, differing from town to town, institution to institution and text type to text type. For example, compare the marked decline of the number of theological printed texts after the second half of the sixteenth century, the change from LG to HG in city chanceries, and the change in schools:

Low German Theological prints

1550–1559	157
1620–1629	53
1670–1679	1
1699	none

(Lindow 1926, cited in Stellmacher 2000: 75)

Language change in city chanceries

Berlin	1504	Brandenburg	1525	Danzig	1550
Wernigerode	1550	Goslar	1565	Kiel	1570
Madgeburg	1570	Münster	1571	Göttingen	1590
Rostock	1598	Bochum	1599	Braunschweig	1600
Hamburg	1600	Schleswig	1600	Husum	1608
Dortmund	1610	Lübeck	1615	Emden	1640

(Stellmacher 2000: 70)

Change from LG => HG in schools
    Mark Brandenburg   1550
    Magdeburg   1580
    Braunschweig, Westfalen, Lüneburg   1630
    Mecklenburg, Pommern   1640
    Lübeck, Hamburg, Bremen, Schleswig.-Holstein   1650
    Oldenburg, Ostfriesland   1670/80

(Gabrielsson 1932/3: 78f.)

Thus, here we see a general process in the form of the change from LG to HG which can be witnessed in many different smaller changeovers (processes) dependent on a range of factors.

Plattdeutsch – 'ein Grund zum Lachen'[5]

By the seventeenth century, LG survived only privately and orally with very few exceptions where it was printed, such as in poems commissioned specially for family events such as funerals or weddings (Ahlmann 1991) or in comic or mocking references to peasants in Baroque drama. LG underwent the process of sociolinguistic stigmatization. Not only was it not considered fit to be used in formal writing, but its use also brought up a range of connotations which identified the speaker as being of lower birth, poorer education, ill manners, and so on. The transformation from an international lingua franca to an undesirable dialect had taken less than 200 years.[6]

As a spoken language, LG survived in private conversations even amongst the bourgeoisie until the late eighteenth century. From then on, however, the upper and middle classes would use LG only when addressing servants, peasants or craftsmen (Niebaum 1986: 21). Peters (1998: 124) places the change from LG to HG in oral language in the mid-nineteenth century for the bour-

---

5   Sanders 1982: 174.
6   *Meißnisch* or Upper Saxon underwent a similar loss of prestige from being the most revered variety of German in the seventeenth and most of the eighteenth century to being the least esteemed dialect in the twentieth and twenty-first centuries.

geoisie and city population, and for the rural population from the 1930s onwards. This change has not yet been completed (there are still a number of native speakers of LG), but neither has the trend from LG to HG has been reversed, despite the efforts since the 1970s (see below). This change from LG to HG over the last 400 or so years has led scholars to suggest that LG underwent the process from language to (a collection of) dialect(s) (e.g. Gernentz 1980: 85).

Support for Low German

Despite the radical decline of Low German as a written and official language from 1500 onwards, there were still learned voices, albeit rarely, who objected to the dominance of HG and who lobbied to promote LG:

> [S]eit Ende des 17. Jahrhunderts namentlich aber seit Beginn des 18. Jahrhunderts [tritt] neben dem Stolz und der Freude am Heimischen auch das gelehrte Interesse am Niederdeutschen hervor, das den neuen Aufschwung einleitet. (Lasch 1926: 422f.)

In his *Veer Schertz Gedichten* (1652), Johann Lauremberg presented a dialogue between a HG and a LG speaker who discuss the merits of their respective languages. In the following excerpt, the LG speaker wonders why HG appears to be worth more than LG. He opposes the claim to higher value, arguing that it is LG which is consistent and which has not changed over the years, in contrast to HG, which changes every fifty years or so, as can be seen from older texts.

> Ick spreke als myns Grotvaders older Môme sprack.
> Wat kann man bringen her vôr Argument und Grûnde,
> Darmit jemand von juw richtig bewisen kunde,
> De Mening, dat van der Hochdûdschen Sprake mehr
> Als van unser Nedderdûdschen tho holden wehr?
> Unse Sprake blifft altidt bestendig und vest,
> Als se ersten was, even so is se ock lest.
> Juwe verendert sick alle vôfftig Jahr,
> Dat kônen de Schrifften bewisen klar.   (cited in Stellmacher 2000: 79)

The most prominent 'virtues' of LG over HG are presented as being its greater antiquity[7] and a purer pronunciation. In his dissertation *Von vnbilliger Verachtung der Plat-Teutschen Sprache* (1704), Bernard Raupach complains about the general discrimation which LG suffers: old LG texts were used as food for mice or packaging material by shopowners! He also claims that the pronunciation of LG is clearer and more exact that the hissing (*Zischen*) of the High Germans. The appeal of LG pronunciation was also noted by HG grammarians such as Adelung: LG is

> unter allen deutschen Mundarten in der Wahl und Aussprache der Töne die wohlklin-gendste, gefälligste und angenehmste, eine Feindin aller hauchenden und zischenden und der meisten blasenden Laute, und des unnützen Aufwandes eines vollen mit vielen hochtönenen Lauten wenig sagenden Mundes. (Adelung 1782: 79)

The support for LG continued in a different way with the publication, in the 1850s, of original poetry by writers such as Klaus Groth (1819–1899), whose work was also partially translated into Dutch, West Frisian and HG, Fritz Reuter (1810–1874) and John Brinckman (1814–1870), who collectively achieved a re-evaluation of LG as something positive (Debus 1996: 20). Their poetry, novels and plays were important for the 'LG-movement' in the second half of the nineteenth and the first half of the twentieth century and they are still read and performed in schools and amateur theatre today.

Not everyone agreed with the praise of LG, however. In the early nine-teenth century, Ludolf Wienbarg (1834, 'Soll die plattdeutsche Sprache gepflegt oder ausgerottet werden? Gegen Ersteres und für Letzteres beant-wortet') and Jonas Goldschmidt (1846, 'Ueber das Plattdeutsche als ein großes Hemmniß jeder Bildung') argued strongly against the use of LG. Goldschmidt asserted that HG was the official language of Northern Germany and hence political debates and official acts were conducted through the language. This, he felt, prevented monolingual LG speakers, who were still the majority amongst the lower classes of his area, from participating in political processes: '[W]ahre Bildung und Plattdeutsch [gehen] heut zu Tage *nicht* Hand in

---

7   This is a *contemporary* argument which was very popular in the seventeenth century to 'show' that one language is 'better' than another, as greater antiquity 'proved' greater proximity to the Original Language(s) of Babel (see also McLelland and Jones, this volume).

Hand!' (Goldschmidt (1846) in Schuppenhauer 1980: 14). He gives the example of a farmer unable to express his views clearly at a council meeting, simply because he does not know HG, rather than because of any lack of intelligence. Thus Goldschmidt's proposal to extinguish LG is based on rather modern ideas of an 'applied' democratization of the people, though nowadays, we would not necessarily agree with his conclusion that one must extinguish LG in order to achieve the goal of spreading democracy.

Thus during the process of decline in actual usage and prestige, a lobby of LG supporters initiated a process of increasing prestige which resulted in the renewed use of LG as a literary and poetical language from 1850 onwards. However, this movement did have its opponents and up until the 1970s, the promotion of LG had little effect in the non-academic population, in that it did little to stop the decline of LG as a native language.

Low German today: 'An de Wöörd vun Menschen dörf nich röökt warrn'

This LG version of the first sentence of the German constitution[8] was stamped on all outgoing letters from the previous Prime Minister of Schleswig-Holstein. It shows that today, LG is highly valued as a 'high status' token of northern identity and culture.

Despite the efforts by Klaus Groth and his colleagues in the nineteenth century to make LG acceptable in written and poetical discourse, and despite the strong movements to promote Northern-ness and LG (cf. the *Aldietsche Beweging*, Debus 1996), the suspicion that LG is not a language to be used in official discourse has not (yet) been overturned. Its connotations remained 'rurality' and 'backwardedness'. Knüppel (1997) reports on the transition from LG to HG in his home village. He contrasts the time during WWII, when children from the city of Bremen were sent to the countryside for protection, with the postwar period, when a very high number of German refugees from

8   HG: 'Die Würde des Menschen ist unantastbar.'

the East arrived in Northwestern Germany. During the war, the HG-speaking city children had to acquire the countryside LG in order to fit in with the other schoolchildren, whereas after the war the incomers, that is, the refugees, appeared to have a better command of HG[9] and were thus at an advantage in school lessons (which had been taught in HG since the seventeenth century). According to Knüppel's informants, the native children of the village were ridiculed by the refugee children for their poor command of HG in schools, to the extent that parents who had gone to school in the late 1940s and early 1950s chose not to speak LG to their own children to prevent them from undergoing the same experience that they had. Knüppel's study rests on interviews and hence it is difficult to determine how accurate the informants' assessment of the situation is. For our purposes it is sufficient to note that the actual speakers of the language perceived it to be such a disadvantage to speak LG that they decided not to pass on the language to their children, despite the notable efforts by 'respectable' men such as Klaus Groth and others to promote the language and to persuade speakers that LG is a 'real' language. This episode shows the distinction that we have to make between language promotion in learned circles and language use in 'real' discourse. The former continues today and has found plenty of support since the 1970s, with the foundation of the *Institut für Niederdeutsche Sprache* (INS) in Bremen, the inclusion of reading in LG in the school curriculum, the continuation and establishment of professorial chairs at northern universities and the performance of LG play by amateur drama groups in virtually all major villages and towns. The use of the language, however, continues to decrease despite all this. The typical native use of LG is still restricted to private conversations to speech amongst the elderly and in the countryside. In some areas, such as East and North Frisia and Dithmarschen (SW Schleswig-Holstein), children still become native speakers to some degree, but this is very much an exception.

A 1984 survey conducted to find out to what extent LG was still a living language (Stellmacher 2000: 102ff., cf. also Stellmacher 1997) asserted, to the surprise of many, that 56% of the informants claimed to speak LG

9   This is somewhat surprising since most refugees who settled in the North came from East Prussia and Pomerania, which were also LG-speaking areas. Therefore it is not immediately clear why they would have a better command than the local children in Knüppel's village.

(35% speak it well or very well) and 66% said that they could understand LG well or very well. These results, implying that 8 million people still knew LG, did not tie in very well with the overall perception that LG was a language on its deathbed. Menge has criticized parts of the survey and its figures, noting for example that in the crucial discourse between parents and children, only 3–5% of parents use LG, while the survey contains no figures at all on the use of LG between children (1995b: 667). Menge claimed that in fact, we can only speak of 2.5 million LG speakers, of whom perhaps as few as 124,000 speak LG to their children, thus confirming the overall impression that LG is a dying language.

The European Charter of Minority or Regional Languages

Since 1999, LG has been protected by the *European Charter of Minority or Regional Languages*. It is the only variety of German that is protected and was eligible only because it was 'decided' that LG was an independent language, not a dialect of HG: 'Das Niederdeutsche ist bis heute eine eigenständige Sprache geblieben, ist also keine Dialektform des Hochdeutschen' (Erster Bericht 2000: 10). The impossibility of distinguishing in any rigid and convincing way between *language* and *dialect* is well known amongst academic linguists but not 'folk-linguists'. That the Federal Government's First Report on the European Charter simply states that LG has remained an independent language rather than being a dialect may well have more to do with the political ambition to have LG included in the Charter, rather than attempting to make a scholarly statement on the linguistic status of LG.

The case for protection was brought forward by Northern parliamentarians, and debates on the issue in parliament, both at federal and regional level, were conducted in LG by those who were able to speak it, both to demonstrate how serious they were about the issue and to show that LG was a proper language suitable for serious debate. Thus LG underwent a process of extension of text type, from only spoken in the eighteenth century, to literature and poetry from 1850, and to official political debates in the 1990s. However, all participants and observers were aware that the parliamentary debates had a 'light-hearted' flavour and they were clearly seen as 'one-off' affairs.[10]

It is debatable to what extent the Charter will initiate or promote processes of extension to other text types, reversal of the decline in native speakers, or achieve acceptability in formal discourse for LG. In general, the Charter promotes the idea of language protection without requiring governments or authorities to take any active steps. In the case of LG, most of the actions to support the language, such as the inclusion of LG matters in schools at primary and secondary level, had already been in place before the Charter. Due to the federal nature of Germany, its member states deal with the issue of language protection in different ways. Whilst in Schleswig-Holstein, the German department at the University of Kiel requires all students to take at least one unit in LG or Frisian, the University of Hamburg teaches LG but prohibits students of German from including LG units in the assessed part of their degree. In schools, the Land Mecklenburg-Vorpommern reports that over 80% of all primary schools make LG an important part of their teaching – a figure that is envied by other regional states. In her tentative study, Buchanan (2002) found that very few kindergartens and schools used LG in any way. She reports that teachers generally estimated the percentage of children that speak and understand LG at under one percent, or at most between zero and five percent, with one notable exception from a Rostock primary school where the teacher estimated that 10% spoke LG and 60% understood the language. The authorities do not force the promotion of LG, for example in the form of mandatory classes in schools or bilingual signposting on the roads, but rather rely on private initiatives to stage plays, or interested teachers in schools to bring LG to the speakers. This will not stop the decrease in the number of native speakers, but it will increase the prestige of LG. Most people in Northern Germany would nowadays agree that LG is part of the cultural identity which should be cherished and protected – but few go to the trouble of promoting the language or even learning it.

---

10   During the two debates in the Schleswig-Holstein Landtag (Bericht: 65–83), parliamentarians from different parties speaking in LG addressed each other by first names, lending support to the general 'feel' of LG as a warmer, friendlier language than the official language, HG.

The overall impression is that fighting for the protection of LG is like fighting a losing battle but also a battle worth fighting. Schuppenhauer (1994: 7) soberly states that it has not been possible to stop the decline of LG in everyday use, but he feels that its decay has certainly slowed. Peters (1998: 126) predicts that the present dialect decay will eventually lead to a dialect loss and that, despite the dwindling numbers of native speakers, no serious efforts are being made to introduce the teaching of LG as a second native or first foreign language in schools. One can only concur. However, due to the increasing prestige of the language, LG will not be subject to ridicule as it was until the 1970s and its part in the cultural heritage and North German identity appears safe:

> Wer heute ein Stück Sachprosa niederdeutsch abfaßt, sei es ein wissenschaftlicher Aufsatz, ein kunsttheoretischer Text oder bloß das Wahlprogramm einer Partei, erregt sicher nach wie vor Aufsehen. Einfach auslachen oder für hoffnungslos überspannt erklären, dürfte man ihn aber schwerlich. (Schuppenhauer 1994: 6f.)

Conclusion

The history of LG demonstrates a range of linguistic processes. It changed from a tribal language in the Old Saxon period to an international language in the Middle Ages and then became almost extinct in the Early Modern Period. Its revival began in the mid-nineteenth century, and although this development gained substantial momentum very recently, it seems unlikely that its death as a native language can be prevented in the mid-term future. LG has undergone linguistic processes in relation to changes in the area in which it was used, the number of speakers who spoke the language, the mode in which it was used (from oral to written to oral to written over the period of a thousand years), the functional domains, text types and situations in which its use was appropriate and folklinguistic prestige which was attached to the language. Thus LG shows what kind of linguistic processes can take place in a language's history, but also how linguistic processes can be both the cause and the result of a changing history.

References

Adelung, J.C. (1782), *Umständliches Lehrgebäude der Deutschen Sprache*, Leipzig. (Reprinted by Olms Verlag, Hildesheim).

Ahlmann, G. (1991), *Zur Geschichte des Frühniederdeutschen in Schleswig-Holstein im Spiegel von Gelegenheitsdichtungen des 17. und 18. Jahrhunderts*, Stockholm: Almqvist & Wiksell.

Betten, A., Besch, W., Reichmann, O. and Sonderegger, S. (1998–2001) *Handbuch Sprachgeschichte*, 2nd ed., Berlin and New York: de Gruyter.

Bericht zur Situation der Niederdeutschen Sprache in Schleswig-Holstein 1996–2000, Kiel: Landtag.

Borchling, C. and Claußen, B. (1931–6), *Niederdeutsche Bibliographie. Gesamt-verzeichnis der niederdeutschen Drucke bis zum Jahre 1800*, Neumünster: Wachholtz.

Braunmüller, K. and Diercks, W. (eds) (1993), *Niederdeutsch und die skandinavischen Sprachen I*, Heidelberg: Winter.

Buchanan, E. (2002), *A regional comparison of the implementation of the European Charter for Regional or Minority Languages*, Undergraduate essay. University of Bristol.

Debus, F. (1996), *Von Dünkirchen bis Königsberg*, Göttingen: Vandenhoeck & Ruprecht.

Dollinger, P. (1989), *Die Hanse*, 4th ed., Stuttgart: Kröner.

Erster Bericht der Bundesrepublik Deutschland [...] der Europäischen Charta der Regional- oder Minderheitensprachen (2000), Berlin.

Francis, T. (2001), '"Schyr van worde tho worde" or "Reyne sprake"? How "Pure" Was the 1534 "Bugenhagen" Translation of Luther's Bible into Low German?' in: *'Proper Words in Proper Places.' Studies in Lexicology and Lexicography in Honour of William Jervis Jones*, M. Davies et al., Stuttgart: Heinz.

Friedland, K. (1991), *Die Hanse*, Stuttgart: Kohlhammer.

Gabrielsson, A. (1983), 'Die Verdrängung der Mittelniederdeutschen durch die neuhochdeutsche Schriftsprache', in: *Handbuch zur niederdeutschen Sprach- und Literaturwissenschaft*, edited by G. Cordes, and D. Möhn, Berlin: Erich Schmidt, 119–53.

Gernentz, H.-J. (1980), *Niederdeutsch – gestern und heute*, 2nd ed., Rostock: Hinstorff.

Glück, H. (2002), *Deutsch als Fremdsprache in Europa vom Mittelalter bis zur Barockzeit*, Berlin, New York: de Gruyter.

Hammerich, L.L. and Jakobson, R. (1970), *Tönnies Fenne's Low German Manual of Spoken Russian Pskov 1607*, Copenhagen: Munksgaard.

Haugen, E. (1994), 'Standardization', in: *The Encyclopedia of Language and Linguistics*, edited by R.E. Asher, Oxford: Pergamon, 4340–2.

Hermann-Winter, R. (1992), 'Urteile über Niederdeutsch aus dem 18. und 19. Jahrhundert', *Niederdeutsches Jahrbuch* 115, 123–44.

Jahr, E.H. (1995), 'Niederdeutsch, Norwegisch und Nordisch', in: *Niederdeutsch und die skandinavischen Sprachen II*, edited by K. Braunmüller, Heidelberg: Winter, 125–44.

Knüppel, K. (1997), *Niederdeutsch / Hochdeutsch in Martfeld* [...]. Hausarbeit (1. Staatsprüfung), University of Oldenburg.

Langer, N. (2003), 'Low German', in: *Germanic Standardizations Past to Present*, edited by A. Deumert and W. Vanderbussche, Amsterdam: John Benjamins, 281–301.

Lasch, A. (1926), 'Die literarische Entwicklung des Plattdeutschen in Hamburg im 17. und 18. Jahrhundert', Sonderdruck aus 'Nordelbingen', *Beiträge zur Heimatforschung in Schleswig-Holstein, Hamburg und Lübeck* 5, 422–49.

Menge, H.H. (1995a), 'Rehabilitierung des Niederdeutschen', in: *ZGL* 23, 33–52.

Menge, H.H. (1995b), '"Wie ist es bei Gesprächen mit Ihren Kindern ...?" Zu Frage 26 der GETAS-Umfrage von 1984', in: *Lingua Theodisca* [...], edited by J. Cajot et al., Münster: ZNS, 655–68.

Niebaum, H. (1986), 'Niederdeutsch in Geschichte und Gegenwart', in: *Niederdeutsch. Fünf Vorträge zur Einführung*, edited by H.-W. Jäger, Leer: Schuster.

Niederdeutsch. [...] *Umsetzung der Verpflichtungen aus Teil III der* [Sprachen-]*Charta in Schleswig-Holstein*, Document for Discussion (*Tischvorlage*) in the 'Ministerium für Bildung, Wissenschaft, Forschung und Kultur Schleswig-Holstein', Kiel. undated.

Peters, R. (1987), 'Das Mittelniederdeutsche als Sprache der Hanse', in: *Sprachkontakt in der Hanse – Aspekte des Sprachausgleichs im Ostsee- und Nordseeraum*, edited by P.S. Ureland, Tübingen: Niemeyer, 65–88.

Peters, R. (1998), 'Zur Sprachgeschichte des niederdeutschen Raumes', *Zeitschrift für deutsche Philologie*, 108–27.

Peters, R. (2000a), 'Soziokulturelle Voraussetzungen und Sprachraum des Mittelniederdeutschen', in: Betten, Besch, Reichmann, and Sonderegger (1998–2001), 1409–22.

Peters, R. (2000b), 'Die Rolle der Hanse und Lübecks in der mittelniederdeutschen Sprachgeschichte', in: Betten, Besch, Reichmann, and Sonderegger (1998–2001), 1496–1505.

Raupach, B. (1985), *De Linguae Saxoniae Inferioris Neglectu* [...].edited by W. Lindow, Leer: Schuster.

Reichmann, O. (1988), 'Zur Vertikalisierung des Varietätenspektrum in der jüngeren Sprachgeschichte des Deutschen', in: *Deutscher Wortschatz*, edited by Munske, Horst et al., Berlin and New York: de Gruyter, 151–80.

Sanders, W. (1982), *Sachsensprache, Hansesprache, Plattdeutsch. Sprachgeschichtliche Grundzüge des Niederdeutschen*, Göttingen: Vandenhoeck & Ruprecht.

Schuppenhauer, C. (ed.) (1980), *Jonas Goldschmidt und andere, 1845/46.* [...], Leer: Schuster.

Schuppenhauer, C. (1994), *Plattdeutsch als Auftrag. Das Institut für niederdeutsche Sprache*, Leer: Schuster.

Sodmann, T. (2000), 'Die Verdrängung des Mittelniederdeutschen als Schreib- und Druckersprache Norddeutschland', in: Betten, Besch, Reichmann, and Sonderegger (1998–2001), 1505–12.

Stellmacher, D. (1997), 'Sprachsituation in Norddeutschland', in: *Varietäten des Deutschen*, edited by G. Stickel, Berlin: De Gruyter, 88–103.

Stellmacher, D. (2000), *Niederdeutsche Sprache*, 2nd ed., Hamburg: Weidler.

GERALDINE HORAN

Gendered and Political Discourses:
Women in National Socialism

Introduction

How and why does women's discourse in National Socialism represent a land-mark in the history of the German language? National Socialist rhetoric has been the subject of great interest in the latter half of the twentieth century, but women's discourse seems at first sight too specialized an area to enjoy a representative status. The purpose of this paper is to illustrate that this topic is of landmark importance for understanding the German language in the twentieth and twenty-first centuries. To begin with, it draws together two major themes in modern language history: women as a linguistic group and National Socialist rhetoric. The combination of these two vast areas of study alone would justify the title of linguistic 'landmark', however there are more specific reasons for regarding the topic as unique and worthy of study. It offers insight into women's discourse in a historical context and helps us to under-stand the complex nature of National Socialist discourse as a whole, with its variety of organizational and group discourses. Most importantly, though, the landmark status of the topic lies in the choice of methodological approaches for characterizing National Socialist women's discourse. The analysis aims to show how a combination of approaches, in particular discourse analysis, pragmatics and feminist sociolinguistics, can prove useful in identifying and interpreting women's language use. This paper begins with a consideration of how a combination of the three above-mentioned approaches can provide an insight not only into the language produced by National Socialist women, but also into the factors influencing the formulation and interpretation of their language. The paper then places the lexical, pragmatic characteristics of women's texts into a context which interprets the usage according to factors such as group membership, status of writer/reader, and text-type. Material for the study is taken from books, articles from NS women's magazines, and from correspondence by women involved in National Socialism in the early years of the movement, 1924–34. It is during this early period, before organizational *Gleichschaltung* took effect, that the women's discourse is at its most dynamic and diverse, reflecting plurality of opinion and expression.

Analytical approaches

As the title of the paper suggests, the focus is on women's *discourse*, and although similar expressions may be used, such as 'women's language use', the choice of the word *discourse* is deliberate. A discussion of possible uses and definitions of *discourse* within the confines of this paper is not feasible, so for the purposes of this analysis, I will define my use of the term as follows: 'language use in context', 'the language of a particular group in society' (Brunner and Graefen 1994: 7), and I draw on Norman Fairclough and Ruth Wodak's definition of discourse as 'a form of "social practice"' in which 'the discursive event is shaped by situations, institutions and social structures, but it also shapes them' (Fairclough and Wodak 1997: 258).

In analysing women's discourse, it is important to explain why a combination of the above-mentioned ways of looking at language is most successful. More traditional approaches would involve the analysis of morphological and lexical patterns, including word-formation patterns, and the frequency and semantic properties of key terms and expressions. Indeed, some of the most prominent post-war research on language in National Socialism from the late 1940s to the early 1970s focused on lexical and stylistic approaches and identified a 'Nazi language', consisting of a body of key words and expressions, including biological, racial, religious and sporting metaphors, euphemisms, the use of superlatives and substantival style, for example (Berning 1964, [Schmitz-] Berning 1998; Bork 1970; Klemperer 1966; Seidel and Seidel-Slotty 1961). Although lists or dictionaries of vocabulary are useful in providing an overview of rhetorical features of NS usage, they also risk presenting an isolated view of language as devoid of context, detached from its creators and users. It is therefore important to embed these characteristics in social, historical and linguistic contexts and to recognize, as many studies since the late 1960s have, that there is no single 'language' in National Socialism, but rather many registers and discourses within National Socialism (von Polenz 1999: 547), including women's discourse (Horan 2003). However, that is not to say that a lexical analysis is of no use with this material, and in fact the analysis of women's discourse will attempt to place lexical and metaphorical characteristics in a socio-historical context. Given the volume and variety of National Socialist texts available to the researcher, an analysis which only identifies key words and phrases, or which offers a stylistic or textual analysis of a single text, is unsatisfactory. What is needed is an interpretative framework which recognizes the hetereogeneous elements of the discourse, including group membership and text-type.

Discourse analysis and pragmatics

Discourse analysis as a methodological framework acknowledges texts as communicative entities, shaped and influenced by socio-historical factors, power relations, hierarchies and dominant ideologies in society and seeks to explain the factors influencing the production of language as well as the end-product itself, that is, the spoken word, or words on the written page. In addition to group membership and a consideration of power and status of the speaker/writer, the type of text is also a determining factor in analysing discourse. Most linguistic analyses of National Socialist discourse focus on monologic or 'one-way' texts, for example, books, articles, posters, pamphlets or speeches, where there is no ongoing communication between writer/speaker and addressee. However, some National Socialist texts (and some examples of women's texts) are in fact letters, dialogic texts, which have the potential for communicative continuity. Letters, similar to conversation, do not merely consist of phrases and sentences designed to convey information, but also of utterances which facilitate successful communication between participants. Thus, in addition to examining linguistic characteristics in the context of power relations and the negotiation of status within the framework of discourse analysis, one must also consider pragmatic characteristics, more typical of spoken interaction. Politeness strategies are of particular relevance to correspondence both between women and between women and men in National Socialism. In communicating ideas or requests, praise or criticism, the women express themselves in ways which could be interpreted as saving or threatening the 'face' of the addressee(s).[1] Penelope Brown and Stephen Levinson (1987) refer to positive and negative politeness: expressions categorized as belonging to positive politeness express solidarity and intimacy with the listener or reader, emphasize shared goals or group identity, whereas expressions associated with negative politeness tend to show respect for the reader or listener (Brown and Levinson 1987: 103, 129).

Feminist sociolinguistics

Having outlined the importance of discoursal and pragmatic characteristics, we must now consider how to evaluate the role of gender in the production of discourse. Gender as a sociolinguistic category is problematic, not least because, as Sally Johnson has pointed out, women cannot be easily categorized as a sociolinguistic group, given that they do not form a segregated group in society (Johnson 1995: 87). If we look at women in National Socialism, we can see that they also came from diverse social and political backgrounds: indeed a unified National Socialist women's organization (the *NS-Frauenschaft*) did not exist until 1931 (Stephenson 1981: 50–8). Prior to this, women belonged to a variety of groups and organizations including the *Deutscher Frauenorden, Frauenarbeitsgemeinschaften* (Berlin and Munich), local *Frauengruppen* and conservative, nationalist women's organizations which lent their support to the NSDAP, such as the *Bund Königin Luise*, the *Neulandbund* and the *Stahlhelmfrauenbund*. In addition, one must also have regard to the considerable level of male involvement and interference in organizational, ideological and linguistic matters. Yet, taking these factors into account, I believe the case

---

1   George Yule defines 'face' as 'the public self-image of a person. It refers to that emotional and social sense of self that everyone has and expects everyone else to recognize' (Yule 1996: 60).

can still be made for regarding women in National Socialism as a linguistic group, as their female gender determined their organizational membership, their status and activities and their communicative networks.

In previous sociolinguistic analyses of women's language use, the 'dominance/difference approaches' have been employed as an interpretative framework (Cameron 1992: 70–8; Coates 1993: 12–13). The 'dominance approach' effectively regards women as victims, using a specific women's register, a powerless language, which entails that they are not taken seriously in society or, to be more precise, by men (Lakoff 1975); the 'difference approach', whilst also acknowleding that women are an oppressed group in society, attributes to women's language use a positive, even superior (if not necessarily highly valued) quality, worthy of emulation by women and men alike (Trömel-Plötz 1996: 369). The dominance and difference approaches are not necessarily mutually exclusive, and both are useful for an understanding of NS women's discourse. The dominance approach sees women as writing and communicating within a discriminatory, at times hostile, environment, and may to some extent explain why women produced a discourse which objectified and discriminated against other women. As suggested by the difference approach, however, NS women turned their marginalized status and position into the expression of a positive women's community, and there is archival evidence to suggest that male National Socialists felt threatened by women as a group within National Socialism.[2] The problem with both the dominance and difference approaches, however, lies in the assumption that women represent a subordinated group, irrespective of whether this has positive or negative repercussions on their language and sense of group identity, and does nothing to promote the perception of women as autonomous communicators. In recent studies in feminist sociolinguistics, the emphasis has shifted to regard gender as something which can be performed by the speaker (or writer). In performing gender, one can draw upon, reject or redefine existing dominant ideologies and discoursal patterns:

---

2   See for example, the exchange of letters between Scholtz-Klink, the *Reichsfrauenführerin* from 1934–45, Bormann and Ley in August 1937 on the question of whether the title *Zellenfrauenleiterin* should be permitted. The issue at stake was whether the use of *-leiterin* would challenge the authority of the *Zellenleiter* (Bundesarchiv NS22/923).

Most of us spend very little, if any, time thinking about gender, and we are rarely aware of 'doing'/'performing' gender [...] We just take for granted that we are women. But we assume that 'being a woman' is a unitary and unified experience – in other words, we think of ourselves as 'I'/'me'; that is, as singular. However, the woman we perform is not the same woman in all circumstances [...] We change because different audiences require different performances – and also because we sometimes feel like playing a different role. All kinds of different 'self' are possible, because our culture offers us a wide range of ways of being – but all these ways of being are *gendered*. (Coates 1996: 232)

The performative interpretation of gender is also problematic, however, as it assumes that the writers or speakers have the opportunity to select and plan their utterances and to control their language behaviour in an environment that is often determined by unequal power relations. Despite this, I would argue that regarding gender as performance is useful for explaining the semi-autonomous, semi-adherent nature of women's discourse in National Socialism. There is evidence to suggest that women in National Socialism draw upon the discourses created by the women's movements of the nineteenth and early twentieth centuries as well as NS ideological discourse to negotiate their roles and status as women. That is not to say that women were not discriminated against practically and linguistically, and that the male-dominated discourse was not to some extent reproduced by women. But the emphasis is placed on women as active communicators rather than passive recipients and mouthpieces of the NSDAP. Sara Mills's research on women's colonial travel writing suggests that women in male-dominated environments often employed discourses that appeared to adhere to dominant discourses and ideologies, but in fact were subversive in their nature and enabled women to gain access to a medium and genre which otherwise would have been denied them (Mills 1993). Thus, as will be illustrated in the analysis of NS women's discourse, even apparently traditional expressions of women's behaviour and activity could be interpreted as challenging to male authority.

Women's discourse(s). Discourse of self-definition and self-promotion

Lexical characteristics

In their texts, women in National Socialism adopt differing positions and styles: co-operative, submissive, subversive, openly oppositional and confrontational. And more than one type of discourse can be adopted within a text. Examining women's texts, it becomes clear that women consider it necessary to define and explain their activities to those within the NSDAP and to a female and male readership in the general public. As a minority, marginalized element within or peripheral to the NSDAP, women create a women's community, a linguistic *Frauenwelt*, through shared key topics, themes and expressions. Topics in articles for NS women's magazines and pamphlets range from the practical to the political and even linguistic, and include cooking, housework, fashion, consumer activities ('aryan shopping'), 'racial hygiene', motherhood, childcare, employment outside the home, and even ('pure', 'aryan') dancing. Women's membership of a cohesive gendered community is communicated through nouns denoting familial relationships, such as *Schwester*, *Mitschwester* or even *Stadtschwester*, and through compounds and derivatives with *Frau* and *Mutter*.[3] Compounds with *Frau* as the first element include formations denoting NS women's organizations, institutions activities, women's characters, behaviour or situation, including: *Frauenamt, Frauengruppe, Frauenfunk, Frauenschafts-bibliothek, Frauenarbeit, Frauenaufgabe, Frauenehre, Frauenherz, Frauenkraft, Frauenseele, Frauenwille, Frauenwürde*. Compounds with *Frau* as the second element identify 'types' of women, for example, *Arbeiterfrau, Berufsfrau, Blockfrau, Dorffrau, Erwerbslosenfrau, Hausfrau, Vertrauensfrau*. These formulations serve to label characteristics, ideas and activities as specifically female and integral to the women's NS community. What is more, however, in identifying these types of women in the singular (*die Berufsfrau, die Blockfrau*), the writers create objectified models for their readership. Within

---

3   Women also signal the existence of a female community through the use of nouns bearing the *-in* suffix, for example *Führerin, Großstädterin, Volksgenossin*. See Horan (2003: 122–39).

the women's NS community, these models have a regulatory, normative function in enforcing consensus in discourse and behaviour. Derivatives with *Frau* such as *Frauentum, Fraulichkeit, fraulich* similarly establish patterns of behaviour to be admired and followed.

Compounds with *Mutter* also denote organizations, institutions and activities, including *Mütterdienstwerk, Mütterheim, Mütterschulung*, as well as motherly qualities and characteristics, for example, *Mutteraufgabe, Mutterliebe, Mutterwille*. As with *Frau*-compounds, formations with *Mutter* as the second element establish types of mother and include: *Blockmutter, Kriegsmutter, Landesmutter, Volksmutter, Zellenmutter*. Derivatives with *Mutter* parallel the formations with *Frau: Muttertum, Mütterlichkeit, mütterlich*. The parallels between formations with *Frau* and *Mutter* serve to highlight the conceptual and semantic overlap between womanhood and motherhood, which is an important characteristic in NS women's discourse. Women's identity is frequently defined according to motherhood and, drawing upon the ideas of social motherhood propagated by the conservative wing of the *bürgerliche Frauenbewegung*, all women can be defined as a 'type' of mother, whether biological, spiritual or social (Korotin 1992: 190–1; Peters 1984: 46; Wittrock 1983: 12–13).

Self-definition in the women's discourse is not always articulated through the theme of motherhood, but in 'public' texts, for example magazine articles or pamphlets, motherhood is a prominent theme. It does not suffice to explain this by saying that because of their gender, NS women were bound to talk about motherhood: it is more complex than that. In promoting women's status as mothers, NS women could be seen as adhering to dominant ideologies in society which emphasized women's role as mothers. But at the same time this characteristic could also be interpreted as a 'performance' of motherhood that allowed women to engage in activities in the political sphere. It has a semiotic function in signalling to male National Socialists that women do not intend to encroach upon traditionally male areas of activity and power, e.g. politics and the military, yet paradoxically it provides women with an opportunity to participate (albeit in a minor capacity) in National Socialist activities. The women are also negotiating their separate status by communicating that there are domains of activity and authority which specifically exclude men. As such, terms and expressions used to denote motherhood, as well as defining female identity in National Socialism, also point towards an oppositional, potentially subversive discourse (see below).

Pragmatic strategies

As previously mentioned, feminist linguistic analyses have often pointed to all-female interaction as having model qualities in fostering equality and solidarity amongst participants. In NS journal articles and pamphlets in particular, strategies akin to positive politeness found in conversation and letters are employed to establish an informal women's community, which shares common concerns and ideas. The use of the pronoun *du* to address readers, for example, creates an intimate relationship between reader and writer, and specifically excludes male readers. The singular pronoun appeals to readers as individuals, yet also has a coercive function, assuming and even prescribing stereotypical female behaviour and ideas, as the following example illustrates:

> [D]ie Erfrischungshalle bietet eine so angenehme Verknüpfung des Nützlichen mit dem Schönen, eine Freundin findet man dort sicher, mit der es sich plaudern läßt, und die billigen Mittagessen und Imbisse, liebe deutsche Schwester, die bietet man Dir nicht an, weil man weiß, daß Du Hunger hast, sondern weil der Jude Deine Schwäche kennt und weiß, daß Du dem Zauber seiner gleißenden und glitzernden Auslagen erliegst. (Auerhahn 1932: 57)

The informal pronoun also serves to connect a discourse of everyday female activity with a more ideologically-charged, racist discourse. In correspondence between women, cohesiveness and solidarity is established through positive politeness strategies including informal greetings and comments, even in official party correspondence. References are made to joint activities and to family members or acquaintances, for example:

> Liebe Frau S!
> Wir haben so lange nicht von einander gehört, seit den schönen Tagen in Dessau – wie geht es Ihnen noch? Hoffentlich gesundheitlich gut [ ] Ich wurde heute an Sie erinnert, als ich las, dass ein Herr S./W. gestorben sei; war das nicht ein Verwandter Ihres Herrn Gemahls? Werden Sie da zur Beerdigung kommen [ ] Wie sieht es sonst in Berlin aus? Ist S.-A. und Gau alles wieder in Ordnung? [ ] Grüßen Sie bitte Ihren Herrn Gemahl und Sohn bestens von mir, besonders aber seien Sie selbst herzlichst gegrüßt von Ihrer L Rühlemann
> u. Mutter u. Schwester. (L. Rühlemann 1930)

Liebe Fräulein S!

Bin gut nachhause[sic] gekommen, allerdings mit grandioser Verspätung, weil das Zügle hinter Bayreuth nicht über den Berg gekommen ist. Vom Fern D=Zug war nichts mehr zu sehen in Nürnberg. Um 8h kam ich in München an, konnte noch eine Viertelstunde auf der Strasse die Rede des Führers hören, um 3/4 9h stieg ich in Bruck aus am Marktplatz, wo ich die Übertragung dann zu Ende hören konnte. Mein Mann war natürlich in Ängsten und Nöten, wo ich wieder geblieben bin.

Ich möchte Sie gleich, damit Sie's nicht vergessen an verschiedenes[sic] erinnern, was wir besprochen haben [...] Ich danke Ihnen und Herrn S noch einmal, daß Sie mir so viel Zeit bei meinem Aufenthalt in Bayreuth gewidmet haben!

Heil Hitler und herzliche Grüsse auch von meinem Mann; grüssen Sie bitte auch Herrn S. (Reber-Gruber 1934)

Discourse of integration and solidarity

Lexical and metaphorical characteristics

One of the many functions of women's discourse is to express loyalty and commitment to the NSDAP. Integration and adherence to National Socialist ideology is communicated through the use of vocabulary and expressions which we now typically associate with NS usage, including metaphors taken from biological/racial lexical fields, for example *Blutopfer, Erbe, erbgesundheitlich, nordisch-germanisch, Rasse, Urquell nordischer Kraft*; negatively-charged expressions to defame and criticize opponents, with *Bolschewismus, Jude, jüdisch*, as key words, for example: *Henkerbeil des Bolschewismus, jüdische Greuelpropaganda, jüdische Lüge*. Military metaphors are also employed by women, including *Einsatz, einsatzbereit, Einsatzfähigkeit, erringen, Front, mobilisieren, Mobilmachung, Ringen/ringen, Schlag, Sieg, Waffe, wehrhaft*, reflecting the central role of military language in NS rhetoric. The military metaphors found in women's texts denote a range of diverse activities including political campaigning, the provision of support and assistance for mothers, the renewal of women's honour, sewing and cooking for members of the SA. Women's references to battle and combat could be categorized as belonging to several strands of discourse. In describing themselves as *Kämpferin(nen)* and their battle as specifically female (*Frauenkampf, Mutterkampf, unser*

Kampf), women are contributing to a discourse of self-definition and self-promotion. Their use of military metaphors could also be defined as part of an oppositional or even rebellious discourse, with women claiming their role as combatants, even warriors, and this is certainly the case for the so-called NS feminists (see below). But I have categorized the women's use of military metaphors, particularly the lexeme *Kampf*, as part of the discourse of integration and loyalty. Military terminology signals a shared belief in National Socialist ideology which portrays every activity as a battle or struggle (infamous examples include *Arbeitsschlacht, Geburtenschlacht*, Keller 1981: 130), but through the use of expressions that define the battle as 'female', it also communicates an acceptance and promotion of women's secondary status. Women portray themselves as female fighters or warriors and indicate that they regard themselves as occupying a supportive role:

> Dieser große politische Kampf ist aber auch die erste Aufgabe der deutschen Frau im Nationalsozialismus. Sie kann nicht mit dem Arm und mit äußeren Mitteln bei solchem Kampf mitwirken. Aber sie erfüllt diese Kampfesaufgabe im Geist, in ihrer ganzen Haltung im Alltag und in ihrer Werbetätigkeit für die politischen Ziele. Daß sie den äußeren Kampf pflegend und helfend in rechtem Frauendienst begleitet, ist selbstverständlich.
> Der zweite Mitkampf, den wir Frauen zu leisten haben, ist der große Kampf um die deutsche Seele, der Adolf Hitler und seinen wahren Mitkämpfern im Mittelpunkt des Ganzen steht [ ] Als Drittes aber wendet sich unser Frauenkampf den besonderen Belangen unseres eigenen Geschlechtes zu, und zwar nach zwei Seiten hin. (Diehl 1933: 81–2)

> Nun sein Manneskampf die Straße frei gekämpft und sich in schwersten Saal- und Straßenschlachten unter furchtbaren Blutopfern sein Daseinsrecht erzwungen hatte [sic], rief er [der Nationalsozialismus] auch uns deutsche Frauen zum Mitkampf herbei. Nun sollte nicht nur die fürsorgende helfende Frauenaufgabe weitergeführt werden, sondern die Frau sollte sich wieder als Mutter des Volkes fühlen und ihren Mutterkampf um ihres Volkes Seele aufnehmen. (Diehl 1933: 71)

> <u>Die alten Kämpferinnen werden auch gern an die Tagung 1925 in Magdeburg denken, wo wir als Frauen zum ersten Mal den Führer der Bewegung unter uns hatten.</u> (Zander 1933, underlining in original.)

Pragmatic strategies

In correspondence between women and men, both positive and negative politeness strategies are employed to ensure that the message of the letter is understood, that the addressee will act on any requests or suggestions and that the relationship between writer and addressee is successfully established and/or maintained. Where there is an imbalance in power and status between the participants or where they are not (well-)acquainted, the women are 'conventionally indirect' (Brown and Levinson 1987: 130) and include hedging statements in their letters to save face and to avoid causing offence. These take the form of apologies for imposing upon the addressee's time and the showing of deference and respect through flattering remarks and comments about the addressee, as well as expressions of personal commitment to National Socialism:

> Sehr geehrter Herr Strasser, ich bitte sehr um Verzeihung, wenn ich Sie nunmehr mit einer Reihe von Schreiben belästigt habe. Ich bin mir bewusst, dass Sie als Reichs-Organisationsleiter nicht Zeit und nicht die Aufgabe haben, sich mit einzelnen Ortsgruppenangelegenheiten zu befassen. (Gauleiterin, DFO Mecklenburg and Lübeck 1931)

> Es wurde diese Tage davon gesprochen, dass Sie, hochverehrter Führer, hier in München eine Frauengruppe, wie eine solche in Berlin schon längere Zeit besteht, zu gründen beabsichtigen. Zu diesem Zwecke möchte ich mich Ihnen zur Verfügung stellen. Seit Jahren werbend für die N.S.D.A.P. tätig, würde ich meine ganze Kraft einsetzen, um aus dieser Frauengruppe eine der Bewegung würdige und nützliche Organisation zu machen [...] Auskunft über meine Person und Gesinnung können Ihnen, hochverehrter Herr Hitler, die Herren Armbrüster, Fiehler und Ostberg geben [...] Es ist mein innigster Wunsch von Ihnen, Herr Hitler, wert befunde[n] zu werden der Bewegung zu dienen. (R. St-S. 1928)

In outlining some of the characteristics of the discourse of self-definition and self-promotion, I stated that as a means of establishing solidarity, women make reference to familial connections in their correspondence with other women. In correspondence with men, they also mention personal connections, frequently husbands or male National Socialists in leadership positions. However, the purpose of these strategies is not to establish intimacy and connection but rather to enhance their own status and to ensure that the addressee takes note of their ideas or requests.

Mein Mann ist einer der ersten, wenn nicht der erste angestellte Richter im Reich (Landgerichtspräsident), der sich offen [...] zum Nat. Sozialismus bekannt hat – auch er hat stets die Frauenarbeit im allerhöchsten Maaße [sic] anerkannt und oft Gelegenheit gehabt zu sagen: es wird zu viel von manchen Frauen verlangt. (Leiterin, NSF 'Probst-heida' Leipzig-Osten 1934)

Although this strategy of 'patronage' is typically used in any formal or political situation where there is an imbalance of power between communi-cating participants, within this context it is the gender as well as the status of the 'patron' that is of particular significance for NS women, as they do not refer to their acquaintance with other NS women as a means of negotiating a higher status.

Discourse of challenge and opposition

Lexical characteristics

By 'discourse of challenge and opposition', I do not mean discourse that opposed or rebelled against National Socialist ideology from the outside but rather a discourse within the NS community which rejected the attempts of male National Socialists to subordinate women and women's role in the party and society, or which, on a modest scale, questioned male dominance and authority, particularly over women's affairs. Historians have identified a particular group of women who promoted women's equality within National Socialism, referring to them as NS 'feminists' (Koonz 1976; Kater 1983) or 'oppositionelle Faschistinnen' (Wittrock 1983). A leading figure of this group is Sophie Rogge-Börner, who edited *Die Deutsche Kämpferin*, from 1933 until 1937, when it was banned by the Gestapo (Wittrock 1983: 170). Articles and correspondence by Rogge-Börner in particular reveal a discourse which pro-motes a redefinition of femininity and motherhood, rejecting the bourgeois *Mütterlichkeitsverehrung* of the late nineteenth and early twentieth centu-ries. Rogge-Börner claims equality between women and men on the basis of relations between the sexes in Germanic tribes, in which women were warriors and took part in military activities. In her texts, racial vocabulary is

employed, not as a signal of integration and loyalty but rather to challenge
National Socialist ideas of 'romantisch verschwommene "Weiblichkeit" und
"Mütterlichkeit"' (Rogge-Börner 1933b: 33). Vocabulary includes *germanisch*,
*Germanen, nordisch, nordisch-germanisch, Artgesetz, Bluterbe, Blutgemein-
schaft, blutlich, rassen-seelisch, rassebewußt*, and is combined in some women's
texts with romantic, pseudo-religious, philosophical language. References to
women's connection to the cosmos and to nature serve to emphasize female
uniqueness and even superiority:

> [S]ie [die Frau] revolutioniert nicht, sondern läuft mit; sie setzt nicht ihren sittlicheren,
> beseelteren Willen als Hebel an die Dinge, sondern läßt sich mit durch alle Untiefen
> des Staatsmaterialismus und des Berufsmaterialismus ziehen. Sie setzt sich noch nicht
> durch in ihrer weiblichen Willensrichtung.
> Und doch muß die Frau heranreifen zu ihrer eigenen Wesenheit, wenn anders ihr Eintritt
> ins öffentliche Leben Sinn haben soll. Eben weil sie noch eine stärkere kosmische und
> übersinnliche Bindung hat, sich noch nicht ausschließlich verengt hat auf die Materie,
> noch müheloser hindurchblickt durch Sein und Geschehen, noch Aufnahmestellen hat
> für die unsichtbaren Strahlungen, von denen alles Greifbare, Stoffliche durchströmt
> wird, eben darum ist ihr Fehlen in der Führung und Bestimmung des volklichen und
> staatlichen Lebens zum Unglück und Verhängnis der Völker der weißen Rasse geworden.
> ('Selbsterziehung der Frau', no author given 1932: 97)

> Unendlich Schweres muß die Gefährtin des Arbeitslosen durchmachen, und doch bleibt
> ihr eines erspart: die Arbeitslosigkeit selbst. Dieser Zustand der Beschäftigungslosigkeit,
> diese endlose Zeit des Grübelns, der Minderwertigkeitsgefühle, der Selbstqual.
> Ob die Frau nun einen Beruf ausübt, oder ob sie im Haushalt tätig ist, immer doch hat sie
> Verbundenheit mit der äußeren Welt und ihren Aufgaben. Diese Verbundenheit, dieses
> An-ihrem.Platz-arbeiten-dürfen macht sie – trotz aller Entbehrungen – unendlich reicher
> als den Gefährten. Und die Aufgabe, die sie an dem Mann erfüllen kann, die seelische
> Hilfe gibt ihr das Wichtigste des Lebens: den Sinn des Daseins. (Fiebig 1932: 152)

An important part of the discourse of opposition is the use of terms
and expressions denoting male activity, including fatherhood (a *Männli-
chkeits-* and *Väterlichkeitsdiskurs*), to counteract the predominance of the
Mütterlichkeitsdiskurs (these parallels are not generally found in 'mainstream'
women's texts). Negatively-charged compounds and derivatives with *Mann*
also occur and references are made to a singular, objectified *Mann* as a parallel to *die Frau*. Compounds and derivatives with *Vater* are used to highlight
the neglect of fatherhood as a topic in NS texts and a failure to address the
role of fathers and fatherhood in society:

Meines Erachtens wären die Volkshochschulen die Stelle, die mit dem Versuche eines Unterrichts über Ehe und Vaterschaft vorangehen sollten. (Martens-Edelmann 1933: 21)

Wo liegen die Ursachen der seit 1922 ständig steigenden Kinderarmut in Deutschland? In der Annahme des Versailler Abwürgungsdiktats durch die Männermehrheit der Weimarer Nationalversammlung, die entgegen den Frauenwünschen aller Parteien Bedingungen unterzeichnete, die vom Feindbund selber für unannehmbar gehalten wurden [...] Versailles mit all seinen Folgen ist ein rein männerpolitisches Werk, ein Ausschnitt aus der Geschichte, die von Männern gemacht wird [...] Es ist üblich geworden, die Frau für den Geburtenrückgang verantwortlich zu machen. Wie kann man das, solange die Frau im Staat, vor dem Gesetz und in der Ehe nichts als der Gegenstand des männlichen Machtwillens ist? [...] Aber mit scheinheiligem Pathos wird die Frau angerufen als 'Hüterin des Blutes'. Die Frau allein kann das deutsche Blut nicht hüten, das der Mann im nebenehelichen Leben verludert. (Rogge-Börner 1933a: 29)

As was mentioned in the outline of the discourse of self-definition and self-promotion, a *Mütterlichkeitsdiskurs* was employed to promote shared interests and activities within the community of women. Part of this *Mütterlichkeitsdiskurs*, however, belongs to the discourse of challenge and opposition: metaphors of nature are employed to communicate the fact that motherhood represents the model for women's authority and power, and that it is an area in which they cannot be challenged by men. In particular, the personified *Natur* (rather than National Socialism) is invoked by women as an authoritative source:

Die Frau ist sich heut im allgemeinen garnicht bewußt, welche ungeheure Verantwortung, aber auch welche große Macht ihr von der Natur durch die Mutterschaft verliehen ist. Von ihr hängt der Fortschritt und der Aufstieg der Völker – oder auch ihr Verfall ab. (Schmidt 1933: 341)

In previous research on NS rhetoric, religious language is often cited as a major characteristic, which was used to emphasize the legitimacy of NS ideology. In women's texts, references to God are employed but could be interpreted as a means of challenging National Socialist authority over women:

Wir richten dagegen einen deutschen Frauenwillen auf, der verwurzelt ist in GOTT, Natur, Familie, Volk und Vaterland und ein eigenes Frauen-Kultur-Programm, das seine Ausgestaltung im 3. Reich finden soll. ('Grundsätze der N.S. Frauenschaft', [no author given] 1932, underlining in original)

Die Nationalsozialistische Frauenschaft hat genau wie in der Kampfzeit unserer Bewegung und damit unserem Volke zu dienen mit all ihrer Kraft. Wir wissen, dass dazu viel Glaube und Wegdenken vom eigenen Ich erforderlich ist. Und wir wissen auch das andere, dass die letzten Kräfte uns immer wieder geschenkt werden müssen von Gott. (Scholtz-Klink 1934)

Alles hat letzten Endes sein Erdreich im Gefüge der mütterlichen Seele. Ist das Gefüge der mütterlichen Seele in Ordnung, d.h. eingeordnet in Gott, sind diese Worte da, sonst niemals. (Schloßmann-Lönnies 1933: 512)

Pragmatic strategies

As women considered themselves active and committed National Socialists, they often held strong opinions and ideas about the role of women in the NSDAP. With the creation of the unified *NS-Frauenschaft* in the early 1930s, many women took the opportunity to communicate their ideas on National Socialism, and to voice criticism of provision for women's participation in the party, believing erroneously that they would be able to have a say in how women were to be organized in the NSDAP. In expressing ideas and criticism in letters to male National Socialists, they engage in a potentially face-threatening act, which might challenge the addressee's authority and position. As we have seen in the analysis of pragmatic strategies in the discourse of integration and solidarity, many women choose to use expressions associated with negative politeness. When expressing criticism to male National Socialists, however, they employ a range of strategies, from openly hostile, face-threatening statements (see the first example below) to more subtle, face-saving remarks, involving qualifying and modifying expressions (as illustrated by the second example):

Soll sie [die Frau] wieder nur Haushalt machen, gewissenlos Kinder kriegen und im ewigen Sparenmüssen frühzeitig alt und hässlich werden? [...] Oder wenn unverheiratet [...] zu Hause hocken, stricken, auch Haushalt machen [...] und auf König Blaubart warten? Wir protestieren energisch gegen diese Knebelung!
(Obrist 1933, underlining in original)

Es liegt mir durchaus fern, irgendwelche Ausführungen zu monieren *aber* ich kann mir nicht vorstellen, dass man Mitglieder, die nachweislich im idealen Sinne für die Sache arbeiten und arbeiten wollen, zurückweist. (Göbel 1931, italics mine)

These examples, whether polite or impolite, represent expressions of opposition and challenge, and the choice of face-threatening or face-saving utterances is dependent on a variety of factors, including level of acquaintance between writer and addressee and the positions of power and status held by both parties. But interpreting the utterances according to these factors is not necessarily straightforward. A woman who voices criticism to an addressee she knows, for example, may feel that she can express herself forcefully, but on the other hand, she may feel obliged to be indirect and polite in order to maintain their relationship in the future.

Conclusion

As the analysis has endeavoured to show through its identification of types of discourse in NS women's texts, women's discourse in National Socialism does represent a landmark in German language history. The focus on the discourse of women is particularly justified if one considers the previous neglect of the topic in analyses of NS rhetoric, despite the fact that women were articulate members of the NS community and created a variety of texts promoting NS ideology. The key to decoding women's discourse lies in the combination of analytical approaches outlined above. The combination of discourse analysis, feminist sociolinguistics and pragmatics enables us to see the women's texts not merely as end-products that convey ideas and information but as part of an ongoing process of creating identity, status and power, determined by factors such as gender and organizational status. Women's discourse is characterized through its use of shared topics, themes and common key vocabulary, which marks the users not only as members of a female community but also as National Socialists. Reading a variety of texts created by NS women, one can conclude that the women employ vocabulary denoting female characteristics, activity and behaviour, with a particular emphasis on femininity and motherhood, but also on war and battle, for example. However, identifying thematic and lexical patterns alone will not explain the context and the motivations for their usage. A number of factors influence their language behaviour, including their marginalized organizational status defined by

gender and their adherence to aspects of National Socialist ideology. Their
status as a gendered group results in a variety of different discourses being
employed in their texts. These texts represent expressions of self-promotion,
negotiation and challenge, in which women test the boundaries of activity
and the acceptability of their own ideas. Women's discourse appears to be full
of contradictions: women express intimacy and solidarity with other women,
yet also objectify women and seek to exclude those who do not comply with
the characteristics associated with the in-group. Similarly, the women express
their loyalty to the NSDAP, yet also challenge its authority, even through
apparently compliant means such as the promotion of motherhood. The
discourse displays evidence of National Socialist male influence and even
interference but also characteristics of autonomy and linguistic, textual and
expressive inheritance from other women's sources, including the women's
movements of the late nineteenth and early twentieth centuries. The combination of analytical approaches allows us to see that women's discourse in
National Socialism is as complex as the position and motivation of the women
who created and used it.

References

Primary sources

Auerhahn, K. (1932), 'Das Warenhaus – der Untergang des deutschen Mittelstandes', *NS-
    Frauenwarte*, 1 August.
Diehl, G. (1933), *Die deutsche Frau und der Nationalsozialismus*, 2nd ed. (revised),
    Eisenach: Neuland.
Fiebig, I. (1932), 'Die Gefährtin des Arbeitslosen', *NS-Frauenwarte*, 1 October.
Gauleiterin, DFO Mecklenburg/Lübeck (1931), letter to G. Strasser, 13 July (Bundes-
    archiv NS22/430).
Göbel, A. (1931), letter to G. Strasser, 6 October (Bundesarchiv NS22/431).
'Grundsätze der N.S. Frauenschaft' [no author given] (1932), 1 October (Bundesarchiv
    NS44/55).
Leiterin, NSF 'Probstheida', Leipzig-Osten (1934), letter to Dr Krummacher, 22 January
    (Bundesarchiv R.15.01/26334/1/1721).

Martens-Edelmann, A. (1933), 'Erziehung zur Ehe und Vaterschaft', *Die deutsche Kämpferin*, May.

Obrist, L. (1933), letter to Reichsminister Frick, 23 December (Bundesarchiv R.15.01/ 26332).

Reber-Gruber, A. (1934), letter to E.S., 14 July (Bundesarchiv NS12/1315).

Rogge-Börner, S. (1933a),'Die vorderste Linie', *Die deutsche Kämpferin*, May.

Rogge-Börner, S. (1933b), 'Die dritte der Stufen', *Die deutsche Kämpferin*, June.

Rühlemann, L. (1930), letter to Frau S., 23 November (Bundesarchiv NS22/431).

Schloßmann-Lönnies, K. (1933), 'Volkspolitische Aufgaben der Mütter und Frauen', *NS-Frauenwarte*, 15 May.

Schmidt, M. (1933), 'Mutter sein heißt!', *NS-Frauenwarte*, 1 February 1933.

Scholtz-Klink, G. (1934), Rundschreiben Nr. F 50/34, 20 December (Bundesarchiv NS44/33).

'Selbsterziehung der Frau' [no author given] (1932), *NS-Frauenwarte*, 1 September.

St-S., R. (1928), letter to Adolf Hitler, 22 May (Bundesarchiv NS22/431).

Zander, E. (1931),'Unsere SA. Reichsordenstag 1931. Der Kampf im Zeichen "Roten Hakenkreuzes"', *Opferdienst der deutschen Frau*, September (BA NSD47/15).

Zander, E. (1933), 'Rückblick und Ausblick', *Informationsdienst der NS-Frauenschaft*, 15 February (Bundesarchiv NS44/54).

Bibliography

Berning, C. (1964), *Vom 'Abstammungsnachweis' zum 'Zuchtwart'. Vokabular des Nationalsozialismus*, Berlin: de Gruyter.

[Schmitz-]Berning, C. (1998), *Vokabular des Nationalsozialismus*, Berlin and New York: de Gruyter.

Bork, S. (1970), *Mißbrauch der Sprache. Tendenzen nationalsozialistischer Sprachregelung*, Bern and Munich: Francke.

Brown, P. and Levinson, S.C. (1987), *Politeness. Some universals in language use*, revised ed., Cambridge: Cambridge University Press.

Brunner, G. and Graefen, G. (eds) (1994), *Texte und Diskurse. Methoden und Forschungsergebnisse der funktionalen Pragmatik*, Opladen: Westdeutscher Verlag.

Cameron, D. (1992), *Feminism and Linguistic Theory*, 2nd edn, Houndmills, Basingstoke and London: Macmillan.

Coates, J. (1993), *Women, Men and Language*, 2nd ed., London and New York: Longman.

Coates, J. (1996), *Women Talk. Conversation between Women Friends*, Oxford: Blackwell.

Fairclough, N. and Wodak, R. (1997), 'Critical Discourse Analysis', in: *Discourse as Social Interaction*, edited by T.A. van Dijk, London, Thousand Oaks and New Delhi: Sage, 258–84.

Horan, G.T. (2003), *Mothers, Warriors, Guardians of the Soul. Female Discourse in National Socialism, 1924–34*, Berlin and New York: de Gruyter.

Johnson, S.A. (1995), *Gender, Group Identity and Variation in the Berlin Vernacular. A Sociolinguistic Study*, Bern: Peter Lang.

Kater, M.H. (1983), 'Frauen in der NS-Bewegung', *Vierteljahreshefte für Zeitgeschichte* 31, 202–41.

Keller, R.E. (1981), 'The Impact of Ideology on the German Vocabulary', *Transactions of the Philological Society*, 118–35.

Klemperer, V. (1966), *Die unbewältigte Sprache. Aus dem Notizbuch eines Philologen. 'LTI'*, Darmstadt: Melzer.

Koonz, C. (1976), 'Nazi Women before 1933: Rebels against Emancipation', *Social Science Quarterly* 56, 553–63.

Korotin, I.E. (1992), *'Am Muttergeist soll die Welt genesen'. Philosophische Dispositionen zum Frauenbild im Nationalsozialismus*, Cologne, Vienna and Weimar: Böhlau.

Lakoff, R. (1975), *Language and Woman's Place*, New York: Harper and Row.

Mills, S. (1993), *Discourses of difference: an analysis of women's travel writing and colonialism*, London and New York: Routledge.

Peters, D. (1984), *Mütterlichkeit im Kaiserreich. Die bürgerliche Frauenbewegung und der soziale Beruf der Frau*, Bielefeld: Kleine.

Polenz, P. von (1999), *Deutsche Sprachgeschichte vom Spätmittelalter bis zur Gegenwart*, vol. 3, Berlin and New York: de Gruyter.

Seidel, E. and Seidel-Slotty, I. (1961), *Sprachwandel im Dritten Reich. Eine kritische Untersuchung faschistischer Einflüsse*, Halle an der Saale: Niemeyer.

Stephenson, J. (1981), *The Nazi Organisation of Women*, London: Croom Helm.

Trömel-Plötz, S. (1996), 'Frauengespräche – Idealgespräche', in: *Frauen-gespräche: Sprache der Verständigung*, edited by S. Trömel-Plötz, Frankfurt am Main: Fischer, 365–77.

Wittrock, C. (1983), *Weiblichkeitsmythen. Das Frauenbild im Faschismus und seine Vorläufer in der Frauenbewegung der 20er Jahre*, Frankfurt am Main: Sendler.

Yule, G. (1996), *Pragmatics*, Oxford: Oxford University Press.

C.J. WELLS

Language in Limbo? Post-1945 German

Introduction

This paper examines features of German immediately after the end of the
Second World War, between 1945 and 1950, as the basis for some subsequent
linguistic developments.[1] To describe that time as a state of 'limbo' is somewhat arch: it is not so much a 'pre-Hell', as an 'after-Hell', but nevertheless a
state of suspension before linguistic fates become clear. The images of Germany
as 'ein großer Wartesaal', as 'Quarantäne', or 'Niemandsland', a 'Vakuum', or
an 'Interregnum' (Scherpe 1982–3: 41, 46) signal the sense of disorientation.
In fact, the lineaments of limbo – as a transition between one state of being
and another – are indeterminate and blurred. Here in particular the interplay
of continuities and discontinuities will be brought into sharper focus in the
history of German from before and after the Second World War. Although
1945 might seem an obvious periodizing point,[2] there can be no complete
break in any language still in use, and linguistically at least, there was no
Stunde Null, despite many radical political, social and cultural changes in the
immediate post-war years. As Walter Dieckmann put it:

> In Deutschland ist 1932 und 1944 nicht mehr und nicht weniger und insgesamt gesehen
> nicht wesentlich anders Deutsch gesprochen und geschrieben worden als 1934 bzw.
> 1946. (Dieckmann 1983: 91; cit. Kämper 2005: 487, fn.4)

---

[1] See esp. Steger (1989); Dieckmann (1983), and now Deissler (2004); Kämper (2005,
2007), and several other studies on her web-page: www.ids-mannheim.de/pub/autoren/
ids/kaemper.html.

[2] Compare Wells (1985) with Gerhart Wolff (1986) who prefers to take 1933 as a periodizing date, not 1945; and see also Eggers (1980: 603); Henne and Drosdowski (1980: 620);
Moser (1985: 1678–1707).

But before we can answer deceptively straightforward questions such as: What was new after 1945? or What remained? we need to consider the domains of use and the situation of the speakers, the different kinds of social space in which communication happens, and even what is meant by 'German'. There were many continuities in everyday usage, and there were radical innovations in public and semi-public administrative language between 1945 and 1950 which were effectively filtered out before they became established in the standard language. They did not enter the contemporary dictionaries and grammars, not least because the German-speaking population had other concerns than registering them, nor did the Allies intend to establish in Germany their own permanent administration with its characteristic language. Moreover, there were regional differences, ideologically between the western Allied occupied zones and the Soviet zone, and geopolitically between Germany and Austria, and Switzerland, which receive only passing mention in the present context, and which offer other perspectives.

Inevitably, difficulties arise in identifying the form of language to be studied. Referring to 'the history of the language', or 'the German language' is to reify German as an object with established forms and features. But linguists have long been aware of language as process and activity, not object or 'output', an insight that goes back at least to Wilhelm von Humboldt (1836), even if, post-Saussure, structuralists and generativists have focused attention on the abstract structure and system of language, not everyday usage. Inevitably, usage reflects systemic elements and structures which can in turn be legitimised, and indeed, reconstructed only from usage. Here the term 'language' will be understood, then, as communication in progress, rather than as any particular identifiable form of language. Trying to avoid reification makes the description of German difficult, but it proves equally unsatisfactory to follow the contemporary approach of the linguistic critics after 1945, like Victor Klemperer (1946, 1996) or Dolf Sternberger, Gerhard Storz and Wilhelm Emanuel Süskind[3] who accepted unquestioningly the existence of a Nazi language they were attempting to eradicate, whether described as the 'Language of the Third Reich' (*Lingua Tertii Imperii*), or as an excerpt from the dictionary of the individualized (and collectivized) monster – *Unmensch* – who spoke it. This determinist view of language as a system that reflects, or

---

3   Sternberger, Storz, and Süskind (1945; 2nd ed. 1957). For Sternberger, see Dodd (1999).

in the stronger formulation, even creates reality proves unsatisfactory, since it disregards or underestimates the openness of language and the human capacity to adapt to speakers of other languages, cultures or even subsections of our own community. In practice, in his *LTI* Klemperer discusses not only linguistic features, but attitudes to language and the paralinguistic setting, like the wearing of uniforms and symbols, parades and other forms of ritualized public behaviour. His fuller account of life in Nazi Germany as a Jew, *Ich will Zeugnis ablegen*, documents Nazi language as a by-product or ancillary component of Nazism, an indicator, rather than a cause.[4] The present approach starting from language as communication examines the speakers' participation in several distinct but important and linked discourses. Since discourses generally involve perspectives and attitudes of the speakers, their parameters are neither determinate nor unchanging, but that is part of linguistic history, and native speakers themselves are aware of changes in their language over time. They naturally notice new, or unusual, perhaps even antiquated patterns in the discourses they encounter daily. The German cliché *die Gleichzeitigkeit des Ungleichzeitigen* ('the simultaneity of the non-simultaneous') applies to the archaism and neologisms encountered by speakers who belong to different chronological 'cohorts' and social groups with widely differing mastery of and chronological experience in their language and correspondingly different perspectives on it. Consequently, old and new features inevitably co-exist: but they are perceived to be old or new by different speakers in differing degree. To postulate a single system is to move to a level of generality beyond the scope of any individual speaker, and in this respect, writing the history of German language inevitably involves both hypostasizing it and also examining an externalized, generalized language that is outside time.

It proves convenient to draw a further distinction between the generalized language, or *Gemeinsprache* which comprises any varieties of language which may be deemed to be or have been 'German', and the codified language of grammars and dictionaries, or *Standardsprache*. While it may be argued that any variety of language more or less recognizable as 'German' belongs to the general German language, in that German dialects, sociolects, functiolects, i.e. regional social and technical or scientific forms of German can

---

4   Klemperer (1995, 7.Aufl., 1996). It was edited from some 5,000 typescript pages and
     newspaper cuttings etc. now deposited in the *Sächsische Landesbibliothek* in Dresden.

all be called 'German', it also follows that many of them, or many of their special features, are not part of that standard language, although they might become so, for instance if a political or national issue involving technical matters becomes topical, reported in the media and widely discussed in the community at large. Indeed, the vocabulary collected in dictionaries is usually marked to some (varying) extent as technical, specialist, colloquial, regional and so forth, and so may be supposed precisely not to belong to 'standard' German: at the 'fuzzy' periphery, where innovations and archaisms co-exist, it is a matter of judgement on the part of the dictionary compilers what goes into the dictionary, and when.

All languages, then, comprise older and newer elements, most evidently at the lexical, rather than syntactic or morphological level, since the vocabulary is an infinitely extensible 'open system' or 'systemoid', whereas the morphology of German consists of a largely determinate set of inflexions, and the syntax too has recurring patterns. Speakers of different age-groups will develop their own varieties, mostly comprising variables of existing patterns, since languages entail social varieties of communication conditioned by the age, and by the technical or social purposes of the speakers. Consequently, there appear to be differences in the degree to which the various levels of language alter over time. Vocabulary is most obviously open to change, and studies of linguistic influences commonly show that nouns make up some eighty percent of innovations, followed by verbs, under ten percent, adjectives, some five percent, and then other parts of speech. The grammatical structures change less radically over time, and they are, broadly, maintained across the various social and functional varieties, although their frequency and stylistic values alter.

Discourses and societal space

If language is viewed as communication in process, to study linguistic history is to trace dominant forms of human interaction and their verbalization over time. In this respect, a number of 'discourses' can be identified which affected most German speakers in the immediate post-war chaos. Ultimately these discourses involve physical survival, the establishment of political systems of control and the promotion of law and order or political stability. The term 'discourse' may conveniently be understood as Caroline Mayer suggests, as *Zeitgespräch* (2002: 7), rather than as the philosophical ideological analysis of the sociological theorists Habermas and Foucault. But the parameters of a discourse prove hard to determine, since they are open-ended: in practice each of the discourses examined here comprises at least two variant forms, or sub-discourses. The new governance structures of the military occupying forces in 1945 are applied in German and a foreign language – English, Russian or French – and they impact on the civilian population, affecting both occupiers and occupied in a complementary discourse of contact and fraternization. The new denazification measures attempt to identify 'Nazi' behaviour and attitudes, and the degree of complicity and guilt, but they form one strand of the Allies' administrative language with its characteristic terminology; however, in the process the former, supplanted Nazi ranks, organizations and institutions are continually recalled to mind. Finally, the Black Market manifests both criminal slang in its practices and the technical language of economic control used by agencies designed to combat it: the language here is new to most Germans, who have to resort to illegal trading. All sections of the population are affected by these discourses, which however occupy different 'social' spaces.

Discourse is communication about certain 'themes', and the arguments and positions and values associated with those themes are all ultimately reflected in the language used. But a major factor helping to determine discourse is its use in the public and semi-public space. The parameters of a discourse vary with the shifting cohesion of the groups which will comprise speakers with different understandings of the discourses and their 'texts', subtexts and intertexts. While the core elements of a discourse can be identified, the subject, the partisan approach, and so forth, not all spaces of discourse are directly accessible for scrutiny. We distinguish public space in which the whole population is governed through the exercise of political power and public opinion, the mass media, and literature. As Dieter Felbick notes, the public discourse of this space is accessible to everyone via the mass media, and indeed engagement with it is virtually synonymous with engagement with the mass media, although communication has been, until recently, one-way.[5] The public-space language is certainly able to inform all the other communicative spaces, in differing degree, whereas the reverse is not true. Beside this public space and certainly drawing on its discourse, then, there is a semi-public space in which individuals relate to other individuals whom they do not know or to whom they are not related. This space comprises social and regional varieties, interface levels of scientific and technical registers, and differing degrees of formal and informal language. Next, in semi-private space activities take place outside private space but with a desire to restrict scrutiny of them or to preserve some personal or private component of the behaviour. Both semi-public and semi-private spaces entail social networking, the participation in groups or one-to-one relationships which may involve linguistic varieties. Lastly, private space may be subdivided into private and personal, and private and intimate space (the so-called *Intimsphäre*). Networking, if it occurs at all in private space is unlikely to involve much change of linguistic variety. However, private space is by definition not publicly available, and generally therefore not accessible to linguists.[6] Semi-public space, on the other hand, where interactions between speakers and people not personally well known to them take place, is where so-called 'everyday language' – *Alltagssprache* – is used; it is governed by forms of politeness, taboo, convention. In semi-public space speakers are communicating in public, but not with (potentially) all the other speakers, merely with the relatively small number of individuals encountered in everyday life and interactions. Semi-private space covers places like public toilets, changing rooms, hairdressers' or doctors' surgeries, and the

5   Felbick (2003: 71). In a democracy, the discourse is freely accessible to all, dialogic in character with reciprocal participation – in theory – and pluralistic, with many differing shades of opinion; in a dictatorship, like that of the Russian zone, however, the discourse is controlled, the prerogative of the ruling party, unfree, monologic and uniform.

6   The boundaries between personal private space and public and semi-public space change and differ in the different German-speaking states. In present-day West Germany the personal (sometimes private and intimate!) invades public space in chat-shows and the celebrity 'culture' of *Promi-Blätter*. After 1989, the more conservative *Ossis* whose limited private space was controlled by the Communist state were disorientated in the *Wessi* social landscape where state receded behind private interests. Between 1945–50, post-war chaos also affects the borders of the linguistic socio-spatial structures I am investigating.

confessional, where forms of behaviour take place which are personal and even intimate yet outside the personal living space. By extension, forms of behaviour which are criminalized and illicit occur in semi-private space also, although they also occur in private space. This will be elaborated on below.

The present study, then, outlines three principal sets of 'discourses' between 1945–50, and to these may be added the discourse about German collective guilt treated by Heidrun Kämper (2005).[7] Kämper's subtle and complex study examines a *Diskursgemeinschaft* ('discourse community') also comprising 'Sub-Diskurse' used by *Opfer*, *Täter* and *Nichttäter*, the victims whose sufferings are described, the perpetrators and their strategies of exculpation, and those not implicated who were attempting to establish the truth and create a new German identity. The discourses of these groups constitute a triangulation of perspectives within the force-field of which individual concepts and terms are to be understood, and our sets of discourse – Allied administration, denazification, Black Market – constitute a similar, if less coherent field of forces.

So far, we have assumed that linguistic features can be recognizable and can consequently be 'instrumentalized' by the speakers to identify themselves and to promote that identity. In this respect, after the war using the 'right language' in semi-public space played a key part in survival, by not compromising oneself politically. But this was true in the Nazi period itself, and here again it is helpful to distinguish between public and semi-public, private and semi-private spaces. The speakers' language also identified their political allegiances, and, as Utz Maas has shown, the Nazis used language to stage-manage (*inszenieren*) themselves and their regime and to promote their image.[8] The identification of a 'language of National Socialism' or a 'language of totalitarianism' as such turns out, however, to be a chimaera. When the Nazis had been defeated, the immediate power-vacuum in the public space might indeed be described as a 'Stunde Null', since the regime change entailed a complete replacement of one political system by another. In fact, there were two caesuras: a 'vertical' one, breaking with the previous political system, but then, as Germans began to establish their own administration,

---

7   Kämper (2005); now narrowed into a critical dictionary in Kämper (2007).
8   Maas, Utz (1983) 'Sprache in der Zeit des Nationalsozialismus', and now Maas (2000: 1980–90).

an increasingly acrimonious 'horizontal' West-East split between the western zones and the Russian zone which intensified through the use of polarized public-space language, a feature which attracted notice from the outset. At first, the victorious Allies concurred in seeking to extirpate all trace of the previous system (of Nazi government) from all communication.[9] However, they had neither the resources nor the time to do the same for the language, although there was no doubt that purifying the language was perceived at the time as a desirable, if concomitant aim of replacing the regime. Who should carry out the linguistic re-education, and how? Moreover, the Allies shared uncritically with the Nazis a tendency to hypostasize language and a penchant for fulsome phrases about national and human values. With literally millions of members of the Nazi Party, the process of denazification was complex and could hardly be carried through without crippling the running of the country. Many minor state and government officials remained in post, part of a bureaucracy which had been perverted, for example in the case of those concerned with the transportation programmes to the death camps, for the purposes of murdering Jews.[10] The Allies could still speak unselfconsciously of human rights and values and the responsibilities of their mission and often used language in public in the same hyper-symbolic way as the National Socialists, notably in the Russian Zone, where the militaristic structures of youth movements, and the paraphernalia of parades and collective rituals remained more evident than in the West and constituted a continuity of symbolic control of the public and semi-public space.

The Nazis had established a state totally controlling the public space, and indeed defining it through their use of language, for instance by excluding and stigmatizing Jews and political opponents as outside the *Volksgemeinschaft*. Hitler and Goebbels both deployed language consciously as a propaganda

9   'Wie schon [...] notiert, stellt das Jahr 1945 eine deutliche Zäsur in der dt. Sprachgeschichte dar. Es ist festzuhalten, daß das Vokabular des NS-Regimes mit einem Schlag tabuisiert wird. So löste noch 1983 die Wendung kulturelle Entartung eine Welle des Protests aus.' Moser (1985: 1679).

10   Railway workers and others, *Transportleiter* etc.: cf. Raul Hilberg, in Hilberg/ Söllner (1988: 542–3). See Kämper (2005: 187–9) on *Transport* and compounds, drawing on Adler (1955: XLI). Ironically, an innocent *Blockstellenleiter* ('pointsman') spent some time interned at Neuengamme because Mil.-Gov. thought he was a *Blockleiter*! (letter to *Der Spiegel*, 07.07.1949).

weapon.[11] This idea was, again, reflected by their enemies the Allies who also had an uncritical, stereotypical view of 'the Germans' under Nazism and in the light of what they saw as German collective guilt. Indeed, there is another continuity here, because linguistic stereotypes of Nazism have been used since the war symbolically to discredit opponents by identifying Nazi attitudes, mostly in order to dissociate from them, but also, in the case of Neonazis, sometimes to forge spurious links to the Nazi past. Language is in essence a symbolic system, but here we have effectively a secondary layer of symbolism with a political function. At the same time, the apparently holistic and uniform view of language promoted makes Nazi Germany seem linguistically monolithic, notably in public space. Utz Maas (2000), and Peter von Polenz (1999) have shown that this is fallacious: German under Nazism was not a monolithic system, nor is it chronologically unchanging: instead, we can distinguish phases and varieties in the use of German under the Nazis, something Maas calls 'polyphony'. In any case, no language can be monolithic, not least because speakers of different chronological 'cohorts' (*Jahrgänge*) have their own historically conditioned forms of their language for their various communicative purposes in different communicative spaces.

Social Reality 1945–9

The four zones of Occupied Germany and the four sectors in Berlin differed in character and situation, and it is not possible to sketch all their complexities here. A valuable contemporary account of life in 1947 distinguishes even a characteristic 'Zonenmentalität': 'apolitische Unzufriedenheit in der französischen, hämische Kritik in der englischen, Furcht in der russischen und berechnende Erwartung in der amerikanischen Zone' (Rümelin 1948: 3). In whatever zone, however, all sections of the population were affected by hunger, homelessness, the rigours of the climate and general lack of resources

---

11   See Hitler (1925–7; repr.1943), *Mein Kampf*, esp. chapters 6 ('Kriegspropaganda') and chapter 11 ('Rasse'), and Josef Goebbels, speech of 1933 to the Rundfunkintendanten. Goebbels (1932–45), vol. 1, Nr. 13, 25.03.1933.

and were subject to military government, denazification and military restrictions on their movements from zone to zone and within zones. They were also dependent, more or less, on the Black Market to survive, and this dependence only really diminished when the western zones introduced a currency reform on Sunday 20 June 20 1948 – known at the time as *Tag-X* – without warning. This replaced the official *Reichsmark* by the *Deutsche Mark*, with a hand-out of DM 100 per household and new rates of exchange. The weekly news magazine *Der Spiegel* (Nr. 27, 1948: 2) punned on the *D-Markationslinie* between Germans and the French visitors who suddenly found currency-reformed Germany too dear. Goods which had been hoarded for bartering appeared in the shops overnight, but were expensive to buy. However, this also precipitated the Russian attempt to close off Berlin and seal the border for all transit, not least for economic reasons. On 24 June 1948, the Soviet authorities began the Berlin Blockade, which lasted until 12 May 1949.[12] The resulting air-lift (*Luftbrücke*) mounted by the Americans and British between 1948–9 broke the blockade, and hastened the founding of the Federal Republic incorporating the American and British zones which had by then formed themselves into a single United Economic Area (*Vereinigtes Wirtschaftsgebiet* or *Bizone*, planned to include eventually the third, French zone). The Federal Republic's Basic Law (*Grundgesetz*) was ratified in May 1949; this in turn encouraged the Soviets to establish the German Democratic Republic (*DDR*) from the Soviet zone (*SBZ, Sowjetische Besatzungszone*) which was not recognized by the Federal Republic until 1972. The growing antagonism between the two nascent German states was to have, increasingly, linguistic effects on the political discourse of the public space. At the outset, the Allies and their civilian administrations in the western and eastern zones had very different conceptions of *Demokratie*, of course: in the West anti-democratic forces often meant Communists, whereas in the East, the enemies of Communism included bourgeois and land-owning circles, who might also be termed 'fascist', and so be subjected to denazification, whether or not they had been complicit in Nazism. Indeed, the imprecise term *demokratisch* was used by the Allies as a compromise formula to paper over fundamental differences of opinion.[13]

---

12   For the historical detail, see Angelika Königseder in Benz (1999: 114–17).
13   See Eschenburg (1983: 51); Felbick (2003: 175–206).

In what follows, the focus will be on three major public, semi-public and semi-private discourses and related sub-discourses that affected Germans in general.

Mil.-Gov.: *Control* and *Kontrolle* – A public variety

Public space (and semi-public space which will be elaborated below) is itself actually defined and therefore created by language and other social codes – dress, politeness, taboo – and is essentially 'political' in the broad sense of *politeia*,[14] since politics regulates social interactions that occur there. Consequently, the end of the Nazi tyranny entailed a break in continuity because of the replacement of one regime by another, which indeed resulted in a period of chaos. While the term *Stunde Null* was not unreasonably applied to this, the label remains a nebulous concept without the association of English 'zero hour', since it appears to mark not the culmination of an operation, but the beginning of a new phase. Perhaps an analogous term might be the use of 'ground zero' in the USA after the terrorist attack of 9/11.

The administrative language of the British and American Zones represents an Allied control discourse with two aspects, a German one and an English one, since orders and directives were usually issued in both languages, occasionally as hybrids, such as *Besatzungszone* beside *Okkupationszone*. In the Russian and French zones a comparable bilingual administration was applied. In the process, many words of foreign origin and some complexity and many new abbreviations became temporarily current in German: *Denazifizierung, Demarkationslinie, Demilitarisierung, Demontage, Entnazifizierung, Internierung, Okkupation, Sektor, Transitverkehr; CARE-Paket, DP, GI, US.* etc. In all zones, East (Soviet) and West (British, US and French), many defeated Germans reacted to the central administration by seeing it as a continuation of the previous tyranny: more of the same, *das Vierte Reich*. With black humour, Klemperer himself sarcastically named the language of

14   From Greek *polis* 'city', the public domain mediated by political control and the media, and by public opinion, but also the semi-public space.

the Soviet Military Administration *LQI*;[15] elsewhere in public discourse the term *Demokratur* mocks the Allies' supposed *Demokratie*.[16] Naturally there were conflicts between the prohibition of political parties in the early post-war stages, and the need to promote independent, democratic institutions and practices, and also between the self-interested *Demontage* and the need to establish a viable German economy. In such circumstances, frustration and downright disaffection in some quarters were inevitable. Despite the apparently innocuous statement of the British military administration in its official organ, the *Neuer Hannoverscher Kurier* (*NHK* Nr. 1, 29.05.1945), published under Allied control from May 1945 to July 1947, the exercise of power is made clear to the population:

> 'Die Besatzungsarmee wird nicht verwalten, sie wird die Kontrolle ausführen', erklärte Oberst B.K.Thomas, Mitglied der Operationen- und Planungsabteilung der britischen Militärregierung.

Subsequently, we find new terminology embodying 'control' in all zones: *Der alliierte Kontrollrat für Deutschland, in Kontrollangelegenheiten, Zentralkontrollrat* etc., but the '*Kontrolle*' turned out to be no mild overseeing: it involved searching persons, documents, homes and offices, checking personal details, censorship of letters, the press and the media, strict limits ('controls', *Sperren*) on going out at night, limiting freedom of movement, the introduction of the *Kennkarte* (ID-card, *Personalausweis*), and many other restrictions, so that public space was entirely regulated and 'controlled'. It became clear that the English 'control' meant something quite other than mere 'supervision':

> Die Bes. Mächte haben aber [...] in Anlehnung vor allem an den angelsächsischen Kontroll-begriff, der Kontrolle einen ganz anderen Inhalt gegeben als es dem deutschen Sprachgebrauch entspricht, Kontrolle im angelsächsischen Sinne ist *Lenkung*, Kontrolle

---

15   *Lingua Quarti Imperii*, 'The Language of the Fourth Reich', by analogy with his earlier work *LTI*. See esp. Heidrun Kämper (2001).

16   In Austria, Herbert Kraus in 1946 terms the rigid coalition government of SPÖ, ÖVP and KPÖ a *Demokratur* (cf. http://cla.calpoly.edu/~mriedlsp/Publications/VdU.html), but in no zone were democratic freedoms fully implemented; later the term *Demokratur* was applied (by Karl Loewenstein) to Adenauer's West Germany, it is currently *en vogue* for several regimes cf. Willett (1992: 6).

im deutschen Sinne Überwachung [...] Begrifflich aber sind K. und Überwachung voneinander zu trennen.[17]

Some of this was dictated by security: bands of Displaced Persons, refugees, released internees and soldiers roamed the country, and some of them were dangerous. There were also health concerns, to avoid epidemics of typhoid and tuberculosis, and food production and distribution had to be re-started. But some punishments seemed Draconian – three months prison for infringing the curfew, for example – and several former German soldiers were executed at Wolfenbüttel because of gun crimes (*NHK* Nr. 1, 29.05.1945: 4). The broadened semantics of *Kontrolle* can also be inferred from a regional source: in June 1946, an agreement of the *Viermächterat* in Austria virtually abolished the demarcation lines – zonal borders – in Austria, and this was commented on by the *NHK* (Nr. 52, 02.07.1946: 3) 'Das Abkommen kann als der Wechsel vom System der Kontrolle zum System der Überwachung bezeichnet werden'.

Most of the terminology introduced at this period was ephemeral and has long since disappeared, including many compounds with *Zone*, *Sektor* and *alliiert*, *Besatzung* and so forth, which exist in the transcripts of proceedings, in the laws, directives and edicts of the occupying forces (*Direktiven*, *Anordnungen*, *Verordnungen*), without necessarily ever being recorded in dictionaries. Similarly, the associated German vocabulary showed developments and variant forms for more or less the same thing: the *Ausgehverbot* and the *Sperrstunden* involved *Ausgangsbeschränkungen* or *Ausgehbeschränkung*, but the *Ausgehzeit* which ended with *das Curfew*[18] was gradually increased (Bein and Vogel 1995: 82–3). The collaboration between British and American zones led to the formation of the *Bizone* and there was talk of a *Trizone* with the French zone. In fact, the *Bizone*, or *Bizonien* as it was humorously called, was absorbed into the new Federal Republic in September 1949 and *Trizonesien* existed only in a popular carnival parody of 1948 by Karl Berbuer which viewed it as a banana-republic, the refrain ran: 'Wir sind die Eingeborenen von Trizonesien/ Hei-di-tschimmela-tschimmela-tschimmela-bumm! ...'

17   Cf. Schmoller, Maier and Tobler (1957: 22), *Kontrolle*.
18   In the British Zone, e.g. Schnelsen/Hamburg: cf. http://www.kollektives-gedaechtnis. de/texte/nach45/haji.htm

(cf. a variant in Eschenburg 1983: 507, 515). Inevitably, there were linguistic implications, with terms like *bizonal,* alongside *interzonal, Interzonenhandel, -konferenz* etc. Under the disingenuous headline 'Anschluß. Der Übel kleinstes', *Der Spiegel* rather provocatively referred to the 'Zone Française' as 'Mariannes jüngste Tochter, [die] sich mit dem anglo-amerikanischen Bizonenmichel verbinden [wird]', and to the population of the French zone being 'anschlußfreudig', even to the 'Gleichschaltung des Verkehrswesens' (*Spiegel* 1948, Nr. 40, 02.10.48: 16–17). Here the loaded terms *Anschluß,* and *Gleichschaltung,* and the erotic metaphor of *verbinden* (see below) (and possibly *Verkehr*) both suggest and undermine a continuity with the Nazi past. Space prevents pursuing the technical administrative terminology of this period further in this paper. It remains relatively unexamined by linguists.

Everyday language in the discourses of semi-public space: New contacts and contexts

In the semi-public space of contact between occupiers and the occupied, the daily language of both sides was enriched but not always enhanced by the circumstances in which they encountered each other. At the same time, the non-fraternization edict originally in force in 1945 was already collapsing in the first weeks: 'Die Verbindung deutscher Mädel mit alliierten Soldaten beginnt sich anzubahnen', as one source puts it, 31 May 1945 (Bein and Vogel 1995: 83). The authorities capitulated in the face of blatant disregard for the edict: 'Umgangsverbot gelockert' (*NHK* Nr. 9, 17.07.1945). The official terms 'non-fraternization'/ *'Verbrüderung'* and *'Verbindung'* were hopelessly inadequate, even euphemistic, compared with the everyday usage. In fact, in US service slang 'non-fraternization' was known as 'non-fertilization', and 'Fräuleins' were known as 'Furlines' or 'Frowleins' or 'Fraternazis': to go out with one was 'goin' frattin', and sleeping with the enemy was 'to frat'. Among British soldiers, an army-issue cheese or corned-beef sandwich, 'a proven way to a hungry Fräulein's heart' was known as a 'frat sandwich', and a 'frat-song' was current, to the tune of *Lili Marlene*: in fact, *frat* meant 'fuck' (Botting 1986: 304, 308). Newspapers sometimes glossed the new vocabulary: *NHK*

(Nr 36 19.10.1945: 2) discusses *Escapist* and other terms – *Sex Appeal, Pin-up-Girl* and *sweetheart* – which are unknown in German but show the social impact of the Occupation forces. Cartoons also reflect the linguistic clash, as when two 'Fräuleins' meet at a dance: 'Hat sich denn dein Tommy vorgestellt?' – 'Natürlich!' – 'Wie heißt er denn?' – 'Haudujudu.' (*NHK* Nr. 25, 29.03.1946: 3).

The younger generation in particular was interested in everything American, from unselfconsciously – and positively re-interpreted – *Negermusik*, with *Blues, Swing, Jazz* and *Jitterbug* and *Boogie-woogie* (all pre-war), to American films, cars, coke and chewing-gum, and especially cigarettes. This cultural influence was one of the mainsprings for the continuing borrowing of American words and phrases in social and recreational use by Germans after the war, as occasionally attested, not always approvingly, in the newspapers of the time. Later, in June 1949 as the Cold War intensified, *Boogie-Woogie* was used by the SED in the East Zone in attacks on the increasing American influence in the western zones, viewed, along with Surrealism, as one of the 'Verfallserscheinungen der sterbenden bürgerlichen Kultur' (Felbick 2003: 139–43). Fraternization, of course, evoked negative reactions in the older generation, was seen as immorality, disloyalty, betrayal, and women who consorted with the occupying troops were stigmatized linguistically in all zones. Uwe Timm sees the humiliation and loss of moral authority of the fathers in particular as one of the reasons for the youthful rebellion against German traditions:

> Die tiefe Empfänglichkeit für die amerikanischen Lebensformen, für Film, Literatur, Musik, Kleidung, dieser Siegeszug hatte seine Ursache darin, daß die Väter nicht nur militärisch, sondern auch mit ihren Wertvorstellungen, mit ihrer Lebensform bedingungslos kapituliert hatten. Die Erwachsenen erschienen lächerlich, selbst wenn das Kind noch nicht fähig war, eine begriffliche Begründung dafür zu finden, aber es war spürbar, die Degradierung der Väter. (2003: 69–70)

Timm's own father remained a tyrannical despot at home, impotently raging against the new history lessons in school which attacked *Kadavergehorsam* and the *Militärfimmel der Deutschen* in a new counter-discourse. With the founding of the *Bundesrepublik* in 1949, the older generation of *Bildungsbürger* looked back to a period before Nazism and looked down on the inferior culture, in particular of the Americans, so that there was a great vogue for Goethe, Schiller and the German classics (*Der Spiegel* 48, 2005: 62),

part of what has been seen as a restorative cultural trend in the Adenauer era
which promoted a safe, bourgeois and essentially non-political withdrawal
into private space: but this contrasted with the taste of the younger generation. Letters to the *NHK* (Nr. 56, 16.07.1946: 2), pro- and contra-, contrast
Jazz and *Swing* with the 'harmless' military music or German 'folk dances'
that turn out not actually to be German in origin (mazurkas, polkas, the
Wiener Walzer etc!). Protests against such cultural decline emanated, it was
claimed, from 'Bornierte' and 'Unbelehrbare'. An article by Wilhelm Süskind
in the *Abendpost* (Nr. 2, 10.02.1947: 3) 'Das Nackte Leben / Ein Tagebuch-
blatt', discusses the coarse language of the young as overheard in a Munich
café in the US-zone:

> 'Die Zenzi ist ein Luder geworden ...' – '...die war immer ein Luder...' (Das ist alles, auch
> die starken Worte, ganz unbeteiligt hingesagt, ohne Empörung, ohne Erheiterung; es
> hat doch nicht einmal die Lust des Klatsches ... Beachtenswert ist die starke Sprache,
> die sie führen. Gefressen, gesoffen – anders geht es nicht.)

In the same article, one girl was referred to as *Zucker* ('Gehst du noch mit
dem, Zucker?' for US 'sugar'), but this seems not to have survived, and 'honey'
has not replaced it. Although the direct linguistic influence of the Allies'
administration was largely ephemeral in the western zones, Dirk Deissler,
following Steger, and von Polenz, Stötzel and Schlosser, emphasizes the crucial role of their press officers in developing a new political awareness among
German journalists, so creating a 'Zäsur im Sprachbewußtsein der Sprecher',
even if there is no radical break in the language they were using (Deissler
2004). Ultimately it is this change of mentality which conditions the later
democratic values of journalism in West Germany.

Denazification procedures and Nazi discourse in the semi-public space[19]

Denazification was a legal and administrative process primarily with the purpose of removing Nazis and others opposed to Allied aims from public office, from the economy and from positions of power and responsibility, so its domain is public space. It was not immediately directed against language, although possessing Nazi or militaristic books was forbidden, and street and other topographical names were also 'denazified' (cf. Bein and Vogel 1995: 150–4). But, the process of denazification inevitably entailed the recalling and perpetuation not just of ranks, institutions, formal and informal bodies associated with Nazism, such as the *HJ*, *BDM*, *Jungvolk*, *Pimpfe*, *Winterhilfswerk* (*WHW*), but also of the attitudes of the speakers towards them, their *Gesinnung*. This had been anticipated by Carl Brinitzer in his pocket dictionary for Allied servicemen:

> The Third Reich has produced a new language, which is sometimes confused by those who know no other German, with the German language itself. [...] It is a rough and hard language, clumsy and unwieldy, an unmusical language, consisting of nothing but an arbitrary sequence of sounds. As is the Nazi language, so are the Nazis [...] Nazi German will disappear. But these words will still be heard for decades in the law courts of each of the United Nations, and in all sorts of papers and official documents [...] The history of the Third Reich will be studied. Out of a forgotten world, out of some far distant, sunken world of National-Socialism, the fossilized linguistic monsters will have to be dug up. (1945: 7–9)

Beside this ostensible continuity – some terms have become more associated with Nazism after the war – there are obvious discontinuities and innovations in the procedures and mechanisms for eradicating the Nazi system, although some words and phrases used for this cleansing sound themselves suspiciously 'Nazi-like': words like *austilgen, ausmerzen, ausrotten, Bereinigung, Säuberung*! Positive and negative associations have been lent to some terms which have been, and still are, used to shock and attract attention. Günter Grass recently spoke of the '*Entartung* der deutschen Presse' and called his

---

19   See, for example: Vollnhals (1993); and Henke and Woller (1993).

reviewers *Scharfrichter*, apparently in reminiscence of the Nazi judge Eissler and his ilk. *Der Spiegel* (Nr. 13, 2007: 157) suspects Grass of using lexical associations with Nazism to depict himself as a victim of persecution because of his recently revealed membership of the Waffen-SS ('Grass schleicht sich ins Lager der Opfer', ibid. p. 154). Apparently, the term *entarten*, especially in *entartete Kunst* 'degenerate art' was not immediately identified as a Nazi term after the war. Like most other vocabulary used by the Nazis for their own purposes it was derivative, in this case from earlier and semi-technical usage within genetics/ animal breeding, but also as a term for perceived sexual deviance (Skinner 1999: ii, 100–1). It was even applied uncritically to the 'verwahrloste Jugend', or lost generation after the war (Hahn 1995: 213). But it has become taboo in some contexts, and, ironically, in 1965 Grass had himself objected to its use by Ludwig Erhard to criticize contemporary German art as 'decadent'.[20] The post-war pre-occupation with Nazi usage involves, then, both the deconstruction and (re-)construction of discourses and the perspectives of their speakers. As Kämper points out, this must properly also include the usage of the victims of Nazi terror, for example in the language of the concentration camps.[21] At the same time, the construction of such discourse, and even the (apparent) reconstitution of a so-called 'Nazi language' may involve misunderstandings and distortions in good and bad faith: words and expressions used by the Nazis are held to be 'Nazi', whatever their origins, and whatever their contexts, and they are then invested with positive and negative associations; the collecting of these words in word-lists and dictionaries reinforces the process, e.g. by Schmitz-Berning (2000). In this way, to refer to those works of art which the Nazis dismissed as worthless by their formulation *entartete Kunst* can be a form of recognition for those artists, identifying them as a historical group

20   Grass (1990, 119). Typically, Grass objects to other 'Nazi words', but those he quotes, *durchführen*, *ausmerzen* and *volklich*, are not listed in Schmitz-Berning (2000) in that form, moreover, *volklich*, as opposed to the common, discredited *völkisch*, is expressly said to be rare by Seidel and Seidel-Slotty (1961, esp. p. 95), and an exactly parallel Danish form *folkelig* has no negative overtones. See also Stötzel (1989).

21   Kämper (2005: 492). For Kämper, this usage of the victims can only be established as *Schulddiskurs* through a retrospective analysis, since the victims were conscious of the illegal and inhumane treatment by those directly carrying it out, without necessarily asking the more abstract questions of guilt and responsibility and culpability under natural justice (pp. 492–3).

and perhaps even dignifying their status as anti-Nazi. On the other hand, to apply the words *entartete Kunst* to later or contemporary artists is clearly taboo, defamatory and ill-intentioned and provocative. Intention and context are all-important in determining how the words are used, and often presuppose (and to an extent even create) 'a Nazi language' *post-hoc*.

Denazification itself – *Entnazifizierung* – is a new word introduced by the Allies (cf. Wember 1991) to mean a purge of all compromised individuals from public office, so far as this was possible: since there were according to some sources as many as 13 million card-carrying members of the Nazi Party, the task was formidable. Among competing designations were: *Denazifikation, Entnazisieren,*[22] *Entnazifizieren, Reeducation, Umerziehung, Wiedererziehung, Neuerziehung, Rückerziehung, Umbildung, Umstimmung* ('reconstruction'). The term *Entnazifizierung* is 'asymmetric', because no 'positive' **nazifizieren* 'nazify' existed under the NS regime,[23] instead the Nazis had used *arisieren*, 'Aryanize', or occasionally *germanisieren* for the theft of Jewish property and the removal of Jewish control of businesses, which might explain why

---

22   Rare: see *NHK* Nr. 12, 08.08.1945: 3; also in *Neuer Zürcher Zeitung* 17 May 1945, see Falkenberg (1989: 16).

23   Apparently the word *Nazi* was not used by the Nazis themselves in public. It has been compared with other pejorative political terms like *Sozi* for *Sozialist*, but also with the south German/ Bavarian use of such hypocoristic suffixes in a more familiar and not necessarily negative way, e.g. *Spezi* from *Spezialfreund*. The *NHK* Nr. 47, 14.06.1946, p. 3, does have a heading *Plünderung und Nazifizierung*, and the Nazi criminal Seyß-Inquart is accused by the French prosecutor Debenest at the Nürnberg War Tribunal of attempting to nazify – *nazifizieren* – the Dutch. However, in his response, Seyß-Inquart uses the words *germanisieren, arisieren*. 'Germanisiert habe ich die Niederlande überhaupt nicht.' (*Nürnberger Prozeß* 1949: Bd. XVI, p. 87, 12. Juni 1946). It seems that the use of the ('back-formation' from *Entnazifizierung*) *Nazifizierung* is a projection from a non-Nazi perspective. He also diverted attention from the deportation and murder of Jews from the Netherlands by interpreting 'Germanisierung' as 'Verdeutschung', which he denied was necessary: 'Wenn wir von Germanisierung gesprochen haben, haben wir nicht an *Verdeutschung* gedacht, sondern an eine politische und kulturelle Zusammenfassung der sogenannten "Germanischen Völker" unter gegenseitiger Gleichberechtigung'. (Prozeß 1949: Bd. XV, pp. 701–2, 10. Juni 1946). However, the principal French prosecutor, M. François de Menthon, noted that this 'Germanisierung' and 'Nazifizierung' based on Nazi race mythology differed from the earlier 'Pangermanismus' by involving the removal of rights from, and physical destruction of so-called inferior races (Prozeß 1949: Bd. V, p. 460).

denazisieren, with obvious and perhaps unfortunate similarity to these two terms, failed to catch on; however, note that the Nazi *entjuden, Entjudung* equally appear to anticipate *Entnazifizierung*. Of course, *Entnazifizierung* might also evoke *desinfizieren*, or *infizieren* and the pathological metaphors which qualified the murder of the Jews – including *judenfrei*, on the analogy of *keimfrei* – this formation was also transferred to the denazification process itself, and the *NHK* reported (Nr. 4, 19.06.1945: 2): 'Münchener Stadtverwaltung nazifrei'.

The categories of complicity, for what Alexander and Margarete Mitscherlich termed a *Schuld der Handlung* and a *Schuld der Duldung* (Mitscherlich and Mitscherlich 1977), were naturally new, but it must be said that despite the US *Gesetz zur Befreiung vom Nationalsozialismus und Militarismus* and *Directives 24* and *38* of the Allied Control Commission in 1946, there were considerable differences in the way the denazification process was carried out in the four Allied zones, and the advent of the Cold War brought its curtailment.[24] Theodor Eschenburg draws attention to the differing understanding of commonly used terms like *demokratisch*, which was vague and compromising, or *antifaschistisch* which in the Russian zone meant 'anti-anti-Communist', since *faschistisch* implied opposition to Communism. Unsurprisingly, therefore, interpretations of denazification diverged:

> *Entnazifizierung* bedeutete im Sinn der Amerikaner vorübergehende Absetzung und Verhaftung (automatischen Arrest) von Mitgliedern der Partei und deren Oganisationen sowie ihr verbundenen Personen. Die endgültige Bestrafung sollte nach einem Gerichtsurteil erfolgen. Nach sowjetischen Vorstellungen konnte Entnazifizierung aber zu Enteignung ohne Urteil führen. Die konträren Gerichtsorganisationen in Rußland und in den westlichen Ländern schufen die unterschiedlichsten Verfahrens- und Entscheidungsarten. Nach den politischen Grundsätzen des Potsdamer Abkommens waren alle Personen, die den alliierten Zielen feindlich gegenüberstanden, von ihren Posten zu entfernen sowie die, die für die Besatzung und ihre Ziele gefährlich waren, zu verhaften und zu internieren. Jeder Nichtkommunist konnte in der Sowjetzone unter diese Bestimmung fallen, jeder Kommunist in der englischen und amerikanischen. Die Sowjetunion hatte kein Interesse an exakter terminologischer Unterscheidung,

---

24   For details, see Benz (1999: 114–17). The Soviet Occupied Zone (*SBZ*) formally ended denazification in February 1948, restoring voting rights to minor Nazis in 1949. In the West, the newly formed Federal Republic followed suit in 1951.

die angelsächsischen Mächte wagten nicht, sie zu fordern. Die weite Fassung war eine Blankovollmacht. (Eschenburg 1983: 51)

In the French zone, 'la dénazification' was viewed as 'un processus culturel et non pas seulement comme l'entreprise d'épuration qui a consisté à éloigner de la vie publique et économique les cadres nazis' (Vaillant 1981: 12). The categories of participation and complicity used in the process of purging in the three western zones were: I. *Hauptschuldige*; II. *Belastete*; III. *Minderbelastete*; IV. *Mitläufer*; V. *Entlastete*. The first of these, for major criminals, entailed mandatory removal or debarring from public office and probable indictment, whereas the second, covering activists, militarists and beneficiaries of the Nazi regime meant discretionary removal, especially on adverse recommendations. The last three categories depended on often arbitrary circumstances.

In the West, the machinery of denazification was placed in the hands of Germans, so far as possible, who formed tribunals, so-called *Spruchkammern*, to examine individual cases of involvement in Nazism and militarism, while the most serious crimes against humanity were examined by professional judges, notably at Nürnberg. So the process of denazification involved both the continuity of prolonging the preoccupation with Nazi structures, terms and ideas and attitudes to them – this time to extirpate them – and also new bureaucratic structures, a sub-discourse of denazifying. One, probably timeless element of continuity was the practice of denunciation, even to similarities in the text-types involved, the mostly anonymous *Denunziantenbrief* (cf. Wells 1999). Those who had denounced fellow citizens for being Jewish or having insulted Nazism or having listened to foreign radio stations or other unpatriotic acts were now themselves denounced to the tribunals. This prompted an early contribution to the *Frankfurter Hefte* 1. Jg., 2, 1946 by a Dr G., in which the act of denouncing is bitterly attacked, again, partly in the same emotive and pathological style found in Nazi writings:

> Die *Schädlinge* müssen gesellschaftlich und politisch *ausgemerzt* werden. Wenn sie sich verbergen, um Zeit zum Überdauern zu gewinnen, damit sie *ihr Handwerk eines Tages erneuern* könnten, soll eine *klare, männliche Aktion* – notfalls in Form einer namentlich gezeichneten Anzeige – *sie ans Licht schaffen*; sie müssen *gefaßt* werden. Aber Mißbrauch der Politik zu privaten Zwecken hat aufzuhören...; ... Ob es einen Wert hätte, auf einen der vielen Fragebogen die zusätzliche Frage zu setzen: 'Haben Sie jemals denunziert?

Wenn ja: wen, wann, warum und bei welcher Dienststelle?' (p. 7: *Recht und Denunziantentum* [Verf.Dr.G.]; italics mine)[25]

This *Fragebogen* was introduced in the American zone, prompting a bitter account from a conservative perspective by Ernst von Salomon who used the 131 questions as the framework for an autobiographical account of his experiences and (rough) treatment by the Americans who interned him and his wife Ille (Salomon 1951). Moreover, the purgation-process itself – a *Säuberung* or *politische Bereinigung* (*der Wirtschaft*) (Bein and Vogel, 1995: 132) – was sometimes alluded to as a *Charakterwäsche* (Schrenck-Notzing 1965*)*, since the *Spruchkammern* could exculpate or minimize the penalties for lesser offences. Indeed, Lutz Niethammer describes these tribunals as *Mitläuferfabriken*, factories churning out relatively minor offenders (Niethammer 1972/1982). Klemperer also records his exasperation with the many requests for exculpation and exoneration, *Leumundszeugnisse*, known popularly as *Persilscheine*, people asked of him ('Widerwärtig, dieses Winseln um Zeugnisse' 1996: vol. 2, 876). Other colloquial terms included the *weiße Weste*, as opposed to the *braune Vergangenheit*, or *braune Flecken*, and the whole denazification process was termed an *Entbräunung* with improbable antonymic associations to *Bräunung*.

The Duden entry for *entnazifizieren* (Duden 1999: 1043) quotes *Der Spiegel* (1966, Nr. 21: 73); 'Wiewohl SS-Angehöriger ... und NSDAP-Mitglied ..., wurde Kurt Krittel zum "Mitläufer" entnazifiziert.' Whereas for the Nazis *Germanisierung* was primarily a process of removal and replacement of individuals by other individuals, because it was racist, based on having the 'right' blood, the *Entnazifizierung*, again in this respect asymmetrical, did by implication allow for re-habilitation and re-education through a change of 'Gesinnung'.

There was considerable discontent with the denazification processes, because the American *Fragebogen* (*USFET*-directive of 07.07.1945) and later *Meldebogen* ('Gesetz Nr. 104 zur Befreiung von Nationalsozialismus und Militarismus', 05.04.1946), and the operation of the *Spruchkammern* were slow and bureaucratic. Those languishing in internment or without jobs, pensions

---

25   Widmer (1966) analysed a corresponding continuity of style and diction in the journal *Der Ruf.*

or housing complained at the time taken to process their case: but there were 13 million *Meldebögen* alone to be processed. A common claim was that the small fry were pilloried, while the major offenders were allowed to go free: *Die Großen läßt man laufen/ Und die Kleinen hängt man auf*, which remains a cliché. The phrase *Das Vierte Reich* which had been used subversively in Nazi Germany to imply that the Third Reich would not last for ever, was now sometimes applied to Mil.-Gov. to mark it as truly the successor to the Nazi regime. Disaffection was rife. Subsequently, the denazification process has been compared with the de-Stasification after the fall of the Wall in 1989, and here again, continuity with a (post-)Nazi past is being insinuated.

While it is not the contention here that there was a distinct 'linguistic variety' of Nazi German, a weaker formulation without an indefinite article – 'recognizably Nazi language' – might cover certain Nazi-held ideas, for example, a nationalistic racism expressed in biological terms was identified by the defeated and demoralized German population as typically (but often not exclusively) 'Nazi'. Hitler himself rebuts the false assumption that 'Germanization' involves language, since according to him 'Volkstum' and Rasse' are inherent only in 'the blood' which is immutable (1943: 428–9). But there was inevitably some continuity of usage because of the whole forensic process of purging the public space of the vestiges of the Nazi regime; there was also a criminalization, with more or less justification, of all Party members and many other Germans. Although before 1945 there had been collections of words drawn from Nazi discourse by contemporaries (Klemperer) and jokes that satirized the Nazi usage, it was, it appears, left to post-war speakers to supplement this discourse *post-hoc* by identifying 'Paläonazismen' for their own purposes. Typically, the aim was to condemn those who were using 'Nazi' vocabulary and hence 'Nazi' thought-processes, as an act of moral cleansing. Here real and supposed 'Nazi' terms from *Abstammungsnachweis, durchraßt*[26] and *Entartung* to *Selektion, Kinderlandverschickung*, or *Zuchtwart* (often pre-dating Nazism) become taboo and are given 'indicator status' to attack political opponents. But in the case of Neo-Nazi groups the words constitute links to what their adherents suppose to be/ to have been 'Nazi' language and symbols, including, improbably, the wearing of 'LONSDALE'-sweat-shirts,

26 Used by Edmund Stoiber in 1991, it became the 'Unwort des Jahres'! (Schlosser 1995: 200).

(un)suitably displayed under jackets to read 'NSDA[P]'! Trivial and crude though these symbolic uses of 'language' may be,[27] they constitute an instrumentalization (and reinterpretation) of the history of German and create a spurious and occasionally disturbing and exaggerated sense of a linguistic continuity which must inevitably exist in the vast majority of everyday communication in the semi-private and private spheres.

Black Marketeering discourse – illegal activities in semi-private space

Since everyone was affected by the problems created by the collapse of Germany, everyone was forced to resort to illegal activities one way or another to keep body and soul together. Between 1945 and 1947 the British Zone alone took in 9 million refugees of all kinds, raising the population from 14.4 to 23.4 million, thus comprising some 55% of the total population of all three western zones, and creating a logistical nightmare. Naturally, there were continuities also in the mechanisms for controlling and rationing foodstuffs and goods in scarce supply, including the rationing categories into which consumers were divided. Most of these regulations derived from measures introduced by the Nazis in the course of the war, although the punishments meted out for those caught infringing them were less severe. Of 13,087 people tried by the *Volksgerichtshof* between 1939 and 1944, 5,142 were executed (Boelcke 1986: 12). The *Normalverbraucher* (still recalled in the phrase 'Otto Normalverbraucher') were those with no other regular means of income or sustenance who depended on the allocation of calories they were entitled to purchase according to their ration-cards: the allocations seldom exceeded 1,500 calories per day, and sometimes sank below 900. The *Selbstversorger* were usually farmers or others with direct access to supply: the label was perhaps unfortunate in implying ruthless self-interest. Additionally, there

27   For the occurrence and instrumentalization of dubious theories of Sprachkritik ('fragwürdige[n] Reflexionstopoi') in public space, and their possible effects on public opinion, see Mayer (2002: 253–4 and passim).

were *Teilselbstversorger*, with access to allotments, for instance, and special provisions were made for some workers by *Sondermarken* and *Schwer(st) arbeiterzulagen*. These *Marken/Sondermarken*, *Raucherkarten* and *Erlaubnisscheine*, such as *Holzscheine* or *Pilzscheine*, were often eagerly sought after on the Black Market. The allocated items themselves were mostly given a bureaucratic designation (cf. Schlosser 1995: 197) which sometimes sounded ridiculously convoluted: *Brennmaterial/ Brennstoffe* (*Kohle, Koks, Bricketts*); *Hausbrand*, which included wood; *Spinnstoffe*, for a range of textile goods; *Fette* – butter and margarine; *Süßstoffe* – which included *Ersatzstoffe* for sugar. *Ersatz* itself became associated with many items in short supply, notably with coffee with which it sometimes became synonymous, when this was not known as *Muckefuck*. The various *Ernährungs- Wirtschafts-* and *Wohnungsämter* placed announcements in the press regarding the *Zuteilungsperioden*, the qualifications for *Zulagen*, etc., while new arrivals, displaced persons and refugees were referred to as *Zugänge*. All of these terms formed and informed everyday discourse in the semi-public space as people struggled to survive and provide for their families. Since contacts were often the basis for getting work or access to food or ration coupons, *Vitamin-B* was a common term: *B* for *Beziehungen*, an example of the metaphorical and literal interaction of public rationing and semi-public survival.

Although the summer of 1945 was glorious, it heralded a cold winter, and in 1946–7, an even colder one: people needed to find shelter, to find food and to keep warm. Evidently, the official sources of supply were inadequate, and this massively encouraged an already flourishing Black Market that spread forms of language across the population which were not new, but which had hitherto been restricted to very limited circles of those who dealt in illegal goods, in theft, extortion, prostitution, drugs and fraud, as well as to the police, customs and excise branches that combated these crimes. But now all classes and kinds of people were involved in illegal acts simply to survive, as well as to profiteer. The sociology of the Black Market could offer surprises: in 1946 a Black Market ring was broken up in Wiesbaden whose members included Agathe Prinzessin von Preußen, Elisabeth Prinzessin von Preußen and Luise Henriette Schmalz, geb. Prinzessin von Preußen (Boelcke 1986: 199). Individuals recoiled from the humiliation of thieving, as in Margret Bouveri's reportage 'Ich stehle Holz', or Kyra Stromberg's account of an expedition to 'Zeche Greif' ('the grabbing pit'), where respectable members

of the community encountered each other shamefacedly as they stole from
coal trucks (Scherpe 1983: 44): the term *Kohlen-Stoppeln* 'abgefallene Kohlen
auflesen' (Wolff 1982–3: 32) might seem more euphemistic and even biblical, evoking gleaning in fields of stubble, than the more accurate and brutal
term *Kohlenklau*. For even middle-classes were forced to pilfer, to sell what
they had – and sometimes themselves – *schwarzvögeln/Schwarzvögelei* was
common, and venereal disease was rife, including among the occupying troops.
As anti-syphilis measures, Allied wives and families with young, pre-school
children were shipped to Germany from September 1946, but the authorities
also launched campaigns to promote the use of contraceptives to avoid V.D.,
including, in the American Zone, books of matches with a young *Fräulein*
on them by the name of *Veronika Dankeschön* and instructions to 'use cover'.
The name *Veronika* for 'prostitute' remained current for some time, beside
less complimentary terms – *Amiliebchen, Tommyliebchen, Amine, Amisette,
Ami-Flittchen, Ami-Hure, Frolleins, Negerbraut, Neger-Hur*, and in the Russian Zone and Austria *Iwanelle, Russenhur(e)*.

Black Marketeering is probably always found in times of crisis, and certainly the vocabulary was not new. The use of black – *der schwarze Markt
/der Schwarzmarkt* – was distinguished from the legal 'white' market and
the semi-illegal 'grey' market by involving bartering with goods restricted
by rationing or acquired dishonestly. Consequently the shady business was
conducted in particular places where illegality might flourish and yet where
there could be a measure of safety in numbers, since parties to illegal transactions were always open to pressure via blackmail, force or simple theft with
or without violence. Bus- and train-stations provided places where people
could loiter, apparently waiting for trains or buses, but approaching passers-
by to make deals, as drug dealers still do at terminuses of all kinds today. In
Bremen the tram conductor used to call out the railway station 'correctly' as
'Schwarzer Markt' (Lenzner 1988: 76), while the *Karolinenplatz* in Munich
was once referred to as the *Kalorienplatz* (Wolff 1982–3: Anhang). Accounts
of the Black Market draw on contemporary newspaper articles or essays,
such as Heinz Rümelin's collection of documentary essays *So lebten wir... Ein
Querschnitt durch 1947*, or Karl Scherpe's later study of post-war 'Reportage'
(Scherpe 1982–3), on works of literature (see esp. Siegfried Lenz, Heinrich
Böll), academic studies (such as Boelcke (1986), Wolff (1982–3)), or are based
on eyewitnesses, *Zeitzeugen*, or autobiography (such as Lenzner (1988)), or

fictional accounts using documentary research, as in the TV series and book *Die Magermilchbande* by Frank Baer, or even on films. Periodically exhibitions like the fiftieth-anniversary exhibition revive memories of the dwindling number of *Zeitzeugen* (Bein and Vogel 1995).

The determinative element *schwarz-* was added to many verbs – *schwarzhandeln, schwarzfahren, schwarzarbeiten* – including the improbable forms *schwarzbuttern*, 'to make or sell butter illegally', *schwarzbrennen* 'to make illegal spirits',[28] and *schwarzschlachten* 'to slaughter animals without declaring them', which gave rise to the English translation 'black-slaughtering'. The adverb or determinative prefix is still common today, for instance in *schwarz(fern)sehen*, 'to watch TV without a licence'. As Thaddäus Troll noted (Rümelin 1948: 62), the adjective/ adverb *schwarz* can be added to any noun or activity to qualify items acquired or supplied illegally.

Various sub-professions of the *Schwarzhändlerei* evolved, from small-fry (*kleine Schieber*), to the *Schieber en gros* (large-scale dealers), to con-men or so-called *Spritzer* who pretended to buy in bulk, pocketed the wares and then refused to pay up, threatening to call in the police (cf. *Der Spiegel*, 24/01/1947, 19: 'Beruf: Spritzer. Arbeitsteilung in dunklen Geschäften'), to *Schlepper* or *Schnapper* who attracted the customers, arranged the deals and then took the punters to the bargaining place; this last category included young boys pimping for their mothers and sisters. *Aufspringer* jumped onto lorries and trucks and threw down the cargo to waiting accomplices. The transactions were *Kompensationsgeschäfte* where goods were paid for 'in kind', but foreign cigarettes were the principal currency – *die Zigaretten-Währung* – often *Lucky-Strike*, *Chesterfield* or sold by the pack or *Stange Ami, Amis*. At one point, an *Aktive* ('an unsmoked new cigarette') cost 12 RM, as opposed to

---

28   Sometimes, in the Hannover area, by fermenting the remains of sugar-beet (*Stippes*) in a broth (*Maische*) to be distilled, sometimes, improbably, by 'refining' V2-fuel: see Schmid (1951: 111–12): 'V2-Sprit: ... Da brauchte man das Benzol nur durch ein paar Stunden Luftdurchblasen und Kohlefiltern zu entfernen, und fertig war das schönste Feuerwasser! ... Gott strafe England und Euch Unabkömmliche (denn wieder schöpfen diese Landwirte das Fett ab: im Kriege waren sie mehr zu Hause als bei uns draußen (*sc.* im Feld CJW), und jetzt fressen sie sich auch wieder als Einzige satt, und nehmen im Tausch der restlichen Bevölkerung das Letzte weg.) Neulich hat einer zu Grete gesagt, als sie mit einer Kaffeebüchse ging: ihm fehlte nur noch n Teppich für n Kuhstall! Krepieren müßten die Schweine! Alle Bauern...!'

a German *Dreherburg* valued at 8 RM. Coffee and cameras were also sought after: *die Leica-Währung*, while the US *Scrip-Dollars* could be used in *PX* stores (*Post Exchange*) in the US zone.

The population – possibly as many as 40% of all Germans – who were dealing operated in semi-private space because of the illegality of the transactions. The 'black' discourse is generally conducted in typical fashion (Wolff 1982–3: 76–91) and is characterized by its illicit, secretive quality, conducted hastily, often in whispered form, with elliptical utterances that remain ambiguous and non-committal until the last possible moment when the deal is done. The complicity involved extends to the use of the familiar '*du*'-pronoun. Siegfried Lenz notes that complete strangers shook hands:

> wie alte Bekannten oder Komplizen...der Schwarze Markt verband die Zeitgenossen in einer ganz bestimmten Art von Rabentraulichkeit. Er rief tatsächlich etwas wie eine schwarze Familiarität hervor. (1964: 34–5)

Doubtless this was also part of the attempt to mislead any authorities who might be watching. At the same time, the deals are conducted often in a semi-private environment; public enough for there to be some element of protection, yet the business involves essentially private and secret activities.

The vocabulary is obviously regional in some instances. The terms of bargaining could vary; *maggeln, makeln* was more northern, in particular Rhenish word (Cologne), often associated with *schmuggeln*, but *kunkeln* also occurs, with variants, for instance in Berlin, *kungeln, Kungelei*. These words show morphological and syntactic development, e.g. *etwas heranmaggeln, etwas erkunkeln*, 'durch Verhandeln erwerben', and *kunkeln* is associated with other words: *im Dunkeln ist gut kunkeln, munkeln und kunkeln* etc. and conveys the illicit, clandestine nature of the activity. In the south, the verb *fuggern, fuckeren*, nouns *Fuggerei, Fuckerer* etc., from the late medieval Augsburg banking family occurred.

Other forms are more obviously from *Rotwelsch*, the language of the criminal twilight or underworld, like *Masematte machen* ('to burgle') from the Rhineland (Wolff 1982–3: 120) which became widespread as the population were constrained to resort to illegal forms of bartering and smuggling in order to survive, words like *meschugge* 'mad', *Pinke* 'money', *Sores, schieben, Schieber* ('push', 'pusher'). An article in the *Rheinische Post* from 1946 about a gang, the Hellweg-Bande, notes: 'Schon das ganze Vokabular dieser

Burschen entstammt der Verbrecherwelt. Da wird von 'Sore' [for 'goods'] gesprochen, von 'Bullen' und 'Polente' [for 'police']; but this language was not restricted to young people.[29] Even attempts to gather food for bartering or personal consumption by travelling on *Hamsterfahrten* were illegal, so that das *Gehamsterte* was not always brought home, having been confiscated in some *Razzia* ('police raid') or another.

Throngs of *Hamsterer*, their knapsacks bulging, went 'hamstering', often to exchange whatever they could get (*verhamstern*), conveniently at the bus and train terminuses. Trains, the favoured means of reaching the more outlying and therefore less stripped areas, had various popular names: the *Kartoffelzug* ran from the Ruhrgebiet to Niedersachsen, scavengers from Ludwigshafen, Pirmasens and Speyer areas alighted from the *Äppel-Expreß*, the *Interzonenzug* Osnabrück-Magdeburg-Berlin was known as the *Fisch-Expreß*, while trains in the other direction were called *Seidenstrumpf-Expreß*. But many more people went by night and illegally across the demarcated and patrolled, but not in those days mined, borders: the popular phrase *schwarz über die grüne Grenze gehen* referred to illegal, clandestine and nocturnal excursions simultaneously. There was considerable friction between the town and country populations, since life was generally easier for the 'Bauern', who were then accused of cheating and stuffing themselves at the expense of the suffering population of 'Normalverbraucher'. Denunciatory letters in the police files confirm this, for example a 'Bauernball' at Damme in January 1948 was extravagant:

> Die Bauerntöchter hatten für diesen Ball nur lange Abendkleider und wurde der Stoff
> für so ein Kleid mit 6–8 Pfd Fett bezahlt. Die Schneiderinnen hier in Damme konnten
> den Ansturm nicht bewältigen. Die Gestaltung des Abends bestand nur aus Saufen und
> Fressen, ja man feierte sogar hinter verschlossenen Türen. Große Mengen von Rinder-
> und Schweinebraten, Würsten usw. riesige Berge von Kuchen und den feinsten Butter-
> creamtorten waren vorhanden ... Es ist eine Schande, wo 90% der deutschen Bevölkerung
> am verhungern ist, das[s] es nicht möglich ist, den Bauern richtig zu erfassen ... [Nds.
> 600 Ac. 45/55 Nr. 1].

Loss of self-esteem, fear and degradation lamed the population and left them sometimes in self-destructive mood, particularly the menfolk. In the

---

29 Hahn (1995: 213), some of this vocabulary (*Bulle, Polente* for 'police') surfaces later in the 1968 student revolt.

initial plundering and raping by the victorious armies – also in the American zone (cf. Salomon 1951: 635) – some kind of self-loathing seemed to manifest itself: in the Berchtesgadener Land there was even some satisfaction that older, respectable women were being raped (*Von Hitler zu Adenauer* 1976: 261). In the anonymous diary of a woman in Berlin, the remarkable author speaks of 'sleeping food into the house' (*Essen anschlafen*), and uses the compounds *Majorszucker, Schändungsschuhe, Plünderwein* and *Klaukohle*.[30] In a rebuttal of the attempts promoted by Karl Jaspers and others to get back to a period of German before Nazism and somehow reassert the positive values of the culture, Lenzner is bitterly dismissive in his Black Market memoirs:

> in der Sprache der damaligen Generation. Nicht nur Zeitgenossen, auch Leser aus der heute jungen Generation werden jener Ausdrucks- und Denkweise mit Betroffenheit folgen ... Von anfänglichem Tauschen und Hamstern streifen die Aktivitäten schließlich kriminelle Bereiche: Spiegelbild der eskalierenden Entwicklung. Goethes Zeiten sind dahin.[31]

This is echoed by the views from inside and outside the country, from Adorno's famous dictum that there could be no poetry after Auschwitz, to the more extreme view of George Steiner, that words like *spritzen* were no longer useable,[32] while Borchert's *Das ist unser Manifest* asserted that the language of the returning soldiers was not beautiful: 'Nein, unser Wörterbuch, das ist nicht schön. Aber dick. Und es stinkt. Bitter wie Pulver. Sauer wie Steppensand. Scharf wie Scheiße. Und laut wie Gefechtslärm': the high-flown phrases of the Nazis were replaced with a coarser rhetoric.[33] This applied to other literary texts: Urs Widmer (1966) examines the literary output of the *Junge Generation* of writers born circa 1915 and later who began writing under the

---

30 Cf. Phillips (1982: 22); *Eine Frau in Berlin. Tagebuchaufzeichnungen*, 1959; repr. Eichborn Verlag, 2003.
31 Lenzner 1988: 15. But Lenzner cynically leaves his text with Goethe quotations from *Reinecke Fuchs*.
32 Handt 1964: 12–13. As correctives (in the same volume): Betz, 'Nicht der Sprecher, die Sprache lügt?' 38–41, and Marcel Reich-Ranicki, 'Nicht der Schimmer eines Beweises', 42–3.
33 Borchert 1959: 312. Cf. Widmer (1966) who contrasts this desire for crude, obscene, yet somehow unvarnished and frank expression with an escapist, old-fashioned and sentimentalizing strain of language that also represents a reaction against the Nazi past.

NS regime and who now recoiled from its tainted language and 'Phrasen-
haftigkeit': 'Die Sprache von 1945 wird, so wie sie ist, als krank empfunden'
(Widmer 1966: 18). Writers including Wolfgang Borchert, Heinrich Böll,
Wolfdietrich Schnurre, Alfred Andersch, Ilse Aichinger and other members
of the *Gruppe 47* called for a break with the past and a new beginning from
scratch – 'tabula rasa' – which presumed a discontinuity, and earned them
the name *Kahlschläger* or *Kahlschlägler* (Widmer 1966: 14).

The terrible winter of 1946–7, with temperatures in the minus 30s, and
thousands dead from cold – while bonfires were lit on the ice of the *Stadtpark*
in Braunschweig for British troops to skate round! – caused people to resort
to desperate measures to keep warm. In Cologne some 18,000 hundredweight
of brickettes was stolen every day (Bein and Vogel 1995: 285). Cardinal Archbishop Frings notoriously gave his name to a term for stealing coal from coal
trucks (*fringsen*), since he declared from the pulpit in his New Year's speech
that such theft was 'Mundraub', that is, justifiable through extreme necessity.
Klauen, especially *Kohlenklau* was not classed as stealing if it was for personal
use. The Black Market effectively ended in 1948, on 20 June, 'Tag X', with
the *Währungsreform*, but the 'moral damage' had been done, although not
without some positive effects, since a sense of civil disobedience had sometimes been provoked.

Conclusions

Hardly surprisingly, the public, semi-public – and by inference the private,
domestic – spaces in which German was used post-war all show considerable continuity with what went before. The discontinuity arises in the public
arena, where the regime change was radical and necessitated a new discourse
of administration in several languages beside German, a discourse which
was progressively replaced as Germans in West and East regained control of
their affairs. The 'Institutionen' were new (Schlosser 1995), and for Kämper
(2007: 485) so is the 'Schulddiskurs' which could only come into being after
the collapse of Nazi-Germany in 1945 and which reflects a 'Phase sprachlichen Umbruchs' in the first post-war decade. With hindsight, a number

of subsequent trends in the interrelationships among German varieties may be interpreted against this background. The 'interpretations of possible consequences' are scarcely capable either of proof or disproof, at best they are plausible – sufficient – whether they are necessary will remain a matter of opinion. There appear to be two areas of effect, a more general one affecting the German-speaking communities as a whole, and a more differentiated set of factors distinguishing West and East Germany and the other German-speaking states.

First, a general and understandable desire to emphasize, indeed create a linguistic break with the immediate past, ranging from at times naive attempts to pillory former Nazi usage, which in the early stages were often couched in the same radicalized pathological imagery of disease and eradication used by Nazis and others before them, to less direct effects, such as the desire for new modes of dress and speech, especially among the young who, where possible, emulated American popular culture in film, music, dress and behaviour. This continued into the 'rebellious' 1960s and 1970s where many cultural influences on West Germany in particular came from America: anti-war protest, civil liberties, sexual and women's liberation, gay rights and so forth. Paradoxically these American-influenced trends co-exist with emancipation from American domination and increasing criticism of the continuing American military presence. But commercial, military, and intellectual influences still received a cultural boost from America. However, the general loosening of morals and language under the privations of the immediate post-war had both disseminated linguistic features of the vulgar and coarse language of the black marketeering world across much of the society in the West and prompted a backlash against this in the Adenauer period. Then, there were efforts to impose more 'civilized' standards, to salvage an acceptable national identity and to revert to mores and language of the past, as well as to traditional roles in the relations between the sexes such as the woman's place in the home, a reversion to the position pre-dating the Nazi excesses, to expunge and to some extent cover up, rather than confront the crimes.

Secondly, the German-speaking states differed. Austria, Switzerland and Luxemburg, all in their different ways and for more, and sometimes less valid reasons have sought to distance themselves from Germany and all things German, including the German language. This has perhaps been one over-riding effect of National Socialism. Austria's 'cultural cringe' reflecting a sense of linguistic inferiority on the part of Austrian speakers in relation to standard German speakers of German has a long history (Clyne 1995: 31), dating perhaps from the Empress Maria Theresia in the eighteenth century, when Gottsched's Leipzig German grammar was introduced in Austrian schools. But after the war Austria's position was quickly seen (indeed actually promoted) as that of the first victim of Nazism in 1938, and there were attempts to distance the state from Germany as far as possible, not least in order to avoid further political dismemberment by the Allies, especially the Russians. Even the German language of instruction used in the schools was for a time referred to not as 'Deutsch', but as the 'Unterrichtssprache' (see McVeigh 1988). Later, Austrian literary writers avoided the period 1934–45, which only reinforced the sense of discontinuity:

> Die spezifische Situation der literarischen Moderne in der unmittelbaren Nachkriegszeit mit den Etiketten 'Nullpunkt' oder 'Bruch' zu beschreiben, wäre also keineswegs verfehlt. Die literarische Moderne der 50er und 60er Jahre in Österreich stand, literaturhistorisch gesehen, in der der Nachfolge derjenigen Tendenzen der österreichischen Kultur, die den autoritären Ständestaat und die Diktatur Hitlers zwischen 1934 und 1945 auszurotten versuchten. (McVeigh 1988: 124–5)

Nevertheless, in both Austria and Switzerland, the print media retain essentially 'standard German' as the educated norm, and, not least because it is more widespread, editors in major German-publishing houses edit out local linguistic features (Ammon 1991). In Switzerland, a polyglot state, the majority German-speaking areas vigorously promote *Schwyzertüütsch*, much leavened by American borrowing for all the same culturally imperialistic reasons reflected in other European countries. However, less admirable aspects of Swiss political relations with the Nazi state in the past have also fostered antipathy to 'German-German'. In Luxemburg, which suffered Nazi occupation, the Rhenish Franconian dialect *Letzebuergesch* has been elevated to prominence as the official national language.

But not only regional variants of standard German have declined in popularity. Apparently, dialects on the Dutch side of the German–Dutch linguistic borders in the north have increasingly drifted away from the German dialects and become more oriented towards the hegemony of standard Dutch. Thus a 'dialect continuum' often cited as an example of the incongruence between linguistic and state boundaries is in fact being replaced by differentiation along state lines, which even a post-Schengen period of open borders might not reverse.[34] The same holds for the German–Danish situation in the north, although in both instances this may also reflect the general decline in the use of the dialect in favour of regional colloquial forms more closely linked to the overarching national standard varieties.

Thus, the ideational effects of political ideology and identity looked at in terms of continuity and discontinuity within a reified linguistic system appear to have palpable, if only partly intended effects on linguistic behaviours and consequently on the linguistic forms and features used in different societal spaces and varieties. This is most clearly seen in a period when both the vanquished and the victors alike were prone to impose monolithic interpretations on the speakers as 'Germans' and on the language they were using and the attitudes it was held to embody, although in fact, none of the discourses discussed here is, so far as it may be reconstructed at this remove of time, consistent, coherent, monolithic or in any way actually corresponding to all the perceptions of contemporary speakers. Nevertheless, it is surely not without legitimacy to try to understand trends and attitudes in the German-speaking areas today by looking at the early post-war conditions that shaped the first stages of the modern states, particularly the fragmented and now once more unified Germany. For diversity and differentiation have always characterized German, and they remain constants in 1945–50, whereas the supposed monolithic, coherent, system is an ideological, even totalitarian simplification. In the 'democratic' western zones, initial chaos reveals itself as the re-assertion of diversity in public, semi-public and semi-private spaces, often to the consternation of the Allies. In the East, control of the public space increasingly extends to semi-public, semi-private and even, thanks to the *Staatssicherheit*, into private space.

Finally, while the discourses discussed here do inform the histories of the different cohorts of most German speakers in the Federal Republic of Germany, the seven million or so immigrants whose pasts are not encumbered with the baggage of National Socialism (though there may be other issues) will facilitate a more distanced confrontation with the infamy of Nazism

34   See Kremer (2004: 3401): it is explicitly not stated that the now discernible 'sprachliche Bruchstelle' along the state boundary-line was caused by distancing from German because of Nazism and its 'Germanisierung'.

which is conducted less and less in linguistic terms. Whatever the eventual outcome of multiculturalism, which has come to constitute in all spaces a major break in continuity after the period 1945–50, for the linguistic historian the bewildering diversity of varieties in public, semi-public and private space – indeed, the constant re-drawing of their boundaries in the German media of communication – appears as a welcome escape from the totalitarian myth of a coherent, all-pervasive, controlling, reified, monolithic public form of German. It does not simplify the task of analysis.

References

Adler, H.G. (1955), *Theresienstadt 1941–1945. Das Antlitz einer Zwangsgemeinschaft*, Tübingen: J.C.B. Mohr (Paul Siebeck).

Ammon, U. (1991), *Die internationale Stellung der deutschen Sprache*, Berlin and New York: de Gruyter.

Baer, F. (1979), *Die Magermilchbande. Roman*, Hamburg: Albrecht Knaus Verlag.

Bein, R. and Vogel, B. (eds) (1995), *Nachkriegszeit. Das Braunschweiger Land 1945 bis 1950. Materialien zur Landesgeschichte*, Braunschweig: Döring. [Begleitbuch zur Ausstellung des Gymnasiums Neue Oberschule im Städtischen Museum Braunschweig vom 12. März bis 17. April 1995].

Benz, W. (ed.) (1999), *Deutschland unter alliierter Besatzung 1945–1949/55. Ein Handbuch*, Berlin: Akademie Verlag.

Berning, C. (1961–3), 'Die Sprache des Nationalsozialismus', *Zeitschrift für deutsche Wortforschung* 16 (1960) 71–118; 178–88; 17 (1961) 83–121; 171–82; 18 (1962) 108–18; 160–72; 19 (1963) 92–112.

Berning, C. (1964), *Vom 'Abstammungsnachweis' bis zum 'Zuchtwart'. Vokabular des Nationalsozialismus*, Berlin: de Gruyter.

Boelcke, W.A. (1986), *Der Schwarzmarkt 1945–1948: Vom Überleben nach dem Kriege*, Braunschweig: Westermann.

Borchert, W. (1949), *Das Gesamtwerk. Mit einem biographischen Nachwort von Bernhard Meyer-Marwitz*, Hamburg: Rowohlt.

Botting, D. (1986), *In the Ruins of the Reich*, London and Glasgow: Grafton.

Brinitzer, C. (1945), *Cassell's War and Post-War German Dictionary [...] With Foreword by N.F. Newsome*, London, Toronto, Melbourne and Sydney: Cassell and Company Ltd.

Clyne, M. (1995), *The German Language in a Changing Europe*, Cambridge: Cambridge University Press.

Dieckmann, W. (1983), 'Diskontinuität? Zur- unbefriedigenden sprachkritischen und sprachwissenschaftlichen Behandlung der Nachkriegssprache in Deutschland 1945–1949', in: *Nachkriegsliteratur in Westdeutschland*, 2, edited by J. Hermand, Berlin, Argument-Verlag, 89–100.

Deissler, D. (2004), *Die entnazifizierte Sprache. Sprachpolitik und Sprachregelung in der Besatzungszeit*, Frankfurt am Main: Peter Lang.

Der Prozess gegen die Hauptkriegsverbrecher vor dem Internationalen Militärgerichtshof. Veröffentlicht auf Weisung des Internationlen Militärgerichtshofes unter der Autorität des Obersten Kontrollrates für Deutschland, Nürnberg, 1947–9 [42 Bde].

Dodd, B. (1999), 'Down but not out: Dolf Sternberger's critique of "Sprachwissenschaft"', in: *From Classical Shades to Vickers Victorious: Shifting Perspectives in British German Studies*, edited by S. Giles and P. Graves, Bern and Berlin: Peter Lang, 123–38.

Duden (1999), *Das große Wörterbuch der deutschen Sprache in 10 Bänden*, Mannheim etc.: Dudenverlag.

Eggers, H. (1980), 'Deutsche Standardsprache des 19./20. Jahrhunderts', in: *Lexikon der Germanistischen Linguistik*, 2., vollständig neu bearbeitet und erweiterte Auflage, edited by H.P. Althaus, H. Henne and H.E. Wiegand, Tübingen: Niemeyer, 603–9.

Ehlich, K. (1998), '"LTI, LQI". Von der Unschuld der Sprache und der Unschuld der Sprechenden' in: *Das 20. Jahrhundert. Sprachgeschichte – Zeitgeschichte*, edited by H. Kämper, and H. Schmidt, Berlin and New York: de Gruyter, 275–303.

Eschenburg, T. (1983), 'Jahre der Besatzung 1945–1949', in: *Geschichte der Bundesrepublik Deutschland in fünf Bänden*, edited by K.D. Braher, T. Eschenburg, J.C. Fest and E. Jäckel, Stuttgart und Wiesbaden: Deutsche Verlags-Anstalt / F.A. Brockhaus.

Falkenberg, G. (1989), 'Zur Begriffsgeschichte der deutschen Spaltung zwischen Deutschem Reich und zwei Deutschen Republiken', *Sprache und Literatur in Wissenschaft und Unterricht* 20, H.64, 3–22.

Felbick, D. (2003), *Schlagwörter der Nachkriegszeit, 1945–1949*, Berlin: De Gruyter, 2003.

Goebbels, (P.) J. (1932–45), 'Reden', in: *Goebbels Reden, zwei Bände*, [i.: 1932–9; ii.: 1939–45], (1971, 1972) edited by H. Heiber, Düsseldorf: Droste Verlag.

Grass, G. (1990), *Deutscher Lastenausgleich. Wider das dumpfe Einheitsgebot. Reden und Gespräche*, Frankfurt am Main: Luchterhand.

Hahn, S. (1995), '"Halbstarke, Hippies und Hausbesetzer" Die Sprache und das Bild der Jugend in der öffentlichen Betrachtung', in: *Kontroverse Begriffe. Geschichte des öffentlichen Sprachgebrauchs in der Bundesrepublik Deutschland*, G. Stötzel, M. Wengeler et al., Berlin: de Gruyter, 211–44.

Handt, F. (ed.) (1964), *Deutsch – gefrorene Sprache in einem gefrorenen Land? Polemik. Analysen. Aufsätze*, Berlin: Literarische Colloquium.

Henke, K.-D. and Woller, H. (eds) (1993), *Politische Säuberung in Europa. Die Abrechnung mit dem Faschismus und Kollaboration nach dem Zweiten Weltkrieg*, München: Deutscher Taschenbuch Verlag.

Henne, H. and Drosdowski, G. (1980), 'Tendenzen der deutschen Gegenwartssprache', in: *Lexikon der Germanistischen Linguistik*, 2, edited by H.P. Althaus, H. Henne and H.E. Wiegand, Tübingen: Niemeyer, 619–32.

Hermand, J., Peitsch, H., and Scherpe, K.R. (1982–3), *Nachkriegsliteratur in Westdeutschland 1945–49: [vol. 1] Schreibweisen, Gattungen, Institutionen; [vol. 2] Autoren, Sprache, Traditionen*, Berlin: Argument-Verlag.

Hilberg, R. and Söllner, A. (1988), 'Das Schweigen zum Sprechen bringen. Über Kontinuität und Diskontinuität in der Holocaustforschung', *Merkur* 42, 535–51.

Hitler, A. (1925–7, 1943), *Mein Kampf*, 2 vols (1925, 1927; nachgedr. in einem Bd.; Zentralverlag der NSDAP) München, Franz Eher Nachf.

Hoffmann, C. (1992), *Stunden Null? Vergangenheitsbewältigung in Deutschland*, Bonn etc.: Bouvier. [Schriftenreihe Extremismus u. Demokratie 2].

Humboldt, W. von (1836), *Über die Verschiedenheit des menschlichen Sprachbaues, und ihren Einfluß auf die geistige Entwickelung des Menschengeschlechts* (Berlin, 1836; reprinted Bonn: Dümmler, 1967–8).

Jung, M. (1995), 'Amerikanismen, ausländische Wörter, Deutsch in der Welt. Sprachdiskussionen als Bewältigung der Vergangenheit und Gegenwart', in: *Kontroverse Begriffe. Geschichte des öffentlichen Sprachgebrauchs in der Bundesrepublik Deutschland*, G. Stötzel, M. Wengeler et al., Berlin: de Gruyter, 245–83.

Kämper-Jensen, H. (1993), 'Spracharbeit im Dienst des NS-Staates 1933 bis 1945', *Zeitschrift für Germanistische Linguistik* 21, 151–81.

Kämper, H. (1998), 'Entnazifizierung BB Sprachliche Existenzformen eines ethischen Konzepts', in: *Das 20. Jahrhundert. Sprachgeschichte – Zeitgeschichte*, edited by H. Kämper and H. Schmidt, Berlin and New York: de Gruyter, 304–29.

Kämper, H. and Schmidt, H. (eds) (1998), *Das 20. Jahrhundert. Sprachgeschichte – Zeitgeschichte*, Berlin and New York: de Gruyter.

Kämper, H. (2001), '*LQI* – Sprache des Vierten Reichs. Victor Klemperers Erkundungen zum Nachkriegsdeutsch', in: *Sprache im Leben der Zeit. Beiträge zur Theorie, Analyse und Kritik der deutschen Sprache in Vergangenheit und Gegenwart. Helmut Henne zum 65. Geburtstag*, edited by A. Burkhardt, and D. Cherubim, Tübingen: Niemeyer, 175–94.

Kämper, H. (2005), *Der Schulddiskurs in der frühen Nachkriegszeit: ein Beitrag zur Geschichte des sprachlichen Umbruchs nach 1945*, Berlin and New York: de Gruyter. [Studia linguistica Germanica; 78].

Kämper, H. (2007), *Opfer – Täter – Nichttäter. Ein Wörterbuch zum Schulddiskurs: 1945–1955*, Berlin and New York: de Gruyter.

Keller, R. (1990), *Sprachwandel. Von der unsichtbaren Hand in der Sprache*, Tübingen: Francke Verlag.

Klemperer, V. (1946), 'LTI', Die unbewältigte Sprache. Aus dem Notizbuch eines Philologen, 3rd ed., (1969) München : Deutscher Taschenbuch Verlag.

Klemperer, V. (1996), Ich will Zeugnis ablegen bis zum letzten. Tagebücher 1933–1945. 2 Bde.: 1. 1933–1941; 2. 1942–1945, 7th ed., edited by W. Nowojski and H. Klemperer, Berlin: Aufbau-Verlag.

Kremer, L. (2004), 'Geschichte der deutsch-friesischen und deutsch-niederländischen Sprachgrenze', in : Sprachgeschichte edited by W. Besch et al., 2nd ed., vol. 4, (2004) Berlin and New York: de Gruyter, 3390–404.

Lenz, S. (1964), Lehmanns Erzählungen, oder : So schön war mein Markt. Aus den Bekenntnissen eines Schwarzmarkthändlers, Hamburg: Hoffmann & Campe.

Lenzner, J. (1988), Brennende Kehle, oder: Der authentische Bericht eines Kenners der dunkelsten Schattenwirtschaft zwischen Stunde Null und Währungsreform von ihm selbst aufgezeichnet. Schwarzer Markt 1945–1948, Bremen: Joh. Heinrich Döll Verlag.

Lilge, H. (ed.) (1967), Deutschland 1945–1963, Hannover: Edition Zeitgeschehen.

Maas, U. (2000), 'Sprache in der Zeit des Nationalsozialismus', in: Sprachgeschichte edited by W. Besch et al., 2nd ed., vol. 2, Berlin and New York: de Gruyter, 1980–90.

Mayer, C. (2002), Öffentlicher Sprachgebrauch und Political Correctness. Eine Analyse sprachreflexiver Argumente im politischen Wortstreit, Hamburg: Verlag Dr Kovač.

Mayer, H. (1988), Die umerzogene Literatur. Deutsche Schriftsteller und Bücher 1945–1967, Düsseldorf: Siedler Verlag.

McVeigh, J. (1988), Kontinuität und Vergangenheitsbewältigung in der österreichischen Literatur nach 1945, Wien: Wilhelm Braumüller.

Mitscherlich, A. and Mitscherlich, M. (1977), Die Unfähigkeit zu trauern Grundlagen kollektiven Verhaltens, München: Piper.

Moser, H. (1985), 'Die Entwicklung der deutschen Sprache nach 1945', in : Sprachgeschichte, vol. 2, edited by W. Besch et al., Berlin and New York: de Gruyter, 1679–1707.

NHK = Neuer Hannoverscher Kurier – the official organ of the British Mil.-Gov. between 29.05.45 and 16.07.46. See Felbick, D. (2003), Schlagwörter der Nachkriegszeit, 1945–1949, Berlin: de Gruyter, 90.

Niethammer, L. (1972), Entnazifizierung in Bayern, Frankfurt: S. Fischer. (2nd ed. renamed: Die Mitläuferfabrik: Die Entnazifizierung am Beispiel Bayerns, Dietz, 1982).

Phillips, D. (1982), 'The language of Stunde Null. A note on post-war German vocabulary', Treffpunkt 14: 2, 22–3.

Polenz, P. von (1999), Deutsche Sprachgeschichte vom Spätmittelalter bis zur Gegenwart. Bd. III 19. und 20. Jahrhundert, Berlin and New York: de Gruyter.

Rümelin, H.A. (ed.) (1948), So lebten wir ... Ein Querschnitt durch 1947, Willsbach: Scherer-Verlag. [mit Genehmingung der Milit.-Regierung].

Salomon, E. von (1951), Der Fragebogen, Reinbek bei Hamburg: Rowohlt.

Scherpe, K.R. (1982–3), 'Erzwungener Alltag. Wahrgenommene und gedachte Wirklichkeit in der Reportageliteratur der Nachkriegszeit', in: *Nachkriegsliteratur in Westdeutschland*, edited by H. Jost et al., Berlin: Argument Verlag, 35–102.

Schlosser, H.D. (1995), 'Gab es sprachlich eine Stunde Null?', *Muttersprache* 105, 193–209.

Schmid, A. (1951), *Brand's Haide*, Frankfurt am Main: S.Fischer Verlag.

Schmitz-Berning, C. (2000), *Vokabular des Nationalsozialismus*, Berlin and New York: de Gruyter.

Schmoller, G. von, Maier, H. and Tobler, A. (1957), *Handbuch des Besatzungsrechts*, Tübingen: J.C.B. Mohr (Paul Siebeck).

Schrenck-Notzing, C. (1965), *Charakterwäsche. Die amerikanische Besatzung in Deutschland und ihre Folgen*, Stuttgart: Seewald.

Schwarz, H.-P. (1983), 'Die Ära Adenauer, 1949–1957', in: *Geschichte der Bundesrepublik Deutschland in fünf Bänden*, edited by K.D. Braher, T. Eschenburg, J.C. Fest and E. Jäckel, Stuttgart und Wiesbaden: Deutsche Verlags-Anstalt / F.A. Brockhaus.

Seidel, E. and Seidel-Slotty, I. (1961), *Sprachwandel im Dritten Reich. Eine kritische Untersuchung faschistischer Einflüsse*, Halle: VEB Verlag Sprache und Literatur.

Skinner, J.D. (1999), *Bezeichnungen für das Homosexuelle im Deutschen. 1: Eine lexikologische Analyse und eine lexikographische Aufgabe; 2: Ein Wörterbuch*, Essen: Die Blaue Eule.

Steger, H. (1989), 'Sprache im Wandel', in: *Die Geschichte der Bundesrepublik Deutschland. Band 4: Kultur*, edited by W. Benz, Frankfurt am Main, 13–52.

Sternberger, D., Storz, G. and Süskind, W.E. (1945, 1957), *Aus dem Wörterbuch des Unmenschen*, München: Deutscher Taschenbuch Verlag.

Stötzel, G. (1989), 'Nazi-Verbrechen und öffentliche Sprachsensibilität. Ein Kapitel deutscher Sprachgeschichte nach 1945', *Sprache und Literatur in Wissenschaft und Unterricht* 20, H.63, 32–52.

Stötzel, G. and Wengeler, M. et al. (1995), *Kontroverse Begriffe. Geschichte des öffentlichen Sprachgebrauchs in der Bundesrepublik Deutschland*, Berlin: de Gruyter.

Stötzel, G. and Eitz, T. (eds) (2002), *Zeitgeschichtliches Wörterbuch der deutschen Gegenwartssprache*, Hildesheim, Zürich and New York: Olms.

Timm, U. (2003), *Am Beispiel meines Bruders*, Köln: Kiepenhauer & Witsch.

Vaillant, J. (1981), *La Dénazification par les vainqueurs: La politique culturelle des occupants en Allemagne 1945–1949*, Lille: Presses Universitaires de Lille.

Vollnhals C. (ed.) (1993), *Entnazifizierung. Politische Säuberung und Rehabilitierung in den vier Besatzungszonen 1945–1949*, München: Deutscher Taschenbuch Verlag.

Von Hitler zu Adenauer. Deutsche Geschichte von 1945–1949, Hamburg: John Jahr Verlag, 1976 [A pictorial popularizing documentation].

Wells, C.J. (1985), *German: A Linguistic History to 1945*, Oxford: Oxford University Press; translated by Rainhild D. Wells: *Deutsch: Eine Sprachgeschichte bis 1945*, Tübingen: Niemeyer, (1990).

Wells, C.J. (1999), 'Sprachhistorische und soziolinguistische Überlegungen zu einer dubiosen Textsorte: Der Denunziantenbrief', *Sociolinguistica. Internationales Jahrbuch für Europäische Soziolinguistik*, 13, *Historische Soziolinguistik*, edited by U. Ammon, K.J. Mattheier and P.H. Nelde, 209–34.

Wember, H. (1991), *Umerziehung im Lager. Internierung und Bestrafung von nationalsozialisten in der britischen Besatzungszone Deutschlands*, Koblenz: KlartextVerlag.

Widmer, U. (1966), *1945 oder die 'Neue Sprache'. Studien zur Prosa der 'Jungen Generation'*, Düsseldorf: Schwan.

Willett, R. (1992), *The Americanization of Germany, 1945–1949*, 2nd ed., London and New York: Routledge.

Wolff, A. (1982–3), *Sprachliche Spuren des 'Schwarzen Marktes' im Jahre 1947*. Unveröff. Schriftliche Hausarbeit zur Wissenschaftlichen Prüfung für das Lehramt an Gymnasien der Technischen Universität Carolo-Wilhelmina zu Braunschweig.

Wolff, G. (1986), *Deutsche Sprachgeschichte. Ein Studienbuch. Originalausgabe*, Frankfurt am Main: Athenäum Verlag.

Notes on Contributors

WINIFRED V. DAVIES is Reader in German at Aberystwyth University and has published on variation and language attitudes in German, the language awareness and linguistic knowledge of teachers, differences between lay and academic discourse about language, and the contribution of linguistic myths to the construction of sociolinguistic norms. A major recent publication, co-authored with Nils Langer, was *The Making of Bad Language: Lay linguistic stigmatisations in German, past and present* (2006).

MARTIN DURRELL is Emeritus Professor of German at the University of Manchester, having retired from the Henry Simon Chair in January 2008. He has been President of the Forum for Germanic Language Studies (1993–2007), Treasurer of the Philological Society (1994–2008) and Vice-President of the *Internationale Vereinigung für Germanistik* (2004–5). He has published widely on German dialectology and sociolinguistics, German grammar and the history of the German language.

JOHN L. FLOOD is Emeritus Professor of German in the University of London. A past president of the Bibliographical Society, he has published widely, particularly in the field of the history of the book in early modern Germany. His publications include *The German Book 1450–1750* (1995), *Johannes Sinapius (1505–1560). Hellenist and Physician in Germany and Italy* (1997), and, in four volumes, *Poets Laureate in the Holy Roman Empire. A Bio-bibliographical Handbook* (2006).

GERALDINE HORAN is Lecturer in German at University College London. She has published on the role of the new media in language teaching, on women's discourse in National Socialism, theoretical approaches to analysing National Socialist discourse and on the regulation of cursing and swearing in German. Current research projects include a sociolinguistic history of cursing and swearing in German since the sixteenth century and the language of nationalism and anti-Semitism in Germany, 1871–1914.

WILLIAM JERVIS JONES has published mainly on German phonology, lexical influences, purism, kinship terms and lexicography, with a focus on the medieval and early modern periods. Since retiring in 2001 as Professor of German at Royal Holloway University of London, he has been compiling a historical lexicon of German colour terms (now nearing completion in several volumes) with the support of a Leverhulme Emeritus Fellowship.

MARIA B. LANGE is a researcher in the field of historical linguistics, currently affiliated to the *Wissenschaftskolleg zu Berlin*. She has recently published a book on the influence of seventeenth century grammarians on the standardization of the German language in which she investigates a corpus of contemporary handwritten minutes. Her interests range from (German) handwriting and the legal position of business women to the language of science fiction, and to long-running television series.

NILS LANGER is Reader in German Linguistics at the University of Bristol, having obtained his doctorate from the University of Newcastle on Tyne in 2000 with a study on prescriptive grammarians from the seventeenth century. He is the current President of the Forum for Germanic Language Studies (FGLS) and is one of the co-founders of the Historical Sociolinguistics Network (HiSoN). His main interests lie in German historical sociolinguistics, in particular the notion of 'bad language' and the use of language to create identity in minority communities.

ROSAMOND MCKITTERICK received the degrees of MA, PhD, and LittD from the University of Cambridge. Since 1999 she has held the Chair in Medieval History in the University of Cambridge and is a Fellow of Sidney Sussex College, Cambridge. In addition to many books, articles and chapters in books on early medieval history and culture her most recent monograph is *Charlemagne: the formation of a European identity* (Cambridge, 2008) also published in German as *Karl der Grosse* (Darmstadt, 2008).

NICOLA MCLELLAND studied at the universities of Sydney (Australia), Bonn (Germany), and Cambridge (UK). Following her first post at Trinity College Dublin, in 2005 she moved to the University of Nottingham where she is currently Associate Professor in German linguistics. She has published widely on German grammatography, especially on the seventeenth-century grammarian Schottelius, but also works on German medieval literature and German sociolinguistics. She is editor of the journal *Language & History*.

FALCO PFALZGRAF is Lecturer in German Linguistics and Medieval German at Queen Mary, University of London and Convenor for Language and Linguistics at the Centre for Anglo-German Cultural Relations. He completed his doctoral thesis on linguistic purism in Germany (University of Manchester, 2003). His main research areas are the influence of English on German, linguistic purism, and the relationships between politics, language, and culture.

SHEILA WATTS is a graduate of Dublin University who now lectures in German linguistics at the University of Cambridge. She has worked on the expression of time within the verb phrase, on verbal prefixes, the development of the perfect, and on other phenomena linked to grammaticalization in the older Germanic languages, particularly Old Saxon. Another interest concerns ideas about the German language in the seventeenth century, and she has published on both the grammarian Justus Georg Schottelius and the lexicographer Caspar Stieler.

C.J. WELLS was Lecturer in Germanic Philology and Medieval German Literature at Oxford University from 1967 to 2008, and is now an emeritus fellow of St Edmund Hall. He first learnt German as a child in the post-war occupation of Germany in 1946 and has been fascinated by the language ever since. His publications include *German: A Linguistic History to 1945* (1985) and articles and reviews on the spelling of Merovingian Frankish personal names and on the spellings in the editions of Luther's Bible translation at Wittenberg and Frankfurt am Main after Luther's death.

Index of Historical Persons

General Index

Nr. 1 Geoffrey Perkins: Contemporary Theory of Expressionism, 1974. 182 S.

Nr. 2 Paul Kussmaul: Bertolt Brecht und das englische Drama der Renaissance, 1974. 175 S.

Nr. 3 Eudo C. Mason: Hölderlin and Goethe, 1975. 145 S.

Nr. 4 W.E. Yates: Tradition in the German Sonnet, 1981. 98 S.

Nr. 5 Rhys W. Williams: Carl Sternheim. A Critical Study, 1982. 282 S.

Nr. 6 Roger H. Stephenson: Goethe's Wisdom Literature, 1983. 274 S.

Nr. 7 John Hennig: Goethe and the English Speaking World, 1983. 288 S.

Nr. 8 John R.P. McKenzie: Social Comedy in Austria and Germany 1890–1933, 1992. 262 S., 2nd Edition 1996.

Nr. 9 David Basker: Chaos, Control and Consistency: The Narrative Vision of Wolfgang Koeppen, 1993. 352 S.

Nr. 10 John Klapper: Stefan Andres. The Christian Humanist as a Critic of his Times, 1995. 188 S.

Nr. 11 Anthony Grenville: Cockpit of Ideologies. The Literature and Political History of the Weimar Republic, 1995. 394 S.

Nr. 12 T.M. Holmes: The Rehearsal of Revolution. Georg Büchner's Politics and his Drama *Dantons Tod*, 1995. 214 S.

Nr. 13 Andrew Plowman: The Radical Subject. Social Change and the Self in Recent German Autobiography, 1998. 168 S.

Nr. 14 David Barnett: Literature versus Theatre. Textual Problems and Theatrical Realization in the Later Plays of Heiner Müller, 1998. 293 S.

Nr. 15 Stephen Parker: Peter Huchel. A Literary Life in 20th-Century Germany, 1998. 617 S.

Nr. 16 Deborah Smail: White-collar Workers, Mass Culture and *Neue Sachlichkeit* in Weimar Berlin. A Reading of Hans Fallada's *Kleiner Mann – Was nun?*, Erich Kästner's *Fabian* and Irmgard Keun's *Das kunstseidene Mädchen*, 1999. 236 S.

Nr. 17 Ian Roe and John Warren (eds): The Biedermeier and Beyond. Selected Papers from the Symposium held at St. Peter's College, Oxford from 19–21 September 1997, 1999. 253 S.

Nr. 18 James Trainer (ed.): Liebe und Trennung. Charlotte von Ahlefelds Briefe an Christian Friedrich Tieck, 1999. 235 S.

Nr. 19 Anthony J. Harper and Margaret C. Ives (eds): Sappho in the Shadows. Essays on the work of German women poets of the age of Goethe (1749–1832), with translations of their poetry into English, 2000. 280 S.

Nr. 20 Peter Hutchinson (ed.): Landmarks in German Poetry, 2000. 218 S.

Nr. 21 Rachel Palfreyman: Edgar Reitz's *Heimat*. Histories, Traditions, Fictions, 2000. 237 S.

Nr. 44 Barbara Burns: The Prose Fiction of Louise von François (1817–1893), 2006. 151 S.

Nr. 45 Peter Hutchinson (ed.): Landmarks in the German Novel (1), 2007. 237 S.

Nr. 46–47 Forthcoming.

Nr. 48 Daniel Greineder: From the Past to the Future: The Role of Mythology from Winckelmann to the Early Schelling, 2007. 227 S.

Nr. 49 John Heath: Behind the Legends: The Cult of Personality and Self-Presentation in the Literary Works of Stefan Heym, 2008. 179 S.

Nr. 50–51 Forthcoming.

Nr. 52 Geraldine Horan, Nils Langer and Sheila Watts (eds): Landmarks in the History of the German Language, 2009. 320 S.